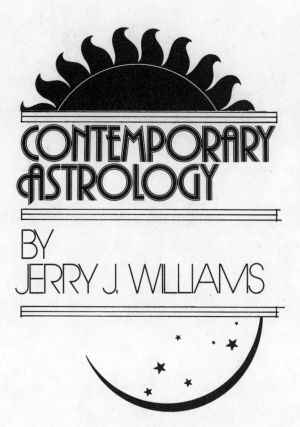

CONTEMPORARY ASTROLOGY

BY
JERRY J. WILLIAMS

CONTEMPORARY ASTROLOGY

JERRY J. WILLIAMS

SHERBOURNE PRESS
NASHVILLE, TENNESSEE

Library of Congress Catalog Card Number 77-77375
Manufactured in the United States of America

For Nola

But, after all, what is a scholar? One who may not break
bounds under pain of expulsion from the academy of which
he is a member.

—Robert Graves, *The White Goddess*

Contents

Illustrations

Acknowledgments

MY FIRST AND greatest debt I owe to my wife, Nola, to whom this book is dedicated. Nola's constant support and patience over the many months in which the book was written and rewritten, her typing of the manuscript (the first draft of which she took entirely in shorthand), her erection of most of the horoscopes, and her wise counsel, made this book possible.

I also owe a great debt to Dr. Robert D. Lynch, who advised me about the psychological implications of the material and who gave me invaluable information about my literary mentor, Aldous Huxley.

I am equally indebted to Lillian Canaan, who provided many of the insights into the chart interpretations.

I wish also to acknowledge my debt to Gina Ceaglio, who was Lillian's, Nola's and my first teacher of astrology, and who also read the manuscript; and my debt to the Self-Realization Fellowship and Sister Karen Lanza of that Order for help with the biographical material about their founder, Paramahansa Yogananda.

Grateful thanks are also due to Shelly Lowenkopf, my editor, long-time friend, fellow tummler, with whom I have long shared the paths of serendipity.

I must also acknowledge the help which our children—Danica, Gina, Kelly and Mark—have provided: J. D. Salinger quite properly referred to children as Zen Masters, for they have not yet learned the separativeness of our rationalist bias.

I am particularly grateful to Dr. Elizabeth Keating, Chairman of the Department of Language Arts and the Humanities at San Diego Evening College, and professor of mythology, for reading the manuscript and for providing knowledgeable—often witty—sidelights on the material.

I also appreciate the yeomanry of Barbara Phillips, who did the copy editing with services well beyond the call of duty.

A special acknowledgment is due the Rosicrucian Fellowship, P.O. Box 713, Oceanside, California 92054, for permission to reproduce several pages of their 1934 ephemeris and several pages of their tables of houses.

There is no clear line between literary debts and debts of friendship or simple charity which make the writing of a book possible. Among these latter, I must gratefully acknowledge my appreciation to the proprietors of the Mithras Bookstore (especially to Elizabeth) in La Jolla, where I spent so many hours in browsing uninterruptedly through arcane literature; to Joe Herweg, in whose San Diego bookstore I found many things I needed, and who found others for me; to Tom Meehan, owner of Paper Book Land, who tracked down many hard-to-find paperback books for me.

Also, there are the many strong and supportive friendships from members of the San Diego Astrological Society.

Finally, I owe a great and continuing debt to my law partner, Don Zellmann, without whose perseverance and unquestioning support this book could not have been written.

Introduction

AN INTRODUCTION IS necessary only to announce that this book is more than just the finest book on astrology in the English language. If one had no interest in the oldest science, astrology, this book might rate as one of the best works of descriptive personality typing since Shakespeare. The author, a practitioner of law, law school lecturer in labor law and jurisprudence, family man and astrologer, has performed the loving task of accurately and sensitively combining all of the important information about humanistic astrology. This book is a scholarly work as could only be written by an attorney.

The author, who has a Sun and Moon posited in Sagittarius in his natal astrological chart, is by his definition a Faustian character whose search for idealism has led him into every possible study. He is an alchemist who with this book has turned base metals into gold. His Sagittarian planets are also located right on the Sagittarian point in the astrological chart of the United States that represents our rollicking, idealistic, willful and determined national character—and the author reflects those national qualities at their best. The straightforward quest for truth and ideals or prototypes found in his approach to this science is what one might expect from Mark Twain, a Sagittarian.

The protean information here about life and personalities is one complete reference book. The how-to-do-it approach to the construction of the reader's own natal chart is still another reference book. This procedure is clear and accurate beyond anything of its kind that is available.

As a work on astrology, *Contemporary Astrology* serves as a major turning point for the science. It becomes clear that astrology is *not a belief system* but is a science. Astrology deals with concepts of time and form as they are found in the cosmos. In this study astrology uses all of the information of astronomy. Astrology also deals with concepts of timing of human events and the structural forms of human life. The cosmic morphology is seen as patterned mathematically and manifested in heavenly bodies and their energy sources. The cosmic timing is viewed by astrology as being synchronous with the timing of patterns of events in human life.

It is not necessary to force a cause-effect explanation upon the relationship between the heavenly bodies and persons. A synchronous and "synmorphological" or just syncretistic relationship can explain the contemporary view. As my friend, Aldous Huxley, discovered: "The universe is fundamentally sane." It is only one step from this discovery to the view that both heavenly bodies and human beings behave in a similar way and are structured in the same way because they partake of the identical higher principle of universal order. This realization has freed my own mind forever of the tedious and not to be fulfilled task of proving cause-effect relationships between planets and persons. The reader will journey through the reasoning ages in history that have produced the cause-effect hang-up. He will discover that Western science, itself built out of cause-effect thinking, is at its highest places abandoning the short-sighted relationship in favor of the ancient concepts of the circularity of time, the ebb and flow of structures and the synchronicity of events. It is science that is becoming contemporary with astrology, science that is growing up to astrology.

Astrology, to become "contemporary," had to go back the way it came; it had to become ancient astrology again. The author traces every detail of astrology's origins to myth, symbols and cultural styles. Where "modern" astrology had become semireligious, requiring belief and faith, contemporary astrology becomes ancient astrology. It is observation with modern telescopes and microscopes of heavenly nature and human nature. Its purpose, more than a parlor game of surprising, meaningful coincidences, is to enable the person to discover his own destiny as promised him by unique patterns of timing, rhythms and personality structure given him at birth. The most well-meaning person who does not know the timing of the build-up of his life pattern can fail to "take it at its flood" and discover too late that his energies and talents have missed their mark and were squandered or were self-destructive.

There are many of us who believe that the *unexamined life is not worth living.* And for us astrology may become a lifelong unfolding of patterns in our lives. It turns out that the architectonic or structure-building scheme of the ancient astrologer, the circle divided into twelve balanced areas of life activities, is the most capable of plugging in both to modern psychology and to electronic computers. The dynamic homeostasis or life-maintaining balancing and counterbalancing recovery system for biological life and for mental health is best represented by a circle with pie slices placed exactly opposite each other for balancing areas of life. This scheme, and no other that I know, can represent limitless diversity and unity in one symbol.

If you were given the task of creating the ten to the tenth power or ten billion persons that will have lived on this earth by the turn of the next century, you could find no more useful system by which to program your computers than the astrological chart of twelve houses, planets, angles, degrees and signs. These variables give almost infinite possibilities for human difference but provide for a unity of form that allows us to survive as a species. This unity in diversity is given birth by the means of expression found in the astrological chart. The message becomes the method. Contemporary astrology has gone back the way it came, and so now is contemporary science: the way of astrology.

Within chapters of this book the reader will discover that a number of prominent psychologists, including Carl Jung, have probably built their entire personality theories on astrology but have denied these origins in clever or perhaps unintentional disguises. These masqueraders have been exposed in these pages and it seems unlikely that anyone will ever try that trick again. That would not be necessary, since psychology and medicine seem close to needing astrology for themselves. I anticipate that medicine will rediscover astrology and will claim it as a long-adhered-to tradition. The rights will have come from Hippocrates, who had an astrological chart prepared for a patient before seeing him.

Medicine has rapidly become aware that the skills and technology at its disposal are useless if the timing of an intervention is wrong. Surgery, scheduled for the convenience of the staff, is being retimed for periods of maximum survival and healing. X-radiation therapy given in the evening when the body is warmer can cure a cancer, but the same dose given in the early morning hours when the body is colder may be fatal.

Psychology is finding that learning may occur in giant breakthrough experiences during certain moments of a pattern. Biorhythm studies have shown that almost all accidents occur on critical days during the cycles. Since astrology is the science of *timing*, it will be central to all other methods seeking to predict the right time for treating an illness, for avoiding an accident or for learning. Eureka learning of a kind we have only guessed about may be possible on a regular basis, once we have identified the time and structural details to allow entry into this special sphere of learning.

Astrologers will recognize that their heretofore poorly sung cause has found its greatest spokesman in our Sagittarian author. But nowhere are concepts forced upon you. Each is discovered by a cool, clear-headed Socratic method which law studies have taught him.

Astrologers will also recognize an entirely new discovery for astrology by the author. This is the correlation of the qualities of past or present or future orientation toward time with the characteristic behavior of the signs of the zodiac. Cancer is viewed as greatly past-oriented: the Cancer person lives through each episode of life with a view to how it will be reexperienced in retrospect. Such a past, present or future orientation of the signs has not been presented in these times. It enriches the already extensive data on personalities as they are found in *Homo sapiens.* Perhaps no other personality theory in existence can approach the ability of the science of astrology to produce data necessary to construct out of facts a personality that really makes up into a human being capable of life.

As a structure which can incorporate our already existing ego theory, astrology with its ongoing descriptions of how balance is accomplished is the most sophisticated model of homeostasis. Character, our interpersonal style, is revealed for us when data from the astrological chart are rearranged, weighed and ordered in "box scores."

By this graphic method of astrological mapping, the geneticists interested in human engineering could not only create a whole race from scratch and never repeat themselves with two identical persons but they could relocate people on the face of the globe either to homes more suitable to their fulfillment of life's destiny or with mates more compatible, as determined by astrological *chart synastry.* Although such engineering of human life remains a dubious moral accomplishment, people are asking to direct their own lives toward useful and possible goals. It is clear to me as a psychiatrist that the data provided by astrological techniques can vastly deepen my understanding of the areas of life, the diversity of human potentiality and the strength and aspirations of my patients.

The book you are about to read will enrich your life if you never become an astrologer. If you *are* an astrologer, *Contemporary Astrology* will become a springboard for your future work. You will have to justify your interest less and you can with confidence build all future work on this scholarly and profound magnum opus, and not have to prove or repeat the heritage which has made ancient astrology and contemporary astrology synonymous.

Within the structures of this book there are surprises and delights everywhere. It is impossible to tell you how to read the book or how to use it. It is a book to own even if you discover yourself to be untied to possessions. This work, so basic, so complete, could make it unnecessary ever to read another book on astrology.

Elsewhere in the book you will meet me again in a different role. By then you will thank me for having urged you to proceed into this adventure with astrology which *Contemporary Astrology* provides.

—Robert D. Lynch, M.D.

PART ONE

What It Is

The Universe begins to look more like a great thought than like a great machine.

> —Sir James Jeans,
> *The Mysterious Universe*

1 Why Another Book on Astrology?

WHEN YOU COMPLETE this book you will be able to erect your own horoscope and interpret it with a delineation based on generally accepted principles of humanistic astrology used by contemporary astrologers. You will know what you are doing and why. Your efforts in horoscopy will be made without resort to spiritualism or esotericism, and without any exercise in extrasensory perception.

When I first became interested in contemporary astrology I looked long and hard for such a book. I was unable to find one. After some years of study and of teaching my own students, I have still been unable to find a readable introductory work which will both instruct the student in the basics of chart erection and interpretation *and* make clear to him what it is that he is doing and why.

This last is very important; in order to have the courage of your convictions as an astrologer, you must know what you are doing.

Some people can learn by rote, doggedly memorizing rules and instructions. I cannot. More important, *no one* who has learned something by rote can adequately defend what he has done when an explanation is sought or needed.

Since I have not been able to find such a work, I decided to write one myself. This is it. It is my goal, which I pass on to you, that you will be able not only to erect and interpret birth charts but to explain to any native whose chart you have delineated the premises on which your interpretation is founded.

What are those premises? That is what the book is all about. The reader is invited to decide for himself which principles make sense, which are acceptable to his personal credo. He is also invited to try out, in his own interpretation of natal horoscopes, any view that is offered, to see whether it works for him. A characteristic of the contemporary astrologer in astrology's present state of flux is his willingness both to attempt new ideas, keeping those that seem to work, and to discard doctrines, new and old, which seem wrong or useless.

A word about the methodology of this book. The first few chapters deal with my personal experiences which led to my present interest in astrology. In a one-to-one relationship, which is the optimum format for instruction of virtually any subject, the student can readily determine whether or not the teacher is someone whom he can respect and from whom he is willing to learn. Even in a large classroom, students quickly and generally perceive whether or not their instructor is genuinely interested in (and capable of) teaching them anything. Their willingness to learn from him is their response to that decision. I realize that this view can be condemned as an *ad hominem* approach, but it is consistent with my view of astrology as an exercise in humanism; and in my opinion, humanistic astrology and contemporary astrology are synonymous.

Therefore, it seemed important to relate the rather odd circumstances which led me away from my comfortable prejudices against astrology to my present rejection of the conventional wisdom, at least insofar as that field of interest is concerned.

Lest there be any doubts, let me emphasize that *all* of the episodes reported involving Lillian Canaan and me are accurate. The events involving the psychiatrist, given the pseudonym of "Dr. White," are not only accurate but have been double-checked in detail by Lillian, the doctor and me. Actually, that episode was even more extraordinary than it appears in chapter two; certain parts have been deliberately omitted to protect the identities of some of the principals. But what is there is factual.

IN ANCIENT TIMES, when parchment was the prevailing writing material, recycling "paper" was popular. Parchment wasn't all that cheap; so when a communication had served its purpose, it was often scraped off and a new message was written over the tough vellum. Parchment reused this way was known as a *palimpsest;* often the old message would show through the new one.

Contemporary astrology is a palimpsest. I have been able to trace many astrological notions to extremely early origins, and it is remarkable to see the extent to which new messages were continuously written over the earlier ones which, for one reason or another, we tried to rub out.

By way of example, consider the zodiacal sign of Capricorn. For millennia before the common era (B.C.E.), the winter solstice, which occurred at about December 21 or 22, was the first day of Capricorn. As you are probably aware, Capricorn is symbolized by a goat; the word itself derives from Greek and Latin cognates meaning goat-horned. Thousands of years ago, it was the custom to sacrifice one goat at the winter solstice to propitiate the nature gods, but to turn a second goat loose to roam in the wilderness, bearing all of the bad karma of the tribe on his head.

Later, this custom became a religious rite of the Hebrews, and is reflected in the Bible. Aaron confesses all the sins of the children of Israel and passes them on to a goat which is permitted to escape into the desert.[1] This rite occurred on the Day of Atonement, Yom Kippur, which coincides with the autumnal equinox. Yom Kippur was originally a time of mourning for Tammuz, the Hebrew fertility god associated with the seasons, who died with the sun at the autumnal equinox and was resurrected the following spring with the vernal equinox, when the sun *passes over* the equinoctial point again and the new world begins with the feast of the Passover. Tammuz, consort of Ashtoreth, was known as the "god who rises" because of his annual rebirth on the vernal equinox, the first day of spring of each year.

The solstices and the equinoxes were the critical astronomical frame of reference for our ancestors for quite a few thousand years. The Hebrew prophets, in scraping off the earlier script, rewrote the story around these same seasonal points, and the earlier story shows through. Later, Christians would write the story anew on the same parchment. This time the "god who rises" is not Tammuz, but the "Anointed One," or *Christos* in Greek, who is reborn at the time of Passover, the feast of Ashtoreth or Easter, measured once again from the vernal equinox.

Of greater significance for our purposes, however, is the concept of Christ as the ultimate *scape* goat, or *scathe* goat, who neither escapes nor is unscathed; indeed, the cognate words and their intermingled meanings are themselves evidence of a palimpsest. Instead, *Christos* willingly accepts all the burden of Man's sins, and it is no coincidence that he was given a birth date of December 25, a date pegged to the commencement of Capricorn at the winter solstice.

To gain some clear idea of the vitalizing premises of contemporary astrology, it is necessary in some degree to see the successive scripts on the palimpsest. It is even more necessary to sort out the truly meaningful (for our purposes) from that which is merely curiously digressive. Thus a considerable process of subtraction must take place to keep to the main line of our thesis. In the above example, comparisons of Mesopotamian vs. Hebrew vs. Christian religious observances are a distraction which must be avoided where possible; but what is significant is the persistent association of the zodiacal sign Capricorn with the notions of the scapegoat, with an overlay of the word "scathe," which means to injure with fire or heat, or to criticize severely. Capricorns as an archetype tend to self-criticism and to the internalization of collective guilt in a social setting.

THE PALIMPSEST CHARACTER of astrology is not just a matter of changing symbols. Analytical psychology, alchemy and literature are involved as well. I have laid aside books on astrology weighted down with obscure Jungian psychology never to pick them up again. In a very real sense, astrology was the forerunner of psychology, with remarkable parallels to the Third Force Psychology of Abraham Maslow, who had the revolutionary and breathtakingly simple idea of studying healthy people psychologically. There are times when these parallels must be touched upon, to show what contemporary astrology is all about.

Jungian psychology is something else again. Jung is one of astrology's greatest heroes, but it is too easy to use his difficult, obscure language to sweep needed analysis of astrological concepts under the rug and to explain an astrological principle with a Jungian term which is even more abstruse. I am therefore cautious about looking to Jung for support of any astrological principle. Beware of that which proves too much!

Alchemy is a puzzle. Like astrology, alchemy dealt with the problems of the mind when there was no psychology as such. As Mircea Eliade has pointed out, it is misleading to think of alchemy as a "protochemistry." I agree. If it's a proto-anything it would be a protopsychology.

There is often an indistinct line between that which is astrology and that which can be attributed to the early alchemists. Sometimes there is no line at all. An example of the last is found in the correspondences between the elements (fire, earth, air and water) and the four humors (choler, bile, blood and phlegm). The elements—and by inference, the humors—are used by astologers in synthesizing the meaning of the various zodiacal signs. According to their relative emphasis in the horoscope, the elements are a valuable tool for the contemporary astrologer, although they originated with the alchemists.

A startling vindication of this alchemist-astrologer typology occurred recently when Dr. Humphry Osmond (creator of the term "psychedelic"), together with Harriet Mann and Miriam Siegler, decided to test Herbert Silberer's notion, later adopted by Jung, that the elements and the humors were designed to reflect basic personality types. The fascinating results of their experiments are reported in chapter seven.

And what about literature? In *The Humors and Shakespeare's Characters*, Professor John W. Draper has provided a compelling analysis of Shakespeare's use of the element-humor personality typology to develop characterization, from the "melancholy" Dane to the "choleric" Laertes. Recently it was pointed out that each of the brothers in Dostoevsky's *Brothers Karamazov* can be clearly identified as a representative of an astrological elemental personality type.[2]

Such astrological analysis of literary forms illuminates both the intent of the author and the application of the astrological principle. A good example is D. H. Lawrence, who, in *Lady Chatterley's Lover*, rejected Western rationalism and the notion of infinite progress through science as counterfeit coin which was bankrupting Mankind. His declared purpose in writing that controversial novel was to advocate sex in the heart, not sex in the head. At first bitterly attacked as a scandalous and pornographic work, *Lady Chatterley* has ultimately triumphed as we have come to see that Lawrence was right.

With his last book, *Apocalypse*, Lawrence carried his thesis to its ultimate astrological conclusion: we are killing ourselves, he declared, because we have lost touch with our natural rhythms, the influences of Sun, Moon and stars, that gave energy and meaning to our ancestors' lives throughout prehistory. This humanistic concern is what contemporary astrology is all about, and Lawrence's contribution cannot be ignored.

Did it ever occur to anyone, I wonder, that *Finnegans Wake*, James Joyce's unread masterpiece, is itself a horoscope? That literary phenomenon combines virtually all the premises of astrology and synthesizes them in a work of genius which provides a remarkable illustration of what takes place in the formulation and delineation of any horoscope.

FINALLY, WE COME to the role of myth and symbol, touched upon in the example of the sign of Capricorn. Each of the zodiacal signs, and each of the planets with which they are associated, is based on one or another of the ideas drawn from our common heritage of myth and symbol. It is a shame that our arrogant dismissal of this rich and meaningful resource has displaced its traditional function in the service of Mankind. Contemporary astrology seeks to recover its values, again running a parallel course with contemporary psychology.

According to psychiatrist Rollo May, "Symbols are specific acts or figures . . . while myths develop and elaborate these figures into a story." Jesuit scholar Michael Novak comments, "Myths are in some not very clearly understood way the bearers of psychic power, life and energy." Both priest and existential psychiatrist see myths as helping the individual experience greater reality in the outside world by drawing out inner reality.[3] Father Novak rightly points out that we do not act according to logical principles but according to the myths that we believe about ourselves.

Without an understanding of the related myths, the concepts of the zodiacal signs are about as papier-mâché as the faddish cocktail coasters they are often imprinted upon. Joseph Campbell summed it up well when he observed that the function of myth "is to serve as a powerful picture language for the communication of traditional wisdom."[4] Contemporary astrologers would agree with all three of these thoughtful men.

TO A LARGE extent astrology is astronomy and always has been. In 1675, when the Greenwich Observatory was founded, the resident astronomer drew up the birth chart of the new observatory as part of his routine function. However, this was also about the time of the incursion into the sciences of mechanistic Western rationalism which has, in its search for objectivity, dehumanized the sciences and made them the Frankenstein they have since become. Himself a victim of Western rationalism, the Greenwich resident astronomer appended to that birth chart the annotation (in Latin): "Friends, can you keep from laughing?"

That was a turning point. Astrology became distinguished from astronomy and was banished to the realm of the occult where other "hidden" things were.

In *The Act of Creation,* Arthur Koestler refers to the "blocked matrices" of science, pointing out that at various points in history, science prefers to ignore realities that appear before it. Contemporary astrologers find themselves in just such a situation. Part of the reason, I suppose, is the God-awful stuff that appears in the daily newspapers; it represents everything that a contemporary astrologer would repudiate, but it is what people think of when the word "astrology" is used.

Another part of the problem is the fact that astrology was seized upon by various cults attracted to any doctrine which the conventional wisdom had rejected. Such usurpation by what Aldous Huxley dubbed "The Secret Society Syndrome" includes various paranoid types and downright frauds. The result is that it is extremely difficult to pursue astrology as a serious study. After all, who wants to be identified with the preacher of the *Decameron* who tours the country exhibiting a tail feather from the Holy Ghost?

Thus the study of our cosmic environment has indeed been one of science's blocked matrices. For this reason, among others, I have avoided relying on the writings of controversial theorists (such as Velikovsky), spiritualists or occultists of any description. I have found that men whose creative ideas have made a generally recognized contribution to our lives have had some remarkable things to say in support of the underlying premises of contemporary astrology.

Finally, I have sought diligently, often through savage self-inflicted editorial wounds, to follow the adjuration of my editor, who said, "Jerry, you can call the book anything you like; but between you and me, it's got to be *The No-Bullshit Book of Astrology.*"

JEAN-PAUL SARTRE, French writer, political activist and philosopher, and one example of a Gemini personality in chapter five, complained about a lady who apologized whenever she let slip a vulgarism. The lady excused herself by exclaiming, "I believe I am becoming an existentialist!" Sartre was also unhappy with a newspaper columnist who signed himself only "The Existentialist." He fretted because the Communists dismissed existentialism as bourgeois, and because the Christians attacked it as atheistic.

Existentialism was a philosophy which made it possible for many Europeans to survive the horror of the Second World War, the despair of concentration camps and the nihilism of the postwar period. In characteristic Gemini fashion, Sartre developed existentialism from its literary antecedents in Dostoevsky, Kierkegaard and others. This philosophy of life had survival value for him and for countless others whose life situations at the time seemed equally hopeless.

Because existentialism filled a need, it flourished; because it flourished, it was criticized. Sartre knew that; but it disturbed him that the criticisms (express and implied) which he had noticed came from people who did not know what they were talking about. What was more disturbing was the fact that if they did understand his philosophy, they might find it helpful in giving meaning and direction to their own lives.

Sartre attempted to inform the public in the simplest terms possible what his philosophy was all about. "Existentialism," Sartre declared, "is a humanism." He went on to explain that far from counseling futility and despair, existentialism is a spur to action, commitment and individual responsibility. "Existentialism Is a Humanism" was Sartre's most popular lecture and essay and has been widely read.

Humanism has been defined as the study of those subjects—including art and literature—that possess human values, helping Man make himself a more fully realized human creature.[5] Astrology meets this definition. It follows that the contemporary astrologer who works from the perspective of his concern for human welfare is a humanist. Until relatively recent times, astrology was in the mainstream of the humanities and was taught as such in universities throughout the world.

In practical terms, the contemporary astrologer does not deal in abstract notions of religious or philosophical principle. For example, he does not look for *evil* in the chart, as some religions professing astrology still do. He does not speak of *malefic* or even of *benefic* planetary influences. Instead, the contemporary astrologer looks for the problems of the human condition as the horoscope might show them. Viewing the chart as a road map for the life of the native whose horoscope it is, he might suggest that where the roads are likely to be rough, the individual might consider alternate routes. No judgment of the road map as being either good or evil is implied or even relevant.

In the Far East, the principles on which astrology is based have enjoyed a tradition continuing to the present day, finding expression in the *I Ching*, in the philosophy of *Taoism*, in the exercises and meditation of the *T'ai Chi Ching* and in the art of acupuncture. These are all manifestations of astrology as a humanism, and the benefit to Mankind in the East is incalculable. We have been denied most of these benefits in our Western tradition because of the preeminence which rationalism and the scientific method have gained in the last few hundred years, and the results have been just as incalculable a loss to us.

It is my hope that this book may make some small contribution to the return of the study and practice of astrology to the mainstream of the humanities where it can provide to Western Man the kind of benefit it has long provided in the Eastern tradition.

2 "Do You Really Believe in Astrology?"

I AM A lawyer and a teacher. As a lawyer I represent individuals and organizations with a variety of legal problems. "The law sharpens the mind by narrowing it," as the old cliché goes, and I have frequently been struck with the truth of that statement.

Teaching has its own satisfaction and rewards. One of these is that the teacher can himself learn if he has a mind to do so.

In the fall of 1969 I was teaching a course in the philosophy of law or jurisprudence. I had never taught this course before, although I had had some graduate and independent study in legal philosophy, and I learned right along with the students. I was struck by the almost compulsive notion of causation which underlies our jurisprudence and our Judeo-Christian heritage. Indeed, the notion is pervasive. The domino theory of foreign policy is an immediate example. We are told that we must protect one country against Communism in order to prevent a whole series of countries from toppling over or yielding to Communist pressures.

But what, I wondered, if the theory of causation was all wrong? I remembered my own study of the law and one professor who was a firm believer in the domino theory of causation. Professor Blank taught torts and would drone on and on about the necessity for establishing causation before the defendant could be found liable for the plaintiff's damages. He frequently used the example of the row of dominoes.

One day the doughty professor arrived in class to find that someone had stacked a row of dominoes on his lecture platform in exactly the manner he had so frequently and tirelessly described. The class watched in breathless silence as our professor sententiously directed his forefinger to the first domino. It quivered momentously, then he briskly struck it over where it clattered against the second domino in the row. And stood there immobile. Some waggish student had glued all the dominoes to the lectern.

At the time it seemed amusing, but now the thought occurred to me: did the professor's concept of causation work because it was true or did it work because those who advocated the idea *made it work* by discarding any circumstance in which it didn't? Certainly a chain of causation could be traced out if the conditions were right for it, and if all examples of its not working could be disregarded, for whatever reason. But was the notion of causation a correct interpretation of reality or was it simply a popular prejudice about it?

Upon discovering in jurisprudence how we use the notion of *cause* to attach blame ("He made me do it!" or "He caused her injury"), I began seriously to wonder about those dominoes glued to the table.

About the same time I received a second blow to my acceptance of the conventional wisdom.

I HAD HAD disturbing signs of internal bleeding which led a specialist to suspect cancer. Barium x-ray tests were scheduled. The day before this uncomfortable examination, I dropped by a neighbor's house to see a friend. He wasn't home, but his wife, whom I knew only slightly, was hard at work at the kitchen table, surrounded by books and papers. I remembered, with a tolerant smile, that Lillian was an astrologer.

I explained about the examination.

"Oh! So you're afraid you might have cancer, huh? Look, if you can wait around awhile for Jack, I may be able to tell you something."

With that, a series of books, treatises and pamphlets appeared, and a form which I was later to identify as a horoscope eventually materialized. Meanwhile, Lillian's husband arrived, and I excused myself to transact some business with him. When I was ready to leave, Lillian called me back to the kitchen.

She favored me with an impish grin. "Relax! Your chart looks good in terms of your health." She tried to tell me why. I found her explanation disconcerting. In her characteristic rapid-fire delivery, and in a vocabulary utterly incomprehensible to me, she described what my horoscope had told her. I understood only the conclusion: "There are no aspects indicating cancer in your chart, so the bleeding has to be something else, probably nothing serious."

I thanked her and left, somewhat bemused. She certainly had put a lot of effort into something so patently ridiculous. I not only did not believe in astrology, I had no interest in it. I never read the daily horoscopic column in the newspapers* and I tended to patronize

---
*I still don't.

anyone who did. After all, how could the stars *cause* good or poor health?

The next day I endured the tests. They were more uncomfortable than painful, although they were certainly expensive. After a week of tense waiting, I got the report from the doctor: no indication of cancer; the bleeding came from some other, probably innocuous source. The doctor's words sounded vaguely familiar, and I remembered Lillian and her analysis based on my birth chart.

But the stars couldn't *cause* good or poor health.

Then I remembered the dominoes glued to the top of the lecture platform.

A MONTH OR so later, I received a call from Lillian. It was the middle of a busy day of dictation, client conferences and telephone calls, and I was perhaps only half listening when Lillian said, "Jer, I just had to call you. I was updating the aspects on your chart and something just sprang out at me. It looks like you will have serious problems with partnerships late in December and early in January. I didn't want to alarm you but it looks so glaringly obvious, I thought I should alert you."

That was October. In December I went to Hawaii on business and returned to the office near the end of the year. One of my colleagues greeted me with the observation that we had a problem. One of our partners was leaving. Another attorney in the office was forming a partnership with him to set up an independent and competitive practice, early in January. It was something that happens from time to time in almost any law firm of any size. Nevertheless, it was a problem which kept us busy for quite some time.

I telephoned Lillian. She seemed quite excited at the news. I wanted to know how she did it. She was most willing to explain, but once again I was hopelessly lost as she rattled on about trines, cusps, squares, transiting planets and other arcane subjects. I thanked her and hung up. Moodily I looked at the doodles on the scratch pad in front of me. Bumblebees. I had been drawing bumblebees. I remembered something an aeronautical engineer had once told me. It had been scientifically demonstrated that the bumblebee was aerodynamically unsound and could not fly.

No one has ever been able to tell the bumblebees that, I thought, so they just go on happily, in their ignorance, flying away.

The next time Lillian called, I felt a pang of apprehension. It was quickly dissipated.

"Jer, I want you to come to astrology class with me."

"Why?" I asked.

"Because I just discovered there is a law on the books against practicing astrology. Sooner or later we're going to need a lawyer. When that time comes, I want you to know something about astrology!"

By special dispensation I attended my first astrology class at the On the Way Astrology Center (now the Academy of Astrological Studies) in San Diego. The instructor was Gina Ceaglio, a handsome and dynamic redhead who had herself been a student of astrology for over twenty years.

In a large, well-lighted room the students sat at tables facing a blackboard on which something called a horoscope had been drawn. Gina did not disclose (or even hint at) the identity of the individual whose horoscope she had charted. As I watched and listened, Gina pointed to the various squiggles placed around the circle and asked the students what, in this particular context, each squiggle meant. By responding to questions from their instructor, the students gradually pieced together the elements of the horoscope which led to the correct conclusion that the individual was J. Paul Getty.

I was impressed. Gina's teaching method was one with which I was familiar. It is the Socratic method commonly used in law schools, and the method which I used in teaching law students.

So far as I could see, there had been no tricks by which the astrologer-instructor had cued the correct answers; indeed, Gina's presentation seemed every bit as straightforward as any law school professor's.

But how had she done it? It was patently ridiculous to consider that the positions of the planets on the day of birth could have anything to do with human behavior. Yet that information was all the students had to work with. I frowned, and noticed the random scribblings I had made on the yellow pad in front of me.

I had drawn another bumblebee.

I MIGHT HAVE maintained an equilibrium of ambivalence created by the tug of my rationalist bias against the impressive events I had recently experienced, but for an event which strangely combined my legal efforts with Lillian's expertise.

Lillian had expressed the desire to do the natal horoscope of a psychiatrist, to establish a rapport which she felt contemporary astrology needed with psychological disciplines. I introduced her to a neighbor, a psychiatrist who had done medical research in paranormal phenomena. Dr. White (as I shall call him) had unimpeachable medical credentials and an open mind for new ideas. However, I doubt that either Lillian or the doctor anticipated the three-hour session that her delineation of his natal chart involved.

"I learned things about myself in Lillian's delineation," Dr. White later declared, "not revealed in my entire practice analysis."

Since I knew that White had found his own practice analysis valuable and enlightening, I was impressed both with Lillian's demonstrated expertise and with the doctor's generous recognition of her abilities.

I thought the psychiatric episode was over, only to find that it had just begun. A drawn and anxious Dr. White sought my advice as an attorney. Some time ago (he said) he had briefly interviewed a young man—let's call him Bill—at the request of his parents. Later, the parents had arranged for Bill to be admitted to a psychiatric hospital—a move in which Dr. White had played no part. They had taken that action on their own initiative because they had become frantic. His behavior had become increasingly erratic, and they genuinely feared that their son might hurt himself and them as well.

Bill had now been released from the hospital. In a *folie à deux* between mother and son, heightened by the mother's fear of her son upon his release, Dr. White became the scapegoat, the one responsible for all of Bill's problems.

It had started some months ago with venomous notes and telephone calls. More recently, there were acts of terrorism directly aimed at White's home (which I deliberately omit describing) which reflected Bill's increasing ferocity toward Dr. White. A certain amount of un-merited hostility is the price of being a psychiatrist; but now the doctor began to fear for the safety of his wife and children.

I exhausted all the procedures that a lawyer uses to investigate a problem. Reluctantly, I concluded that there was no remedy for Dr. White on any accepted legal theory.

Meanwhile, the veiled threats became more direct—not enough so to support a legal action—and the ominous implications worsened. To his question, "What can I do?" I could only shake my head.

I finally referred him to another attorney, a friend with far greater experience in criminal law than I had. Perhaps I'm too close to the problem, I thought hopefully; maybe "Felix" can figure out an ap-proach that I've overlooked.

But Felix came up only with regrets.

Then I recalled something I had once heard: when all rational efforts to solve a problem prove unavailing, it is irrational not to try the irrational.

I telephoned Lillian.

"The situation's impossible, Jer!" she exclaimed. "I've got White's chart, but you don't even know the birth date of this kid, much less the exact time of his birth!"

I remembered Lillian's insistence on an accurate birth date and time, to the exact minute, for casting a valid horoscope. Still, I was determined to exhaust whatever possibilities there were.

"Can't you at least take a look at Dr. White's chart," I implored her, "to see whether or not there is any real danger to him or his wife and children?"

There was a moment of silence while the Taurean fixity of Lillian's Ascendant fought a losing battle with the insatiable curiosity of her Gemini Sun.

"Come on over as soon as you can—let's see what we can do."

LILLIAN WAS ALREADY at work when I arrived, papers and reference books scattered about her kitchen table. "I've already checked White's chart to see what he's got in his twelfth house of secret enemies," she said in the brisk way that always signaled her commitment to a problem. "He's got Venus and the north node both in Pisces, which means that Venus in his twelfth is his guardian angel. Of course, the north node helps."

This was all Greek to me. I had frequently complained to Lillian that her astrological explanations left me more confused than before.

Lillian pressed on. "There's further evidence of that, since Venus trines Pluto in the fourth house of the home. Pluto rules White's eighth house of death, so that means his home will be pretty well protected. Then I saw his Sun and Mars conjunct—"

I interrupted to ask what "conjunct" meant. Lillian explained that a *conjunction* occurred when two (or more) planets were in the same sign of the zodiac, within a few degrees of each other; and that generally a conjunction of planets increased the energy of both. A *trine*, on the other hand, represented an easy flow of energy from one planet to another, and occurred when planets were 120 degrees apart.

"Dr. White has his Sun conjunct Mars in the eleventh house of friends," she resumed, "but they are both in opposition to Jupiter in his fifth house of children."

"What does that mean?"

"Well, Mars rules Dr. White's Ascendant and his Sun rules his fifth house of children. The opposition of his Sun and Mars to Jupiter shows that he has got a preoccupation in the direction of his children."

"I don't follow that jargon of yours, but I do know that White's first concern is his children's welfare," I said.

"Okay. Jupiter in his fifth house of children shows that Dr. White wants everything for his children—Jupiter is the planet of expansiveness and where we place our highest hopes and ideals. That means his kids have got to be aware that he's uptight right now, especially with his Sun conjunct his Mars—that means he would show he's upset."

At that first meeting, Lillian's major concern was for Dr. White; not so much for the threat posed by his estranged patient as for the stress the doctor was experiencing. But Bill's actions led to the basic question: was the doctor in danger?

"I have to have more to go on," Lillian added. "Don't you have any idea of this fellow Bill's birth date?"

I shook my head.

Lillian sighed, then brightened. "I have an idea! I don't know if it will work, but what the hell, we can give it a try." She began bustling about, gathering up her reference works and astrological tables. "We're going to try to figure out what kind of planetary interplay I should look for in Bill's chart, based on Dr. White's chart!"

She became very busy with her calculations.

I used the time to call Dr. White to ask him what sort of personality Bill had. He said that Bill appeared completely rational and charming, that he had a winning personality: you just couldn't believe he wasn't in control of himself—until something happened to trigger his disturbance.

Lillian seemed to be thinking out loud. "I don't know what Bill's mental problems are, and I'm not going to ask. But I'll tell you, I've seen Bill's kind of personality many times. It usually shows up where the native's Sun is in opposition to his Moon. The kid's got a split personality—his head and his heart are disconnected." That was about as succinct—and accurate—a description of schizophrenia as I had heard.

Lillian passed over a piece of paper on which she had made some notations in a cabalistic scrawl that included the glyphs for the planets and the symbols for the zodiacal signs.

"Neptune has got to be powerful in this guy's chart because he's so far removed from reality. Also, there should be some important aspect between the position of Bill's Mars and Dr. White's Uranus."

"Why?" I asked.

"Because Uranus is prominent in Dr. White's chart. Uranus is in his first house near his natal horizon, which means it shows up in his personality. Uranus is the planet of the unusual and our more impetuous impulses. Mars is Bill's sexuality as well as his hostility. So there's got to be some connection between Mars in Bill's horoscope and Uranus in Dr. White's horoscope."

I nodded dumbly. What was there to say to someone who seemed to know what she was talking about and who spoke so confidently about a subject matter which my intellectual conceit told me did not exist?

"Hey! I think Bill has made a suicide attempt," Lillian said, viewing White's chart with renewed interest.

I was genuinely skeptical. "How can you tell that *Bill* made a suicide attempt by looking at *White's* chart?"

"It's easy. Here, I'll show you." She stood over me, and pointed to the pie-shaped divisions of the circle of the horoscope. "It's a process called 'counting houses.' This"—she pointed—"is White's house of secret enemies, which is the twelfth house of any horoscope. Now, since his secret enemy in this case is Bill, Dr. White's *twelfth* house is Bill's *first* house in White's chart. The first house is always the house of the self."

"Lil," I complained, "that boggles my mind. Would you go over that again—slowly?"

She patiently explained that the doctor's house of secret enemies (his twelfth) was the *first* house of the secret enemy himself—in this case, Bill. Since Dr. White's chart was all she had to go on, she counted Dr. White's twelfth house of secret enemies as Bill's first house of self. Counting "one" from that house, she then counted to twelve and arrived at *Bill's* twelfth house—in terms of Dr. White's chart.

"And what do we find in Bill's twelfth house, according to the doctor's chart?" she continued.

I looked. "Mars and the Sun." I was proud that I was able to identify the glyphs she was pointing to.

"That's right," Lil said. "And since the Sun is the basic self, and it's conjunct Mars in Bill's twelfth house of secret enemies, that tells us one thing."

"What's that?" I was hopelessly confused.

"*Bill's his own secret enemy.* In this case, that probably means a suicide attempt. Mars would suggest a knife or gun."

She peered at the chart. "*Two* suicide attempts. He also tried to drown himself." She said something about the planet Neptune, ruling water, located in Bill's seventh house of other people in hard aspect to the same Sun-Mars configuration.

"What do other people have to do with it?"

"Simply this: in his delusion inspired by Neptune, Bill felt that 'other people' were driving him to suicide."

I was frankly incredulous. She had only the doctor's horoscope before her, and no information at all about this so-called secret enemy. Unless she worked by some sort of ESP (which she vehemently denied), Lillian's deductions simply did not seem possible.

I decided to telephone Dr. White. He was surprised at my question, but after a moment's hesitation, confirmed both suicide attempts. The first time Bill had slashed his wrists with a knife. The second time he had swum far out to sea from a nearby beach, late at night, intending to continue until he could swim no farther.

"Lillian," I said when I had hung up the telephone, "this is getting too spooky. I'm going home." I left, promising to try to discover Bill's birth date—and idly wondering why she didn't just get it from Dr. White's chart.

As I drove home, I passed the beach from which a desperate and lonely young man had begun to swim, in an effort to drown himself and all his problems. Was the passerby who noticed his suicide attempt and who called the police also prefigured by celestial influence?

I scanned the heavens and shivered: the Moon and stars loomed close, bridging the comfortable distance at which our usual common sense puts them. For an instant I felt their elemental power as Archaic Man must have felt it. Later I would read Carlos Castaneda's *Teachings of Don Juan* with an uneasy feeling of recognition when the author related the disorientation he felt in experiencing phenomena he could not explain away in terms of his scientific bias.

THE NEXT DAY I had an idea. Anyone who was as troubled an individual as Bill appeared to be must have had some run-in with the law, which should appear on a rap-sheet somewhere. And the rap-sheet should have his birth date.

But how could I, as a lawyer, make inquiries predicated only on a desire to determine someone's birth date? I shrugged. I had come this far and had involved other people; I would have to see it through. Without much effort, I found Bill's date of birth and immediately telephoned the information to Lillian. That same evening I rushed over to see what Lillian had come up with.

She seemed to be in midsentence as she greeted me at the door. "Bill's chart shows that his Neptune went direct when he was nineteen!" she exclaimed. "Do you know what that means?"

Obviously I didn't.

"Neptune is the planet of *illusion*," Lillian explained. "With positive aspects it can mean a helluvan imagination. But with hard aspects it can mean self-delusion."

The position of Neptune in Bill's chart showed hard aspects indeed. Lillian also explained that relative to the motion of the Earth in its orbit around the Sun, Neptune was in retrograde, or backward motion, when Bill was born. Retrograde motion of a planet would give that planet less emphasis than it might otherwise have. However, when Bill was nineteen the retrograde motion was reversed and Neptune "went direct" and its delusive effect became prominent in his horoscope.

"It was when he was seventeen that he made his first suicide attempt. At nineteen, he tried the second time." Lillian thoughtfully regarded the chart.

I knew the dates were correct from my discussion with Dr. White on the telephone, but I hadn't mentioned it to Lillian or to anyone else. "Where do you see that in the chart?"

She pointed to the glyph for Neptune. "When he was seventeen, Bill's rising sign—that's the sign on the first house of the self—conjuncted Neptune by one degree. That was the first self-deluded suicide attempt. When Bill was nineteen, Neptune went direct. That was the second." She paused, and looked again. "Not only that," she added excitedly, "transiting Uranus hit that Neptune late in 1968 and that conjunction set off a basic conflict between Saturn and Neptune in Bill's chart!"

I didn't know what "transiting" meant. Lillian explained that the positions of the planets at the time of birth are called the *natal* positions in the horoscope. The actual movements of the planets in the heavens on a day-to-day basis are described by astronomers and astrologers as *transits*. A planet which appeared at one point in the horoscope at the time of birth could figuratively "hit" another planet in the birth chart by its subsequent *transit* through the heavens as diagrammed in the natal horoscope.

In Bill's case, as Lillian showed me in the chart she had erected, that is exactly what had happened. Uranus, the planet of the unusual and of quick changes, was in the sign of Gemini when Bill was born. In September of 1968, transiting Uranus moved into the sign of Libra and slowly continued through that sign during 1969, and in doing so, "hit" Bill's natal Neptune and set off a hard aspect between Saturn and Neptune in his chart.

Lillian was now musing over other aspects in her newly erected chart for Bill. She pointed to a big red triangle she had inked into the chart, connecting three planets. "See that? That's a grand trine in fire signs. Aries, Leo and Sagittarius are the fire signs and they give a lot of fiery energy and impetuosity when they're prominent in the chart. When they're linked in a grand trine like this—wow!"

As Lillian had anticipated, the chart showed Bill's Sun in opposition to his Moon.

She had also determined that Bill would have Neptune and Jupiter conjunct his rising sign, or Ascendant, in the first house of his horoscope, the one dealing with his self and his personality. I saw that Neptune and Jupiter were indeed in the very pie-shaped segment of Bill's chart where she had expected to find them, and quite close to the division line which she called the first house cusp.

Certain other anticipated points of contact between Bill's and Dr. White's horoscopes were now confirmed. There was a powerful relationship between Mars, the planet of sexual energy in Bill's chart, and Uranus in Dr. White's chart: they were in a close conjunction of three degrees. There was also an intense aspect between Pluto, the planet of emotional intensity (and of physicians!) in Bill's chart, and the Sun and Mars in Dr. White's chart: they were in opposition, within two degrees of each other.

Lillian pointed out that the Mars-Uranus contact between the charts confirmed her supposition that Bill would react strongly to Dr. White's personality.

She referred to Dr. White's "Uranus personality" because, she said, Uranus was near the horizon at the time of his birth, placing it in the first house of personality in his horoscope. Likewise, she had anticipated the Pluto contact to Dr. White's Sun and Mars, because the doctor's Sun-Mars conjunction showed Dr. White as a strongly masculine individual.

"Bill's chart shows that he has doubts about his own manhood, so he relates strongly to the confidence in his male identity that Dr. White's Sun-Mars conjunction indicates." She frowned at the chart. "He also has a violent reaction *against* those very feelings of attraction. It's as if he hates the doctor for the very reason he loves him!"

I was startled. Without so much as an awareness of the psychiatric term, Lillian had described the classic counterphobic reaction of hostility and fear directed toward a forbidden love object. It certainly explained a lot of Bill's erratic behavior.

"Obviously, Dr. White is a father figure for Bill," Lillian mused. "And with all that Gemini emphasis in Bill's chart, he would want to relate to Dr. White by impressing him with his ability to communicate—at the same time that he would be reacting in a fiery way to that very desire to communicate."

She began working rapidly. "Let's see what's happening with him right now. If we progress Bill's Moon to the present date, that puts it in his third house of communications, where it begins to form an opposition both to his Sun and his Uranus."

I asked her what she was doing.

"There are different ways of updating a chart," Lillian explained. "We call it *progression*. The easiest way is to move each planet one degree for each year since birth. That's what I'm doing now."

I remembered something Lillian had told me earlier. Each sign of the zodiac is a pie-shaped segment of 30 degrees, so that all 12 signs make up a 360-degree circle. So in progressing Bill's horoscope, she was adding as many degrees to the Moon's zodiacal sign position as there were years of life since Bill's birth date. By doing that, she figuratively moved the Moon from its position in the birth chart. The new position of the Moon she called the *progressed Moon*.

As Lillian had indicated, Bill's progressed Moon was approaching a zodiacal sign degree exactly opposite the zodiacal sign degree of both the Sun and Uranus in Bill's birth chart. This impending opposition meant to Lillian that there were heavy obstacles developing which would affect his personality. She explained that this was especially so because of a kind of chain reaction created by the opposition of the progressed Moon to the natal Sun and Uranus, inasmuch as the Sun and Uranus, in turn, had hard aspects to other planets in Bill's chart.

"In this case," Lillian concluded, "Uranus represents erratic behavior and since these hard aspects are being set off by the progressed Moon in the third house of communications, I suspect that Bill will be making a lot of telephone calls in the near future. Remember, Uranus is in Gemini, and that means communication—impulsive and a little kooky."

I asked her whether he was likely to hurt someone.

She shook her head. "I don't think so. I think his greatest release is through words. As a matter of fact," she added, "that's why he keeps calling Dr. White: to command attention to his well-phrased communications!"

She scanned other aspects in the chart. "There is a great deal of sexual frustration here. A real conflict in terms of sexual expression, somehow tied into his feelings about his parents.

"A lot of big money through some kind of Plutonian source! Pluto rules the underworld. He's got a friend helping in an undercover way."

She speculated about the source of his income; I am omitting those probably accurate observations.

"He'll spend his money for sex but he won't get any satisfaction out of it. Whatever woman he becomes involved with will intensify his feelings of inadequacy," she continued. "He'll take out his sexual frustrations again through communications—this time by making a scene in public."

Lillian's most recent deductions were promptly confirmed by an unexpected source. Bill did have a lot of money to spend. He had checked into a downtown hotel which at that time was being readied for the Republican National Convention. It was destined not to take place in San Diego, but we didn't know that then—nor did the Secret Service men who were scurrying about, checking out signs and portents in their own way to insure the safety of the President and his party.

They were not at all happy to discover the presence of Bill, who began making vaguely threatening telephone calls, as Lillian had anticipated. They wanted Dr. White, or his lawyer, to do something about Bill; but Felix confirmed that there was still no effective legal action to be taken.

Government agents had telephoned Dr. White directly when they first became aware of Bill's antipathy toward him. Using Lillian's observations, Dr. White suggested that Bill might follow a certain course of conduct. The Secret Service men were amazed at the psychiatrist's predictive ability.

Bill had indeed attempted a sexual encounter with a woman which had resulted in a public outburst reflecting his inner frustrations. Those frustrations intensified his vehemence which was now directed not only against Dr. White but against father figures generally. That included the President of the United States, the ultimate father figure for any American. As always, however, the more ominous implications of Bill's exhortations were always obscured (from a legal point of view) by his erratic delivery.

Finally, almost as if Bill were bent on fulfilling Lillian's chart analysis to the letter, he contacted a local newspaper and expressed his wish to see in print the full story of the abuses he had suffered. A reporter telephoned Dr. White to get his version of what Bill claimed had happened to him. Dr. White gently refused comment, pointing out that for however short a time, the individual in question had been a patient; and that he could not discuss any patient's problems with newspapermen. The reporter must have been impressed with the doctor's refusal to defend himself against Bill's verbal tirade. Bill's story (or fantasy) never appeared in print.

I touched base with Lillian. "How is all of this going to end?" I asked her.

"It already has," she said with finality. "As of January 20, the Moon moves out of orb of that opposition and I don't think Dr. White will be bothered by Bill again after that date."

On January 20, Dr. White received a pathetic letter from the troubled young man. He never heard from Bill again. He did, however, hear from Bill's parents, who came to the doctor to apologize, expressing genuine contrition for the grief they had visited upon him and his family. They admitted that they had used him as a scapegoat because they were afraid of what their son might do if he found out that his hospitalization had been their doing and theirs alone.

"THIS WAS MY first contact with astrology," Dr. White said. "Lillian Canaan's accurate reading of my horoscope has led me to regard her honesty and nonmanipulative style with great respect. Her assurance and astounding insight that the patient's only desire was to communicate with his doctor gave me my first freedom from fear in many months.

"It also gave me a psychiatric tool to deal adequately with any future threats. Let me tell you the perspicacious advice she gave me.

" 'Doctor,' she said, 'if he ever calls you again, I suggest you simply tell him that you've always known that he was an extremely brilliant person, and that you had the capability of helping him. Tell him also that he is wise enough to know that you did not incarcerate him and that it is your greatest wish for him that he use his brilliance for the good of all Mankind.' I consider this good advice.

"In Lillian's view, it was most important that Bill's strong verbal emphasis be respected, in terms of his need to communicate and to be respected for the clarity of his expression. Again, I cannot fault her opinion."

Fortunately, Dr. White has had no occasion to test Lillian's theory.

"LIL, HOW THE hell do you do you do it?" I asked her.

"Jer, I told you: it's all in the chart." She seemed pleased and amused.

I asked her if that meant that our lives were predetermined by the positions of the stars and planets at birth, a thought that was anathema to me.

"No, of course not. The chart is a road map. If you know your horoscope, it can help you find your way, just as any good road map could. Your horoscope is not an excuse for doing things that you know are wrong. I'm a firm believer in God and in free will and nothing I have learned in astrology has ever changed that."

I thought for a moment. "Lil, do you really *believe* in astrology?" I immediately felt foolish in saying that: after all, one or two lucky hits could be passed off as coincidences but the succession of bulls' eyes I had recently observed could not.

Lillian smiled skeptically. "Do you believe in arithmetic?"

I started to answer that arithmetic wasn't a matter of belief. You used arithmetic because it worked and because it was a useful tool; it did not require an act of faith. My jaw snapped shut. I saw her point.

3 Where Did It Come From?

"I'M SURPRISED AT you, Jerry," Charles said. "You wouldn't tolerate such dogma from me. Why are you willing to accept it simply because it's called astrology?"

I stared at him. Charles was a minister and a man I respected. Although he had a broad interest in psychic phenomena, as befit his Aquarian Sun, he professed the greatest skepticism about astrological principles.

"You've got a good point," I admitted. "Frankly, I don't know what the sources or their claims to validity are. But I'm going to find out."

That was several years ago. The search has been labyrinthine, but my vanity had been hurt and my curiosity aroused. I really didn't know whether the underlying premises of astrology were empirical—or whether they were mystically derived from insight and revelation. I didn't know whether I was dealing in the subject matter of religion or of metaphysics. But after all the research that went into this chapter and the next, and a lot more in the process of revision, I did arrive at some conclusions. First, that astrology is neither physical nor metaphysical. Nor is it a normative science. Law is a normative discipline, one that is based on more or less arbitrary *norms* or standards of human behavior, rather than on general conclusions about reality itself.

Nor is astrology an empirical study such as medicine, which likes to think that it is based on facts drawn from scientific observation of the physical world. All too often, however, science is based on the suppression of facts inconsistent with favored theory.

It seems to me that astrology is *metempirical*: that is, it is *empirical* in that it is based on observation of and experience in the real world; but its ultimate concepts generalize well beyond (*meta-*) empirical observation. Perhaps that is what Dane Rudhyar, one of our greatest astrologers, meant when he said astrology was the algebra of life.[1]

The reader must draw his own conclusions after reviewing the evidence. My first question for research was: *where did astrology come from?*

The answer came quickly, although it raised many new questions. Astrology came from everywhere; it started all over the world and all at once.

It started with the Sun.

AS DOCTORS AND scientists have often observed, there is no counterpart in the animal kingdom for the phenomenon known as the human brain. Moreover, despite the remains of hominid (manlike) apes which anthropologists claim are our distant ancestors, science has found no species from which the brain of *Homo sapiens* could have been derived.

What's so strange about the human brain? Just this.

First, the human brain is as large as it can be to allow birth, and the female pelvis has made all possible adjustments to accommodate its size.

Second, within three months *after* birth, the brain of the human infant has trebled in size—and continues growing for years thereafter.

Third, in those thankfully few cases in which the brain does not undergo this strange postnatal development, a pinhead, without human consciousness, is the tragic result.

Fourth, during what Dr. Simeons calls a period of "freakish growth" of the human brain cortex, the period of infancy, childhood and adolescence is remarkably stretched out—again, a phenomenon unparalleled in the animal kingdom—giving Man a proportionately greater period of childhood than any other mammal. This *neotony* as it is called is required to permit the growth and development of the human brain.

Fifth, there is an incredible acceleration of the development of the human brain cortex in the evolutionary scheme—just as if it happened all at once, at the end of the last phase of the current Ice Age.

Sixth, despite the enormous postnatal growth of the human brain, the cerebral cortex, which is a direct measure of human intelligence, is so complexly convoluted, so densely packed into the cranium, that if it were, instead, stretched smoothly over the two lobes of the brain, the brain would have to be the size of a beer barrel to accommodate it.

In *Man's Presumptuous Brain*, Dr. Simeons remarks about this "freakish growth" of the human brain.[2] Freakish? Perhaps more than he realized. We know today that mutation, along with Darwinian natural selection, is the explanation for the evolutionary scheme of things, according to the conventional wisdom of science.

The Sun is our major source of radioactivity, constantly bombarding us with radiation even under normal conditions, and radioactivity causes mutation. Reports by lunar astronauts of the existence of once molten areas of rock on the Moon have prompted naturalist Loren Eiseley to conclude that some thirty thousand years ago, a solar prominence of enormous size may have reached out across space "like the flame of a dragon's breath."[3]

Eiseley speculates that the radiation from such a giant solar flare could explain the sudden extinction of the dinosaurs in the last phase of our current Ice Age; and he raises the question whether this dragon's tongue of radiation changed Man's world in some major way, which perhaps gives credence to the ancient myth of our loss of Eden.

I would answer Eiseley with this: if such a serpent of fire, a giant solar flare, so addled the pea-brains of those giant mammals as to cause their extinction, it most certainly could have caused the mutations of the hominid primates which led to the "freakish growth" of the human brain. Most mutations fail; but mutations of the hominid brain which gave the hominid ape the intelligence to adapt to the demands of a rapidly changing world at a time of retreating ice and changing climates could enable him to survive as a matter of natural selection. And such mutations in the hominid ape could stretch out his infancy, sacrificing his fur to the "freakish" postnatal growth of the brain, leaving our hominid ancestors truly naked and afraid in a world they never made.

Solar cataclysms were not uncommon during the last phase of our current Ice Age, according to Robert Ardrey's *African Genesis.* Solar flares have been credited with having caused the alternating periods of advancing and retreating ice. And although sunspots or solar flares still occur, the enormous flares which melted the Moon's crust some thirty thousand years ago must have rained an enormous amount of cosmic radiation on the heads of our hominid ancestors. The process of mutation, selection, adaptation, leading to the development of a truly human consciousness, may have then begun; so that what appeared at the Caspian Sea, the ancient hub of civilization, some ten thousand years ago was not *Homo erectus,* but *Homo sapiens: perceiving man.* Indeed, the very word "man" may be derived from the Anglo-Saxon for "mind."[4]

What does all this have to do with the origin of the zodiac? Samuel Taylor Coleridge once remarked that it is impossible to think of Man without the concept of a Fall. Aldous Huxley adds that the Fall embodies an important psychological truth. However, Huxley would modify the Genesis myth to make clear that the Fall involves the transition from the timelessness of eternity to the historical time of Man; from the unmanifested Oneness of divinity to the manifest multiplicity of nature. In the East, this religious transformation is called *Maya.*

The zodiac shows the Fall of Man in terms of the dawn of human consciousness, commencing with the *fire* sign Aries, representing the first primitive ego-consciousness of Man. When the Aries consciousness is developed in successive stages, through the next three signs, the *fire* sign Leo symbolizes consciousness as the paterfamilias, the leader of family or tribe. The *fire* sign Sagittarius commences the last evolutionary cycle, the higher consciousness of religion, philosophy and law.

Zodiac is often translated as circle of animals, but it really means *circle of life,* and it shows the *event* of Man the conscious animal in its entirety. "Man is the whole fantastic event" resulting from that consciousness, according to naturalist N. J. Berrill. And the event of Man includes not only the present but his collective past as well.[5] Or, as Eiseley put it, with the dawning of human consciousness, Man became "a dream animal" in the sense that he lives at least partially in a secret universe which he shares with his fellow dream animals who live in their heads as well. And with that, Eiseley concludes, "Symbolic communication had begun."[6]

So what did Man, the dream animal, see when he stepped out of his cave of primeval darkness, his vision aided by the new consciousness of his remarkable brain?

He saw angels.

THE ANGELS OF the Old Testament were actually astrological signs. According to Old Testament teachings, stars were messengers in the service of God.[7] The Hebrew word *malak,* meaning messenger, was translated into the Greek equivalent, *angelos,* thence into Latin as *angelus* and into English as angel. Angels were messages from God, drawn from Babylonian star myths or, in a word, from astrology.

Today we think of angels as people in white gowns with wings. While angels were personified in human form in dreams in the Old Testament and in the Apocalyptic visions of the New Testament, their origin and reality were in what the ancient prophets saw as portents in astrological groupings of the stars. The rampant angelology of the eleventh through the thirteenth centuries has blurred this original authentic vision, but it is rediscoverable by any fair reading of the Old Testament.

The messages of the angels thus provide some of our earliest astrological lore. *Seraph,* the singular of *seraphim,* the highest order of angels, means fiery serpent. It is the *seraph* which has dominion over the element fire, corresponding to the salamander of the Hermetic astrologers. The *Revelation of Moses* speaks of the *seraphim* who "roar like lions." The zodiacal fire sign Leo *is* a lion and, according to traditional astrological principles, is ruled by the fiery Sun itself. Finally, the glyph or symbol representing Leo looks a lot more like a serpent than a lion.

The angelic astrology of the Scriptures gives us tantalizing hints about Man's origins and his Fall. Uriel, an angel whose name translates as fire of God, has been identified as the regent of the Sun, and as the angel who "watches over thunder and terror."[8] But what thunder and what terror? According to one authority, Uriel "stood at the gate of the lost Eden with the fiery sword."[9]

Could it be that the fiery sword of the angel of thunder and terror was Eiseley's serpent's tongue of solar cataclysm that led to our loss of Eden by the acquisition of human consciousness some thirty thousand years ago? One day we may know.

American scholar Samuel Noah Kramer tells us, in *History Begins at Sumer,* that his translations of clay tablets in the ancient land of Ur led to his conclusion that that civilization was amazingly advanced, including, among others, such precedents as: the first schools, the first bicameral congress, the first cosmology and cosmogony, the first farmer's almanac.[10]

Civilization began at Sumer, some eight thousand years before the common era (B.C.E.). The Sumerians were not a Semitic people; they actually antedated the Semites—including the twelve tribes of Israel!— who were the beneficiaries of their extremely advanced culture. Interestingly enough, the Sumerian philosophy did not include the notion of causation.[11]

Sumer was known in the Old Testament as the land of Ur. In the original Hebrew, Ur is *Aur,* which means fire, or light in the context of fire. We can therefore trace the origin of Man, human consciousness and civilization to a common root in fire.

Chapter seven, on the astrological triplicities, deals at length with the elemental qualities of the signs. Each sign of the zodiac corresponds to one of the elements of alchemy—fire, earth, air and water. That sequence is repeated three times, so there are three signs in each of the elements. These sets of three signs by element are called *triplicities.*

For purposes of tracing astrological origins in this chapter, we need only consider the astrological problem presented by the *fiery* triplicity of Aries, Leo and Sagittarius which has confounded many an astrologer. The fire signs are characterized by most astrologers as primarily passionate and sexual, while others consider them primarily signs of *mentation*, or conscious thought processes.

I confess that I was both surprised and delighted when my digging into astrological origins showed such conclusive support for the identification of the fire signs as signs of human consciousness. With the physical evidence of the Deluge and attendant solar cataclysms and with the astrological messages contained in angel myths, it is almost as if the fire signs reflect Man's racial memory, dredged from his collective unconscious, of how his Fall into human consciousness resulted from a baptism of solar fire. However, that conclusion left unresolved the question of the persistent sexuality always associated with the fire signs. Again, research led me back to the Sun, the astrological (and perhaps biological) source of human consciousness.

Biblical scholar John Allegro tells us that the Sun was viewed by Archaic Man, including the Old Testament prophets, as an enormous phallus: the Sun glowed bright red with tumescence at sunrise, white hot with sexual tension at noon, and dull red in detumescence at sunset. Our ancient concept of deity was seen in the fire of the Sun which was equated with its apparent sexuality: the Sun fertilized the Earth with celestial semen in the form of rain. Crops sprouted then, for the Earth had been impregnated by the Sun god and would be bountiful.[12] In *The Psychoanalysis of Fire,* Professor Gaston Bachelard suggests that our earliest ancestors, worshipping the hot and sexual Sun, sought to duplicate its sexuality in ritual by the friction of sticks rubbed together—and real fire was the result. How else, Bachelard asks, would anything so forbidding and so threatening as fire ever be adapted for human use by our primitive ancestors?[13]

Finally, Allegro points out that the root of Ur, the land of our common ancestors, is *U*—the most important word-unit in the whole of Near-Eastern religion.[14] According to context, *U* means copulate, mount sexually or create.

Thus, underlying the *Ur* of fire is the *U* of sex; and the astrological characterization of the fire signs is vindicated in terms of our ancient equation of sex and creation with the fire of human consciousness, a principle just as vital to contemporary psychology as it is to contemporary astrology.

However, Archaic Man saw in the heavens a luminary even more vital to his existence than the Sun, and that was of course the Moon.

LONG BEFORE WE developed any sense of history, we lived according to the cycles of the Sun and Moon, but most especially of the Moon.

Today we think of the Sun as rising in the east, being directly overhead at noon and setting in the west. But its apparent path varies much more than that. In midsummer, the Sun appears overhead; in midwinter, it appears quite low in the sky. To Archaic Man, the Sun *died* every year, but the Moon, although it waxed, reached fullness and waned, was immortal.

From the cycles of the Moon Archaic Man first gained the hope of rebirth—and the concept of the month, a word derived from the Latin *mensis*, the same root for our word "menstrual," another cycle related to the Moon. The menstrual, or Moon, cycle was but one expression of our ancestors' feeling of relationship to the universe, a relationship which is the foundation of astrology.

According to Plutarch's biography of the mythical founder of Rome, Romulus founded the city by first digging a central pit; from this center he described a circle with a plow to mark the city's boundaries. The circle was then divided into quaternities, according to the cardinal compass directions of north, south, east and west. As Carl Jung and C. Kerenyi interpret this myth, the world of Rome radiated in all directions from the universal center that was Man. [15]

This symbolic microcosm remains basic to astrology and can be seen in any conventional horoscope charted by the contemporary astrologer. The central point is the individual at the horizon of his birthplace; the basic division of the outer circle is fourfold, according to cardinal compass directions.

Archaic Man saw an earthly counterpart for everything that happened in the heavens, with Man himself as the center of the universe. *With the first breath of infancy he internalized these cycles and from that moment until death he and the universe were one.* And what happened in the heavens was first marked by the cycles of the eternal Moon, which keyed the tides, the menstrual flow and, when her position was fixed by the clusters of stars surrounding her, the seasons as well. For, as Dr. Hugh Moran has pointed out, the first signs of the zodiac were the clusters of stars surrounding the Moon, or lunar mansions as they were called; by using the lunar mansions as mnemonic aids to the Moon's position, our ancestors first learned how to trace the seasons. [16] Ironically, these signs would eventually lead to the alphabet, which became the single greatest tool of scientific rationalism and its triumphant attack on the astrological symbolism from which it was derived.

Our ancestors noticed that there were certain stars that did not wander; they were the circumpolar stars fixed in the celestial sphere. Others, puzzlingly, seemed to wander across the sky in the same path as the Sun. The Greek word *planet,* meaning wanderer, was applied to them. And since the Sun's pathway through the heavens was the only position at which the terrifying eclipses occurred, the Sun's path became known as the ecliptic. It still is, in astrology (and astronomy) today.

We eventually noticed that when the Sun was at the vernal equinox, it was spring: this is the point at which the plane of the ecliptic and the Earth's equator coincide, so that day and night are of equal length. The identification of this position of the Sun in the heavens was made possible by our ancestors' use of mnemonic images derived from the star clusters that formed the celestial background to the Sun and Moon.

We then noticed that when the Sun reached a standstill, the weather was warm and it was summer. This was the summer solstice—solstice means sun stands still—another important period of the solar year. At harvest time, the Sun's ecliptic crossed the equator again, and this was the autumnal equinox. Finally, in the dead of winter, the Sun reached its final standstill, or solstice.

I have said that the lunar mansions were mnemonic aids first used to locate the ever-changing positions of the Moon, which each month disappeared for a time from the night sky. But, as the use of these star clusters or constellations was eventually applied to the changing seasons of the solar year, the cycles of the birth and death of the Sun, they took on a deeper significance.

In predicting the ecliptic path of the Sun through the heavens, Archaic Man projected onto the night sky the images that we know as constellations and signs of the zodiac. As contemporary psychologists such as Carl Jung and many others have pointed out, we projected on those disparate points of light in the night sky twelve master symbols or archetypes drawn from our collective unconscious and triggered by the cyclic rhythms of Sun, Moon and season. The objection that these twelve constellations or signs hardly resemble the images for which they are named entirely misses the point: *the images came first* and were projected onto the heavens in the same manner that today we project images onto Dr. Rorschach's inkblots. The difference, however, is one of interpretation. Whereas the analysis of the Rorschach inkblots gives clues to the individual personality, the analysis of the meanings of the zodiacal signs provides us with important clues to the enduring relationships of Man, the dream animal, to the universe which engulfs him. Research into the history of the world's religions reveals that these symbols were universal; that the same messages were derived in archaic societies throughout the world from the cyclic repetition of the Sun, Moon and stars, or what Eliade has called the eternal return.

Cosmos out of chaos was the promise of the vernal equinox, when our ancestors saw with vast relief that energizing god return to the world of men after its demise in what we still call the dead of winter, the winter solstice at about December 22. All of Man's religions teach that in the beginning was the Word; but it was more than just a word: it was the Greek *Logos*, essentially untranslatable, but translated in the Book of John as the Word. *Logos* means much more, with connotations of a creative, cosmic order, or the cosmic reason which was seen in the cyclic nature of the universe. Its Old Testament equivalent is *Memra*, meaning world-constructing, world-permeating intelligence, with implications of divine wisdom.

The vernal equinox signaled the commencement of the new year, the rebirth of the Sun and therefore of the entire world in all of the societies of Archaic Man. In Babylon, mourning festivals were held for the dying nature god Dumuzu at the autumnal equinox. In Greece, Dumuzu was revered as Adonis; in ancient Hebrew belief he was called Adonai, or Tammuz. Even today, the holy Day of Atonement, or Yom Kippur, is the tenth day of Tishri, the first month of the Hebrew calendar based on the lunar cycles and commencing with the autumnal equinox.

Recently, an ancient Hebrew horoscope was discovered in the remains of a temple in the biblical land of Chaldea, with all twelve zodiacal signs and also with Hebrew lettering (see fig. 1).

The vernal equinox was also celebrated as the holiday of the Phoenician fertility goddess Astarte, the German dawn goddess Austron and the Teutonic goddess Easter.

Today we celebrate Easter on a date calculated from the first Sunday following the first full Moon occurring on or after March 21, the date on our modern calendars which most generally coincides with the equinox. Indeed, the vernal equinox remained the first day of the year in England until 1752.

The vernal equinox commences the zodiacal year at the first point of Aries, that holy day of beginnings for Mankind throughout history and prehistory.

ALTHOUGH ASTROLOGICAL PRINCIPLES appear to have developed simultaneously and independently throughout the world in all of Man's societies, the land of Chaldea is especially associated with the

FIGURE 1. An ancient Hebrew horoscope
Reprinted by permission of the Jewish Theological Seminary

early flourishing of astrological lore. Chaldea is a generic term which encompasses all of what was southern Babylon; it was also known as the land of Ur, and the Chaldeans inherited the highly developed civilization of the even more ancient Sumerians. Chaldea, or Ur, benefited also by the remarkably clear skies of southern Babylon next to the Persian Gulf, and the Chaldeans built watchtowers, called ziggurats, to observe the heavens more closely. The Babylonians were merchants, and commerce created mathematics, which, combined with their philosophical beliefs based on the cycles of Sun and Moon, made astrology-astronomy a highly sophisticated art thousands of years ago. It is no wonder that the words "Chaldean" and "astrologer" became synonymous.

With the benefit of their Sumerian inheritance, the Chaldeans gave us the division of the circle into 360 degrees and the division of the year into 360 days, both concepts based on their observations of the ecliptic path of the Sun. The division of the ecliptic into 360 degrees led naturally to the further division into lunar periods of 30 days each, to make 12 such cycles in a year: hence the 12 months and the 12 signs of the zodiac.

The Chaldeans were also the first to chart the heavens, to distinguish between the stars and the planets and to determine the dates of the solstices and the equinoxes. Every planet was identified according to its archetypal characteristics, and as such, became a god about whom stories could be told and for whom future events could be predicted. With the invention of the 360-degree circle and the discovery of the zodiac in terms of the ecliptic path of the Sun in which all the planets travel, the Chaldeans were able to cast the first horoscopes.

Consider how the horoscopes we use today reflect their original source. Figure 2 is a typical chart showing the 12 zodiacal signs in their natural sequence. It is a circle with 12 subdivisions of 30 degrees each for a total of 360 degrees. It starts with zero degrees Aries, the point represented by the vernal equinox, which then corresponded to the Sun's position in the constellation Aries, the Ram. The circle of the zodiac commences at the east, where the Sun rises, and east is at the left-hand side of the horoscope, with south at the top because in Chaldea—located at about 32 degrees of Earth latitude in the northern hemisphere—you must face south to see the noonday Sun. As you can see, if the Sun were placed in this horoscope at noon, it would indeed be at the cardinal southern point at the top of the chart.

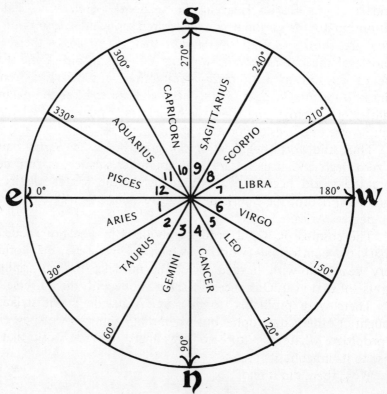

FIGURE 2. Division of the horoscope

At the point of intersection of the vertical and horizontal lines which show the cardinal compass directions and divide the horoscope into quarters, we find the central point, which corresponds to the axial pit from which Romulus plowed his circle to found Rome. For both the Chaldean and the contemporary astrologer, Man is always at the center of the universe, which the horoscope represents.

The signs of the zodiac are numbered from 1 to 12, in counter-clockwise rotation. Just as the 360-degree circle represents the Chaldean year, the 12 zodiacal signs represent the periodic lunar cycles or months. The basic premise of the ever-renewing cycle of life is graphically depicted here. The circle of the horoscope proceeds from the first sign of consciousness, Aries, through the twelfth and begins anew. The horoscope is both a representation of the heavens as they appeared to the Chaldeans and a magic circle symbolizing the cosmic order which was a deeply felt religious principle not only of the Chaldeans but of all our traditional societies.

Such magic circles, with a central point upon which to fix the gaze, have been used for millennia in the Near and Far East. They are called mandalas, meaning magic circles for meditation. In the Chinese mandala of the Earlier Heaven, the sequence of elements and their relationship to the cardinal compass directions and trigrams of the *I Ching* are shown. As an overlay on that magic circle there is the mandala of the Later Heaven, showing the relationship of the seasons, time of day, again with cardinal directions and trigrams from the Chinese Book of Changes. These mandalas show both the palimpsest qualities of astrology and the basic principles of Man in his relationship to a universe of cycles of constant change.

Thus, the world begins at zero degrees Aries, the vernal equinox. At zero degrees Cancer we are at the summer solstice; at zero degrees Libra the world begins to age and die. At the winter solstice, zero degrees Capricorn, the Sun is dead and remains so until it is reborn at zero degrees Aries.

The cosmos or world order symbolized by the horoscope was a remarkably comfortable world in which to live. True, the world died every year; but with it died all of the burdens—the sins, guilts and regrets—of that year. Our ancestors lived at one with the universe.

There were problems, to be sure. A plague might strike, or a drought or other catastrophe, but when that happened we knew enough to propitiate whatever nature god was angry. It was a world that made sense to its inhabitants.

Why, then, did it end?

THE MYTH OF SISYPHUS is the story of a man whose punishment it is to spend eternity rolling a huge rock to the top of a mountain. Once there, the rock rolls down the mountain and Sisyphus must turn back to begin his endless task.

Albert Camus used this myth to represent the absurdity of Man's condition as he saw it. For Camus, rational man confronts an unintelligible universe which he can never hope to know. So the intelligent man must live without hope, struggling through a world that is essentially absurd. Sisyphus has been widely adopted in the humanities as a symbol of Man's present relationship to his universe.

Yeats called suicide the Savage God; and the marked increase in sacrifices to the Savage God in this century has been directly related to Man's growing sense of alienation, or to what Alvarez has described as the artist's sense of personal chaos.[17]

Traditionally, suicide has had two causes: either the individual's inability to live up to the demands of his ego or his altruistic self-sacrifice for an ideal. At the turn of the century, however, French sociologist Emil Durkheim discovered a new, third type of suicide, a phenomenon resulting from Man's present sense of alienation. Durkheim adopted the term *anomie* to describe that sense of contemporary alienation which leads to *anomic suicide*.[18] *Anomie*, or anomy, was originally a theological term, widely used in the seventeenth century to mean disregard of divine law[19] or, I might add, of *Logos* or *Memra*.

This sense of alienation, of chaos, is a symptom of a profound change in Man's temporal perception. We see time as a linear function which holds no promise of cyclical regeneration, and we have lost Archaic Man's sense of relationship to the cosmic order. To discover how this vitally important alteration occurred, let us return to those Chaldean plains, this time to consider certain Semitic tribes which were indistinguishable from the many other nomadic tribes except (as Will Durant once remarked) for one quality: the Hebrew prophets had an absolute genius for religion.

Old Testament visionaries displayed both great wisdom and great dedication; instinctively they understood that their survival as a people required exclusive devotion to their unknown God, a Deity whom they called Yahweh, which, literally translated, means He Who Causes To Be.

The Hebrew prophets exercised their considerable authority to direct their people away from the popular nature gods worshipped by the Babylonians and by the Egyptians. History shows that it was no small task. Indeed, had it not been for the periodic catastrophes by which the Semitic tribes were so regularly afflicted, it is doubtful whether the stern polemics of their prophets could have succeeded.[20]

But succeed they did. By interpreting all catastrophes as the vengeance of a wrathful Yahweh, the rabbinate ultimately convinced their fellow tribesmen that they must reject Baal, Ashtoreth, Tammuz and all the other gods who reflected the cosmic order of Archaic Man, and live instead according to Yahweh's immutable commandments.[21]

The achievement of the Hebrew religion was therefore to firmly establish, *for the first time in Man's history,* the notion of cause and effect in human existence with the intimately related notions of responsibility and guilt. Aided by the conception of the Fall into human consciousness which, according to Genesis, was also an act of guilt—attributing to Man the ability to distinguish and therefore to choose between good and evil actions—the Hebrew prophets ultimately succeeded in transcending the traditional world-view of ever-repeating cycles of death and rebirth and imposed on the consciousness of their people (and eventually, of Western civilization) *the phenomenon of a one-way time.*[22]

Yahweh personally intervened in the lives of his subjects and expressed his pleasure or displeasure with their actions in terms of everything that happened to them—as interpreted by their prophets. The global catastrophes were the vengeance of Yahweh for the wickedness of his people. Whatever their cause, these catastrophes are described in many passages of the Old Testament, as, for example, the fiery serpents which the Book of Numbers (21:6) tells us were sent to punish Israel and killed many people. This incident illustrates a parallel development that made the monumental religious achievement possible. The rabbinate disapproved of astrology because its premises seemed inconsistent with their concept of Man's total responsibility for all his actions; and I suspect that it is for that reason that angels appear with less and less frequency as the Old Testament history progresses.

Instead, astrological symbolism was used in an entirely different manifestation, with results even more profound.

AWARE OF THE fact that for the past two thousand years scholars have sought in vain to trace the origin of the alphabet, Dr. Hugh Moran, a Columbia University professor who had studied Orientology at Oxford, decided to explore. In his remarkable study, *The Alphabet and the Ancient Calendar Signs,* Dr. Moran concluded that the written word originated with the Hebrew alphabet, which had been adapted by Sumerian priests from the signs of the zodiac.[23]

The Hebrew patriarchs succeeded in their religious objective of requiring steadfast devotion to the God of Righteousness by adapting a tool which was part of their Sumerian inheritance. The alphabet, and hence the written word, made the Scriptures possible, and with the Scriptures a linear, cause-and-effect conception of the world emerged—the end of the timeless era of Archaic Man and the beginning of history.

To write history is to interpret history; and the Old Testament is the history of the Jews interpreted as their relationship to their One God Who Causes Everything To Be. Archaic Man vanishes. The Man of History emerges, possessed of the notions of cause and effect, the knowledge of right and wrong, the responsibility for his actions—and a relentless accumulation of guilt. Such is our Judeo-Christian heritage, the foundation of our common law and the beginning of Western civilization.

Historic Man also marks the point of departure from our ties to the ever-repeating cycles of the Sun, Moon and seasons, for the Man of History must accept as meaningful the actions of an unknowable Deity of a world that presses ever forward, that neither ends nor is reborn.[24]

To console their people for the loss of the world of annual rebirth, the Old Testament prophets promised a new Golden Age with the coming of the Messiah. The Apostles of the New Testament claimed that that prophecy had been fulfilled and their adherents constructed a City of God on a foundation of Old Testament doctrine and Greek philosophy.

Because the Ptolemaic conception of a geocentric, or Earth-centered, universe was part of that City of God, astronomy became religious dogma. So that limited knowledge of the heavens was frozen, and any attempt to develop new theories was regarded as heresy.

Essential to our Judeo-Christian religious heritage is the concept of *faith:* for it took faith, and sometimes a great deal of it, to accept as both meaningful and just the actions of an unknowable God who causes everything in a world that goes on and on. And when faith is no longer possible, life becomes both absurd and unendurable, as the many anomic victims of the Savage God have found in our own time.

But what of the Messiah, *Christos* in Greek, Anointed One in Hebrew? Surely when the Messiah comes, the world with all its absurdity will finally end!

Or has he already come? And if he has come, has the world regained its meaning?

To restate the question in terms of our quest, what has Christianity written on the palimpsest of astrological lore?

4 ... And Come Again?

I MENTIONED AT the beginning of the last chapter that my search for astrological origins has been labyrinthine, and so it has. The maze of our human beginnings led me down many corridors that ended in a cul-de-sac; or into a maze of esoterica that brought me full circle.

In retrospect, I find it surprising how closely the Labyrinth parallels my own blind gropings. In that Greek myth, the Labyrinth was the lair of the Minotaur, a monster with the head of a bull and the body of a man. The legendary Greek king Theseus, acting in the service of the god Apollo, found his way into the Labyrinth with a magic ball of thread. Once there, he slew the Minotaur.

Having followed my magic ball of thread, the principles of astrology itself, through its labyrinthine twists, I tug on the thread: the Old Testament ends and the era of the New Testament begins. We are now in the lair of the Minotaur itself. Unlike Theseus, our task is not to destroy the Minotaur but to resurrect him.

There were two major influences in Greek life at the birth of Christianity. One was Apollo, and the other Dionysus, a fertility god, represented by a bull, who ruled wine and vineyards. Later, he was the drunken Bacchus; but as Dionysus, the intoxication he produced was spiritual.

The worship of Dionysus began with the legendary figure of Orpheus, whose devotion to Dionysus required purity of thought and deed—although antic revelry was very much in order when his acolytes were appropriately moonstruck: Dionysus was worshipped by dancing and by theatre. The intoxication sought by the Orphic cult was a mystic Oneness identical to that of the Hindus, from which some claim Orphism was derived.

To the Orphic worshippers of Dionysus, life in this world was pain and suffering. Mortal Man was bound to the wheel of life through endless cycles of birth and death, but by renunciation of this world, he could escape the wheel of rebirth and achieve the ecstasy of Oneness with God.[1]

The Greeks worshipped at one of two shrines. Some worshipped Dionysus, and all that was ecstatic, religious and mystical. Others worshipped Apollo, and all that was rational, empirical and scientific. Those Greeks who were of a religious nature embraced Orphism; Greeks of a rationalist bent worshipped Apollo and despised Dionysus.[2]

Precisely who were these gods? The Roman equivalent of Apollo was the god Sol, a word which means the Sun. The Greek god Apollo is also identified with the Sun. Intriguingly enough, the word "Apollo" has two possible origins, either *destroyer* or *apple*.[3] Apollo was the son of Zeus, the father god whose name means bright sky.[4] Apollo, the Sun god who represented all that was rational in Man, was both the *apple* from the Tree of Knowledge and the *destroyer* of Man's innocence.

Dionysus, on the other hand, was the child of Zeus and Io, a goddess who was also called Semele or Selene, all of whose names mean the Moon. Dionysus, the Moon god, represents Man's original innocence, his existence in a state of nature before he ate that apple.

Genesis tells us that God made men to have dominion over the Earth. Then as now men who worshipped Apollo sought the knowledge to gain dominion over the world with which they were no longer one. Then as now men who worshipped Dionysus sought to return to that state of nature or Oneness, which is achieved not by reasoning but by intuition—or by enthusiasm, a word which quite literally means infused with the god.

Astrology, ancient and contemporary, associates our rational, Faustian drives with the Sun, just as the ancients did in Apollonian and biblical myths. Our intuitive, enthusiastic and spiritual drives are associated with the Moon—again, just as did our ancestors in their Dionysian and biblical myths.

It is a principle of contemporary astrology and of contemporary analytical psychology as well that both of these drives exist in all of us and require expression.[5] In the myth of the Labyrinth, the Minotaur is the child of the Sun and the Moon. His supposed monstrousness is an Apollonian libel: it was Theseus the monarch, Graves tells us, who *invented* the concept of justifiable homicide.[6]

In astrology, the symbol for the *planet* Mercury is based on the caduceus of the *god* Mercury, who is Hermes in the Greek original. Hermes was the god of wisdom, and it is significant that the caduceus, which was the heraldic staff of Hermes, shows two serpents intertwined. As the reader will see in chapter ten, "What Are the Planets?," these serpents show the courses of the Sun and Moon, symbolizing the astrological principle that the archetypal forces these luminaries represent must be integrated for the native to achieve wisdom.

Why, then, did Theseus slay the Minotaur for Apollo?

Perhaps the myth is a simple statement of historical fact, reflecting the early struggles which existed within Christianity itself. Like the Old Testament Jews and the later Christians of orthodoxy, the Orphic worshippers of Dionysus were essentially monotheistic. *Unlike* the Jews, however, the Orphics did not worship the ongoing rationalism of the God of Righteousness. Quite the contrary; the Orphics worshipped the eternal NOW of Unaging Time as it existed before the Fall.

Monotheism is but one of many similarities between Orphism and early Christianity. Both cults emphasized revelation, the founding of churches and the idea of resurrection. "I am the vine," Jesus says in the Book of John, using the symbol most readily associated with Dionysus. In turn Dionysus was often called *Zagreus,* which means *The Resurrected*—a term most often associated with Christ.[7]

Robert Graves is probably our greatest living authority on Greek mythology; he is certainly no sensationalist. Yet his second thoughts about the myth of Dionysus are sensational indeed, providing an even more intriguing coincidence between Dionysian and Christian mysticism. Graves has decided that the nectar and ambrosia on which the gods subsisted—most notably Dionysus and his moonstruck followers— was in fact wine to wash down the hallucinogenic *Amanita muscaria,* better known to us as magic mushrooms.[8] Even more recently, biblical scholar John Allegro concluded that these same magic mushrooms were used by the original Christians to achieve mystic union with God; he also says that the original Dionysian and Christian cults were essentially one and the same.[9]

Be that as it may, the mystic search for Oneness by both the Orphics and the Christians was halted in the name of Apollo. The Christian Word spread by Paul (whose birth date followed the date ascribed to the death of Christ) was rigorously rational, oriented to Hebrew Scripture and to Greek philosophy. St. Augustine, that great professor of rhetoric, was squarely in the Apollonian camp: his *City of God,* which laid the philosophic and religious foundations for the Roman Catholic church, reflects both his love of prose and of Plato.

But what of Christ himself, before the retelling of his message by so many people who never knew him? The search for the historical Jesus has not proved fruitful; a passage from the early historian Josephus, heavily relied upon as evidence external to the New Testament itself of Christ's existence, has been shown to have been faked.[10] Allegro contends that, by tracing the words *Jesus* and *Dionysus* to their philological roots, he has shown that, as with the cults themselves, the very words have a common origin.[11]

Whether they do or not, the astrological significance is the same, for the slaying of the Minotaur accurately symbolizes the vanquished forces of Dionysus, the rise of rationalism and the triumph of Apollo, who would reign supreme both in Hierosolyma, the Sacred City of the Jews, and in the Christian City of God for nigh unto two thousand years.

Dionysus became a fugitive god in Western civilization and the arts and skills attributed to him became *occult*—a word which means hidden. Thus the Kabbalah of the Jewish mystical tradition, another major source of astrological lore, has been considered occult in its devotion to the Orphic concept of Unaging Time or the eternal NOW. .

And astrology? The astrological conception of Man at the center of the universe was first enlisted in the service of Apollo. It was later condemned as irrational (which it is) when it no longer served that Apollonian purpose.

In the East, mysticism continued to flourish throughout the Christian era, and its unbroken tradition provides many clues to its astrological origins. Hindu mysticism expresses the astrological concept of Oneness as *Brahman* or *Atman*.[12] And in Taoist yoga, for example, the yogi achieves the One Reality "by uniting the sun and the moon."[13]

Astrological mysticism has never been more beautifully expressed than in the *Rubáiyát* of the eleventh-century Persian astronomer-astrologer Omar Khayyám. In the forty-third quatrain, Omar relates his divorce from unfruitful Reason, and his second wedding to mysticism, the "daughter of the vine"—the Orphic symbol of wine to achieve the mystical Oneness with God.

In the Far East, time was not a linear succession of centuries, but a cycle of *dynasties*, the time-spiral of the original conception of Archaic Man.

As William James has pointed out, mysticism quite literally defies expression: it is almost totally nonverbal.[14] Hence the need for, and value of, the horoscope, which is an *architectonic expression* of Man's relationship to the universe. Most attempts at verbal expression of mystic relationships fail. In sharp contrast, one consequence of the triumph of Apollo in our Western religious heritage has been that our relationship with the world became emphatically *verbal*, spelled out in Scripture, Scholastic philosophy, literature and other wordy exercises in rationalism. Our universe remained stable on this kind of verbal, rationalistic foundation so long as learning was limited to the religiously orthodox, as it was throughout the Middle Ages. So long as only the pious were learned, all the best arguments were in favor of God. A reading of St. Thomas Aquinas, that greatest of Scholastic philosophers, demonstrates this fact. (We must overlook for the moment the further fact that in later life, St. Thomas had a mystical experience of Oneness, after which he refused to write another word.) [15]

God forbid that any unbeliever should be educated! But in the seventeenth century, the enemy was both pious and orthodox, and well within the gates of the City of God before anyone knew what was happening. When they found out, the foundations of orthodoxy were trembling. It was already too late.

THE SENSE OF the absurdity of Man's condition actually began in the seventeenth century, when, as Bertrand Russell has observed, "Almost everything that distinguishes the modern world from earlier centuries is attributable to science . . ." According to Russell, science achieved its most spectacular triumphs in the seventeenth century, when "the modern world, so far as mental outlook is concerned, begins . . ." [16] To be more precise, it began when *The Revolution of Celestial Bodies,* in which astronomer-priest Nicolaus Copernicus argued for the heliocentric universe, attracted the attention of a shy and pious Catholic scholar named René Descartes.

Descartes had the odd habit of sitting in his oven all day, meditating. He was enchanted with the new physics of Galileo, Newton and others, and became absorbed in the astronomy of Copernicus. After some period in the oven, mulling over these new ideas, Descartes announced that the world was controlled by a rigid determinism based on the laws of physics. Human beings were not excluded, he declared, for the mind was also controlled by the physical laws. [17] To put it another way, Man was simply the Ghost in the Machine. [18]

Today this Cartesian dogma is recognized as both false in principle and internally inconsistent, but Descartes is nonetheless recognized as the founder of modern philosophy and a founder of modern science as well. In fairness, his mechanistic tunnel-vision of the universe made possible much that science has accomplished in the last few centuries. But it did so at a terrible cost to our self-image. Sigmund Freud, in whose work the Ghost in the Machine was expressed as psychic determinism, once remarked that modern man has suffered three major blows to his narcissism, his sense of being the center of the universe: Copernicus delivered the cosmological blow; Darwin delivered the biological blow and psychoanalysis (by which Freud meant himself) delivered the psychological blow.[19]

These three body-blows to the ego of Man have had a devastating impact. No longer the center of the universe, Man was merely an embarrassingly hairless ape, one of a number of animals inhabiting an insignificant planet in a solar system indistinguishable from countless others, and his vaunted ego was controlled by his base and animal impulses.

Our technological wasteland has produced the organization man, the juvenile delinquent and the counterculture as reactions to its spiritual emptiness, according to humanist Paul Goodman in *Growing Up Absurd*. Faith in God became faith in Science until Hiroshima and the growing technological peril to Man as an endangered species made faith in that Apollonian god of Man's dominion over the Earth untenable.

Today it seems incredible that Gordon Brown, Dean of MIT's College of Engineering, could have said as recently as 1967: "I doubt if there is such a thing as an urban crisis, but if there were, MIT would lick it in the same way we handled the Second World War."[20]

Yet now, Brown's statement seems as absurd as Man's present condition. Copernicus was born in 1473. It is ironic that on the 500th anniversary of the Copernican Revolution, we find much more meaningful than Brown's declaration of faith in science the statement of Harvard biologist-historian Everett I. Mendelsohn: "Science as we know it has outlived its usefulness."[21] For we are now in the midst of what Professor Willis Harman has described as a Second Copernican Revolution, whose impact, Harman believes, may be more profound than the one that commenced five hundred years ago.[22]

There has been a growing recognition of the limitations to the conventions of the scientific method. As early as 1925, E. A. Burtt pointed out that the men who founded modern science proceeded on many startlingly unwarrantable assumptions; and their superstitions were at least as gross as those of the Middle Ages.[23]

In *What is Life?*, first published in 1944, Erwin Schrödinger, co-winner of the Nobel Prize in physics, convincingly demonstrated that physical models are wholly unsatisfactory when it comes to explaining human consciousness. It was Schrödinger who first captured the attention of modern science with the observation that traditional mysticism provides a far more satisfactory explanation of consciousness, with its view that the personal self equals the omnipresent, all-comprehending self, or what mystics over the centuries in all cultures have described as a sense of Oneness with God.[24]

Schrödinger was perhaps the first modern scientist (Jung excepted) to reintroduce the original astrological conception of Man as the microcosmic center of the universe. More recently, Harvard astronomer Owen Gingerich acknowledged the possibility of non-causal things in the universe, and rejected the "tunnel-vision" of a linear, non-mystical approach to science. German physicist-philosopher Carl Friedrich von Weizsacker adds that he is convinced that mysticism is one of the great discoveries of Mankind.[25]

As Professor Harman accurately observed, the New Copernican Revolution is well under way,[26] and questions related to Man's transcendental experience are at the forefront of our attention. Heretofore excluded by the nihilistic bias of the conventional scientific method, long neglected (and derided) fields of inquiry are receiving respectful note. Mentors in all disciplines are approaching the recognition that the solution to the alienation, disaffection and general sense of chaos in our contemporary civilization cannot be had through political solutions, but must involve an exalted image of Man as a numinous and striving creation whose spirit is very much a part of the universe.

Does it sound as if science is taking on a mystic slant? I think it is; and I think it long overdue. Part of the Ghost-in-the-Machine view of Descartes was his enchantment with the Greek atomist philosophers, who flourished at the time of Socrates and Plato. The atomists were rigid nihilists who believed that all life, including Man, evolved from the primeval slime, and that everything in the universe was divisible into tiny particles called atoms. If this sounds familiar, it should, since it is part of the original Cartesian dogma, a keystone of modern science and the origin of its nihilistic bias.

There was therefore no room for the subjective or transcendental experience of Man in the Cartesian formulation of scientific method. Today, that is no longer so. It is no accident that Professor Harman's article, "The New Copernican Revolution," was reprinted in the official publication of the Self-Realization Fellowship, a religious organization dedicated to spreading the teachings of Hindu mysticism in the Western hemisphere.

I have, I hope, demonstrated that astrology is the study of cycles of various lengths. Today Apollo's star is setting and that of Dionysus is rising, to use an ancient astrological metaphor. Or, to return to our original myth: the Minotaur has been resurrected and returned to the center of the Labyrinth, which is, after all, a mythologem of the Ptolemaic universe with its seven circles of planetary orbits and Man at its center. I prefer the myth of the Minotaur in the Labyrinth, because it expresses my humanistic and astrological goal of the integration of

Man's rational and intuitive functions, the offspring of the Sun and the Moon of astrological symbolism.

No sane person would be willing to give up our cultural heritage, with all its limitations. The example of Nazi Germany shows that that kind of regression is both disastrous and insane. Nor can we ignore the common religious background which is part of that cultural inheritance and with which, in a very real sense, history began.

But looking at the Scriptures from a humanistic perspective, as psychoanalyst Erich Fromm has done recently, is very much in keeping with the New Copernican Revolution. From his standpoint of radical humanism, Fromm concludes that in the idea of the One God, contemporary Man can find his own Oneness with the universe by the development of his uniquely human qualities of love and reason.[27] His is perhaps the best expression of the rationalist viewpoint in contemporary terms.

At the end of the last century, the Orphic phase of the New Copernican Revolution began in earnest when German pharmacologist Ludwig Lewin discovered that American Indians and Mexicans ate a cactus root called peyote, which, he wrote, "they venerate as though it were a deity."[28] With that discovery, we commenced a cycle that may yet unite Man's Sun and Moon in an integrated Oneness, both within himself and with his universe. From the peyote cactus came mescaline, and the term coined by Humphry Osmond, "psychedelics," to describe states of altered or expanded consciousness. Those experiences led Leary and others to reinterpret the mystical *Tibetan Book of the Dead* as a rite of passage not from life to death, but from life to transcendental rebirth.[29] In *The Joyous Cosmology*, Zen Master Alan Watts points out that "one of the greatest of all superstitions is the separation of the mind from the body," and proves his point with his report of the use of psychedelics as an aid to consciousness-expansion.[30] The self which emerges mirrors the microcosm of the astrological conception of the horoscope.

And finally, to the outrage of medical orthodoxy, Dr. Andrew Weil argues in *The Natural Mind* that "the desire to alter consciousness periodically is an innate, normal drive analogous to hunger or the sexual drive."[31] This remarkable work includes a discussion of what he terms the *shared consciousness* of certain Indians, who perceive the collective unconscious of Mankind as an immediate reality. "There is nothing special about these Indians, except their relative lack of attachment to ego and intellect," Dr. Weil remarks,[32] placing himself squarely at the forefront of the Second Copernican Revolution, along with fellow scientist, anthropologist Carlos Castaneda.

In a trilogy of works of anthropological research culminating with *Journey to Ixtlan,* Castaneda explores shamanism of the Indians of the American Southwest from the inside, as an apprentice. There is no better illustration of the conscientious struggle of the Western scientist against his rationalist prejudices than this classic account of one man's genuine efforts to see the universe in the astrological conception of an integrated whole, and himself as a part of its cyclic pattern.

Contemporary astrology, in its immemorial conception of the essential Oneness of Man and his universe, is a potent force in the New Copernican Revolution. As recently as December of 1972, *Today's Health,* a publication of the American Medical Association, reported that research conducted at the Temple University School of Medicine has turned up a hormone which is triggered at birth to set out biological clocks to the Earth's circadian rhythms, just as (I would remind the reader) Chaldean astrologers postulated thousands of years ago in formulating one of the basic tenets of astrology.[33]

With contributions totalling in excess of one million dollars, Edward Dewey established the Foundation for the Study of Cycles. A grant of a half-million dollars more funded the research for his recently published *Cycles.* Dewey's findings vindicate Giorgio Piccardi's declaration, which he quotes:

> Only by understanding the mechanism which connects him to the earth and the sky will man be able to understand his physical and psychic position in the universe today. In the context of the universe as it is, man will find his natural role.[34]

Dr. Piccardi heads the Institute for Physical Chemistry at the University of Florence, but his statement might just as easily have come from the lips of a Zen Master, a Hindu mystic—or a contemporary astrologer.

5 What Are the Signs?

IF I HAVE learned anything as a teacher, either of law or of astrology, it is that no one can learn something which he already knows, no matter how erroneous that knowledge may be. The most difficult subject to teach is the one with which the student has some familiarity.

This problem applies with force in astrology. We have all become familiar with the zodiacal signs and know the popular catch phrases for them. Aries is headstrong and stupid; Libra is indecisive; Scorpio oversexed and vengeful. In actual fact, Aries is identified with intellection, albeit willful; Libra with an innate ability to initiate things through partnerships; Scorpio with religious leadership such as Gandhi and Billy Graham.

In order to truly understand the significance of each of the signs of the zodiac, it is vital that you learn their sequence and their polar opposites. For every sign of the zodiac, there is an opposing sign, and the totality of the zodiac reflects the equilibrium achieved by the bipolar opposition of the six sets of signs, called the *antipodes*—simply, something which is the polar opposite of something else.

Every horoscope expresses the constant change which the astrologer has seen in the universe, with its comparable manifestation in Man. These same concepts of universal change, and the changelessness of change, are also found in the *I Ching*, which has a common origin with astrological principles.

Therefore, you should learn the signs in their sequence and with their polar opposites, or antipodes. The symbols following each of the signs are called *glyphs*, or graphic representations of symbols, which you will need to know in order to erect a horoscope. The glyphs are used by astrologers as a kind of shorthand in chart erection, since it is far easier to draw in the glyphs than to write out the words for the signs and their planetary rulers.

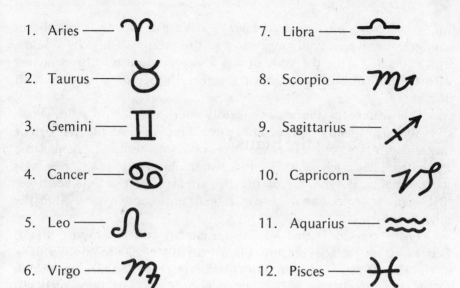

1. Aries
2. Taurus
3. Gemini
4. Cancer
5. Leo
6. Virgo
7. Libra
8. Scorpio
9. Sagittarius
10. Capricorn
11. Aquarius
12. Pisces

As an aid to understanding the signs, and remembering how to write the glyphs, here are their origins and meanings.

ARIES

Sequence. Aries is the first sign of the zodiac. Zero degrees of Aries coincides with the vernal equinox. The word *aries* comes from the Latin, meaning Ram; and the Ram displaced the Bull for first place in the zodiac thousands of years ago. However, even though the names have been changed, the result has been that the docile Ram has many of the astrological characteristics of the more aggressive Bull.

Glyph. The glyph for Aries is commonly viewed as symbolizing the horns of the ram. That might be so, but it would probably be more accurate to say that such symbolism comes by way of the Greek letter Omega, which when inverted looks quite similar to the glyph for Aries.

The *planetary ruler* of Aries is Mars. In Greek mythology, the god Ares was the god of war; his Roman counterpart was Mars.

Melothesia. The association of each sign with a part of the human body is called *melothesia*, or body rulership. Aries is associated with the head or, as astrologers say, "Aries rules the head." It is a conviction of many astrologers that Aries people often sustain injuries to their heads; and a noticeable scar on the native's head may indicate that in that person's chart the Aries configuration is prominent.

Aries *characteristics* are generally described as courageous, head-strong, impulsive, sexually aggressive and pioneering. But why would a sign associated with the gods of war and aggression be also identified with the human head, and with the cerebral processes which the head implies?

Our search for the answer reveals another aspect to Aries which gives this sign quality considerably more dimension. As the first sign of the zodiac, Aries commences the cycle of eternal return, as symbolized by the zodiacal circle of life itself. Thus, the horoscope, and Aries as its starting point, is symbolic of the Fall of Man—of the time when the first man recognized that he was a being different in kind from the other animals.

From the conflation of Mesopotamian creation myths that is Genesis, to the frescoes recently discovered in Mexican tombs, the story of the Fall of Man is told in terms of Man gaining the capacity to think (often with associations of fire), which gives him his godlike powers and results in the loss of Paradise. That power of thought, particularly in terms of impulsive, rebellious acts of will, is very much a part of the archetypal qualities of Aries.

The myth of Lucifer is exemplary. Lucifer was the name given by the Babylonians to the planet Venus. To the Hebrews and Babylonians, Venus or Lucifer was a rebel, because it was the last of the stars to vanish upon the appearance of the Sun, who was the father of the gods. At sunrise, Venus still shone; and it seemed to our ancestors, as they projected their collective unconscious upon the heavens, that Lucifer resisted the dominance of the morning Sun. Hence Lucifer, whose name means light-bearer, was regarded as the most intelligent of the gods, who in his intellectual arrogance led a rebellion against God the Father and was cast down into the underworld in punishment.

The equation of brilliance with intellectual superiority has survived to the present day; so have other aspects of the Lucifer myth I shall presently consider.

I note in passing that Venus was indeed cast down into the underworld every day, when it ultimately disappeared, or set, upon the full rising of the Sun.

The Lucifer myth is the genesis of our concept of Satan, whose name means adversary, and who was the most favored of God's starry angels, but who was cast down from heaven for his intellectual arrogance in daring to rebel against the authority of the Supreme Being.

We human beings feel a lot more sympathy with Lucifer or Satan than we are usually willing to admit. After all, the Fall of Satan is but a retelling of the Fall of Man. Both Satan and Adam, whose name means man in Hebrew, were cast out of heaven or of Paradise for much the same reason: Lucifer-Satan for his intellectual arrogance in daring to compete with God; Adam for his defiance in eating the fruit which gave him knowledge of good and evil, which, as God himself observed, made him "like one of us" (Genesis 3).

John Milton wrote *Paradise Lost* as an exercise in piety. When Milton read this epic to a fellow Puritan, his friend complained that there was a lot more about Hell in *Paradise Lost* than there was about Heaven. As indeed there was. Milton sought to correct his error by writing *Paradise Regained*, but the result was a failure, for Milton tried to do without his most interesting and sympathetic figure: Satan.

Psychoanalyst Erich Fromm points out that there is no mention of sin or evil in Genesis with regard to Adam's action in gaining knowledge of good and evil by disobeying God.[1] Professor Homer Smith has also noticed that the Satan of Genesis appears co-equal with Yahweh, with no mention of sin or evil.[2] It is not until Job that Satan shows evidence of a bad character by being both curious and skeptical.

This evolution is consistent with the idea of Aries as a sign of conscious but impulsive *will*. Willfulness and rebellion are truly Arien and have led to the fall of more than one human being with the impulsive Aries will in prominent configuration in his chart. Aries is also regarded as significant in the horoscope of dictators and tyrants. If this seems inconsistent with any process of intellection, consider another aspect of Lucifer: his pride.

To the early Hebrew tribes the most detested personality trait was something they called *hybris*, meaning intellectual arrogance. (It may have had something to do with their resentment of the intellectual superiority of their prophets, in view of the prophets' insistence on single-minded devotion to Yahweh!) *Hybris* became *hubris* in early Christianity, and ultimately the sin of pride, regarded by the Christians as the deadliest of the seven deadly sins because it separated Man from God. Consider whether any military, political or religious leader who is willing to consign human life to death on principle—whether in wars to end all wars or in crusades to recapture the Holy Land—has not elevated his prideful valuation of an abstract product of his mind so far above his senses as to be separated from God and Man alike. Isaiah said it well:

> How art thou fallen from
> Heaven, O Lucifer, son of
> the morning! how art thou
> cut down to the ground, which
> didst weaken the nations!

> For thou hast said in thine heart,
> I will ascend into heaven, I
> will exalt my throne above the
> stars of God . . .
> Yet thou shalt be brought down
> to hell (Isaiah 14:12-15).

In this passage, the prophet excoriates the King of Babylon for acts of tyranny "that made the world a wilderness, and destroyed the cities thereof," all doubtless performed for what the Babylonian king thought was the highest principle, and earning him the full identification with Lucifer, that god of rebellious will and Aries prototype.

But that is a *negative* manifestation of Aries. To balance the scales, let us consider the following:

> I am the Alpha and Omega, the first and the last, the beginning and the end.

> . . . I am the root and the offspring of David, and the bright and morning star.

The Greek Alpha is derived from the Hebrew Aleph, the first letter of the Hebrew alphabet; and Aleph is itself derived from the sign and constellation Taurus, when Aleph was the first sign of the ancient zodiac. Taurus was displaced by Aries in the ancient Hebrew astrologers' accommodation for the precession of the equinoxes.

Omega is the Greek letter from which the sign Aries is drawn, and is the last letter of the Greek alphabet. In its graphic form, Omega was Aries, which became the first sign of the zodiac when Taurus became the last sign. Also, it happens that the last letter of the Hebrew alphabet is Taw, meaning bull, and the root of our word "Taurus."

Thus, we can see that the references to the first and the last, the beginning and the end, are references to *Aries* both as the beginning of the zodiacal cycle of eternal rebirth—and also its end, when the cycle begins anew. This meaning is confirmed three verses later, where the speaker identifies himself with Lucifer, "the bright and morning star."

And who is the speaker? The quotation is from the Book of the Revelation of John, also called the Apocalypse. In the quoted passage, from the thirteenth and sixteenth verses of the last chapter, Jesus reveals to John a vision of the New Jerusalem—a vision of the world when it begins anew, with Jesus catasterized (transformed into a star) as Lucifer, the bright and morning star. Could there be a more positive manifestation of Aries consciousness than that of Jesus Christ, preeminent and inner-directed religious leader who drove the money-lenders from the temple, defied the establishment religion and held the un-swerving conviction that he was the Messiah promised in the Old Testament?

Prototypes. Marlon Brando had his Sun, Moon and Mercury all posited in Aries at his time of birth on April 3, 1924. He rose to fame with the original stage version of *A Streetcar Named Desire,* in which he made the name of his character—Stanley Kowalski—synonymous with egocentric willfulness. Brando quickly gained notoriety as the actor who refused to take direction. Another Aries foible is Brando's insensi-tivity to the feelings of others despite protestations to the contrary and his sexual competitiveness.[3]

In a famous *New Yorker* profile, Truman Capote noted that Brando, with his weight-lifter's body and too-pretty face, might never have had the wide appeal he has enjoyed as an actor but for his broken nose: the injury to his face marred the regularity of his features just enough to give him the image of male aggressiveness. An injury to the head is, of course, the Aries trademark.

Brando has the indomitable Aries spirit as well. *Time* Magazine, that omniscient journal of popular bias, had written Brando off follow-ing the release of *Desiree.* According to the *Time* reviewer, there was no place left for Brando to go and it was downhill all the way. For awhile there appeared to be a certain hateful truth to this prophecy; and Brando's Arien *Mutiny on the Bounty* did nothing to improve his career.

However, in 1972 Brando delivered a remarkable performance as Don Corleone in *The Godfather.* While raves were still being heard for that achievement, in November of 1972 Pauline Kael reviewed *Last Tango in Paris* for *The New Yorker* and her ecstatic endorsement both of the film and of Brando's performance were heard around the world. Once again Brando has apparently scored a great success in the role of Paul, who may be characterized as a prototype of primitive sexual aggressiveness—a not unfamiliar role for Brando or for the Aries male.

Karen Dinesen, born in April 17, 1885, in Denmark, is another good example of the indomitable Aries spirit. Karen Dinesen had the misfortune to arrive in this world on one of the Tycho Brahe days: for Danes, April 17 was one of 32 unpropitious days of the year, according to the famous Danish astronomer Tycho Brahe; indeed, April 17 was considered the unluckiest day of the 32!

Although contemporary astrologers rarely consider any calendar date propitious or unpropitious, there certainly seemed to be merit in Brahe's notions about April 17, insofar as Karen Blixen was concerned. By the time she was thirty-five years old, her father had committed suicide; she had been betrayed by her husband, Baron Blixen; her farm in Africa had been ruined by drought and her lover had died in an airplane crash.[4]

But Tanne—her nickname, short for Titania—had Sun, Venus, Mars and the south node all posited in Aries and she was indeed a veritable female Titan. She had run a coffee plantation in Kenya, Africa, where Denys Finch-Hatton, the younger son of an English earl and roustabout aviator, would visit her. Denys became her lover; and she prolonged his visits in the manner of Scheherazade by spinning out tales which so absorbed him that he always lingered longer than he had intended. When the farm failed and she returned to her family home at Rungsted-lund, alone and penniless, she cast about for something to do. Her pioneering Aries spirit inspired her to set down in English the Gothic tales she had spun for her lover. Her efforts to peddle her manuscript at first met with catagoric refusal; short stories were always difficult to sell and, if written by an unknown author, entirely out of the question.

Nevertheless she persevered. Writer Dorothy Canfield Fisher was a family friend who could be persuaded to read the stories and she passed them on to publisher Robert Haas with encouragement. Haas published the book with considerable misgiving; it was not only a collection of short stories but it was written in English by a Dane who was unknown even in her native land. *Seven Gothic Tales* had a meteorlike success and created an instant audience and new career for this remarkable and courageous lady, who under the penname Isak Dinesen continued to spin out stories and tales to the age of seventy-seven.

Remember that every sign has *positive and negative aspects.* Positively manifested, Aries is pioneering leadership, inner-directed consciousness and unflinching acts of will. Negative Aries can be tyrannical, self-centered and a recklessly impulsive egotism. How the Aries qualities will manifest themselves depends upon the configuration of the individual horoscope and—of course—the native's power of choice or free will.

At this point, it is well to remember that we need all of the archetypal qualities represented by the zodiacal signs in our lives. F. Scott Fitzgerald, for example, had his Sun posited in Libra, with no Aries emphasis in his horoscope whatsoever. It seems that if Fitzgerald had had but a little more Aries egocentricity, to balance his compelling Libran desire to share himself in countless partnerships with others, he could have had a longer and more rewarding life.

We will learn more about Aries qualities when we consider the *polar opposite* sign of Libra.

Notable Aries personalities include Charles Chaplin, Béla Bartók, Joseph Campbell, Casanova, Joan Crawford, Aretha Franklin, Vincent van Gogh, Thomas Jefferson, Nikita Khrushchev, J. P. Morgan, Diana Ross, Gloria Swanson, Arturo Toscanini and Leonardo da Vinci.

Element. In a later chapter, we will consider groupings of the signs according to the alchemical typology of fire, earth, air and water. For the present, note that Aries is the first *fiery* manifestation of the consciousness of Man, or of any native whose chart you will consider.

TAURUS

Sequence. Taurus is the second sign in the natural zodiac. The Sun enters Taurus about April 21 of each year. The word *taurus* is Latin for bull.

Glyph. The glyph is said to represent a bull's head; that statement is true only insofar as the Hebrew letter Aleph is itself based on the configuration of a bull's head, especially its horns. Aleph also means bull in Hebrew.

Planetary ruler. The planet against which Taurus is ruled or measured is Venus, which represents the feminine principle. And the archetypal Taurean does indeed have a *venereal* quality in the original sense of that word: a capacity to love sensuously and to *venerate* with heartfelt feeling the object of his love.

Melothesia. Taurus rules the neck and shoulders; for this reason, Taureans often have excellent speaking and singing voices. At the same time, this area is likely to be vulnerable to illness when Taurus is prominently indicated in the natal horoscope or found on the cusp of the sixth house of health. Taurus also rules the thyroid and the metabolic system.

Characteristics. The essential Taurean quality, a kind of durability, may be seen as fixity or inertia. Taurean qualities derive from an acute perception and appreciation of the present; Taureans enjoy and appreciate all the delights of the senses. Because of a contemporary bias in favor of the process of mentation, we tend to discount the virtue of superior sense perception, which is our loss. Taureans don't. They often have an excellent aesthetic sense, a good ear for music, a good voice for singing, a good palate for food and a good eye for a well-turned ankle.

A children's psychiatrist once remarked that of all the children he treated, those who were virtually certain to use marijuana were children whose basic reality-orientation was to immediate sense perception. Although he did not know it, he was describing the Taurean, whose acute perception of present reality is such that *Cannabis sativa*, which heightens the appreciation of the moment and stretches out its duration, has immediate and direct appeal. The qualities of passivity and inertia, characteristic of some Taureans, are also characteristics of being stoned on marijuana, according to Margolis and Clorfene, whose witty *Child's Garden of Grass*, once an underground classic, has surfaced to impress a general readership as well.

In the spring of 1953 Aldous Huxley swallowed four-tenths of a gram of mescaline dissolved in half a glass of water. When the results of that adventure were reported in *The Doors of Perception* in 1954 by this century's consummate essayist, mystic and humanist, the Taurean sub-age began. For the first time in our history, a large and growing segment of our population called a halt to the popular notions of the American manifest destiny—our fiery, Sagittarian head-trip—and declared the supremacy of the moment over the uncertain and ambiguous future.

As Huxley reported his mescaline experience, all of his sense perceptions were heightened so that, gazing at a full-blown Belle of Portugal rose, he experienced what Adam experienced on the morning of his creation: "The miracle, moment by moment, of naked existence." When asked whether the experience was "agreeable," he truthfully responded, "Neither agreeable nor disagreeable. It just *is*."[1]

And so it is with Taurus. When the apperception of reality is acute, it becomes meditation, transcending ordinary reality to achieve a mystical quality. This phenomenon is nowhere better expressed than in *The Doors of Perception*.

Prototypes. The most exact prototype of a Taurus personality that occurs to me is the image of Ferdinand the Bull. As visualized by Walt Disney, Ferdinand was the bull that refused to be goaded into a fight to promote a senseless ritual in which he was sure to be the loser. Ferdinand preferred to smell flowers. In this example, he would nibble on them as well, and they would have psychotropic qualities.

There are less esoteric examples. Orson Welles, once the *enfant terrible* of the cinema, directed *Citizen Kane* in 1941. One of its virtues is Welles' ability to create a superb illusion of immediacy. As film critic Charles Higham has observed, Welles is a *bon viveur* as well as a poet, and in *Citizen Kane* this Taurean emphasis shows up in his gourmand's gobbling up of aural and visual detail.[2] Welles' display of visual and aural effects, Higham notes, often work through the sheer accumulation of grotesque detail.[3]

Welles' Taurean gourmandizing has not gone unnoticed. As Welles himself observed, gluttony may not be the worst sin, but it is surely the most noticeable.

Welles' Sun and Mercury in Taurus are reflected in his 1938 radio production, "War of the Worlds," a Halloween offering. According to Howard Koch, who wrote the script for the Mercury Theatre production, Orson Welles' direction "provided the alchemy which transformed written words into a living experience." His superb Taurean evocation of a Martian invasion as present reality transformed that fantasy into an experience whose terrifying immediacy panicked the nation. Columnist Dorothy Thompson claimed he had done the country a service by showing us how ill-prepared we were in the event of war, and tipped the scales of public opinion in his favor. Welles became an instant international celebrity.[4]

Never before and never since has anyone equalled that feat. Indeed, when the news of the attack on Pearl Harbor flashed around the world on December 7, 1941, many Americans at first dismissed it as another show by Orson Welles. Perhaps Dorothy Thompson was right after all.

In *Chimes at Midnight*, released in 1966, Welles produced, directed and starred in a film biography of Falstaff, that penultimate Taurean whom he so closely resembles, with a script ingeniously drawn from every play in which the Falstaff character appears.

Welles has had a lifelong admiration for Falstaff, his favorite Shakespearean character. And not without reason. "Now, Hal, what time of day is it, lad?" Falstaff inquires of his drinking companion who is soon to become the King of England. The question provokes a response which introduces Falstaff and tells us about his Taurus character:

> ... What a devil hast thou to do with the time of day? Unless hours were cups of sack and minutes capons and clocks the tongues of bawds and dials the signs of [whore]-houses and the blessed sun himself a fair hot wench in flame color'd taffeta, I see no reason why thou shouldst be so superfluous to demand the time of the day (*Henry IV*, Part I, act 1, scene 2).

Is it mere coincidence that in the very speech which introduces the character, Shakespeare has Prince Hal describe Falstaff in terms of the basic Taurus qualities of sense appreciation and indifference to time? I don't think so. Himself a Taurus, Shakespeare was familiar with both alchemy and astrology; indeed, his plays abound with references to both.

In this instance, Shakespeare deliberately uses astrological prototypes to give dimension both to Falstaff and to Hotspur, the Scottish rebel who is the play's antagonist, by ascribing to them contrasting astrological personalities. Thus Hotspur describes his anger as "worse than the sun in March," i.e., when the Sun enters Aries; and Hotspur pledges to slay so many men that Mars, the planetary ruler of Aries, shall be "up to the ears in blood" (act 4, scene 1). By making Hotspur as fiery and impetuous an Aries as Falstaff was an earthy and phlegmatic Taurean, Shakespeare heightens our interest in both characters.

Falstaff's views on courage are truly Taurean, and once again in sharp contrast to Hotspur's. After observing that honor can neither set a leg nor cure a wound, Falstaff decides that it is something that can neither be felt nor heard by the dead who have earned it; he therefore decides that he will have none of it (act 5, scene 1).

Welles' views on heroism appear to be as Taurean as those of his favorite Shakespearean character. The first time he met Ernest Hemingway, Welles had been called to read the narration for a Hemingway documentary about the Spanish Civil War. (An excellent speaking voice, which Welles has, is a notably Taurean trait.) Finding Hemingway's script perhaps even more pompous than Hotspur's, Welles suggested cuts. Hemingway didn't take kindly to the suggestion; besides, he had been drinking. "You—effeminate boys of the theater," he exploded. "What do you know about the real war?"

Welles was as unimpressed with Hemingway the hero as Falstaff was with the concept of valor. With mincing gestures, Welles exclaimed, "Mister Hemingway, how strong you are and how big you are!"

Enraged, Hemingway grabbed a chair; Welles did likewise. With great good humor, Welles recalls how they scuffled in front of the flickering images of the Spanish Civil War on the screen, and ended the battle by giving each other accolades over a bottle of whiskey,[5] in the finest Falstaffian—or Wellesian—tradition.

Polar opposite. The polar opposite sign to Taurus is Scorpio, and we will learn more about the Taurean character when we consider the Scorpio sign emphasis.

Positive and negative aspects. Positively manifested, Taurean natives show stability, steadfastness and follow-through. Their mystical quality, a factor of their appreciation of present reality, is often overlooked. Negatively manifested, Taurean stability becomes inertia; Taurean determination, stubborness; Taurean sense appreciation, sensuality and materialism. Free will plays a principal role, as does the overall configuration of the native's chart.

Notable Taurus personalities. Cher Bono, Irving Berlin, Bing Crosby, Salvador Dali, Ella Fitzgerald, Yehudi Menuhin, Vladimir Nabokov, Sugar Ray Robinson, William Shakespeare, Barbra Streisand and Harry S Truman.

Element. Taurus is the first of the earth signs, in the triplicities of fire, earth, air and water.

GEMINI   ♊

Sequence. Gemini is the third sign of the natural zodiac. The Sun enters Gemini about May 21. The Latin word *gemini* means twins, and there is evidence that more twins are born under this sign than under any other.[1] For many of the startling facts of twinship, astrology may provide the only answer, according to a recent non-astrological examination of the twin phenomenon.

Glyph. The glyph for Gemini is a symbol derived from the constellation of Castor and Pollux, the twins of mythology, who were sons of Zeus and a mortal mother. The twins were catasterized at death as a tribute to the exemplary brotherly love they had displayed in life.[2] Although the twins were originally brothers, the image of Gemini twinship today is of a brother and sister. The universality of the twin image for the constellation has been found throughout antiquity.[3]

The Twins rule the airy element and summon fortunate winds at the behest of sailors.[4]

Planetary ruler. The ruler of Gemini is Mercury, the planet which rules the mind. Mercury is the Roman name given to Hermes, whom Zeus found so ingenious, eloquent and persuasive that he made Hermes/Mercury his messenger. Other gods taught Hermes how to foretell the future. All of these attributes attach to Gemini as well.[5]

Melothesia. Gemini rules the arms and hands—which are, after all, used for expression—and the nervous system.

Characteristics. The basic Geminian quality is one of *duality,* as the Twin myth suggests. If you know anyone who has Gemini prominent in his natal horoscope, you may have noticed that he or she always seems to be doing two things (at least two!) at once. Geminian personalities seem to live in a world of infinite possibilities which they can never resist exploring continuously. Their ability and even insistence on a multiplicity of simultaneous activities can be distracting to natives of more fixed temperaments—Taureans, for example.

"My wife will read a book, knit a sweater and follow a television program, all at once," one hapless husband of a protean Gemini lady complained. "Usually while eating something," he added. "The worst part is that if I'm watching the same program and I'm distracted, she can give me a word for word playback—and never drop a stitch in the process!"

That is not impossible for a Gemini, although the example is perhaps extreme. More common is the Gemini trait which sees these natives at the supermarket, invariably purchasing two of an item, rather than the one that is actually needed; or the tendency to have more than one occupation—simply because it's more interesting, and it helps to keep the mind occupied.

"The next, the new, the promised!" is the battle cry of Gemini—and the beautifully evocative title of a short story by Rachel Maddux, dealing with the climate of potentiality that is the true environment of every Gemini. (It has been pointed out to me that, having Gemini in prominent configuration in my natal chart, I have just illustrated Geminian duality: a battle cry is not just a battle cry; it also has to be something else to satisfy a Gemini.)

Gemini is associated with writing, including both fiction and non-fiction, song lyrics and, for that matter, all forms of communication, written or oral.

There is a distinction which should be made between Gemini and Aries in terms of products of the mind. Aries uses mental effort to impose his conscious rational will on his environment; a kind of ideation of self. Gemini, on the other hand, uses his mind for the sheer delight of doing so; he enjoys communication for its own sake. Gemini types rarely pause long enough to impress their will on anyone or anything.

Taurus can be contrasted to Gemini as well. With his superior aesthetic sense a Taurean can stand absorbed, oblivious of time, before a painting. Not so a Gemini personality; and it isn't just a short attention span. Rather, it is his constant mental exploration of his environment. If the painting is a Picasso of the Blue Period, he may begin by comparing it to other periods and then to Braque. Soon the Gemini native is itching to write down some of the insights he has had about both painters' styles. With Gemini, every experience raises new possibilities to be explored.

The Geminian duality and curiosity are pervasive. In sexual attitudes, Aries is direct, sometimes primitive, propelled by immediate ego needs. Taurus is more likely to be placid, engrossed, at home with the experience of his senses. Gemini is insatiably curious and cool—I can think of no other word for it—about sex, and his sexual interests are likely to be as variable as are his many other attitudes. Often as not, there is more of a brother-sister feeling with his sexual partners, rather than a strong emotional attachment. He probably enjoys talking about sex as much as the experience itself.

Gemini is the gadfly of the zodiac.

Prototypes. In my introductory chapter, I mentioned, as a prototype, Jean-Paul Sartre, born June 21, 1905. With his natal Sun, Mercury and Pluto posited in Gemini, Sartre's life and career have been characterized by duality. He started with a career of teaching and writing, first a spate of imaginative psychological studies, then a series of articles about contemporary literature which popularized Hemingway, Faulkner and Steinbeck for the French audience.

In his early thirties, Sartre published *Nausea,* his first novel, and *The Wall,* a collection of short stories; both dealt with the meaninglessness and absurdity of life as he then saw it. Shortly thereafter, he joined the French army, and was taken prisoner in 1940. He escaped to Paris, joined the Resistance, resumed teaching and produced his first play—in the face of Nazi censorship and despite his fugitive status!

That same year his magnum opus was published: *Being and Nothingness,* the seminal work on existentialism in which Sartre transmuted the pervasive sense of meaninglessness and despair of human existence through the alchemical processes of his mind and art into a philosophy of commitment and action.

In an autobiography of his earliest years, Sartre describes the beginnings of a remarkably Geminian personage. The title, *The Words,* is Geminian enough, and reflects the author's lifelong preoccupation and fascination with words. For Sartre, his grandfather's library was "the world caught in a mirror." He remarks, "I began my life as I shall no doubt end it: amidst books." Learning to read was the greatest thrill of his life; he found "the human heart . . . insipid and hollow, except in books."

In Gemini fashion everything took place in his head. Sartre defended himself from the world with his imagination. Gemini optimism surfaced early: from books and magazines he "derived my most deepseated phantasmagoria: optimism."

His earliest sexual attitudes are remarkably allusive to his zodiacal sign:

> I had an elder sister, my mother, and I wanted a younger sister. Even now—1963—that's the only family relationship which moves me.

He adds in a footnote:

> Traces of this fantasy can be found in my writings: Orestes and Electra in *The Flies,* Boris and Ivich in *The Paths of Freedom,* Frantz and Leni in *Altona.* The last-named are the only ones who go the whole way. What attracted me about this family bond was not so much the amorous temptation as the taboo against making love: fire and ice, mingled delight and frustration; I liked incest if it remained platonic.[6]

Sartre's insouciant description of his sexual feelings says more about Geminian attitudes in lovemaking than pages of exposition: curiosity is the primary motivation, making that which is forbidden the most appealing.

Sartre also feels the Gemini joy in experience for its own sake. He remembers a sculptor who was struck down and seriously injured by an automobile, but whose first reaction was one of joy: "Something has happened to me at last!"

Sartre well understood that bizarre response, as can any Gemini. "I admire that will to welcome everything," he comments. "If one likes surprises, one must like them to that degree, one must like even the rare flashes which reveal to devotees that the earth is not meant for them."[7]

The reader is also acquainted with my second example of the Gemini character, Lillian Canaan. Little more need be said about Lillian except to point out that her extraordinary prowess as an astrologer illustrates the fact that intuition is an archetypal Gemini quality.

In a later chapter I shall have considerably more to say about the nature of intuition. In current usage, the term has acquired a deplorably ambiguous connotation; I view it as one of several basic and indispensable modes of functioning which we all have in greater or less degree. For present purposes, it is enough to observe that Lillian's intuitive skills enable her to see both the forest and the trees, to relate the particular to the whole, and from this mediation to forecast the most likely possibilities for future events.

Polar opposite. The polar opposite sign to Gemini is Sagittarius, a sign emphasis which seems superficially similar. However, we shall better understand Gemini duality and versatility when we explore the characteristics of Sagittarius.

Positive and negative aspects. Positively aspected, Gemini is versatile, adaptable, imaginative and creative. However, if the native yields to the excesses of the Gemini sign emphasis, Geminian versatility is dissipated in many projects begun and none completed. Creative curiosity becomes mere superficiality and verbal skills, verbosity and glibness. At worst, the Gemini can become so distracted by the manifold stimuli that barrage his mind that his reason may be completely unhorsed.

Notable Gemini personalities. Marilyn Monroe, Cole Porter, John F. Kennedy, Frank Lloyd Wright, Judy Garland, Isadora Duncan, Hubert H. Humphrey, Allen Ginsberg, Walt Whitman and William Butler Yeats.

Element. Gemini is the first of the air signs in the triplicities of fire, earth, air and water.

CANCER

Sequence. Cancer is the fourth sign of the natural zodiac. The Sun enters Cancer about June 21. The word *cancer* means crab, deriving from the Latin *cancer* and the Greek *karkinos.* Because the word was also applied to a kind of creeping ulcer—suggested by the presumed crablike motion of a malignant tumor, or *carcinoma*—the word *cancer* came to mean a disease that has nothing to do with the fourth sign of the zodiac. Because of this use of the word, Carroll Righter has substituted the term "Moon Children" for "Cancer" as a zodiacal sign.

Glyph. The glyph for the sign is said to represent a crab, although some authorities believe it depicts the scarab sacred to the Egyptians. To me it has always seemed more closely to resemble a woman's breasts, which may be a helpful mnemonic aid to the reader. Cancer rules the breasts and is very much associated with the concept of maternal thought and feeling. Most likely the derivation of the glyph is from the Hebrew letter Zayin (Zeta in Greek), whose meanings include being and living creature. As Dr. Moran has demonstrated, Zayin is derived from the constellation Cancer as seen by the ancient Hebrew astrologers.[1]

Planetary ruler. The Moon is the ruling planet for Cancer, representing as it does the feminine principles of watery fluctuation and deep sensitivity.

Melothesia. Externally, Cancer rules the breasts; and internally, the stomach and the uterus.

Characteristics. As the Moon rulership suggests, the basic Cancerian quality is feminine or maternal feeling. When emphasized in the natal chart, Cancer indicates a subjective, highly sensitive evaluation of all of life's circumstances. The Cancerian woman is very much a lady who enjoys all of the conventional feminine roles. She does not find the obligations of home, family and children onerous; nor does she feel that she must have other activities to assert her individuality. If she works in an office, she is the secretary who is forever planning little lunches for the clerical staff and bringing in home remedies for the boss when he has a cold.

In men, a strong Cancer emphasis has often produced individuals of considerable wealth. There has been much speculation as to why this is so. One suggestion is that Cancer is an acquisitive sign; the Cancerian rarely lets go of anything. It is true that most Cancerians seem to have a culch of personal possessions, oddments and snippets of various cherished items whose only value can be in terms of personal reminiscence.

This trait is not limited, however, to things which are worthless. To put it crassly, Cancers are *hoarders:* and they hoard money as everything else. While generous with their feelings, their milk and cookies and home remedies, they tend to parsimony with cold, hard cash, perhaps because they are always unconsciously storing things up for a long winter. The concept of home is important to natives with a Cancer emphasis.

Many Cancer men have achieved success in politics. Whether that is because politics is a source of wealth or for some other reason such as a maternal, protective attitude toward their country depends on the individual natal chart. Certainly, if Drew Pearson is to be believed, *The Case Against Congress* suggests that in the United States, at least, the economic motivation is not inconsiderable.

Cancer men often have great attraction for women, probably because they intuitively understand them so very well—and vice versa. For this reason, the Cancer male represents in some cases what psychiatrists have termed a male lesbian. Cancer men typically have a lifelong devotion to their mothers; but if love is not possible, they will hate their mothers just as passionately.

Prototypes. Anne Morrow Lindbergh is a good example of a lovely, intuitive Cancer lady. In *Gift From the Sea,* her Cancer warmth expresses itself in a comforting mysticism with which she was able to surmount the overwhelming tragedy of the loss of her first child.

She ruminates about the role of women today, her thoughts oriented to the milky opalescence of the moon shell before her, much as a seer might gaze at a crystal ball. She remembers the advice of an ancient mystic that to achieve the possession of the self, one must go inward. Woman must be the pioneer in this turning inward for strength, she concludes, and her Cancer insight is amplified by the moon shell's suggestion.

Among Cancerian males, Marcel Proust is representative of one type of Cancer expression. Born July 10, 1871, Proust had his Sun, Mercury, Jupiter and Uranus all posited in Cancer. At the age of seven Proust experienced a trauma which influenced all his later life, when his mother denied him a good-night kiss. That may seem absurd or even grotesque to us, until we remember the lifelong devotion which Cancerians typically feel for their mothers. Proust ultimately retired to a cork-lined room (womb?), where he spent the rest of his life nourishing his grief over his mother's death, and re-creating his personal past in his classic *Remembrance of Things Past.*[2]

Ernest Hemingway is an excellent example of another type in which a strong Cancer emphasis is manifested in a very different way.

He is a fabulous figure in the literal sense of that word; it is frequently difficult to separate the image of the big-game hunter, bullfighter, soldier (in the Spanish Civil War) from the man who wrote fiction about those things, often in first-person narration. The prevailing image of Hemingway is of a big, bearded man emerging from the African bush after a plane crash, with gin bottle in one hand and stalk of bananas in the other: "My luck, she is running very good"—perhaps the best prose he ever composed.

How does Ernest Hemingway stand as an example of a Cancer male? He and Proust could hardly be more different! Proust was an admittedly and apparently exclusive homosexual male, Hemingway an exclusively heterosexual male who believed a young man had to be prepared to kill any man who made homosexual advances, in order not to be bothered.[3]

Hemingway was unlike Proust in still another way: he apparently feared and hated his mother. This attitude is evident in many of his clearly autobiographical stories and nowhere more so than in *Now I Lay Me*, an artistic recapitulation of an actual episode from his child-hood.[4] The narrator recalls coming home with his father one day from a hunting trip. They found that his mother had destroyed all of his father's cherished relics—including pickled snakes and Indian arrow-heads—in a bonfire. Special attention is paid to the irreplaceable arrow-heads, which his father attempts to rescue from the fire with a rake. The castration fear of his mother and therefore of all women dramatized by this episode is clearly evidenced by the phallic symbolism of the snakes and arrowheads destroyed in the fire of the mother's hostility.

Hemingway emerges as a man obsessed by the fear of castration. Yet it is the more usual manifestation of Cancer sensitivity in the male: the hard outer shell of *machismo* pretense protects the tender feelings inside. For most men, those feelings must be concealed at all costs; expressing them in any direct way could be overwhelming.

A. E. Hotchner's sympathetic portrait, *Papa Hemingway*, estab-lishes that Hemingway had both the Cancerian devotion to his home and a disposition to hoard money in amounts far beyond any realistic need.

Hotchner also tries to solve the riddle of Hemingway's suicide but he cannot, nor could the doctors who treated Hemingway at the Mayo Clinic. Perhaps maintaining that *machismo* Cancer shell required more energy than sixty-two-year-old Hemingway possessed. And without the shell, every close friend was a threat, and the de-pression and paranoia deepened, so that Hemingway was no longer able to live life on his own terms.

Hart Crane, American poet, while returning by ship from Mexico on April 27, 1932, threw himself into the ocean. There was no doubt about the reason for his suicide; an aggressive homosexual who rejected himself just as his father had rejected him for his Proustian attitudes, Crane was a committed alcoholic given to violent rages and had destroyed most of his important relationships with the people who tried to help him. Crane could neither change the way he felt, nor the way he felt *about* the way he felt. That old whore, death, provided the only answer.

Crane had been born on July 21, 1889, in Garretsville, Ohio, the same month, day and year of birth as Ernest Hemingway, and with the same Cancer emphasis. Indeed, their solar charts are identical.

Polar opposite. We shall learn more about the qualities of Cancer when we consider the characteristics of Capricorn, its polar opposite.

Positive and negative aspects. Positively manifested, Cancer qualities produce individuals of great warmth and depth of feeling, with a capacity to nourish and shelter those less fortunate than themselves, both materially and psychically. They are great providers, both for themselves and for their families, and often amass considerable wealth.

Negatively manifested, a strong Cancer emphasis may produce men of blustering over-aggressiveness who seek to reject feelings that they find repulsive in themselves by overreacting in an opposite direction. In women, negative Cancer expression more often takes the form of maternal possessiveness of the kind described in *Portnoy's Complaint.* However, bizarre and contradictory reactions to Cancer sensitivity are not limited to men, as French novelist Baronne Dudevant, born July 1, 1804, illustrates. Assuming the name George Sand, she wore men's suits, smoked cigars and became Chopin's mistress.

Notable Cancer personalities. John Quincy Adams, Pierre Cardin, Jean Cocteau, Calvin Coolidge, Hermann Hesse, Lena Horne, Rose Kennedy, Wanda Landowska, Gina Lollobrigida, Gustav Mahler and John D. Rockefeller.

Element. Cancer is the first water sign.

LEO

Sequence. Leo is the fifth sign of the natural zodiac. The Latin word *leo* means lion. The Sun enters Leo about July 23.

Glyph. The glyph for the sign Leo is the graphic depiction of the constellation Leo found in the Hebrew letter Lamed (Lambda in Greek).

Word associations to Lamed include the notions of learning and impatience, and the latter is particularly notable as a Leo quality. In the context of the former, Lamed is generally associated with *Malmed*, meaning ox goad, on the theory that learning takes compulsion.[1]

Planetary ruler. The Sun is the planetary ruler of Leo.

Melothesia. Leo rules the heart and cardiac system. Externally, Leo rules the upper back.

Characteristics. The fact that the ruler of Leo is the Sun itself gives us some idea of the fiery nature of this sign. Whereas the fire of Aries finds expression in egocentric will, Leo's fiery consciousness has a patriarchic character. As a leader, Aries is a lone wolf. But Leo wants an audience. Depending on the context, that audience can be his children, his troops, his followers, his flock or, quite literally, a theatrical audience. Leos are great actors.

Leo is indeed the king of beasts. As such, he must have progeny—be they the actual children of the native or his brain children. Implicit in the concept of Leo, as in any other fire sign, is the imposition of the conscious will on the environment.

In the Leo rulership of the heart and cardiac system we can trace the connection of Leo's mental fire to the fire of his passions. Norman Brown has rightly observed, "In the unconscious, cerebral is genital."[2] Brown notes that the word "cerebral" has the same cognate as *cresco*, to grow, and *creo*, to create. Stated succinctly, "The erection is in the head."[3] Thus it is that Leo's desire to create, to grow, may find expression in his offspring or in the creative fire of his consciousness. Or, as D. H. Lawrence put it, "Maybe all basic thought takes place in the blood around the heart, and is only transferred to the brain."[4]

Leo is the second fiery expression of Man's consciousness, Aries being the first. Leo is always identified with a crown. It's his mane, or his hair style or some sort of headdress—often of gold—symbolizing his royal status. But it tells us something more as well. Many cultures, especially the Chinese, represent fiery consciousness by a dragon.[5] The Egyptians, as Lawrence notes, used the *Uraeus*, a gold serpent worn as a headdress. Other cultures have used horns, such as "the gold horns of power that bud on Moses' forehead . . ." But for the commonality, Lawrence concludes, the horn of power has always been the phallus, the cornucopia or horn of plenty.[6] There is also that aspect to Leo.

Leo needs an audience to recognize his royal status and to do obeisance, to honor his performance. If he doesn't get it by virtue of his royal status alone, the Leo native will demand it by antics ranging from the outrageous to the bizarre. While Leo emphasis may express itself in the native's imperious demands for attention, the same Leo emphasis may see the native as easily hurt and wounded. Leonine vanity is prodigious.

Prototypes. Alfie did not question his instructions when his father gave him a note to take to the police station. Nor did he open the folded paper to look at the message his father had written. To say the very least, he was surprised when, after reading the message, the inspector at the desk directed Alfie to accompany him. Alfie followed him down the corridor; the inspector beckoned, and Alfie proceeded into the cell. The door clanged shut; the keys rattled and Alfie found himself a prisoner. Surely it was a horrible mistake! But the inspector's tread faded down the hall, another door clanged shut and all was silence.

It seemed an eternity before the inspector returned with an explanation: Alfie's father had asked in the note that his son be shut up in this manner. "This is what we do to naughty boys," the inspector rumbled, reading the note. But Alfie had no idea what he had done wrong.

Nor does he know to this day. Whatever the offense, the discipline seems grotesque. In another child, the trauma could have been disabling. But Alfred Hitchcock, born August 13, 1899, is very much a Leo. As such, it is important for him to be in the forefront of public attention. Do you know any other movie director whose trademark is his appearance in every picture he directs?

With a view to his Leo Sun, I see Hitchcock as a regal figure, who, far from being cowed by that early childhood trauma, has re-created it, again and again, in a succession of brain children commencing with his early haunting story of Jack the Ripper, where his innovations were such as to cause the film to be shelved for over a year.

GOLD AND THE Sun are always associated with Leo, as they were with Zelda Sayre, who became Zelda Fitzgerald in one of the great love stories of the 1920s. Born July 24, 1900, when the Sun and Mercury were both posited in Leo, Zelda, at fifteen, was already a golden-haired beauty; at eighteen, she met Scott Fitzgerald at a country club dance. Scott was an Army lieutenant then, and Zelda had just graduated from high school. Fitzgerald was immediately drawn to this golden girl, and she to him.[7] When the Army sent Scott North, Zelda's attention-getting antics drove him into a frenzy. But attention and homage were due her by Leo birthright: was it her fault that a special society known as Zeta

Sigma (for Zelda Sayre) was formed, whose initiation rites included pilgrimages to her home?[8]

When Fitzgerald's first novel, *This Side of Paradise*, was published in March of 1920, Scott and Zelda were the king and queen of each other's fantasies and of the reading public. His literary success enabled them to be married, and their story truly began where other fables ended.

With a due regard to her Sun and Mercury in Leo, Zelda's character is more easily understood—including her penchant for highly publicized, attention-getting antics such as splashing about in public fountains.

But her princess quality was her most attractive feature to Fitzgerald, who used it again and again in his fiction. She was Daisy in *The Great Gatsby*, where she was "High in a white palace the king's daughter, the golden girl . . ." She was also Sally Carrol Hopper, the Southern heroine of "The Ice Palace," in which the sun-and-gold of Zelda-the-Leo are apotheosized: her home "took the full sun" and over it "the sunlight dripped . . . like golden paint . . ."

The obvious competition for recognition that developed between Scott and Zelda has been documented many times. After her tragic descent into schizophrenia, the major medical goal was "to get her to distinguish between her fantasies, illusion and reality."[9] That was not easy for Zelda; indeed, the task was never accomplished.

In her novel, *Save Me the Waltz*, Zelda became Alabama Beggs, and Scott was originally Amory Blaine, the hero of his first novel, *This Side of Paradise*. That name was later changed, on Scott's demand. The novel shows Zelda's search for an identity independent of her childhood subservience to her father, who is Judge Beggs in the novel.

Save Me the Waltz is truly a remarkable piece of Leo narcissism. Alabama is "the wildest of the Beggs" but "a true thoroughbred." When she falls in love with David during their first kiss, she creeps into his head and "stares about the deep trenches of the cerebellum," where she becomes hysterically lost. She loved him so much that her vision became distorted, as if she were "pressing her nose upon a mirror and gazing into her own eyes."[10]

Save Me the Waltz is Zelda's autobiography as she saw her life: a fairy tale, with Zelda the princess and Scott the knight who carries her away from her thralldom to her imperious father; that competition she could never win.

There are evidences of Zelda's insight into the excesses of her own Leo character, as when she mentions that "Alabama's peculiar genius lay in possessing a rapacious engulfing ego that swallowed the world . . ."[11]

In her quest for identity through creations born of her own ego, Zelda wrote *Save Me the Waltz* from a sanitarium in a frantic six weeks in 1932. It was her last great burst of creative fire. She had driven herself well beyond the point of collapse with her ballet lessons, determined to achieve stardom as a ballerina, to achieve public recognition equal to her husband's literary fame. An erratic, .disorganized work, *Save Me the Waltz* has flashes of brilliance that show Zelda Sayre Fitzgerald with the best and worst of the Leo archetype. It was her tragedy to recognize her excesses and to be unable to cope with them other than in the schizophrenic fashion which is Leo at its worst: to draw attention to herself by destroying those around her. For it was Zelda, in the anxiety of a homosexual crush on her ballet teacher, who accused Scott of a homosexual liaison with Hemingway. She invented that calumny to maintain her own Leonine ego, which could not bear the thought of having any human frailty which her spouse did not have at least in equal measure. [12]

Narcissism is an essential Leo characteristic; it is however, an elemental part of human nature, which can be positively or negatively expressed by every one of us. I think Hitchcock is a delightful man whose Leo narcissism has been a source of satisfaction to generations of moviegoers. Zelda Fitzgerald's narcissism overwhelmed her, and brought unhappiness to her and to everyone around her.

THE FINAL BIOGRAPHICAL note on Leo characteristics deals with Aldous Huxley, born July 26, 1894, a figure whose humanism broke through the bondage of his Leo will.

Serious problems with his eyesight barred him from a career in medicine; instead, he became a man of letters, whose early novels reflected his heritage of scientific rationalism. *Point Counter Point*, published in 1928, was the best of these.

Then Huxley underwent what psychiatrist Henri F. Ellenberger would probably describe as a *creative illness:*[13] a long period of psychic pain from which he emerged permanently transformed with mystical enlightenment.

Prior to that enlightenment, there had been various evidences of Huxley's dissatisfaction with his own Leo brilliance and with the brain children that his intellect had produced. The first of these was the devotional act of gathering, editing and publishing D. H. Lawrence's letters, which-hé arranged to tell the story of Lawrence's life. In his introduction to that work, Huxley defended Lawrence from the savage attack by John Middleton Murry in the form of pseudo-Freudian analysis; and his staunch defense of his deceased friend was just the kind of commitment he had earlier avoided in his posture of intellectual detachment.

Then there was the death of his brother Trevenan, for which he felt some inchoate responsibility. Trevenan was the member of his own family to whom Huxley felt the strongest bond. With Trevenan and Lawrence both dead, and no sustaining personal belief, Huxley's sense of despair deepened, but for him conventional religion held no answer; indeed, it never had.

The agony he felt from 1932 to 1936 is expressed in *Eyeless in Gaza*, the quasi-autobiographical novel which dramatizes his mystical conversion. He recognized that the intellectual freedom which had been so important to him, the hubristic freedom from commitment, was a form of slavery in the guise of freedom; a spiritual vacuum in the pretense of intellectual detachment. The novel's hero—Huxley in thin disguise—is a spiritually blind man who receives an inner vision of mystical enlightenment. (It is no accident that the Old Testament concept of Sammael, Satan or Azazel, whether in the form of demon, god or beast, was always seen as blind.)

Thus *The Perennial Philosophy* (1945) expresses Huxley's recognition that the very intellectual brilliance that made literary excellence so easy for him itself imposed a serious limitation.

He finally realized the dangers of his own Leo narcissism, and surmounted them by embracing a nontheistic mysticism.

Huxley knew Leo narcissism very well, and from the inside. Thus, in his remarkable novella, *The Genius and the Goddess*, he describes the intellectual Leo he could have become but did not.

In the forties, Huxley developed an interest in Vedanta, an American version of Hindu mysticism, which takes as a guiding principle the view that "Religion is not in doctrines, in dogmas, nor in intellectual argumentation; it is being and becoming. It is realization."[14]

Under the supervision of Dr. Humphry Osmond, Huxley experimented with mescaline and with lysergic acid to augment his mystical experiences, and once again the Leonine self-will was very much involved. In a letter to Father Thomas Merton, Huxley pointed out that such experiences were not necessarily pleasurable, and indeed not altogether pleasant, inasmuch as they all involved *the death of the ego;* but the benefits of the essentially mystical experience, the transcendent sense of Oneness, greatly outweighed whatever disadvantages there were.[15]

Aldous Huxley, mystic, humanist, man of letters, surmounted the bondage of a Leonine will by precisely the means he advocated in *The Perennial Philosophy:* he willed it out of existence. As a result, he became the unintended leader of an entirely new following; he was lionized anew, this time as the symbolic mentor of the counterculture of alienated youth who were oriented toward the same mysticism and humanism, with a like disaffection for technology and religious formalism.

Few traces of the original Huxley Leo survived this remarkable transformation. However, there was one: for Huxley, the crown of power described by D. H. Lawrence in *Apocalypse* was not the archaic crown of antiquity; it was instead the beautiful Gunn and Latchford neckties made from Chinese tapestry, for which he maintained a fondness until his death in 1963.

Polar opposite. We will have a better understanding of the further reaches of Leonine qualities when we consider its polar opposite sign, Aquarius.

Positive and negative aspects. Positively manifested, a Leo emphasis can produce leaders and actors of great devotion who have a compassionate concern for their subjects or a like dedication to their audiences. Negatively expressed, a strong Leo emphasis may be seen in a native whose demands for attention make him a nuisance at best and a megalomaniac at worst; and whose boundless narcissism can be both destructive of the self and of those close to him.

Notable Leo personalities. Napoleon Bonaparte, James S. Copley, Raymond Chandler, Benito Mussolini, Herbert Hoover, Carl Jung, Jacqueline Kennedy Onassis, Emily Brontë, Ray Bradbury, Yves Saint Laurent and Mae West.

Element. Leo is the second fire sign; the first was Aries. With Leo, the second cycle of sign elements begins.

VIRGO

Sequence. Virgo is the sixth sign of the natural zodiac. In Latin, *virgo* means virgin. The Sun enters Virgo about August 24 each year.

Glyph. The glyph for Virgo is derived from the Hebrew letter Mem,[1] which became the Greek letter Mu and ultimately the M of our alphabet. In the context of Heaven, Earth and Water, Mem means Waters, a fertility symbol.

Mem, Mu and M are all originally based on the constellation Virgo at a time when the Sun's entrance into that constellation coincided with the harvest feast. Virgo is still often represented by a virgin holding a sheaf of wheat, symbol of the harvest.

Planetary ruler. The ruler of Virgo is the planet Mercury, which also rules Gemini.

Melothesia. Virgo rules the abdomen and the intestines.

Characteristics. Natives with a Virgo sign emphasis often possess an intuitive analytical ability. However, I think it is a mistake to conclude that simply because *Virgo* means virgin that it is a barren or unfruitful sign. After all, Virgo was the goddess of fertility! When the sign and the constellation were originally conceptualized, "virgin" simply meant any unmarried girl. The Christian concept of the Virgin Mary, added to the astrological palimpsest much later, expresses the better-known Virgo qualities of loyalty and devotion. Here the palimpsest concept is helpful, for the symbols of Virgo as the young girl of the harvest festival and as the Holy Mother illustrate the twin Virgo needs for *the real and the ideal.*

There is another aspect to the palimpsest which sheds further light on Virgo. Just as sailors of an earlier age relied on Polaris, the polestar, to give them direction at sea, so Virgo finds direction from its own polestar. In that earlier time a second polestar beloved of sailors was known as *Stella Maris,* the Star of the Sea.[2]

The Moon was the root for the Hebrew *Miriam,* who became the Christian Mary, still revered as *Stella Maris* in Catholic teaching. And it is *Stella Maris,* the Holy Mother and the Virgin Mary of our Virgo palimpsest, who is the polestar* of Virgo natives. Without her to guide the native, the Virgoan is truly lost at sea.

As a sign quality, Virgo is often damned with faint praise. For too many people, analytical ability and dedicated service say everything there is to say about Virgo, none of it very interesting.

The implication is that Virgo personalities are perhaps the least colorful natives of the zodiac. There is even the notion that Virgoans are a bit stupid. One of the relieving qualities of Virgo, and a frequently overlooked attribute of this sign emphasis, is the remarkable sense of humor which many Virgo natives possess. More often than not, the Virgo sense of humor has an incisive edge of comic genius, which places Virgo among the wittiest people of the zodiac.

While Virgoans may be extremely tidy, they may also be the reverse. Again, the reason lies in idealism. Where Virgo is untidy, it is likewise in the extreme, and usually because of his concern for order. Realizing that he will never be able to be as orderly and well organized

---

*The Moon as the Virgo *polestar* should not be confused with the *planetary ruler* of Virgo, which is Mercury.

as he would ideally prefer, he throws up his hands and abandons the effort completely.

Idealism makes hypochondria a characteristic Virgo ailment; and those Virgoans who are not clearly hypochondriacal may be fanatic about health foods and organic foods, dietary regimens, exercise, physical fitness and the like. Yet many Virgo people suffer great intestinal distress, including duodenal ulcers, in steadfast devotion to an idealized goal far beyond its intrinsic worth. It all seems to point to that admixture of present reality and its idealization.

Prototypes. English-American novelist Janet Taylor Caldwell was born September 7, 1900, in Prestwick, Manchester, England. A Roman Catholic, Taylor Caldwell exemplifies many Virgo qualities, together with the conflicts which they create. She has a chronic abdominal complaint[3] and cheerfully describes herself as "an enthusiastic hypochondriac."[4]

Her family, comfortably situated in England, found itself in reduced circumstances in the United States. Caldwell's early life was one of poverty, a status which continued into her first marriage. However, poverty was not a state she willingly endured; and at this point we are reminded that Virgo is, after all, an earth sign. She swore that she would have all the money she wanted and needed when she grew up.[5]

Taylor Caldwell's first book, *Dynasty of Death*, was completed in January of 1938 and rejected by the first publisher to whom it was sent. The day after receiving the rejection, Caldwell wandered disconsolately into a spiritualist meeting, more or less by accident, where to her surprise her name was promptly called by the speaker. Without asking any questions, the spiritualist advised her that her book would be sold on April second to another publisher. It was; and on the very terms specified by the spiritualist.[6]

Such eerie episodes have continued throughout her life.* Her husband, Marcus Reback, promised some sign to her if there was an afterlife. The day before Marcus died, the family gardener had suggested removing an old resurrection lily that had failed to bloom in the twenty-one years of its existence. Taylor Caldwell demurred out of sentiment. And the day after Marcus's death the resurrection lily burst into full bloom.[7]

After this incident she sought out Jess Stearn, the author-journalist best known for his eminently readable accounts of psychic experiences and whose work includes *Edgar Cayce: The Sleeping Prophet* and *Adventures into the Psychic*. She asked Stearn's help in setting up a program to attempt her hypnotic regression to see whether there was some sort of survival of the personality after death.

---

*Attributable to her Pisces Ascendant.

The results have been recorded in Jess Stearn's absorbing documentary account, *The Search for a Soul: Taylor Caldwell's Psychic Lives.* Through hypnotic regression, Janet Taylor Caldwell vividly recalled past lives as the lover of Savonarola, the Dominican friar condemned to death at the stake for urging Church reform; as the scullery maid of George Eliot and as many others, including existences in the ages of Atlantis and of the Incas.

In view of Caldwell's recurrent literary theme of religious and historical romance, her own psychic experiences and the convincing evidence of her hypnotic regressions into seemingly past lives, not to mention her own energetic efforts in setting up the entire project, we might expect that she would pronounce herself satisfied as to the existence not only of the soul but of reincarnation as well. Not so. After reading the original manuscript of *Psychic Lives,* Caldwell penned an epilogue of her own, the upshot of which is her flat statement that she was not convinced.

At this point we see a Virgo native who has spent the greater part of her life fulfilling a vow to achieve financial success which she now repudiates; and who has evidenced considerable preoccupation with psychic and religious themes, both in her work and in seeking out a psychic researcher for regression into past lives—who now disclaims any belief in reincarnation, and expresses some doubt about the existence of the soul itself![8]

The key to the puzzle lies in the nature of the Virgo character. Like all Virgo natives, Taylor Caldwell *needs an ideal,* someone to serve with devotion, who will be the polestar for her orientation in present reality. Usually that polestar is *Stella Maris* personified as the native's mother.

The Virgo native will perform that devoted service to his parental ideal whenever the parent fulfills the polestar role of providing guidance and love. However, if the parent frustrates the native's devotion by withholding love or by otherwise failing as a parental model, the native becomes disoriented—at sea with himself and his universe. The result is what we may call the Three A's of Virgo: *ambivalence, anger and analysis.*

A reading of Taylor Caldwell's autobiography, *On Growing Up Tough,* shows that she has indeed used her mother as her polestar, perhaps regrettably, in the usual way of internalizing her mother's values and accepting them as her own. But in her epilogue to *Psychic Lives,* Caldwell admits that she hates her mother, who was "always anxious to put a kid down—notably me."[9] That is perhaps the least of it. She describes her mother as "vicious, vicious . . . I used to wish she would die."[10] Throughout *Psychic Lives,* there are passages in which she vehemently recalls the abuse she suffered at her mother's hands and her parents' total lack of affection for her. She concludes: "My life has been tragic and disastrous from birth." She regards her childhood as "appalling. I knew nothing but fear, cruelty and rejection from my parents."[11] Taylor Caldwell has reason to be an angry lady.

Ambivalence? Although Caldwell deplores charity, she admits that she gives not just a tenth of her income to charity, but a *full third* of her large estate to the needy; and she also concedes that she has helped "many thousands" anonymously.[12] Although she scorns Liberals, her actions (if not her stated opinions) are those that anyone who styled himself a Liberal should be proud of. Her views on organic foods, food additives, the IRS, establishment hypocrisy and formal education would rank her with the long-hairs she professes to deplore.[13]

When a person has an internal tug of war going on inside him—or her—between two opposing goals, he is termed ambivalent. He wants something, yet he wants the opposite; clearly he cannot have both. We see this ambivalence in Caldwell's conflicting attitudes on many subjects.

Taylor Caldwell struggled hard to achieve financial success, and she prevailed over considerable hardship. Her religious orientation and her devotion to her dead husband give her stern commands: money cannot buy happiness; she must reject her goal of wealth in favor of the (to her) conflicting goal of piety. As she sees it, it would be disloyal for her to be happy, to enjoy her life and hard-earned wealth after her husband's death.

The goal of proving the truth of her religious convictions thus surfaces, and we see the considerable effort, imagination and dogged determination that went into her search for a soul with Jess Stearn. That search was clearly an act of love, a devotional service to the memory of her beloved husband. And what is the result? Once again, Taylor Caldwell rejects her desired goal when it is within reach; for after all, psychic experiences and reincarnation are ridiculous; they conflict with her polestar mother's no-nonsense values which Caldwell has loyally—if unconsciously—followed throughout her life.

Moreover, her nature is far too critical to accept the things which she longs to believe. But what *is* criticism? Simply stated, *criticism is analysis accompanied by anger.* In Taylor Caldwell we see that Virgo criticism is analysis infused with the anger of the native who has been deprived and whose devoted service is not acknowledged or even appreciated. *On Growing Up Tough* is a highly critical book by an angry lady who tells us that her parents did not love her and did not want her.

A lesser person might not have survived; but Taylor Caldwell's very survival is a tribute to her strength of character. Her outlet for her tragic childhood circumstances was characteristically Virgoan: she would become a writer.

Writing is one form of analysis; and many Virgo natives are outstanding writers. For Taylor Caldwell, becoming a writer gave her a new goal, that of economic success, which she idealized in terms of a vow to give one-third of everything she earned to the poor, if God would permit her to succeed.[14]

By substituting one ideal for another, she thus regained orientation in life; but not without difficulty, for the original polestar was now seen as false, leading the native astray. Where the first polestar is shown to be false, the Virgo native can never quite believe any other, so that her reliance on the substitute is always provisional. To some extent, the Virgo native thus deprived of the guidance of her own *Stella Maris* will always be lost at sea. Only today, we used words like "inconsistent" and "ambivalent."

A disillusioned Virgo can be extremely cynical, doubtful of the genuineness of all the good things life has to offer. That is why Taylor Caldwell disclaims the implications of her psychic lives on the ground that she sees no proof of reincarnation. Yet she freely admits in her foreword to *Dialogues with the Devil* that *if* she were superstitious, "I should say that two personalities took over the book in mid-passage . . . Certainly the thoughts in the book are not my thoughts," while in the same breath confirming that she is "of course" superstitious.

It is also significant that Taylor Caldwell spent forty-six years, by her account, in writing her novel about St. Luke. She wrote the first version at the age of twelve, the second when she was twenty-two and the third when she was twenty-six. The fourth was published in 1959 as *Dear and Glorious Physician.*[15] St. Luke represents the kind of ideal service which this native and every Virgo native seeks.

Her Virgo need to render devoted service appears to have found a more rewarding outlet in her marriage to Marcus Reback, her husband of some forty years whose death she so sincerely mourned. Her husband's passing deprived her of her polestar and the result was a prolonged and suicidal depression.

The regressions described in *Psychic Lives* seem to be her Virgo way of continuing to serve her husband even after his passing. As a result of these episodes, she reports that her good spirits have returned, together with her appetite and some of her hearing. She has met a man whom she regards with matrimonial interest. And yet—her dearest, fondest wish is for death![16] Has the experiment been a total failure after all?

Perhaps. And perhaps not. Taylor Caldwell concedes that as a result of her journeys into past lives she has recaptured a joy of living unknown to her since her husband's passing. How strange, then, to wish for death!

Unless of course she has found her polestar, that worthwhile someone to serve with the kind of devotion that only a Virgo can provide. Perhaps now she knows that that ideal is simply waiting for her . . . on the Other Side.

DAVID HERBERT RICHARDS Lawrence[17] is about as unlikely a candidate for a Virgo prototype as anyone could imagine. Yet Lawrence, born September 11, 1885, in the Nottinghamshire coal-mining town of Eastwood, was a Virgo by Sun sign; and Virgo is the key to his character.

It was generally held that to befriend D. H. Lawrence was to incur his wrath; that he returned every favor with a corresponding slight to show his ingratitude. Even his close friend Aldous Huxley did not go unscathed. Lawrence didn't like Huxley's books, he freely admitted, adding, "But again I feel that only half a man writes the books—a sort of 'precocious adolescent.'"[18] When John Middleton Murry founded a magazine called *Adelphi* to serve as a vehicle for Lawrence's work at a time when Lawrence very much needed it, Lawrence's response was typical: he derided the publication.[19]

How do notions of loyalty, service and devotion square with the known facts about D. H. Lawrence? Aldous Huxley gives us the answer. In his introduction to his collection of Lawrence's letters, Huxley declares:

> . . . he remained through thick and thin unshakeably loyal to his own genius. The *daimon* which possessed him was, he felt, a divine thing . . . This loyalty to his own self, or rather to his gift, to the strange and powerful *numen* which used him as its tabernacle, is fundamental in Lawrence and accounts, as nothing else can do, for all that the world found strange in his beliefs and his behavior.[20]

One definition of a daimon can be found in Plato's *Symposium*, in which Socrates says that Eros, or Love, "is a daimon"—often translated as great spirit—who "is intermediate between the divine and the mortal."[21]

Contemporary psychiatrist Rollo May agrees with Socrates, and contributes some ideas of his own on the nature of the daimon Eros:

> In my definition, Eros is the daemon which constitutes man's creative spirit, the drive that not only impels him to sexual union and to other forms of love, but also . . . drives him to . . . become poet, or artist, or scientist.[22]

Sex and love, anger and rage, the quest for power—all are daimonic, because all have the power to take over the total personality; and daimonic possession, Dr. May points out, is "the traditional term through history for psychosis."[23]

Eros was the daimon that took possession of D. H. Lawrence; indeed, there were many times when he seemed psychotic, so intense was his commitment. But his loyalty was unwavering. "The daemon is the power of nature," Goethe said, and it was that power that Lawrence the Virgo praised and served. His friend Lady Cynthia Asquith described his Virgo character precisely, when she said that Lawrence was

> A *mystical materialist,* he wanted to make sex valid, devout—beautiful instead of ashamed . . . His method may often have been mistaken, but *his intention*—to release humanity from that degradation of sex which gives so many a fear of it—was *always burningly idealistic.* [24]

Could there be any other way for a Virgo native in service to his daimon?

As biographer Mark Schorer observed, "Nowhere was this idealism pursued more intensely than in *Lady Chatterley's Lover.*"[25] It was Lawrence's intention to serve his daimon by protesting the industrialization which had reduced that great force of nature to the modern Cupid—the insipid, childish and banal—and to urge the daimon which could restore Man to his former proud estate. Thus Constance Chatterley is married to an impotent and crippled mine-owner, but she escapes the deadening influences of her overcivilized society and her husband's life-denying intellectualization by falling in love with her gamekeeper, who embodies the Lawrentian daimonic vitalism.

The daimon Eros has never been so profoundly expressed in terms of Lawrence's understanding of his commitment as in *Lady Chatterley.*

Our Western culture has engaged in a polite conspiracy, Rollo May reminds us, to enforce the illusion that nice feelings are all there is to love, whereas throughout Man's history we have known there is much more. There is, for example, the dread that the new relationship will destroy us, as expressed in the early nature myth of Adonis slain by the boar's tooth of winter. As May points out, every kind of mythology relates the sex act to death.[26] The idea of surrender, of dying and being reborn, is basic to the daimon Eros, and the true experience of love is more than a little frightening. Kate Millett and *Sexual Politics* notwithstanding, male aggression is essential, and May points out that "the erection is a powerful daemonic symbol. ... Both man and woman need this self-assertion to bridge their separateness and to achieve union with each other."[27]

It is this true Eros which Lawrence celebrates with accuracy in *Lady Chatterley's Lover,* where his announced intention was a rejection of sex in the head in favor of sex in the heart.

Sons and Lovers demonstrates that Lawrence's mother was indeed his *Stella Maris,* his guiding star throughout his life. Had he deliberately sought to explain his characters on the basis of astrological principles, he could have done nothing more to stress the Virgoan Moon-Mother relationship.

Paul's sweetheart is Miriam, the Old Testament version of the *Stella Maris.* The name Miriam is particularly appropriate, inasmuch as Miriam is the competitor of Paul's mother for the devotion of the Virgo son; for the competition to be real, they must be well matched.

Later, Paul has an affair with Clara ("Moonlight") and despairs of his relationships with women. His mother seeks to comfort him, saying, "You haven't met the right woman."

In astrological terms, *Sons and Lovers* is the story of the struggle of a Virgo native to find his true guiding star, his *Stella Maris,* personified in his mother, his girlfriend, his lover and his art. Such was Lawrence's own struggle, and his daimon gave him the uncanny intuition to use the Moon throughout this autobiographical novel to illuminate and add dimension to the struggle. In *Sons and Lovers* as in life, Lawrence served with Virgo devotion.

This astrological view of Lawrence makes comprehensible much that biographers and friends have found puzzling. Acts of apparent disloyalty, such as his criticism of Huxley's earlier books and his derision of Murry's *Adelphi,* can be seen in terms of what Huxley called his unshakable loyalty to his daimon.

Lawrence's Moon at birth was conjunct (in close proximity to) his natal Venus, the planet representing the native's ability to give and to receive love. Both the Moon and Venus were in the sign of Libra, the sign of love and the aesthetic sense, especially in literature.

With this configuration, his polestar Moon was at once his mother, his art and—Eros: and the Moon-Venus conjunction in Libra accounts for his darker moods as well. As his friend Richard Aldington observed, of all his dark moods, "Among the most extraordinary was his response to the influence of a full moon."[28] Lawrence's polestar in the context of a Moon-Venus conjunction caused lunacy in the original and literal sense, and accounts for many otherwise inexplicable aspects of his character.

Lawrence paid a great price for his Virgoan servitude. Today he is regarded as an Aetna of modern literature. His insight into the human condition, his prescience of the problems created by industrialization in human life, the achievements of his literary work and its remarkable volume in his relatively short lifespan fill us with awe.

But in his own lifetime, Lawrence was denied recognition for these achievements. He saw his works condemned as obscene, his writings censored and banned, exhibitions of his art suppressed and his paintings threatened with burning. He lived in penury and in exile. He was ridiculed by much of the literary establishment, most especially the effete Bloomsbury group, which represented all the forces in reaction to his daimonic celebration of the life force of nature.

But he remained Virgo to the end in devoted service to his daimon, a great and tortured spirit whose contributions are only today being fully recognized.

Polar opposite. The polar opposite of Virgo is Pisces. When we consider the archetypal qualities of that watery mutable sign, we will see the outside dimensions of Virgo.

Positive and negative aspects. Positively manifested, Virgo personalities express steadfast devotion to a person or to a cause, utilizing an innate analytical prowess for constructive ends, with an extra dimension of wit and humor often present. Negatively manifested, Virgo qualities result in ambivalence, destructive criticism, irascibility, nit-picking fussiness and self-defeating idealism.

Notable Virgo personalities. Leonard Bernstein, Christopher Isherwood, George Hegel, Theodore Dreiser, Goethe, Charlie Parker, Jean-Claude Killy, Walter Reuther, Lyndon B. Johnson, Arthur Koestler, Sid Caesar, Peter Sellers, Leo Tolstoy, Sophia Loren, Max Beerbohm, Mort Walker, Walt Kelly, Martha Raye and Buddy Hackett.

Element. Virgo is the second earth sign; Taurus was the first.

AT THE BEGINNING of this chapter I observed that it is impossible to teach anyone something he already knows. Because of the popularity of Sun-sign astrology, an understanding of the signs of the zodiac is assumed by most people; any real comprehension of the signs is therefore beset with obstacles.

The popular conception of the zodiacal signs is wrong because it views the signs as stereotypes, which they are not. An *archetype,* on the other hand, is a basic theme or motif which can be seen in all things of its kind; the variations on the archetypal pattern are infinite.

The contemporary astrologer views the signs of the zodiac as archetypal themes which, in the psychological sense, show instinctive trends. When the contemporary astrologer knows the sign emphasis in the native's chart, he looks for that archetypal pattern which can illuminate otherwise puzzling aspects of the individual's life or character. The demonstration of the *archetypal* nature of the first six signs in this chapter has, I hope, disabused the reader of any preconceived notions of zodiacal stereotypes.

6 What Are the Polar Opposites?

THE NEXT SIX signs of the zodiac have both their own unique qualities and the added weight of being the archetypal opposites of the signs considered in the previous chapter. By dealing with the signs in a traditional perspective, in relationship to each other, I hope the reader will gain not only a fuller understanding of each sign but will ultimately conceive of the signs of the zodiac as antipodes, or six sets of bipolar opposites.

LIBRA

Sequence. Libra is the seventh sign of the zodiac. The Latin word *libra* means a measured weight, suggesting the scales of justice with which the sign is often identified. The Sun enters Libra at about September 23 each year.

Glyph. The glyph for Libra is based on the Hebrew letter Ayin[1] (the Greek O Mikron), originally derived from the constellation Libra. Ayin means an eye, a well or a spring of water.

Libra commences with the autumnal equinox, which has also been the Hebrew New Year since the first century B.C.E. The Kabbalah advises that the first manifestation of God from the void was "Ayin."[2] With this pronouncement the world begins. Since Libra is based on Ayin, it is my conclusion that the glyph represents the rising Sun of the beginning of the universe.

Planetary ruler. The planetary ruler of Libra is Venus, the planet which also rules Taurus. Thus the ability to give and to receive love, the basic meaning of Venus in astrology, finds dual expression in Libra and in Taurus, although in different ways.

Melothesia. Libra rules the kidneys, the organs responsible for maintaining the equilibrium of the personal seas which we took with us when we emerged from the primordial oceans to walk on land.[3] Even today we could not survive as land creatures without the constant harmonizing efforts of our kidneys.

Characteristics. Libran qualities include a desire for harmony and balance in both a judicial and an aesthetic sense. One way in which such harmony is achieved is in relationships with others, a need which is very much a Libran quality.

In the *Symposium,* Aristophanes complains that men don't understand the true nature of the daimon Eros; and he proceeds to set out his view of the power of this great and good friend of Man. He explains that Man was originally constituted not as two sexes but as three. There were Man, Woman and a third sex, an Androgyne, or Man-Woman combination. Aristophanes is relating an ancient astrological myth about the sexual nature of Mankind, explaining that the sexes were three because the Sun, Moon and Earth were three. Man was a child of the Sun; Woman was a child of the Earth and the Androgyne was the child of the Moon, which was made up of the Sun and the Earth. Because of the arrogance of the Androgynes, the gods debated whether to annihilate them. Reflecting that if he destroyed them there would be no one to do him homage, Zeus decided instead to split each of them in two.

When the division of each of the three creatures was complete, Aristophanes continued, the present state of humankind was the result. Everyone was divided in two, with each of us seeking to be reunited with his severed other half according to his original sex, and both halves longing to grow back into one whole person.

This Platonic myth is a good illustration of Man's Libran yearnings for relationship. It also tells us that the daimon Eros is no respecter of social mores, which do change from time to time. On the basis of such ancient myths, both Freud and Jung concluded, independently of each other, that the nature of Man was essentially bisexual[4]—a fact known to astrologers from immemorial times.

It is therefore surprising to read in *Medical Astrology* the statement of Omar Garrison that astrology still categorizes homosexuality as "an abnormality of morbid origin."[5] Garrison cites no authority for his statement, nor does he set out whatever credentials he may have for his medical judgments.

For the contemporary astrologer who recognizes that just about everyone who consults him has some concern about how his sexual feelings correspond to whatever the current notions of normality may be, the myth told by Aristophanes provides an answer: we all have the

Sun and the Moon in our horoscopes, in which the Sun represents the male principle and the Moon the female principle. Our Libran needs for relationship to achieve emotional balance are universal and innate; how we act to satisfy those needs is a matter of individual choice in the exercise of our free will.

Many Librans struggle to achieve balance in all of life's situations to the point of appearing hesitant and indecisive. It mischaracterizes this sign emphasis, however, to dismiss Librans as indecisive; for the essential quality is the relentless search for harmony and balance—whether the Libra native is an attorney seeking balance in the scales of justice or an artist seeking balance in the harmonious interaction of line and color.

Too often overlooked is the Libran aptitude for interpersonal skills. Here the contrast to Aries becomes apparent. Whereas Aries is characterized by headstrong aggressive action, Librans work judiciously *through others* to persuade rather than to compel. They are often masters of inducing others to carry out their wishes; more often than not, the other person is unaware of what is happening.

Prototypes. The sense of fairness, the dedication to art, the love of luxury over thrift, the acting through others and even the attribution of his better qualities to persons other than himself—Libran qualities all—are apparent in F. Scott Fitzgerald.[6] His Libran nature was a source of concern both to his wife, Zelda, and to his sometime friend Hemingway. He thought Fitzgerald was too pretty, especially his mouth, which worried Hemingway. Zelda accused her husband of a homosexual liaison with Hemingway.

It is true that Fitzgerald, born September 24, 1896, at 3:30 P.M., with Sun, Venus and Mercury all posited in Libra in the eighth house of sex, was attractive to women; but there is no evidence that his Libran need for partnerships with men (as well as women) ever found sexual expression. It was perhaps his Libran failing that his interest in, and concern for his friends was such that he was indifferent to the dangers that they sometimes posed for his own self-interest.

Fitzgerald has traditionally been regarded as an American expatriate writer who symbolized the so-called Flaming Youth of the 1920s in its revolt from social restraints and conventions. In recent years, literate Americans have grown to realize that this stereotyped view of Fitzgerald has shortchanged an outstanding artist and his considerable literary contribution.

In F. Scott Fitzgerald we see an artist with most of the Libran attributes—and failings. He loved luxury, he wrote with genius, his sense of fairness placed the interests of others above his own and he had an intense and compelling need for fulfillment through others.

With all of its much-publicized idiosyncrasy, his life was true to the basic character of the Libran archetype. In a very real sense, Fitzgerald acted out his art by the way he lived. This fact is brought home again and again by a variety of incidents recounted by his many biographers.

Arthur Mizener describes how Fitzgerald acted out the role of the protagonist in his first novel, *This Side of Paradise,* riding down New York's Fifth Avenue with Zelda, the beautiful girl he had wooed and won—as had Amory Blaine in the novel—on the top of a taxi because it was a hot day. Or diving into the fountain at Union Square, presumably for the same reason. Or trying to undress with the girls at the *Scandals*— was it that hot? Or crying as he rode through New York, "because I had everything I wanted and knew I would never be so happy again."[7]

Leading the expatriate American colony on the French Riviera from 1926 to 1929, Fitzgerald remarked that everything that happened there had something to do with art.[8] His Libran sense of fairness would not permit him to divorce or otherwise abandon Zelda, although as her illness deepened she tried to destroy him. Long before schizophrenia overwhelmed her personality, Fitzgerald had incorporated her life as well as his own in his stories and novels.[9] In one instance, he took a letter Zelda had written to him and used it almost word for word in his first novel, attributing it to one of his characters. He protested her use of her own biographical material in her literary efforts, because he felt it somehow belonged to his art.[10]

On the French Riviera he became close friends with Gerald and Sara Murphy, whom he admired[11] and whose positive sense of good taste gave direction to the American expatriate colony. In Libran fashion Fitzgerald incorporated both the Murphys, himself and Zelda in what many critics now consider his greatest work, *Tender Is the Night.* The amalgamation of the Fitzgeralds with the Murphys into Nicole and Dick Diver was attacked by knowledgeable critics and by Gerald Murphy as well. Fitzgerald's reply was that the book was inspired by the Murphys and by his admiration for the way they lived: ". . . the last part is Zelda and me," he added, "because you and Sara are the same people as Zelda and me."[12]

Fitzgerald's response to Gerald Murphy discloses what I regard as the key to his Libran character: "When I like men, I want to be like them—I want to lose the outer qualities that give me my individuality and be like them."[13] This Libran quality of achieving identity through

others can also be seen in Fitzgerald's choice of classmate Edmund
Wilson as his intellectual conscience, Ernest Hemingway as his artistic
conscience and Gerald Murphy as his social conscience.[14]

What Fitzgerald believed to be Hemingway's dedication to his art
attracted Fitzgerald to him; and Fitzgerald advanced the literary career
of the unknown Hemingway with Scribner's, his own publisher. When
Hemingway later attacked him at a time when he was most vulnerable,
Fitzgerald's Libran sense of fairness, coupled with his appreciation of
Hemingway's worth as an artist, forbade his doing anything other than
paying his respects to Hemingway's achievement, as his letters to
Hemingway disclose.[15]

But what about Libra women? After careful consideration and
close personal investigation and commitment, I am prepared to stand
on the following observations. A Libra lady is a lady who:

> Bursts into tears when cleaning squid because they are so hideous.
> Bursts into tears when given an African violet because it is so
> beautiful.
> Charms you into doing what *she* wants and makes you glad you did.
> Charms herself into doing what *you* want and is glad she did it.
> Is so beautiful in spirit that she makes you feel beautiful too.
> Is so happy when you're happy that you're happy for both of you.
> Whose entrance into the room wafts the scent from the roses on the
> table near the door.
> Whose departure reminds you that the roses are overblown and
> ashen.
> Is this a valentine? Yes, I suppose it is.

Polar opposite. Libra is the polar opposite of Aries and by contrast
gives further dimension to the qualities of both signs. The Libran need
for relationship to achieve balance is contrasted with the Arien need for
self-assertion. Where either extremity of these bipolar opposites is
reached, the native suffers from the excess of the one and the lack of
the other.

Positive and negative aspects. Positively manifested, Libran qualities include a well-developed aesthetic sense, an ability to harmonize
life's situations, to apply judicious reasoning to insure fair play and to
use interpersonal skills to good advantage. Negatively manifested,
Libran qualities are indecision, a preoccupation with aesthetics of
bizarre proportions, self-defeating manipulation or a pathological uncer-
tainty amounting to a total inability to act.

Notable Libran personalities. Henri Bergson, Lenny Bruce, Truman Capote, Dwight D. Eisenhower, T. S. Eliot, William Faulkner, John

Lennon, Emily Post, Eleanor Roosevelt, Gore Vidal, Oscar Wilde, Thomas Wolfe and Nola Williams.

Element. Libra is the second air sign; the first was Gemini.

SCORPIO ♏

Sequence. Scorpio is the eighth sign of the natural zodiac. The Latin word *scorpio* means scorpion. The Sun enters Scorpio about October 23 each year.

Glyph. The glyph for Scorpio is based on the Hebrew letter Samekh, with connotations of offering religious sacrifices in both Chinese and Phoenician applications. The most distinctive feature of the glyph is its tail, which is derived from the comparable Chinese ideogram representing a two-day ancestral feast in autumn. At that time the Chinese celebrate the ascension of the spirits of their ancestors and the tail symbolizes a vanishing spirit.[1] The tail also symbolizes the venomous tail of the scorpion, in the astrological palimpsest of zodiacal signs.

Planetary ruler. Mars was originally held to be the planetary ruler of Scorpio; however, with the discovery of Pluto in 1930, Pluto has been assigned rulership of this sign. Many astrologers still consider Mars the co-ruler.

Melothesia. Scorpio rules the genitals and the bowels.

Characteristics. Legend has it that the original symbolic association of this sign was to an eagle, reflecting Man's ability to soar high above his origins through the creative force of Eros. The degeneration of Man's sexual passions led to the substitution of the Earth-bound scorpion—or so the story goes. The symbolism of the deadly scorpion should not be overlooked, since Scorpio as an archetype deals with Eros in its original daimonic sense: a natural force which involves both birth and death.

The ancient religious associations of Scorpio are just as meaningful. Although popular notions about this sign emphasize sexual power, that power can be transformed into spiritual intensity. As the contemporary astrologer would observe, how that energy is used is an exercise of the free will of the native, for it can be consciously directed.

A remarkable example of the sexual-spiritual polarity of Scorpio is reported by George B. Leonard in *Education and Ecstasy.*[2] Leonard, an educational consultant, is touring a grade school. The principal has taken him to a room of fifth-grade children, and is pointing out the balanced illumination of the room when Leonard feels a "vinegary tingle" at the back of his neck which tells him that there is a witch in the room.

He spots her soon enough—she is a little girl in the fourth row— and she returns his stare boldly, telling him wordlessly that she knows everything she needs to know about him. Leonard ruminates that this little girl, with the right kind of education which she probably won't get, "might foretell the future, read signs, converse with spirits." Instead, her conventional schooling will endeavor to make her adjusted—that is, to make her fit into our Western rationalism. This incident illustrates how our rationalist society hobbles the Scorpio native, the intensity of whose passion always permits him to transform Eros into Agape.

For Scorpio, the choice is always between love sacred or profane. That passion can be a tremendous creative force. Henrik Ibsen, the vitriolic Norwegian poet and playwright, kept a scorpion under a bell jar on his desk. When the scorpion began to look sickly, he would put a soft fruit into the jar. The scorpion would discharge its poison into the fruit and feel well again. It was the same way, Ibsen said, that he worked: he discharged his energy into his work—and felt well again.[3]

Another manifestation of Scorpio passion is the vampire of ancient myth. The vampire of our earliest folklore was a woman—a fact implicitly recognized in the word "vamp," meaning a woman who deliberately arouses men by her alluring attitudes. Vamp is short for vampire, and it was used as both noun and verb in the 1920s when Theda Bara—whose name is an anagram for Arab Death—was synonymous with sexual allure.

The vampire is an archetype of woman as the bloodsucker, the drainer of Man's vital energy, the harbinger of death. The vampire is a Scorpionic version of the Eve of Genesis and the Pandora of Greek myth, both of which express Man's bitterness that Woman can always exhaust his potency, can always take more than he can give.

In the Genesis version of the myth, Eve (life) requires the rib (the phallus) of Adam (a man) to exist; once created, her conniving nature (the serpent) brings about Man's grief. In the Greek version, Pandora (all gifts) opens a jar (her vulva) which releases all the world's demons to Mankind; it was a trick played on Prometheus (forethought) by Zeus (the father) in revenge for his having given fire (consciousness) to Man.

These original vampire myths reflect Man's fear that Woman's power is limitless and Man's is not. That feeling survives today in the comic-strip notions that we have about Scorpio women. Interesting, is it not, that you rarely hear Scorpio *men* libeled?

As it developed, the vampire became a Scorpio legend: vampires became *revenants*, dead persons returned to life on All Hallow's Eve, October 31 each year, shortly after the Sun enters Scorpio. The following day, however, is All Saint's Day, a Christian religious holiday.[4]

Thus the pagan lust of the darkest night of the year is transformed into the love of God with the rising Sun: the Hallowe'en vampire is but a retelling of the conflict between love sacred and profane. It is also a good illustration of two aspects of Scorpio, the deadly energy of the Earth-bound arachnid and the lofty energy of the soaring eagle.

Prototypes. With Scorpio we see the daimon Eros as the three faces of Eve: the vampire of deadly sexual passion, the poet of powerful creative force and the saint who transformed Eros to Agape.

Although Abraham was destined for greatness, it is doubtful that he ever knew it. A Scorpio born in Dublin in November 1847, in his early years he suffered such ill health that it seemed unlikely that he would survive at all, much less make a contribution to the humanities that would leave an indelible—and peculiarly Scorpionic—mark on Mankind.

But love and nurture can accomplish wonders. His adoring mother was a fixture at his bedside during those early years, and she filled his waking hours with many an Irish fairy tale and ghost story. To everyone's surprise, Abraham grew to be, by his own description, "immensely strong" and a strapping six-foot-two inches in height.

After graduation he entered the Civil Service as his father had done before him. He also pursued his father's interest in the theatre. Impatient with the quality of local reviews, which seemed less than knowledgeable, he volunteered his own services as a theatre critic without fee; they were promptly accepted.

One of his first reviews was an enthusiastic appreciation of Henry Irving;* who would eventually become a legendary figure, the first actor to be knighted and the first to be buried in Westminster Abbey. However, his theatrical innovations had not been well received by Dubliners; in fact, Irving had been hissed off the stage during his last visit to Dublin. Perhaps in gratitude for Abraham's role in gaining him a warmer reception, Irving invited the young critic (Abraham was thirty at the time) for dinner. They became friendly, and other visits followed.

One night, as a gift to Abraham and other guests at his apartments, Irving recited the currently popular narrative poem by Thomas Hood, "The Dream of Eugene Aram." Aram, the narrator, is haunted by the

---

*Scorpio Ascendant.

murder of a man whose corpse he could not keep hidden. After a number of attempts to conceal the corpse, Aram realizes that it is fruitless. Abraham remembered vividly how Irving's eloquent hands spread fanlike around his face and how his eyes were fixed as inflexible as fate, and

> Then the awful horror on the murderer's face as the ghost in his brain seemed to take external shape before his eyes, and enforced on him that from his sin there was no refuge.[5]

Irving concluded the performance by a dramatic fainting collapse. Abraham—to his own amazement and chagrin—went him one better: he burst into a fit of violent hysterics.[6]

That night Abraham and Irving became friends for life; for, as Abraham declared in a volume of personal reminiscence about his life with Henry Irving, "Soul had looked into soul! From that hour began a friendship as profound, as close, as lasting as can be between two men."[7]

Indeed, it lasted until death.

For a time Abraham continued to write theatre reviews for the local newspaper. His particular fondness for Irving's performances in roles of Gothic horror or the supernatural suggests both his Scorpio emphasis and the evocation of his delicious childhood shivers at the tales of the counterpane told by his adoring mother. In his review of *Vanderdecken,* he noted that the play itself lacked something; it wasn't eerie enough. Irving as the doomed Flying Dutchman, however, was magnificent:

> In his face is the ghastly pallor of the phantom Captain and in his eyes shines the wild glamor of the lost—in his every tone and action there is the stamp of death. Herein lies the terror . . . The chief actor [Irving] is not quick but dead.[8]

At Irving's invitation, Abraham soon left his Civil Service job for a full-time position as Irving's personal secretary. Eventually, Abraham became the manager for the Lyceum Theatre, Irving's theatrical company in London. The two men were inseparable; Abraham serving Irving's limitless ego, and Irving somehow satisfying Abraham's Scorpio ardor.

Although Abraham was unhappy with *Vanderdecken* and tinkered with the play to make it spookier, he was very much pleased with *Eugene Aram.* A blackmail plot had been added to give theatrical form to the poetry, and a romantic interest to highlight the intensity of Aram's conflict. Reminiscing about the play, Abraham tells us that as the blackmailer made greater and greater demands on Aram, the growing pressure transformed the character played by Irving "from his gentleness to a ravening tiger; he looked the spirit of murder incarnate . . ."[9] The blackmailer, Abraham adds, was "a veritable 'daughter of the horseleech.' "[10] That phrase is little used today. Bloodsucking horseleeches were common throughout Europe (and see Proverbs 30:15).

Neither Irving nor Abraham was ever really satisfied with *Vanderdecken,* and when they later met its author in 1895, they urged him to write a new play of Gothic horror as a vehicle for Irving.[11] By 1897 Abraham reports that it was clear that the new "work of weirdness" that Irving had hoped for would never materialize.[12]

Or did it? In that same year a marvelous work of weirdness *did* materialize, for Abraham, or Bram, Stoker somehow found the time to write *Dracula.* In 1890 Arminius Vambery, professor at Buda-Pesth University, had been Irving's and Stoker's guest at the Lyceum Theatre, and had stayed to a private supper in the Beefsteak Room.[13] He regaled his hosts with hair-raising stories of Vlad, a bloodthirsty military genius dating back to the fifteenth century in his native Hungary.[14] Vlad was called *Vlad Tsepes*—Vlad the Impaler—because his favorite punishment was to impale his victims on stakes. He was also known as Count Dracula, from the Rumanian word *Dracul,* which means dragon or devil.

Two years earlier, in 1888, Stoker had met the legendary Sir Richard Burton,* whose translation of *Arabian Nights* included a vampire story—and whose remarkably pronounced canine teeth very much impressed Abraham.[15]

That Count Dracula seized control of Abraham Stoker's excited fancy seems clear enough; but his archetypal Scorpio passionate intensity created the visionary novel that became *Dracula.*

The original Count Dracula was a real psychopath and sadist of the fifteenth century; but he was not a vampire, nor was he thought to be. Transylvania was also real—once a province of Hungary, now modern Rumania, but the area attributed to Dracula in the novel is not the area in which Vlad Tsepes reigned.[16]

It was Bram Stoker's genius that combined disparate elements from so many sources to create *Dracula.* His mother's ghost stories and tales of the London plague merge in Scorpio fashion with the suggestive

---

*Scorpio Ascendant.

canines of Burton and fellow Dubliner Sheridan Le Fanu's classic vampire story, *Carmilla.*

But Dracula was a different kind of vampire from any the world had seen before. No longer a *revenant* appearing only on All Hallow's Eve, or a bloodsucking female patterned after the Eve of Genesis, he is a figure remarkably like Henry Irving both by day and by night.

By day, Dracula is as powerless as any actor away from the magic of the footlights. But by night, Dracula is the "incarnate power, incarnate passion" of Irving as Eugene Aram in that first private performance which so inflamed Stoker's Scorpio imagination and passion.

Jonathan Harker (read Stoker) is the young Englishman who is the first to tell the story of Dracula. Harker's first discovery of Dracula in his coffin is evocative of Irving's persona. Harker notices again the "deep, burning eyes" and that Dracula "lay like a filthy leech . . ."[17] A horseleech? For it was Irving who was the biblical horseleech to Stoker, "crying give, give!" and whose demanding ego could never be satisfied.

The vampire legend as we know it today is the Dracula myth created by Stoker with all of its ambiguous but pervasive sexuality: the bloodthirsty kiss, the stake through the heart (two and one-half inches thick), the sharp canine teeth, the noctural restlessness, the enslavement and the many brides and above all the feast of blood. Truly a Scorpio love story.

There are other elements as well. *Dracula* reflects the Scorpio conflict between love sacred and profane. In his second role as Van Helsing, the book's true protagonist whose first name is also Abraham, Stoker uses science and above all Christianity to free Harker from the evil passion that Dracula represents. It is the Christian Abraham—Van Helsing—whose crucifixes and Holy Wafers prevail against the daimonic force that is Dracula.

Infused with the daimon that possessed Stoker in his adoration of the greatest theatrical figure of his time, *Dracula* was both love-offering and sexual phantasy. Had Irving not fallen ill in 1897, bringing on a feebleness from which he never fully recovered, *Dracula* would indeed have been the great "work of weirdness" that Irving was looking for. The epistolary form of the novel—letters, diaries, journal entries—gives it an immediacy which readily translates to the scenes of a play.

But Irving did fall ill in that year of *Dracula's* publication and could not assume any new projects.[18]

So *Dracula* passes into history and into the collective unconscious of the human race where it continues to thrive. For *Dracula* has been called a visionary novel in the sense that Carl Jung used that term, in that it "squirms with such primordial, dark or forbidden news from the abyss"[19] that surpasses Man's conscious understanding, but appeals directly to his unconscious desires and primordial urges. *Dracula*, which has never been out of print since its publication seventy-five years ago, has become a twentieth-century myth. And the figure of Count Dracula is an evocation of the Scorpio archetype, for *Dracula* deals directly with the interwoven themes of sex, love and death. It is a story of passion which enslaves men and women alike in polymorphously perverse sexuality that merges with Stoker's unconscious perceptions of his genuine enslavement to his real-life master. After all, by his own testimony, he was not only the business manager for the Lyceum, the most important theatre in England, who planned the acting itinerary for a company that played thirty provinces in five months, he also answered fifty of Irving's letters *every day!*[20] Dracula's first commands to Harker are to write a series of letters.

If only Irving had lived long enough to perform the role that was truly his own, fulfilling before the footlights the fantasy of his adoring slave and crowning his life of achievement with the role that instead made Bela Lugosi immortal, Stoker's Scorpio dreams would truly have been realized. As it was, Stoker wrote a book that would gain him immortality; and in his own time he had the satisfaction of knowing that it pleased that great teller of ghost stories—his mother—who thought *Dracula* "was splendid."[21]

IN BRAM STOKER we see Scorpio passion in its preoccupation with sex and death, but also as a creative artistic force.

Another Scorpio native to express the daimonic energies associated with the sign is Sylvia Plath, born October 27, 1932, when the Sun was in early degrees of Scorpio, and Mercury in the third decan of that sign. On February 11, 1963, she committed suicide. Although she had been treated for schizophrenia and had attempted suicide some ten years before, no one really knows why she killed herself. But her schizophrenia may be reason enough. As R. D. Laing has said,

> I have never known a schizophrenic who could say he was loved, as a man, by God the Father or by the Mother of God or by another Man. He either *is* God, or the Devil, or in hell, estranged from God.[22]

That means that none of the daimonic life force can escape into passionate love either of Man or of God. The schizophrenic is like

Ibsen's scorpion in a bell jar, with no opportunity to discharge his creative force into the fruit of any relationship.

I cannot help but wonder if Sylvia Plath had not heard about Ibsen's scorpion in choosing the title of her autobiographical novel, *The Bell Jar.* True, the bell jar of the book is a symbol of the feeling of "shutupness," Kierkegaard's term used by Laing to express the schizophrenic sense of isolation, but the coincidence is nonetheless striking.

The bell jar also symbolizes solipsism, an archetypal Scorpio characteristic I have not yet discussed. Solipsism is a philosophy which holds that only the "I" is real. The individual who maintains this attitude doubts the reality of the world about him; there is no way in which he can prove it exists, and he concludes that he himself is the only reality. Many adolescents experience solipsism for a time; it is almost a part of growing up. Some people, however, feel that way all their lives. Solipsism is very much a part of the Scorpio character and has made possible much that Scorpio genius has produced in art and in religion. Thus the artist re-creates the world in his head, and the religious zealot views the world as a testing ground for his spiritual growth.

Solipsism is very much in evidence in *The Bell Jar;* and it is exemplified in "Mad Girl's Love Song," the poem Sylvia Plath sold to *Mademoiselle* while she was still a student at Smith College. The opening lines tell the story: "I shut my eyes and all the world drops dead/(I think I made you up inside my head.)"

Used creatively, this attitude can produce greatness in directing Scorpio passion toward religious zeal; or in directing the daimon Eros toward visionary efforts. But when the Scorpio native is not in control of his creative energies his solipsism does become a bell jar which imprisons him. Then, there is no direction for the daimonic Eros symbolized by the scorpion's tail but inward where it poisons the Scorpio native and produces attitudes already too well known. The native himself reacts to the sting of the scorpion with feelings of persecution and vengefulness.

For Sylvia Plath, the most momentous event in her life was the death of her father when she was eight years old; and for that, she never forgave him. "Daddy," perhaps her most famous poem, sets forth her love/hate feelings for her deceased father. "I was ten when they buried you," she declaims. "At twenty I tried to die." That was the occasion of her first suicide attempt.

She describes her father as a vampire, herself as the victim, and concludes: "Daddy, daddy, you bastard, I'm through."

"Daddy" is a powerful and intense poem, in which Sylvia Plath recognizes both her schizophrenia and the neurotic love and hatred of her father which poison her and distort her view of the world, as if she were within a bell jar. As A. R. Jones put it, with "Daddy," "She manages to elevate private facts into public myth, and the sheer intensity of her vision lends it a kind of objectivity."[23]

The venom poisons the scorpion in the bell jar and it becomes powerfully death-obsessed. One poem begins with her description of herself as "vertical," to which she immediately adds, "But I would rather be horizontal." The opening sentence of *The Bell Jar* tells the reader that the summer she spent in New York was "the summer they electrocuted the Rosenbergs . . ."

Alvarez, in his study of suicide, begins with a prologue on Sylvia Plath, whom he knew personally, especially in the months just before her death. Impressed with her tremendous productivity in the last few months of her life, he is reminded that "the passion for destruction is also a creative passion . . ."[24]

EROS AND THANATOS, the gods of love and death, are inseparably linked, both Freud and the contemporary astrologer remind us. Rollo May points out that the genuine experience of the daimonic Eros means death in terms of an entirely personal sense of annihilation:

> This intensity of consciousness has something in common with the
> ecstasy of the mystic in his union with God.[25]

In the *Symposium*, Socrates defines Eros as Man's desire for union with the divine. In this Platonic view, the highest expression of Eros, the natural force which can break the limbs' strength, is *Agape*, the love of God. Yet such love exists, Rollo May assures us, whether labeled Agape, selfless love or the love of God for Man.[26]

The life of Aurelius Augustinus[27] is an example of the spiritual rebirth occasioned by the evolution of Scorpio passion from Eros to Agape. Born November 13, 354 C.E., with Sun and Mercury in Scorpio,[28] Aurelius was a source of distress to his mother, a pious Catholic. At the age of sixteen he journeyed to Carthage where, he later admitted, "a cauldron of illicit loves leaped and boiled about me. I was not yet in love, but I was in love with love . . ."[29] He took a mistress, who bore him a son. When his mother reminded him that it was time to marry, he became engaged to a girl of whom she approved. He gave up his mistress; but, since his fiancée couldn't marry him right away, he took another. His conscience bothered him a great deal, and he used to pray, "Grant me chastity and continence, but not yet."[30]

He went to Rome to teach rhetoric, and then to Milan, where he met St. Ambrose, one of the early Catholic saints. His mother and St. Ambrose brought him into the faith after he endured passionate inward struggles. He was baptized by St. Ambrose himself. Thus at the age of thirty-two, Aurelius Augustinus, better known to us as St. Augustine, was converted to Catholicism and gave up his professorship, his mistress—and his bride.[31]

In his *Confessions,* long regarded as a religious classic, St. Augustine relates in some detail the evils of lust; he explains his rejection of the daimonic Eros in favor of Christian love, which is defined in terms of the Agape of Platonic philosophy. Later, St. Augustine's *City of God* would be based on the Platonic ideal. Passionate man and passionate saint, Augustine was one of our first great Scorpios.

"Do not understand me too quickly," Edith Wharton begged a new acquaintance. So it is with Scorpio, the most misunderstood sign of the zodiac. The archetypal forces that Scorpio symbolizes exist in all of us; indeed, they must if we are human. The popular notions of Scorpio as mysterious and secretive result from our belief that deep feelings must be hidden, that they are socially unacceptable or somewhat embarrassing. But we all feel what Scorpio represents as an archetype, and, once again, we all have all twelve of the signs of the zodiac in our horoscopes.

Polar opposite. The polar opposite of Scorpio is Taurus. Taurus is *sensuous,* a receptor for all the senses. Scorpio is *sensual,* and like Ibsen's scorpion in the bell jar, the potent force of Eros demands expression for the native's health. Thus Taurus tends to inertia; Scorpio requires action.

Positive and negative aspects. Positively manifested, Scorpio qualities bring a depth of feeling that breathes life into whatever matter captures the native's interest. Scorpio ardor can be expressed in the passionate love of another human being, in religious or scientific zeal, in poetry or art.

The negative expressions of Scorpio result from our denial of Eros or the reverse: when Eros is suppressed, Scorpio expression may be secretive, vengeful and counterproductive. If Eros is too powerful for the native's internal controls, we see the daimonic possession of which Socrates spoke, which can truly break the limbs' strength.

Notable Scorpio personalities. Margaret Mead, Billy Graham, Theodore Roosevelt, Indira Gandhi, Pablo Picasso, Marie Curie, Joni Mitchell, Fyodor Dostoevsky and George Patton.

Element. Scorpio is the second water sign; the first was Cancer. Cancer and Scorpio are both signs in which the native functions through his feelings. However, in Cancer that feeling is maternal and sentimental, whereas in Scorpio it is passionate and fixed.

SAGITTARIUS

Sequence. Sagittarius is the ninth sign of the natural zodiac. The Latin word *sagittarius* means archer. The Sun enters Sagittarius about November 23 each year.

Glyph. The glyph for Sagittarius is based on the constellation of the same name, which became the eighteenth letter of the Hebrew alphabet, Tsade. Tsade depicts the shooting of an arrow; it has no Greek or Roman equivalent. Originally, Sagittarius was a lunar constellation, and the eighteenth Chinese lunar station equivalents, pronounced *Tsang* or *Chang,* mean to shoot an arrow.

Planetary ruler. Jupiter is the planetary ruler of Sagittarius.

Melothesia. Sagittarius rules the lower back and hips.

Characteristics. The season marked by the lunar constellation of Sagittarius was universally the start of winter. In ancient times, early winter was the time of the hunt and a time of sacrifice to ancestral heroes. All the words for Sagittarius—*Tsade, Tsang* and *Chang*—are onomatopoetic, in that they *sound* like an arrow being shot from a bow.[1]

Sagittarius has been variously depicted as an archer, a horseman, an archer on a horse and finally a centaur with a bow and arrow who, more often than not, is directing his arrows at the stars.

"Ah, but man's reach should exceed his grasp,/Or what's a heaven for?" asks Andrea del Sarto in Robert Browning's poem about the Renaissance artist known as the Faultless Painter. Del Sarto's philosophy sums up the Sagittarian quest. Browning, in any event, had a Sagittarian Ascendant in close conjunction with a Sagittarian Neptune—the planet which rules the imagination.

Jupiter, the planetary ruler of Sagittarius, was named after the father god who was the lawgiver; Sagittarius is the sign associated with religion, philosophy and law.

The Sagittarian has a penchant for forever seeking new fields to conquer. This sign tends to excess and is not particularly conscious of its limitations. The Sagittarian's optimism is unquenchable. This fire sign seeks to impose upon the world the ideals which are the product of its conscious will.

Prototypes. Georg Faust was a German alchemist who blew himself into oblivion while attempting to make gold in 1539. The Faust legend tells of an old man who has spent his life in scholarly pursuits and who yearns for the experience of life he has missed. The most vivid example is dramatized by Christopher Marlowe in a scene in which Mephistophilis summons Helen of Troy at Faust's request. When she appears, Faust exclaims:

> Was this the face that launched a thousand ships
> And burnt the topless towers of Ilium?
> Sweet Helen, make me immortal with a kiss.[2]

In astrological terms, Faust has pursued the archetypal Geminian quest for knowledge at the expense of the Sagittarian quest for experience.

By black magic, usually dramatized as a pact with the devil, Faust regains youth and power sufficient to embrace all the experience his heart desires. While in some versions of the legend the devil takes his victim at the appointed hour, in Goethe's version Faust is redeemed at the end. Why? Because Faust is never satisfied with the knowledge he has gained or the delights of experience. For Goethe, speaking through his angels, declares that

> Whoever
> Strives forward with unswerving will—
> Him can we aye deliver . . .[3]

Goethe, an enthusiastic advocate of astrology, commenced his autobiography with his precise natal information—which reveals Pluto, the planet of intensity, in Sagittarius in the first house of the self. It seems more than mere coincidence that in his masterly re-creation of the Faust legend, Goethe has presented the world with the ultimate Sagittarian whose endlessly striving will is his salvation.

Oswald Spengler, writing in Germany in the gloomy years after World War I, saw the West in terms of what he called Faustian Man, whom he defined as an archetypal figure motivated by a boundless will to power and locked in endless strife to overcome the world's obstacles.[4]

In *The Will to Power* philosopher-poet Friedrich Nietzsche extolled the concept of the indomitable will, which he derived from Arthur Schopenhauer. There was a marked difference of attitude, however. For although Schopenhauer recognized that Man's will was a more powerful motivating force than his intellect (anticipating Freud somewhat), Schopenhauer was a Piscean who deplored what was to him such a regrettable state of affairs, and urged a characteristically Piscean solution: we should learn Eastern mysticism as a palliative for the overweening demands made by the will. Nietzsche, on the other hand, had a Sagittarius Ascendant, and waxed poetic about Man achieving greatness through his aspiring will.

With his Sun in Libra, Nietzsche wrote about human nature with great literary skill and intuition. His first work contained the brilliant essay on the Apollonian/Dionysian duality of human nature which Jung used in the delineation of his functional personality types. But with his Sagittarius Ascendant, it is no surprise that notions about Man's aspiring will captured Nietzsche's poetic imagination. Nietzsche believed that by exerting the will we could transcend our all-too-human nature and become the Man-Above-Man—usually mistranslated as Superman—which was our divine birthright. As envisioned by Nietzsche, the Superman is a mixture of energy, intellect and pride, unified by a great purpose. Is that not also a definition of Sagittarius?

Nietzsche the man was full of the contradictions suggested by his Libran love of poetry, art and literature; his Sagittarian striving for omnipotence is indicated by his Ascendant. With Sagittarian zeal and bluntness, Nietzsche attacked all the cherished ideals of his age. He especially deplored the Christian religion because he felt it led men away from coping with the problems of this world by distracting them with notions of the next. Belief in God is dead, he said; any meaning of life in terms of a supernatural purpose is therefore also dead, and we should get on with the business of perfecting that unfortunate mixture of inertia and cultural conditioning which we call human nature!

"Become what thou art!" Nietzsche cried and in this categorical imperative we find a key which may provide a Sagittarian answer to the essentially Sagittarian excesses which bedevil the United States of America.

WHEN WAS THE United States born? Mundane* astrologers generally agree on the date of July 4, 1776, but argue endlessly about the time. Perhaps the most common chart used shows Gemini on the Ascendant,[5] but that places the signing of the Declaration of Independence at about 2:13 to 2:17 A.M.

While veteran astrologer Barbara Watters has given an ingenious explanation for this birth time,[6] I find the research reported by astrologer Sybil Leek more convincing. Leek suggests that the Gemini Ascendant may be more an act of patriotism than historical fact.

She reports the finding of an unpublished letter from Thomas

---

*From the Latin word *mundus*, meaning world. Mundane astrology deals with the birth charts of nations. Genethliacal (*genethle*, Greek for birth) astrology deals with birth charts of individuals.

Jefferson to a friend who asked him, in his later years, when the Declaration of Independence was signed. Although his recollection was cloudy, Jefferson did say definitely it was in the "late afternoon." Other Jeffersonian correspondence relates that the Declaration was signed in early evening, after which everybody went off to dinner.[7] From this and other evidence, Leek concludes that 5:00 P.M. is the correct birth time. That produces a Sagittarian Ascendant in early degrees; I agree because the Ascendant reflects the basic *personality* of the entity, individual or nation, for whom the horoscope is made. And the personality of our country is, in my view, emphatically Sagittarian.*

In the Statue of Liberty—with her welcoming invitation to all the disenfranchised of the world, and the American Museum of Immigration in her base—we can readily find symbolism for the Cancer Sun of our basic national character. But our personality can be identified with the Faustian Man, who has been credited with the technological success of Western civilization, of which the United States has always been the chief exponent; I believe that "Faustian Man" and "Sagittarian" are precisely interchangeable terms.

Whether our persona be expressed in terms of Faustian Man or Sagittarius, the United States is usually held up as the best example of what Man has achieved by constant striving to master the environment. (In this context, it is worth noting that one of Faust's acts of redemption, as retold by Goethe, was to reclaim land from the sea upon which to found an ideal society; regrettably, the plan fails.)

"Personality" is derived from the Latin word *persona,* meaning mask, especially the mask worn by an actor. In psychology, the term "persona" refers to the role assumed by the individual to display his conscious intentions to himself and to others. As personality or persona, the roles which we Americans have traditionally favored add further verification to our Sagittarian Ascendant.

Boundless optimism, idealism and high achievement characterized Andrew Carnegie, for example. Carnegie was a Sagittarian native whose life we have regarded as exemplary of what we like to think of as the American way, choosing to ignore the hypocrisy and brutality with which he crushed a long-overdue strike by his underpaid employees working under incredible conditions at the mill which we now call United States Steel.[8]

Winston Churchill was regarded by his countrymen as a national nuisance, a blood-and-thunder jingoist about whom one of his countrymen declared, *"No* one, not even the wildest Tories, would dream of trusting power to Winston."[9] Yet in the United States Churchill was

---

*Dane Rudhyar has also suggested that the United States has a Sagittarian Ascendant.

first totemized and ultimately apotheosized in the American motion picture, *Young Winston*.

Why do Americans cherish the memory of a man so admittedly bombastic, outspoken and belligerent; a man whose memoirs, according to book reviewer and fellow Englishman Malcolm Muggeridge, are, like all his literary efforts, gaseous and overwritten?[10] The question answers itself: we identify with Churchill the Sagittarian native, and embrace him as a national hero.

Our love affair with Western badmen likewise characterizes our essentially Sagittarian personality. William H. Bonney was Billy the Kid and the Robin Hood of the Old West in Walter Noble Burns's popular *Saga of Billy the Kid;* but he was actually Henry McCarty—he took the name William H. Bonney as an alias—and no hero,[11] much less a Robin Hood. Very likely, Billy the Kid was a psychopath. Yet he was born November 23, 1859, and was a Sagittarian through and through; and was apotheosized in countless films, such as *The Outlaw,* produced by that enigmatic American billionaire, Howard Hughes. Although Hughes had his Sun posited in Capricorn, he also had a strong Sagittarian emphasis in his natal chart.

And what of that old Indian fighter whose last stand is an epic mural on many a barroom wall? George Armstrong Custer, graduated last in his class at West Point, was either a fun-loving prankster or a dangerously disordered personality—depending on your point of view— but certainly an inept military strategist. It was probably a doubtful charity that saw him graduate at all. Nonetheless, he was a Sagittarian by birth and in character and fit our American concept of our persona.

The less attractive side of our American personality can be summed up in the stereotype of the wealthy Texas braggart; and this is the negative aspect of Sagittarius as well. It seems, then, that too much of a good thing is no good at all. Too much technology endangers our environment; too much idealism sees us wreaking havoc in other countries to impress our ideas upon them. Too much optimism deludes us into believing that somehow we will always be able to afford our mistakes without paying for them, and that we shall survive indomitably, forever.

This last point was made most tellingly in the film version of *Catch-22.* Somehow director Mike Nichols managed to construct a fine story from that unwieldy novel. Yet it was Nichols's only commercial failure.

It is easy to understand why. As Nichols reconstructed the story, the theme of *Catch-22* was our American (and Sagittarian) refusal to recognize our own mortality. Only Yossarian, the main character, understood that death was real, and sought to escape the insanity of war; but because his desire to escape death demonstrated his sanity, he fell victim to Catch-22. One of the film's most memorable scenes was an interview with an old Italian gentleman who finds American attitudes about death amusing. Looking straight at the camera, he asks us whether we don't think that we can die—don't all countries eventually die, just like people? There was a drollery in his voice and a twinkle in his eye; but it was a thought that struck me (Sun and Moon in Sagittarius, conjunct the national Ascendant) with a chill.

According to Roberto Vacca in *The Coming Dark Age,* an era of disorder and destruction is the manifest destiny (what a marvelously Sagittarian notion!) to which our yearly multiplying millions have brought us. Systems engineer Vacca points to the great power blackout in the Northeastern United States in 1965, as evidence of impending technological breakdowns which will, he believes, incapacitate all other human systems—such as rail, road, fire, police emergency agencies—as well. With scores of people dying and no means of disposing of their remains, pandemic disease will ultimately capture the entire American megalopolis in demographic catastrophe. Like Faust, we will be destroyed by our own alchemy.

Or will we? Molecular geneticist Gunther S. Stent has reached entirely different conclusions from what appear to be essentially the same data. There will indeed be an end to technological progress, Stent declares, but the result will be not doom but a new Golden Age.

How could two scientists, each with impeccable credentials, reach such contradictory conclusions? The difference, I submit, is in Stent's comprehension of the sea-change in the persona of the American people which is now taking place.

AS A NATION we have treated our writers abominably, further evidence against a Gemini personality for our country. We have official mourning for the death of generals; and have even given elaborate ceremonials to a horse: Comanche, the only survivor of Little Big Horn, was commissioned "second commanding officer" of the Seventh Cavalry Division, never to be ridden again, but draped in black and led in state "upon all occasions of ceremony . . . and . . . paraded with the regiment."[12]

Until most recent times, great American literature was regarded as the stuff of children, and names like Nathaniel Hawthorne, Washington Irving and Henry Wadsworth Longfellow immediately recall our elementary-school textbooks. As befits our nurturing and motherly

Cancer Sun, American literary efforts were expected to be bowdlerized on the principle that a book that a child could not read without risk of offense was not to be considered literature.

Samuel Langhorne Clemens,[13] with a stellium of Sun, Mars and Venus in Sagittarius saw his vocation as one "to excite the laughter of God's creatures."

Sometimes his rebellious efforts were quashed, either by the influence of his literary mentor, William Dean Howells, or his wife, Olivia, whose role as Victorian censor has been spun out into an elaborate fantasy by Van Wyck Brooks in *The Ordeal of Mark Twain*, which says much more about the ordeal of Van Wyck Brooks—and of his readers—than that of Samuel Clemens.

Although today we think of *Tom Sawyer* and *Huckleberry Finn* as books for children, no one thought so when Clemens wrote them. *Tom Sawyer* was Clemens's exasperated reaction to the prissy and unreadable Victorian literature then deemed suitable for children. Paradoxically, *Tom Sawyer* was condemned as unfit for children when it was first published. *Huckleberry Finn* is something else again, for it is not a children's book at all.

In *Love and Death in the American Novel*, the seminal work of literary criticism which is well on its way to becoming a classic, Leslie Fiedler points out that the novel form itself is a tribute to the Great Mother or the Eternal Feminine, stemming from the conventions of courtly love which flourished in the Middle Ages.[14] In this regard, Fiedler's views seem close to those of Robert Graves, who has declared that all true poetry is a hymn to the feminine principle, the Great Mother whom Mankind has always seen in the Moon.[15]

Thus the American novel is itself an expression of our basic Cancerian self. But Fiedler goes farther and excites our astrological interest even more. He finds that the hero of American literature, of which the best example is Huckleberry Finn, is a *Faustian* hero. When Huck declares, "All right, I'll *go* to hell!" he aligns himself with all the other American heroes who are willing to be damned in order to have the freedom which challenges the conventions of society and the forces of nature. Huck's journey down the Mississippi takes him, like Faust, into the Gothic darkness of the American soul. The visions in the fog are ghostly; but the lynch mob after Nigger Jim is all too real:[16] over 1,500 Negroes and whites were lynched in the United States in the 1890s.[17]

And yet *Huckleberry Finn* was but one aspect of Sam Clemens's Sagittarian idealism and rebellion, for he is what Fiedler defines as the Faustian artist "caught between bravado and self-hatred."[18] To say all the things he wanted to say, Clemens once remarked, he would need "a pen warmed-up in hell."[19] There is indeed evidence that he had one. Clemens was a perfervid critic of what he termed our nation's imperialistic policies, and his remarks to a newspaper reporter in 1900 have an all-too-familiar ring:

> We have no more business in China than in any other country that is not ours. There is the case of the Philippines. I have tried hard, and yet I cannot for the life of me comprehend how we got into that mess.[20]

Consistent with his archetype, Sam Clemens attacked the corruption of the Gilded Age in which he lived, yet enjoyed its luxury; with undaunted optimism, he plunged into one reckless get-rich-quick scheme after another, all of which were costly to him. He campaigned for better copyright laws to protect writers, and testified in Congress for such reforms; he also rushed to the defense of President Ulysses S. Grant, and insisted on publishing his memoirs because he felt that the former president would otherwise be taken advantage of. That last idealistic venture catapulted him into financial disaster and ultimate bankruptcy.[21]

None of these events cooled his pen, however. He spent the last years of his life attacking the notion of Manifest Destiny, and rewrote "The Battle Hymn of the Republic" to reflect his disgust at our use of war as an instrument of national policy, concluding

> As Christ died to make men holy, let men die to make us rich—
> Our god is marching on.[22]

As Mark Twain, Sam Clemens was a popular hero, seen at his Sagittarian best as a totem-busting, plain-spoken homespun American who would not be taken in by a lot of foreign fuss and feathers. Clemens was much more than that, and it was all consistent with his stellium of Sun, Mars and Venus in Sagittarius. He was an exhibitionist, a passionate foe of social injustice and a grassroots radical whose idealism was so intense that he denounced "the damned human race" in his rage over human folly.

Clemens was equally unrelenting with the Deity. He was no mere atheist, for, as Janet Smith has observed, "Mark Twain, far from denying God, insists upon him, hunts him down, and reviles him."[23]

In its most familiar version, *The Mysterious Stranger* is the story of an angel who comes to Earth as a young man. He becomes a friend to several other youths in an Austrian village named Eseldorf (Jackassville) during the Middle Ages. He is irresistibly charming, and fascinates his companions with his feats of magic. However, his behavior is odd in the extreme. He creates a race of tiny men whom he casually exterminates when their prayerful obeisances annoy him. Beseeched to intercede on behalf of a beleaguered priest, the angel does so by driving him mad. To two individuals the angel extends the courtesy of an early death by drowning.

Only Mankind can do evil, the angel explains to the horrified narrator, because only Man has a moral sense; actually, insanity or death is the best thing that can happen to that hapless creature whom we call Man.

The Mysterious Stranger was a tale over which Clemens labored for more than a decade; indeed, it occupied his attention virtually up to the time of his death, for the last manuscript pages are dated 1908. [24] Clemens wrote at least four versions of the fable, embodied in three manuscripts, none of which was ever completed—by him.[25] The posthumously published book bearing the title *The Mysterious Stranger* was a pastiche in which the second version was bowdlerized, an unfinished chapter omitted and a conclusion which Clemens had intended for a later version tacked on as an ending.[26]

Why did Clemens extend himself in this agonizing way over a story which seems satisfactory enough in the version which has been popularly accepted? The short answer is that Clemens had a characteristic Sagittarian preoccupation with the identity of God. Neither Milton nor anyone else had ever justified God's ways to Man to the man who pursued his Deity in *Captain Stormfield's Visit to Heaven, Eve's Diary, Letters from the Earth* and the various versions of *The Mysterious Stranger.*

The location of the tale varies from Clemens's own hometown of Hannibal, Missouri, to St. Petersburg, Russia, to Eseldorf, Austria, in the version with which we are familiar. But in all versions the angelic hero dominates the action, variously named Philip Traum (Dream), Satan or, cryptically, "Forty-four."

None of the versions was ever finished, for Clemens could never reconcile his own conflicting views about the Deity: on the one hand, God was indifferent to (and unaware of) Man; yet on the other hand, God was patiently explaining all of these things to the young narrator, whom he clearly loved! Consistency has never been a feature of the Sagittarian archetype, and Clemens was no exception. He lived during the founding of Christian Science, which in 1893 he termed "that rational and noble philosophy," when he consulted one of its practitioners and persuaded his wife to send their daughter Suzy to another.[27] By 1901, however, he had become a convert to osteopathy, and declared, "Damn all the other cures, including the baths and Christian Science . . . *this* is the satisfactory one!"[28] Later, he devoted an entire volume to attacking Mary Baker Eddy and Christian Science.

I have said that no American writer has been honored with a state funeral. In the case of Samuel Clemens such a display would have been superfluous, for the Mysterious Stranger with whom he quarreled much of his life made all the arrangements. In 1909, when his heart disease became more troublesome, Clemens remarked, "I came in with Halley's comet in 1835. It is coming again next year, and I expect to go out with it."[29]

Sam Clemens died on April 21, 1910. The night before, Halley's comet had again appeared in the sky.

EARLIER DISCUSSIONS CONSIDERED the egocentric will of Aries and the will-as-leadership of Leo. Sagittarius exemplifies yet a third, the will of the higher mind. This will to meaning is at the heart of the Faustian will to power, and is indicative of the intentional nature of human consciousness.

Colin Wilson provides a striking example of how intentionality works at a level below our conscious awareness of it. The incident is best related by the wife and biographer of that fervently idealistic Greek author of *The Last Temptation of Christ*, Nikos Kazantzakis:

> The women were very beautiful in Vienna, and while Buddha was spurring him on to absolute renunciation of the flesh on the one hand, on the other, in the concert halls, in the streets and restaurants, in the libraries and museums, various caressing, oblique glances were summoning him to enjoy himself. Whether it was by coincidence or, as Dr. Wilhelm Stekel, a disciple of Freud, had told him, by the force of his own spirit, a hideous eczema suddenly broke out over his whole face prohibiting all contact.[30]

As Stekel had predicted, the "horrible sexual mask" disappeared as soon as Kazantzakis left Vienna.[31]

In the Middle Ages, Wilson observes, this syndrome was called the Saint's Malady: saints tempted to leave the ascetic life would break out in running sores.[32] Saint's Malady or sexual mask, it is a striking example of intentionality at the unconscious level, which has led to a revolution in modern thought and a new version of existentialism which is decidedly more optimistic in outlook.[33] If Man can act *intentionally* —both as to the Man within as well as to the world without—he can truly create himself according to his highest ideals.

Third Force Psychology is an expression of the new humanism, and is essentially optimistic, idealistic—or, in a word, Sagittarian. It is *psychology of the will.* "Meaning stimulates the will, fills one with a desire to reach out to new horizons," Wilson declares. He cites Nietzsche in support: "The great man is the play-actor of his ideals."[34]

According to Abraham Maslow, the pioneer in Third Force Psychology, mental health depends upon the will fired by a sense of purpose—the idealism of the Sagittarian archetype. For Maslovian psychology, both the Apollonian (rationalist) and Dionysian (intuitive) faculties are required for a holistic approach either to psychology or to religion;[35] when both faculties are utilized, little if any difference can be found between what a layman would consider mystical or religious and what a Third Force psychologist would refer to as a peak experience.[36]

"Which of you expects to achieve greatness in your chosen field?" Maslow asked his students. When no one answered, he asked, "If not you—*who* then?"[37] This fallacy of insignificance—Wilson's term— reached its height in the despair after the First World War, along with an increasing bias toward the rat-maze reductionism in psychology.[38]

In sharp contrast, Maslow echoes Nietzsche's exhortation,* "Become what thou art!"[39] With its emphasis on the Sagittarian impulse in all of us to strive for meaning, Third Force Psychology can be an effective antidote for depression.

Consider again the gloom of Sam Clemens's last years. Only recently have we been allowed to see the true dimensions of the problems which beset him in the last decade of his life. Clemens could find no meaning in the increasing burden of his tragedies, and raged against a Deity who permitted such senseless things to happen. It is significant that a passage from a letter to a friend expressing his grief about his wife's death became the conclusion of *The Mysterious Stranger.*

Incredibly, Sam Clemens also suffered from the fallacy of insignificance. He identified himself as foremost among the cowards of the human race. That claim is refuted by many passages which reflect rare moral courage; and, as Frederick Anderson has noted, by Clemens's willingness to speak out as often and as openly as he did in many of the major works on which his reputation is deservedly founded.[40]

---

*Actually, Pindar said it first.

But Clemens remained the Faustian artist, caught between bravado and self-hatred; and in the last decade of his life, personal tragedy overwhelmed him, and his obsessions about his inability to find meaning in life poured out in the telling and retelling of *The Mysterious Stranger.* He began the fable about a year after Suzy's death, and wrote the intended conclusion for the last version the summer his wife died. After his daughter, Jean, died in 1909, he told a friend, "It will be the greatest disappointment in my life if I don't go with Halley's comet. . . . Oh, I am looking forward to that!"[41]

Clemens's genuine agony in these last years makes Van Wyck Brooks's Freudian *kitsch* about his ordeal wholly indigestible. For Clemens, as a Sagittarian, the will to meaning was more important than the will to live.

OUR SAGITTARIAN WILL to meaning also provides the solution to the apparently contradictory predictions of a forthcoming Golden Age and an impending Dark Age. Vacca's Dark Age is premised on a breakdown of technological systems as a result of continually increasing demands; Stent's Golden Age is based on the general conclusion that Faustian Man's will to power is, by its very nature, self-limiting.[42]

As Stent sees it, the Faustian—I would say Sagittarian—notion of the infinite perfectibility of Man, which became our scientific religion,[43] has not only run its course but has produced the counterculture in which our youth, alienated from the society produced by technology, has rejected the religion of science. According to Stent, even now profound adjustments are occurring in the psyche of Western Man which will produce the new Golden Age.[44] The result, Stent believes, will be the era predicted more than twenty-five centuries ago by Hesiod:

> For the secular consequences of progress have now readied the Earth
> for that golden race of mortal men who, thanks to technology, will live
> like gods, without sorrow of heart, remote and free from toil and grief,
> but with legs and arms never failing, beyond the reach of all evil.[45]

This is neither the soulless hedonism described in Huxley's *Brave New World* nor Vacca's technological apocalypse, but Polynesia on a global scale as a result of general stasis, and the natural consequence of the strivings of Faustian Man.[46]

There are already straws in the wind indicating that Stent is correct. Something is happening to our view of our Western heroes. We have even come to some belated recognition of our collective guilt in our shameful treatment of those Americans who preceded us—the Indians. In the film *Little Big Man, mirabile dictu,* the Indians are the heroes and Custer just another crazy white man.

Experts in other fields corroborate Stent's view of the evolution of Faustian Man. In *Visceral Learning,* for example, Gerald Jonas gives the lie to the behaviorist dogma of B. F. Skinner that the autonomic nervous system could not be conditioned with trial-and-error techniques.[47] Meditation, alpha waves, yoga and other techniques are now combined with technology to produce personal energy control—the ultimate conquest of self by act of will.

In *Tools for Conviviality,* Ivan Illich blueprints the reconstruction of our technological society in terms of Man's relationship to his tools. For a hundred years we have schooled men in the service to machines on the hypothesis that machines can replace slaves, but the result, Illich observes, has been that machines enslave men.

Since our present use of the tools of technology menaces the survival of Mankind, we must recognize our limits and reprogram our tools to serve individuals rather than productivity. Illich believes that the result will be a new, convivial society.

Taken together, the views of Stent, Illich and Jonas (among many others) acknowledge the failure of technology to master the world because we have failed to master ourselves. By using the tools of technology to look inward and to gain self-mastery, perhaps we shall at last accomplish the ultimate Sagittarian victory: the victory over our own excesses. Kazantzakis yearned for Buddhist asceticism and got it; in Eastern mysticism the honorary title, "Master," denotes one who is *master of himself.*

The Homunculus, or Little Man, was artificially produced by Faust's assistant, the pedantic scientist Wagner, to lead Faust to Walpurgis Night, when witches rendezvous with Satan. We have had our indulgence in Walpurgis Night, with its chaos and absurdity, and have found it not to our liking. With the inward journey of our consciousness revolution, we may yet produce what Third Force psychologists call the New Man, but who is readily identifiable as Nietzsche's Sagittarian hero, the Superman.

Polar opposite. The polar opposite of Sagittarius is Gemini, and at first glance they appear rather similar. Consider, for example, Gemini's running off in all directions and the Sagittarian's continuing search for new realms to conquer. Both signs are associated with travel, Gemini with short trips, Sagittarius with long journeys. And neither sign has a full awareness of its limitations. There are, however, fundamental differences. The air sign Gemini, intuitive and verbal, sees the world in terms of its infinite possibilities; the fire sign Sagittarius is the highest expression of Man's aspiring will by which he seeks to re-create the world (and himself) according to his loftiest ideals.

It is my conviction that each of the signs is but one-half of a master archetype: Gemini *and* Sagittarius make up the whole. So an overemphasis of one polar characteristic may mean a dearth of the other.

Positive and negative aspects. Positively manifested, Sagittarius contributes the gifts of idealized consciousness. Negatively aspected, Sagittarius becomes a god unto himself, detached from the common humanity of which he may forget he is a part.

Notable Sagittarian personalities. Sammy Davis, Jr., Pope John XXIII, Robert Moses, Baruch Spinoza, William Blake, Georges Seurat, Otto Preminger, William S. Hart, James Thurber, Ludwig van Beethoven, Lucius Beebe and Rachel Maddux.

Element. Sagittarius is the third and last of the fire signs.

CAPRICORN

Sequence. Capricorn is the tenth sign of the natural zodiac. The word *capricorn* derives from the Latin words *caper* and *cornu,* which together mean horned goat. The Sun enters Capricorn about December 21 each year.

Glyph. The glyph for Capricorn is related to the Hebrew letter Shin, which became the Greek Sigma, both of which were based on the Chinese lunar station *Chiao,* meaning a horn.[1] Shin has associations to goats and to the related solar zodiacal sign Capricorn, which commences with the winter solstice.

Planetary ruler. The planetary ruler of Capricorn is Saturn.

Melothesia. Externally, Capricorn rules the knees and skin; internally, Capricorn rules the skeletal structure and the teeth.

Characteristics. "Point one finger at somebody else and you point three fingers at yourself!" Gary declared, shaking his own forefinger sententiously back at me. I was amazed. Gary, himself a Capricorn, had defined the quintessential Capricorn character: idealistic to the point of being self-defeating, particularly in social and political situations, critical, cynical. More than anyone I know, Gary fits the Capricorn stereotype. I say *stereotype* advisedly.

First I shall consider the essential—and generally well known—Capricorn characteristics; then I shall discuss the *Other* Capricorn, who is less well known but whose archetypal qualities are all clearly implied by the essential features which are the subject of my immediate consideration.

It is almost as if the Capricorn native had been born old, for his seriousness seems to reflect that essential wisdom which only age can bring. The planetary ruler of Capricorn, Saturn, emphasizes this relationship of seriousness, wisdom, controversy—and age.

Horatio Alger is synonymous with stories of rags-to-riches success and with the essential Capricorn character, not only for the themes of his *Ragged Dick* and *Tattered Tom* stories, but because he had a huge stellium of planets in that sign.

The son of a Unitarian minister, Alger was himself groomed for the ministry (he attended Harvard Divinity School), but he fled to Paris to live the life then called bohemian. His family finally prevailed upon him to become ordained, but he soon gave up his pulpit in Brewster, Massachusetts, to become chaplain to the homeless waifs who lived at the Newsboys' Lodging House in New York City. Alger devoted his life and fortune to the Lodging House and to its inhabitants, the bootblacks and newsboys who became the heroes of over 120 inspirational Capricorn novels in which virtue is rewarded with riches, success and (very often) the boss's daughter.

In Alger we can see beyond the Capricorn concern for wealth and status to a kind of messianic seriousness. Both characteristics are popularly attributed to the desire for security and social position, but that is not always the case.

Consider Joan Baez, a Capricorn native whose concern about social injustice is in deadly earnest, but who has shown no discernible interest in financial security or social position. Yet whether she is troubled about the conflict between generations and the prevalence of hate, as in *Daybreak*, her autobiography, or the terribly repetitive pattern of the slaughter of the innocent, as in *Baptism: A Journey Through Our Time*, Baez is nothing if not serious.

There is also a sense of mission about Capricorn that the popular misunderstanding about the goat has obscured. It is *our* interest in sex, and not the goat's, that has led us to identify that sacred animal with ruttishness. The short season of the goat's sexual excitement has been given attention in complete disproportion to its essential character. Not so in the Scriptures, where its acute vision and essential dignity made it an apt synonym for the Deity,[2] as in Song of Songs, for example.

A further trait implicit in the characters of Horatio Alger and Joan Baez is more clearly seen in Howard Hughes, a Capricorn native (who also has a stellium of planets in Sagittarius). Hughes was born to wealth, and could have eked out a splendid existence by running the Hughes Tool Company. Instead he has spent a lifetime in controversy—with headline-grabbing ventures ranging from *The Outlaw* to the Spruce Goose—and today is a mysterious, legendary figure. He has sequestered himself from public view, Hughes says, to avoid lawsuits and other attempts to deprive him of his wealth. His self-imposed imprisonment, which set the stage for the hoax perpetrated by Clifford Irving, provides the paradoxical figure of a multimillionaire with more money than he can possibly spend in his remaining years as a martyred recluse.

Or consider the case of Muhammad Ali, born Cassius Clay in Louisville, Kentucky, January 17, 1942,[3] when the Sun was in late degrees of Capricorn. Clay demonstrated Capricorn ambition by achieving material success in one of the few ways then available to black men in this country: as an outstanding boxer.

It was the day after he won the heavyweight crown from Sonny Liston that Clay became the Other Capricorn with this messianic announcement: "I believe in the religion of Islam, which means I believe there is not God but Allah, and (Elijah) Muhammad is His Apostle."[4] Clay had become a convert to the Black Muslim religion, and shortly thereafter changed his name to Muhammad Ali.

Clay's public conversion raised a storm of protest, and a flood of hate mail to his draft board which probably led to his 1-A reclassification. When he refused induction because of his religious vocation, the World Boxing Association and the New York State Athletic Commission quickly took back his title. Years of litigation followed over Ali's draft status, and they were years of sacrifice and penury.

This willing martyrdom for a cause, and the religious ideals behind it, is characteristic of the Other Capricorn. It should not be confused with the kind of martyrdom sometimes found in an afflicted Piscean personality, characterized by ambivalence and self-pity, which is an excuse for an inability to act.

CAPRICORN IS USUALLY represented by a mountain goat, but there is another Capricorn symbol which has become less common and is far less understood: the sea-goat, with a fish tail instead of hindquarters. Derek and Julia Parker point out in their beautiful and knowledgeable *The Compleat Astrologer* that the ancient Babylonian god Ea was called the antelope of the subterranean ocean;[5] Capricorn the sea-goat may be a reflection of that Deity.

Ea was the god of Earth and Water who, in the Akkadian *Epic of Gilgamesh*, which parallels the Genesis myth of Noah, warned the ancestor of the heroic Gilgamesh that he must build an ark to avoid the coming flood.[6] Unlike the other gods in the ancient pantheons, Ea was a friend to Man, and rescued him from the catastrophes that the other gods set up for him, often incurring their wrath for doing so.[7]

The amphibian, the Capricorn sea-goat, possibly reflects ancient knowledge of Man's origins. Ea was the Sumerian god of wisdom who provided Sumer with all the necessary elements of civilization[8] and who instructed the gods in the creation of Man.[9] Another myth relates that Ea prompted his son Marduk to fight Typhon, the son of Chaos and god of windstorms, whose name is one source of our word "typhoon." Marduk kills Typhon and creates Man from his blood.[10]

Marduk corresponds to the Greek Zeus, the Roman Jupiter and the Yahweh/Elohim of Genesis.[11] As the god of wisdom who *advises* the other gods, including his own son Marduk, who creates Man, Ea is reminiscent of the *Ain Soph,* or God-Beyond-God, of Jewish mysticism; the wisdom incarnate of the Hindu Brahma and the universal One of the Christian Gnostics.

Thus Capricorn is both mountain goat and sea-goat, two aspects of the same archetypal figure. As mountain goat, Capricorn is our ambition, our concern for our place in society and for security. As the sea-goat, Capricorn reflects those qualities of Ea that made him the protector of Man, to the wrath of his peers.

The mountain goat also has connotations of willing martyrdom. J. D. Salinger is a prototypical case in point, with his self-imposed isolation and his fictional heroes reflecting what I suspect is his own self-image of the sensitive artist bruised unceasingly by a brutal society; his autobiographical hero Holden Caulfield comes to mind. Similar martyrdoms are the fate of all the heroes in his *Nine Stories.* "Teddy" is particularly noteworthy because it shows both the religious aspect of Capricorn martyrdom and Salinger's preoccupation with Eastern mysticism. Teddy is a ten-year-old reincarnation of an Indian whose devotion to God was diverted to devotion to a lady, necessitating another turn on the wheel of karma, instead of the ultimate union with God to which he had been heading.

The idea of Capricorn as a sign of religious preoccupation may not square with the usual stereotype of Capricorn as a sign reflecting Man's interest in wealth, success, status. Capricorn *is* concerned with security, and it is a social sign as well; thus a Capricorn emphasis shows our recognition—consciously or otherwise—of the reality that security must ultimately come from within. For many persons, that means a relationship with the Deity, however we conceive him to be.

Such is the lesson Jabez Stone learns in "The Devil and Daniel

Webster." Stone has one misfortune after another. Sorely provoked, Stone makes a deal with the devil which provides him with all the material success he could wish for—at the price of his soul.

Stone ultimately realizes that all the security he has gained is no security at all, because of the terms of his compact. He retains the legendary Daniel Webster to argue his case before a diabolical jury—based on a failure of consideration for the contract.

Prototypes. Swami Point is a promontory north of San Diego; and the hermitage built for the Hindu swami still stands like a white ship atop the cliff. The hermitage had originally been a gift to Mukunda Lal Ghosh, a Bengali of the *Kshatriya* caste of rulers and warriors, who was born January 5, 1893,[12] in northeastern India near the Himalayas when the Sun had traveled halfway through the sign of Capricorn.

The boy Mukunda manifested the mountain goat aspects of his Sun sign at an early age with a powerful attraction to the nearby Himalayas. From the age of eight until well into his college years at Calcutta University, Mukunda again and again sought refuge in India's sacred mountains.

The sea-goat surfaced even earlier, for, true to his Sun sign, the young Capricorn provoked controversy in the very first society in which he was placed, that of his immediate family. Following the early death of his mother, the aspiring acolyte felt the combined pressure of father and elder brother (a powerful force in Hindu society) to pursue a more establishmentarian career.

For over a year, his elder brother Ananda withheld the deathbed message which their mother had entrusted him to convey to his younger brother: that her own guru had baptized the infant Mukunda with the prediction that he was destined to become a yogi.[13]

Even after this reluctant disclosure, father and elder brother maintained their opposition. Finally, Ananda designed a test of Mukunda's religious vocation which, although weighted heavily against him, Mukunda passed dramatically and unequivocally, convincing his brother he was not to be dissuaded from the course he had set for himself, and converting his brother as well.

Soon Mukunda became a disciple of Sri (meaning holy) Yukteswar, whose guru had in turn been the guru of Mukunda's own mother and father. To Mukunda's dismay, his guru's first direction was for his disciple to enroll in Calcutta University. A resigned but uncomprehending student, Mukunda did as he was told.

Always an indifferent student, Mukunda nevertheless graduated with an A.B. degree from Serampore College in 1914, to his combined surprise and relief.[14] That same year he was initiated by Sri Yukteswar into the ancient Swami Order of which his guru was a member, and was given the new name Yogananda, which means Bliss (Ananda) through Divine Union (Yoga).[15]

In 1920, Yogananda responded to a vision received in meditation by accepting an invitation to attend the International Congress of Religious Liberals in Boston under the sponsorship of the Unitarian Foundation. He appears to have become immediately popular; the swami's personality must have been the major factor in the dramatic and encouraging response he everywhere received to his lectures. In the years following his arrival in the United States, Yogananda was received by President Calvin Coolidge at the White House and by the President of Mexico, Portes Gil, among many other luminaries. Yogananda initiated Luther Burbank into Kriya Yoga in 1924,[16] and Mahatma Gandhi in 1935.[17]

One of his early converts was a Boston dentist, Dr. Minott W. Lewis, who was to become an intellectual pillar of the religious order founded by Yogananda, and its vice-president. Another devotee was J. J. Lynn, a self-made American millionaire, whose wife was so incensed about his conversion to yogic practices that he was forced to meditate behind a locked bathroom door. Yogananda appears to have won that rivalry handily: as Rajarsi Janakananda, Lynn succeeded Yogananda as the head of the Self-Realization Fellowship, which the swami founded in 1925.

The headquarters for the new religious order was Mount Washington Estates in Los Angeles, which Yogananda's fellowship purchased against a large mortgage. Yogananda frequently traveled the Pacific Coast Highway between San Diego and the Mount Washington headquarters. Often he would stop at a serene promontory in Encinitas, just north of San Diego, to meditate before continuing his journey.

In 1935, Yogananda returned to India. While there, his guru bestowed on him the title of *Paramahansa,* the Supreme Swan—a great honor.[18] When he finally returned in 1937, a surprise was waiting for him. J. J. Lynn had purchased the Encinitas property which had been Yogananda's meditation site and had built a hermitage there for Yogananda. By 1952, there were major centers of Self-Realization Fellowship activity in Los Angeles, Hollywood, Pacific Palisades, Encinitas and San Diego.[19]

During the last week in February of that year, Yogananda kept saying, "I have a very important engagement in March." His disciples thought he was referring to the forthcoming visit of the Indian ambassador to SRF headquarters set for March fourth; or possibly to the banquet planned in the ambassador's honor for March seventh at which

Yogananda was scheduled to speak. Each time Yogananda referred to the banquet he identified it as "the banquet on March ninth," despite frequent reminders that it was set for the seventh.[20] Apparently it occurred to no one at the time that his own guru's passing had been on March ninth.

Another hint was broader. On the afternoon of the dinner a box of green coconuts arrived, sent to the guru from a disciple in Florida. [21] He observed that it was the first time he had had green coconuts since his return from India some sixteen years before. After he drank the green coconut milk, he added: "My last little desire has been fulfilled. I wanted to drink coconut milk, just as I used to in India, once more before I go."[22] At the dinner, as *Time* reported,

> the guru rose to make a speech about "spiritual India." He ended it
> with a quotation from one of his own poems:
> *"Where Ganges, woods, Himalayan caves, and men dream God—*
> *I am hallowed; my body touched that sod."*
> As he finished, Paramahansa lifted his eyes, turned slightly to the right
> and slid to the floor, dead.[23]

The *mahasamadhi** of Paramahansa Yogananda certainly dramatized the Capricorn trait of willing martyrdom; it is a convention among yogis that they take on the karmic debts of their disciples and work them out on their own bodies. [24] Yet the Paramahansa was a paragon of other Capricorn characteristics as well.

After his passing, the yogi said, his writings would be the guru for his followers; and Yogananda was a prolific writer, whose published works include *Cosmic Chants, Metaphysical Meditations, Scientific Healing Affirmations, Sayings, The Science of Religion* (Self-Realization Fellowship is the publisher of all of Paramahansa Yogananda's work) and a variety of other literary efforts, such as his commentaries on the Bhavagad-Gita (the Hindu Bible) and on the *Rubáiyát of Omar Khayyám*, serialized in the magazine which he also founded.[25]

By far his most popular work was his own *Autobiography of a Yogi,* which richly fulfills the Capricorn quality of generating controversy. "The narrative is filled with what, in any other context, would be called magic," grumbled *Christian Century,*[26] when the book was first published by Philosophical Library in 1947. In the article "Here Comes the Yogiman," *Time* declared of the book:

---

*A yogi's final conscious exit from the body.

It is not likely to give the uninitiated much insight into India's ancient teachings. It does show exceedingly well how an alien culture may change when transplanted by a businesslike nurseryman from the tough soil of religious asceticism into hothouses of financial wealth and spiritual despair.[27]

Yogananda's *Autobiography* does make great demands on the reader's credulity. There are levitating saints, saints who never eat, who materialize and dematerialize at will; there are incidents of telepathy, telekinesis, teleportation and unerring prophecy. The reader may be both startled and amused when the author, late in the narrative, remarks:

However, in recording the lives of Babaji, Lahiri Mahasaya, and Sri Yukteswar, I have thought it advisable to omit certain miraculous stories.[28]

Throughout his *Autobiography*, Yogananda urged scientific examination of the phenomena he described, with the conviction that such study would provide theoretical support for these apparent miracles. Only recently has research into the phenomena of paranormal experience begun; but the reports now coming in tend to vindicate Yogananda's experiences on a variety of grounds.

Paramahansa Yogananda is a paradigm of the Other Capricorn. At a time when church attendance is in decline, the church he founded is clearly flourishing; lessons in yogic practices are mailed to students of self-realization all over the world from centers in India and in Mexico City and from the Los Angeles headquarters. At least forty schools are known to assign his *Autobiography;* no one knows the actual total.

THE GURU-DISCIPLE relationship described by Paramahansa Yogananda invites comparison to the *brujo**-apprentice relationship described by anthropologist Carlos Castaneda in the trilogy about his apprenticeship to don Juan, a Yaqui Indian, recently completed by *Journey to Ixtlan*. Read in sequence, the trilogy traces the development of a UCLA anthropology student who undertakes the apprenticeship with the Yaqui Indian as a method of gleaning information about peyote for a student paper.[29] Finally giving up his self-defeating reductionism, Castaneda succeeds for the first time in applying what he has learned; he is rewarded with the experience of immanent Oneness.

---

*Sorcerer, medicine man, healer.

This experience seems identical to the ecstasy of *samadhi* so frequently described by Paramahansa Yogananda; and "a state of ecstasy" is the phrase used by Castaneda in reporting his first real step to becoming what his *brujo* calls a "man of knowledge."

As in Yogananda's *Autobiography*, there are in *Journey to Ixtlan* many archetypal figures—the mysterious ally with whom he must one day wrestle; the luminous coyote with whom he converses and who will be his companion for life; la Catalina, the worthy adversary who can transmogrify herself into a blackbird or crow. And, as in Yogananda's *Autobiography*, miracles abound. In *Journey*, Castaneda's experiences are without drugs of any kind.

Predictably, Castaneda's work has made him a controversial figure. "Is it possible that these books are nonfiction?" asks novelist-critic Joyce Carol Oates, who praises their high literary quality.[30]

What the *Time* reporter actually encountered was quite the reverse of "El Freako and Acid Academic," [31] for Carlos Castaneda is a conservatively garbed young professor of anthropology who discourses comfortably on the phenomenology of Edmund Husserl; [32] and whose insight gained from don Juan's teachings was a badly needed corrective for the finger-pointing Capricorn syndrome—as Castaneda's own confession demonstrates:

> I confessed that I had never respected or liked anybody, not even myself, and that I had always felt I was inherently evil, and thus my attitude towards others was always veiled with a certain bravado and daring.[33]

It will be no surprise to the reader to learn that Castaneda was born on December 25, when the Sun was in early degrees of Capricorn.*

Time's correspondent found Castaneda "attractive, helpful and convincing—up to a point," that point apparently being his warning that he would change background data to preserve his (and his guru's) anonymity.[34]

Psychology Today editor-at-large Sam Keen concludes that Castaneda is one of the psychonauts of the new mysticism (his terminology), grouping him with Dr. John Lilly, whose autobiography of inner space, *The Center of the Cyclone*, also reports archetypal figures who counsel the author. The new mysticism sounds much like the traditional mysticism of the East with the addition of a technology;

Time gives the birth year as 1935. However, I investigated farther and concluded that the given year is incorrect but not the December 25 birth date.

here I am reminded that Yogananda hoped to see Western technology combined with Eastern insight for the benefit of the world. Paramahansa Yogananda, Professor Castaneda and Dr. Lilly—all concerned about the fate of Man in an age of nihilism and absurdity, all working in responsible public roles of high visibility (church founder, anthropologist, doctor-scientist) and all highly controversial—were each born when the Sun was posited in the sign of Capricorn.

THE PRESIDENCY IS a uniquely Capricorn goal with its power, public recognition, deadly seriousness and opportunity for self-sacrifice. And four of our presidents have been Capricorn natives by Sun sign,[35] including the thirty-seventh President of the United States, Richard Nixon, who has been the subject of a psycho-historical inquiry by Professor Bruce Mazlish; his conclusion that Richard Nixon is characterized "by an oppressive moralism and air of apology"[36] is consistent with the President's Capricorn character.

Just as astrologically significant is Mazlish's observation that

> There is one other important element in our vague feeling of unease about Nixon, an element that, moreover, corresponds significantly to the inner nature of many other Americans and to crucial aspects of this country's policy at home and abroad. We see this illustrated in Nixon's pervasive belief in his own goodness and morality.[37]

That is of course the *hubris* of our Sagittarian Ascendant; and the *hubris* of President Nixon has not escaped notice.[38]

To an astrologer, the gradual expansion of power of the presidency is but a reflection of the horoscope of the nation itself. But no astrologer would comment on the chart of any president without at least a sidelong glance at the chart of our nation. It is not my purpose to analyze the horoscope of President Nixon. I am interested in the manifestation of those characteristic factors which flesh out the archetype.

At this writing, the only president who has been impeached was Andrew Johnson, who, as it happens, was also a Capricorn, born December 29, 1808. Johnson's *hubris*—his belligerent speeches and contentious bluster—so exacerbated the tensions of that era that an already hostile Congress was virtually goaded into the nonetheless unwarranted impeachment which Johnson survived by one vote.

Woodrow Wilson was a Capricorn, born December 28, 1856. After impressive victories in leading the nation through World War I, Wilson attended the peace conference at Versailles with a high level of *hubris*. He defied the reigning political powers in Congress and was especially unwise in slighting Republican Senator Henry Cabot Lodge, who successfully led the opposition to the ratification of the peace treaty Wilson had engineered. Attempting to take his case to the people, Wilson stumped for the League of Nations and for the treaty—and collapsed a broken and defeated man.

And then there is Millard Fillmore, born January 7, 1800, the thirteenth president of the United States, and our first Capricorn chief executive. Everyone seems to recognize his name as that of one of our presidents; but no one who is not a historical scholar seems to know anything else about him.

Millard Fillmore became president in 1850, and although he served out Zachary Taylor's term, he bears the unique distinction of being an incumbent president who was unable to secure his own party's nomination to run in the succeeding election. But even a lackluster president such as Fillmore must have some claim on our attention; in his case, he was a political martyr in a controversy which polarized our nation.

The 1850s in the United States were a time of bitter internal strife over the slavery issue. One of Fillmore's first executive acts was to sign the Compromise of 1850, regarded by some historians as an act of rare moral courage. But Fillmore, in awe of Daniel Webster, unhesitatingly signed the bill that President Taylor had been expected to reject. Although the Compromise of 1850 kept the Union together for ten more years, by signing the bill, Fillmore joined Webster in the martyrdom which destroyed their party. And Daniel Webster, the lawyer whose ambition took him to the threshhold of the presidency, but who never attained that office because of the sacrifice by which he surmounted his own moral flaws to achieve greatness, was born January 18, 1782, when a stellium of Sun, Mercury and Venus were all posited in the sign of Capricorn.

Polar opposite. The polar opposite of Capricorn is Cancer. Whereas the principal concern of Cancer is the immediate environment of the home, the major concern of Capricorn is the larger social environment in which the native finds himself.

Positive and negative aspects. Positively manifested, Capricorn qualities bring needed ambition to our life and a proper concern for social esteem and the opinions of others. Negatively expressed, Capricorn recalls the iron bed of Procrustes, the mythical Greek robber who either stretched or cut off his victim's legs to fit the iron bed to which he tied them. Destructive self-criticism or unrealistic demands that the Capricorn native makes upon himself may result in Procrustean self-mutilation.

Notable Capricorn personalities. Joan of Arc, Rod Serling, Rudyard Kipling, J. Edgar Hoover, Sir Isaac Newton, Alan Watts, Simone de Beauvoir, Elvis Presley, Joseph Smith, Swami Vivekenanda, Jack London, Albert Schweitzer, John Dos Passos, Julian Bond, Aristotle Onassis and Martin Luther King, Jr.

Element. Capricorn is the third and last of the earth signs.

AQUARIUS

Sequence. Aquarius is the eleventh sign of the natural zodiac. The Latin word *aquarius* means water bearer. The Sun enters Aquarius about January 21 each year.

Gylph. The jagged lines which symbolize the sign have sometimes been interpreted as water, and are often pictured as flowing from an amphora:

However, those jagged lines represent not water, but electricity. Ancient astrologers and alchemists conceptualized that force as vibrations which were first noticed emanating from amber, especially when that strange and exotic substance was polished. The Greek word for amber is *elektron,* and the unknown force which astrologers represented by two wavy lines was electricity.

There is no Chinese lunar station, and hence neither a Hebrew letter nor Chinese character, related to Aquarius.

Planetary ruler. Saturn was originally held to be the planetary ruler of Aquarius. Since the discovery of Uranus in 1781, that planet is regarded as its planetary ruler. Many astrologers assign Saturn a co-rulership.

Melothesia. Aquarius rules the ankles and the circulatory system.

Characteristics. As an archetype, Aquarius is very much an expression of humanitarian love, Agape rather than Eros. Aquarian love encompasses the entire world and all its creatures—all the things embraced in that strange new word "ecology."

Aquarius is also the sign usually associated with astrologers, the notion being that the astrologer at a very early age symbolized humanitarian concern and inspiration as well. There is a certain distance about the affectional nature of persons who have a strong Aquarian emphasis which can be mistaken for coldness or aloofness. Not so; Aquarians have an inherent capacity to take the long view, a characteristic unrelated to pride, vanity or self.

The Aquarian is born inspired and seeks to inspire others with his forward-looking vision. Like all air signs—Gemini and Libra are the other two—Aquarians live in future time. We have seen that the Gemini native tends to respond to manifold stimuli by viewing the world in terms of infinite possibilities. The Libran works through others, and is likewise future-oriented, with a weather eye to achieving the chimera of perfect balance.

Aquarians, on the other hand, are oriented toward the future in their inventiveness, the long view of their fellow men and their humanitarian goals. Such Aquarian attitudes mean compassionate rather than punitive concepts of law and justice, and the notion of the infinite perfectibility of Man. Aquarians are also credited with the notion of applying science and technology to improve the lot of Mankind, rather than to achieve power—the latter being a characteristic of its polar opposite, Leo.

Capricorn, the sign of social consciousness, shrewdly perceives each stratum of society. Contrast the Aquarian whose future vision makes him the most socially indifferent of all the zodiacal archetypes. He sees society as a future interest; indeed, Aquarius is a sign of social change.

The term "Aquarian Age" derives from the astronomical concepts of the Great Month and the Great Year. Because of the Earth's wobble on its axis, which produces the precession of the equinoxes, there is a total change of zodiacal constellations at the start of the vernal equinox every 2,160 years. At this point, known to astronomers and to astrologers as the Great Month, the Sun appears in a different zodiacal constellation when the zodiacal year commences. In 25,000 years or so (the Great Year), the Sun has completely traversed the zodiacal constellations.[1]

At one time the Sun appeared in the constellation of Taurus at the vernal equinox. In Old Testament times, it slipped backward to the Aries constellation because of precession. Then the starting point of the zodiac was changed from Taurus to Aries. When, with the continuing effects of precession, the Sun edged toward the constellation of Pisces at the commencement of the zodiacal year, astrologers decided to fix the signs according to a geometric formula based on the solstices and the equinoxes and to discard the background of constellations as a frame of reference. However, most astrologers still consider that background a relevant factor in determining the overall character of the Great Month.

Today the Sun is approaching the constellation of Aquarius at the time of the vernal equinox, having slipped backward into the constellation of Pisces just about when the New Testament period began.

Because we are moving into the constellation of Aquarius in this fashion, social changes oriented toward humanitarian attitudes are increasing, for Aquarian and egalitarian are synonymous and harmonious. The quest for equality, social justice and fraternity in the realization of a better world for all Mankind is the true aspiration of the Aquarian archetype and hence of the Great Month which bears its name.

Prototypes. Jules Verne, born February 8, 1828, with Sun and Mercury posited in Aquarius, illustrates these Aquarian attitudes. Verne created a body of literature in which speculations about our technological future were dealt with according to scientific premises. The result was science fiction, a new genre of literature which combined those scientific speculations with high adventure. Science fiction is indeed the literature of the Aquarian Age.

Verne's novels have been incredibly prophetic. He anticipated the submarine, the aircraft, space travel and a host of other modern inventions. A lesser-known fact about Verne's literary output is the persistent theme of humanitarian concern. Captain Nemo, for example, invented the submarine in order to monitor and destroy the military arsenals of all nations. Nemo's fulminations about the idiocy of war and the inhumane treatment of Man by Man reflect Jules Verne's own heartfelt Aquarian concerns.

WHEN I DISCOVERED that Dr. Lynch was an Aquarian by date of birth, and after reading about his pioneering new biofeedback center,[2] I went there to interview him.

"Most of this"—Lynch gestured around him—"is prototype equipment which we designed ourselves." I remembered from the magazine article that the clinic was a joint effort in which he was engaged with other psychiatrists, psychologists and educational consultants. Through biofeedback training, a patient can learn to be aware of what his body is doing to itself, and correct the difficulty. In similar fashion, patients with heart disease can learn to control their bodily rhythms to avoid disaster and to reassert their health.

Dr. Lynch was born on the third of February, 1932, in Wichita, Kansas, at 10:00 A.M. At the time of his birth, both the Sun and Mars were posited in Aquarius and in the eleventh house, which is the natural house of Aquarius, adding emphasis to what was already a strongly Aquarian personality.

Dr. Lynch had attended medical school at the University of Kansas Medical Center, with a view to psychiatric residency at the

Menninger Clinic at Topeka. Bob Lynch had decided in the ninth grade that he wanted to be a psychiatrist, after writing a report on psychiatry as a class assignment. In preparing his report, he came to recognize that the counseling function for which people—including many adults—were already seeking him out was the kind of thing at which he wished to spend his life; fortunately, his teacher was encouraging. His near-diversion to surgery was averted by a dramatic and characteristically Aquarian incident.

Outstanding scholarship won him the most coveted of internships available: the Hospital of the University of Pennsylvania, where the most prestigious of the medical specialties was surgery, and Lynch was greatly tempted. He was invited to participate in one of the world's first open-heart operations. As the intern on the case, he worked for twenty hours with twenty doctors on the operation. When the patient died on the operating table, it was Bob Lynch's job to complete the operation, sew up the patient, advise the family, obtain the autopsy permit and make all the other arrangements.

It was the next day by the time all of these tasks had been concluded. An exhausted intern slumped into a chair at the hospital cafeteria. Over his breakfast coffee, Bob read the headlines: "STARK-WEATHER SLAYS THIRTEEN VICTIMS!" He was stunned.

"I realized that while twenty doctors had worked around the clock on the heart of one man who was expected to die, another man who happened to be mentally disturbed had killed thirteen people. I decided then and there that I could accomplish more as a psychiatrist than as a surgeon."

It was an Aquarian decision. At that time, the top ten or fifteen percent of medical graduates in the United States chose surgery as their specialty; psychiatry was the *bête noir* of the profession, and Bob Lynch did not escape derision from his peers and his medical superiors for his decision.

Because of his class position and his excellent record at Pennsylvania Hospital, Lynch was able to achieve his original goal: a three-year residency at the Menninger Psychiatric Hospital. Even better, he had been awarded a three-year fellowship in psychiatry, and was permitted to take his residency and fellowship contemporaneously. That was no small matter. Interns at that time were paid a salary of ten dollars a month; the monthly fee for parking in the hospital lot was thirty dollars. The fellowship made it possible for him to survive financially for three years of arduous effort and intensive training.

"But my interest in what we now call biofeedback antedated my psychiatric training," Bob mused. He had met Gerald Heard in 1949, when he was an undergratuate at Washington University in St. Louis and Heard was his professor of comparative religion. They became friends, and Lynch spent a month or two each summer through college, medical school and his psychiatric residency, at the Heard guest house in Pacific Palisades, California, studying Eastern philosophy, mysticism, social problems—plus all the humanistic concerns that Heard, a scholar whose Sun and Uranus were conjunct in Libra, was interested in.

"It was a remarkable opportunity, and I'm grateful for it," Bob said. "People came to tea every day at three o'clock in the afternoon and the tea lasted till six. And they came from all over the world—people like Martha Graham, Igor Stravinsky and Ethel Barrymore. It was an absolute paradise for a young medical student from Kansas! The discussions were vigorous, and Heard's guests were all people on the growing edge of experience."

One of the guests was Aldous Huxley, and he and Lynch established a friendship which, through the intervening years of medical school, psychiatric residency and other interruptions, could always be taken up where they had left off, and lasted for the last ten years of Huxley's life.

"It was remarkable," Lynch mused. "Aldous always seemed to want to learn from *me*, which was certainly flattering. But more than that, it made my mind operate at its most original and creative level whenever I was with him."

Through Huxley, Lynch learned to trust his mind to be at once innovative and helpful. "I learned that the core thing about myself was that in my dealings with people, I wouldn't hurt anyone by what I would say or do. I learned to trust myself to be therapeutic and to come up with useful ideas based on an inner knowledge of the world and other people."

Lynch and Huxley shared an interest in the potentiality of lysergic acid diethylamide to help humankind long before its street use brought the overreaction of restrictive laws. His thesis, written for his fellowship at Menninger's, was described by Gardner Murphy* as a magnum opus. Entitled *Human States of De-Differentiation*, it was the product of his eight years' research on LSD, plus his own three experiences with the hallucinogen, in which he concluded that the potential benefits of lysergic acid to society were enormous and profound.

His own use of LSD therapy is dramatically illustrated in *Myself*

---

*Although his eminent colleague, Dr. Joseph Rhine, is probably better known in the field of parapsychology, Dr. Murphy is widely regarded as the dean of American psychologists, with the field of parapsychology not excepted. At the time of Dr. Lynch's residency and fellowship, Murphy was director of research at the Menninger Foundation.

and I,[3] written by a patient who ultimately achieved emotional health through the chemotherapy that Lynch and another psychiatrist administered, after a complete Freudian analysis failed to relieve her chronic insomnia, her tension or her frigidity.

I wondered whether Dr. Lynch saw a common link between biofeedback therapy, Karl von Reichenbach's odic force, Reichian orgone energy, the auras described by occultists and by mystics and the energy flowing from all living things described by so many persons who have had hallucinogenic experiences.

"We all have three layers," he said. "The part other people see—the body and all its trappings of personality—is the densest part of us." He touched his chest. "What *we* know ourselves to be includes the dense part plus the less dense extension, which takes in our memories, our fantasies, our wishes and dreams. The least dense part is hardly perceptible, even to ourselves. It emanates from us in an orb that may encompass the entire universe."

I asked Dr. Lynch how he saw himself in this universal scheme.

"I am very much aware of my home base in eternity. I see myself as one slice of a line of people, stretching both backwards and forwards to infinity."

Did he agree with the widely quoted statement by Carl Jung that "astrology represents the summation of all the psychological knowledge of antiquity?"[4]

"I would go even farther than that: astrology is Man's discovery of the universal computer. Through astrology, we can see that the universe operates in cycles and rhythms—and, as Aldous said in his last LSD experience, shortly before his death—all of its manifestations are fundamentally sane."

How would he, as psychiatrist and eclectic mystic, sum up Man's present condition?

"I have described that in terms of *futureshock*," he reminded me, recalling a series of lectures which he had taped at the suggestion of anthropologist Margaret Mead.*

The circumstances present an excellent illustration of Aquarian detachment at its best. In the fall of 1969 *West* magazine, then a supplement of the *Los Angeles Times*, published an article by Rita

---

*The gist of Dr. Lynch's futureshock lecture series was that Man is now living in a time which cannot be designated by such catch-phrases as Space Age or Atomic Age, which could provide an arresting image and identify a period for us. In contrast, our present time is a Period of Perpetual Change, a label which tells us nothing about its contents or what to expect from it. The result is a special kind of disorganization or malaise which Dr. Lynch identified as futureshock. Under such circumstances, adaptability is necessary to survival.

Gustaitis which included an interview with Dr. Lynch and a mention of his new concept by name. Shortly thereafter, Dr. Lynch received a long-distance telephone call from the author of the as-yet-unpublished book *Future Shock.* Alvin Toffler was both surprised and concerned about the Lynch neologism. Toffler had spent years researching and writing his forthcoming book: what was this La Jolla psychiatrist going to do with the term which was both the title and the subject of his magnum opus?

Nothing. "I explained that I was a psychiatrist, not a writer," Lynch said. "Besides, my notion has always been that ideas belong to everybody." His latest idea? All disease is essentially a bad memory, whether it is a psychological or a physical disorder. "What is necessary to change that fixed idea of disease is something that will block that memory—a local anaesthetic, such as procain, or acupuncture. Biofeedback may provide a better way through retraining the patient to produce healthy functioning of the organ system involved."

True to his Sun sign, Lynch has never lingered long enough with one idea to exploit it financially; new ideas always beckon first.

Polar opposite. The polar opposite of Aquarius is Leo. Just as Aquarius expresses humanitarian love, or Agape, so its polar opposite, Leo, expresses the passion of Eros with all the pride and vanity so remarkably lacking in the Aquarian archetype.

Positive and negative aspects. Positively manifested, Aquarius is humanitarian, visionary, prophetic and selfless. Negatively manifested, Aquarius can be domineering, perverse and cold-blooded; or ineffectual and remote.

Notable Aquarian personalities. Francis Bacon, Charles Darwin, Abraham Lincoln, Franklin D. Roosevelt, Vanessa Redgrave, Charles Lindbergh and Gina Ceaglio, the dean of San Diego astrologers.

Element. Aquarius is the third sign in the air triplicity; the first is Gemini, the second is Libra.

PISCES ♓

Sequence. Pisces is the twelfth sign of the natural zodiac. The Sun enters Pisces about February 21 each year. Like Aquarius, Pisces has no equivalent in the Hebrew alphabet or in the original lunar constellations. Our word *pisces* is derived from the Latin word for fish, and is thematically related to *Ichthys*, which means fish in Greek.

Glyph. The glyph for Pisces represents two fish bound together and swimming in opposite directions, symbolizing duality and ambivalence. For Jung, this sign is a basic, primordial archetype which finds its origin in Man's collective unconscious. This view places the Pisces symbol in its proper astrological perspective in the prehistory of Mankind.

Planetary ruler. Jupiter was originally held to be the planetary ruler of Pisces; however, since its discovery in 1836, Neptune has been assigned the primary rulership. Many astrologers still consider Jupiter a co-ruler of Pisces.

Melothesia. Pisces rules the feet.

Characteristics. The fact that the dreamy and nebulous Pisces rules the feet may seem surprising. One explanation is that, in the mystical or spiritual interpretation of the human form, the tree of life is the human body itself, with Man's hair as its roots and his nerves as its branches. In this configuration the feet are closest to the heavens and the soles of the feet are the receivers of all spiritual emanations.[1]

There are less esoteric explanations. The foot has traditionally been symbolic of the human soul, partly in the sense that quite literally the foot keeps the human form upright; and partly in a sense of archetypal symbolism. In Greek and other mythology, for example, lameness has indicated divinity. Zeus and Hephaestus were lame, as was Dionysus; and Jesus has been credited with lameness as well.[2]

The ambivalence represented in the glyph for Pisces is reflected in the fact that, its spiritual connotations to the contrary, the foot stands for Man's direct contact with the Earth; and it is an immemorial phallic symbol as well. It is curious that the fish and the foot have both been dual symbols of the carnal and spiritual aspects of human nature throughout Man's history. In its spiritual expression, the Piscean archetype is otherworldly, supraconscious and unique, for the Piscean personality does indeed march to the beat of a different drummer.

Prototypes. With the holistic vision such natives possess, phenomenal mathematical aptitude often results—as in the case of Bobby Fischer. As he is described by Brad Darrach, Fischer marches to the beat of a very different drummer indeed. A big man, in a padded jacket "his shoulders look so wide his head seems even smaller than it is. 'Like a pea sitting on a ruler,' somebody said." A fast walker, "he walks the way a hen runs—and this hen fills a doorway." His stride may result from his stance: he is described as having his "feet wide apart and toes turned in,"[3] suggesting the Piscean idiosyncrasy of the foot.

Confused by many of the things most of us cope with more or less routinely, Fischer comes alive at the chess board:

When he sits at the board, a big dangerous cat slips into his skin. His chest swells, his green eyes glow, his sallowness fills with warm blood. All the life in his fragmented body flows and he looks wild and beautiful.[4]

But try to get such a man to a chess match in Iceland, and you have the makings of what Darrach himself describes as a plot for "Mission: Impossible."[5]

THE DANCE IS a peculiarly Piscean art, perhaps because of the melothesia of the foot, perhaps also because of that strangely different beat. The two greatest male dancers of this century have been Vaslav Nijinsky and Rudolf Nureyev, each of whom was born with the Sun in Pisces. Either Nureyev or Nijinsky makes an excellent prototype of the Piscean dancer; however, Nureyev has a strong Arien emphasis as well, with Mercury, Venus and Saturn all in Aries and in close conjunction to his Pisces Sun. That stellium certainly explains his impulsive defection to the West; but it makes Nijinsky, with his Sun, Venus and Mercury all in Pisces, a better example for my purposes.

Vaslav Nijinsky was the greatest dancer of this—some say of any—century. Nijinsky was born March 12, 1890, at approximately 10:30 P.M.[6] The birth date is sometimes shown as February 28, 1890, according to the Old Style Russian calendar; with the necessary intercalation, the correct date is March 12.

As a child his shyness was such that he could scarcely answer the examiners' questions when enrolled by his mother in the Russian Imperial School of Dancing; but even at that early age his demonstrable skills prompted the examiners to accept him.

His rise as a dancer was meteoric, and he was soon taken under the wing of the impresario Sergei Diaghilev, who became both his mentor and his lover. Overbearing Aries personality that he was, Diaghilev was nonetheless a brilliant innovator, credited both with bringing the Russian ballet to the attention of the West and with creating ballets which glorified the male beauty Nijinsky exemplified.

Nijinsky soon became the premier danseur of the Ballet Russe of Sergei Diaghilev. Under Diaghilev, Nijinsky developed and performed the balletic art which elevated him to his legendary status. Nor were his talents limited to the performance of the work of others. Nijinsky himself revolutionized the form of the ballet with such works as *The Afternoon of a Faun* and *The Rite of Spring*. Nijinsky choreographed these ballets himself; both scandalized the public when first performed, and both are now classics of ballet repertoire.

Nijinsky was ultimately rescued from his thralldom to Diaghilev by Romola de Pulszky, a lady of Hungarian nobility who joined the Diaghilev Ballet because of her enchantment with its premier danseur.

His wife, Romola, furnished the explanation for Nijinsky's phenomenal and breathtaking leaps: it was the structure of his foot. Nijinsky's foot was not constructed like that of other human beings, but looked like a mixture of the anatomy of man and bird, according to a medical doctor who attended Nijinsky at the time he injured his ankle. After examining the x-rays, the doctor declared that Nijinsky's foot was the secret of his amazing elevation: "No wonder he can fly; he is a human bird."[7]

Romola reports a number of other Piscean qualities of her husband. There was, for example, the amazement of Professor Pichler, the great Hungarian mathematician who used to visit Nijinsky to discuss math problems which the dancer was fully able to comprehend.

Nijinsky's views of life were flavored with Piscean mysticism, for he viewed birth and death as part of a great circle, reflecting God in the universe of which Man was an infinite part. He declared that his art was but an expression of the Deity.[8]

Nijinsky's marriage produced an immediate and irreparable rift with Diaghilev. Diaghilev's antagonism and the barrage of mundane problems which beset Nijinsky once out of the magic circle ended his dancing not long thereafter. Messianic preoccupations—he was found wearing a big gold cross around his neck, urging passersby to church—led inevitably to the psychiatric diagnosis of incurable mental illness, a judgment confirmed with heartbreaking consistency by doctor after doctor, and by his own eerie and otherworldly diary of those later years.

THE PISCEAN SIGN of the fishes marks the beginning of the Christian Era as well. Legend has it that *Ichthys,* the Greek word for fish, was an acronym made up of the initials of the Greek words for "Jesus Christ, Son of God, Savior." In this context, I.Ch.Th.Y.S. (a transliteration from the Greek letters) was supposedly a password used by early Christians who were forbidden to practice their religion. But Jung, in *Aion,* concludes that the Ichthys symbolism was far more complex than this popular legend supposes.

He noted the many astrological and religious correlations of Pisces.

Using talmudic sources which predicted the birth date of the Messiah, coupled with his own astrological expertise, Jung surmised that the appearance of the Christ figure was destined to occur at a conjunction of Saturn and Jupiter in Gemini.[9] Jung found that conjunction significant not only in the duality which Gemini always indicates but also in the fact that the two planets in the conjunction themselves represented a union of opposites: Saturn the restricter, and Jupiter the planet of growth.

Astrologically, then, the Talmud predicted the arrival not only of the Christ figure but also of his deadly opponent, the Antichrist. Or so Jung concluded.

As Christ and Antichrist, or as two fishes bound together and swimming in opposite directions, the archetypes of the Christian and the Piscean Ages are the same. It has been an era of conflict and of duality, of contradictory forces.

Christianity has always been bedeviled by two sets of symbols, Aldous Huxley once observed. The first relates to the brotherhood of Man and the fatherhood of God, but the second relates to class distinction, worship of Mammon and national idolatry. Every Christian nation has worshipped both sets of symbols with characteristic Piscean ambivalence. Christian sects have also been fond of identifying each other as the Antichrist, whose contested identity has been the occasion of many a Christian bloodbath.

Christ and Antichrist, spiritual and carnal, sublime and ridiculous: only the coming of the Aquarian Age can resolve the contradictions of Piscean duality, declares Jung.[10]

DR. RICHARD MAURICE Bucke was at the very least a man of strong convictions. A lifelong believer in the Baconian authorship of Shakespeare, his principal career was as the medical superintendant of an institution for insane persons where he was a reformer and an advocate of nonrestraint. Dr. Bucke has also been described as one of the foremost alienists on the North American continent.

Bucke was also something of a philosopher and literateur, who taught himself French in order to read contemporary developments in philosophy and taught himself German in order to read Goethe's *Faust* in the original.[11] He discovered Walt Whitman's poetry when he was thirty and it "opened a new door in his mind."[12]

He recognized the apparent contradictions of mysticism and supra-consciousness, and yet wrote about them with conviction. His classic investigation of the evolution of individual human consciousness in his psychological study, *Cosmic Consciousness,* explores that evolution from the simple consciousness of animals to the self-consciousness of humans, and then to an even farther evolution which Bucke finds already evident in some human beings. Our next evolutionary step, Dr. Bucke claims, is cosmic consciousness, in which the human mind moves beyond its awareness of self as different-from-other to an awareness of its Oneness with the universe as a whole. In defining cosmic consciousness, Bucke quotes his favorite writer: "[Walt] Whitman . . . speaks of it in one place as 'ineffable light—light rare, untellable, lighting the very light—beyond all signs, descriptions, languages.' "[13]

Riding home after an evening spent with friends, reading poetry—especially Whitman—Bucke had the experience which inspired his investigation into the evolution of our consciousness:

> All at once, without warning of any kind, he found himself wrapped around, as it were, by a flame-colored cloud. For an instant he thought of fire—some sudden conflagration in the great city. The next instant he knew that the light was within himself.
>
> Directly after there came upon him a sense of exultation, of immense joyousness, accompanied or immediately followed by an intellectual illumination quite impossible to describe.[14]

Although the illumination itself continued for only a few seconds, its effects lasted a lifetime. It was his initiation into "the new and higher order of ideas."[15] He had literally seen the light; and sought to share some part of it with his fellow man by writing *Cosmic Consciousness*.

Whitman, whom he once treated, said of Bucke, "It's beautiful to watch him at his work—to see how he can handle difficult people with such an easy manner . . . Bucke is a man who enjoys being busy."[16] These personality traits are remarkable for a man who, at the age of twenty-one, had the whole of one foot and part of another amputated, and was so badly maimed that for the rest of his life he was never free from pain.[17]

Dr. Richard Bucke was born March 18, 1837, when the Sun was in late degrees of Pisces.[18]

WENDY FELLOWS IS as English as her name, with the finely chiseled features such as the English like to see carved on ivory cameos, and a complexion of the same petal white hue. She is the handsome mother of three handsome sons, with the eldest a charter member of what Tom Wolfe called the Pump House Gang.

I shall always remember Wendy's Christmases, with their Dickensian ambience of good cheer and conviviality, and her magical touch in the kitchen.

Wendy is as fabled for her English wit as for her cookery. A friend told her that his psychiatrist had said that hair piled in a topside bun was phallic; and that women who wore their hair that way were revealing their phallic impulses. When told this, Wendy patted her own topside bun—her trademark, usually set off by a gaily colored scarf—and her eyes sparkled as she remarked: "Fascinating, darling! But just how should I go about it?"

Although her interests are wide-ranging indeed, Wendy is a competent astrologer in her own right. However, some of her friends say in good-natured badinage that she doesn't play fair. I know what they mean, for my first meeting with Wendy was far removed from the esculent delights of her kitchen.

That memorable weekend seminar at Kairos in 1968 on contemporary religion proved to be a remarkably serendipitous affair. Bishop Pike was the major event, since his much-publicized demand for a heresy trial was in the air, and his vindication by a special investigating committee had but recently made headlines. Co-speaker was Father Dubay, who had attempted to organize a priest's union, and who had recently written *The Human Church*.

None of us knew Father James Kavanaugh, who had been a surprise encounter of Bishop Pike's at dinner just before the Friday evening session. It was prior to the publication of Kavanaugh's *A Modern Priest Looks at his Outdated Church*, but Pike prevailed upon him to join us, and the audience was delighted that he did.

I noticed the gracious English lady, shyly retiring in one corner of the room, quietly taping the sessions, but Wendy said very little until someone said, later in the discussion, that he thought *psi* data indicating life after death was nonsense. That someone else might well have been the author of this book, who confesses that, until the very next thing that happened that night, his attitude toward such phenomena was one of outspoken skepticism. In Pike's own words, here it is:

> At that point a Mrs. Wendy Fellows, who hadn't said anything that evening, spoke up: "I hadn't wanted to interrupt to mention it before, Bishop, but since we're on the subject, there was standing behind you for a while a man about your height, in church vestments, who repeated several times, 'You're right.' Or at least that's what I thought he was saying. It was red around his chest area. I don't know if that was in the design of the vestments or what."[19]

As Pike himself verified, the wraith was that of his close friend Father Hugh Wright (Hugh Wright = you're right), whose recent death had not been publicized. When he called his friend's widow the next day, Pike discovered the significance of the red around the chest area which Wendy had so vividly described. Father Wright had collapsed in a remote, wooded spot. A hemorrhage had filled his lungs with blood and suffocated him—spreading a red stain across his shirt front.[20]

That is why her friends sometimes accuse Wendy of not playing fair. They suspect that she doesn't really have to *read* the horoscope, but only hold it in her hands as a psychometric device.

Wendy Fellows—Mars, Mercury and Sun all in Pisces—with a congenitally ailing right foot.

AN AFFINITY FOR liquids also identifies the Piscean personality. Take Ben, for example, whose life posed the question which many a parent has asked: why does one son become a man to be proud of, and the other a source of humiliation and shame?

Ben's brother became a respected Beverly Hills physician, but Ben died the gangster's death he had anticipated for himself when he laughingly reassured entrepreneur Del Webb: "Don't worry—we only kill each other."[21]

Ben was no exception to the Piscean affinity for liquids. His career began during Prohibition. He was one of the men who made it by clinging to the big names of the era "like pilot fish to the shark."[22] He was a characteristically unorthodox Piscean, born February 28, 1906, when the Sun, Venus, Mercury and Saturn were all posited in Pisces.

Handsome as a movie star, and appealing to women as such, Ben worried about his appearance. Most of all he was concerned about losing his hair, a problem he dealt with in Piscean fashion.

It was with no plans to become an actor himself that Ben left his New York syndicate to make his way in the distant and unfamiliar territory of Hollywood. The explanation lies in his Piscean nature, for his biographer advises that Ben's mind was prodded by a "nameless emotional turbulence."[23]

Like many Pisceans, he had an insight that might be labeled *prescient ignorance.* It was demonstrated—among other ways—by his phenomenal ability to pick winners at the racetrack. But his most prescient vision was that of a fabulous hotel on thirty acres of desert sand where his companions could only see a dilapidated failure of a motel. Ben pursued his vision, built his extravagant hotel and named it after his girlfriend whose auburn red hair earned her the sobriquet, The Flamingo.

Today the Flamingo Hotel is the cornerstone of the Las Vegas Strip, a garish neon fantasy that inspired Hunter Thompson's book *Fear and Loathing in Las Vegas.* It was Ben Siegel's American dream and his bequest to his countrymen. They called him Bugsy because of his oddly Piscean habits; what would they call him now?

Our last view of him was also Piscean: a photograph of his right foot dominated the front page of the *Los Angeles Herald-Express* for June 21, 1947. The tag on the big toe read HOMICIDE. His name was misspelled.

Bugsy Siegel, the Man Who Invented Las Vegas.

Polar opposite. Pisces is the polar opposite of Virgo. Virgoan dedicated service is unselfish; Piscean devotion is self*less*. Where Virgoan dedication is rooted to the Earth-bound present, Piscean devotion is otherworldly and strangely retrospective. It is as if the Piscean has a pervasive sense of *déjà vu.*

Positive and negative aspects. The Piscean aspects of human character can carry us to the zenith of higher consciousness or to the nadir of degradation. At its best, Pisces attains that holistic vision which identifies the mystic, the poet and the artist.

In negative expression, Pisces tends to an excess of its virtues. Empathy becomes martyrdom; and the Piscean becomes a human tuning fork bearing the stigmata of the suffering of others. Overindulgence in alcohol, drugs or even sex becomes a short cut to achieve a sense of Oneness; higher consciousness becomes a self-defeating otherworldliness in which the native may be unaware of the reality of his own body.

Notable Piscean personalities. Edgar Cayce, Mircea Eliade, Manly P. Hall, Sri Ramakrishna, Jack Kerouac, Piet Mondrian, Arthur Schopenhauer, Albert Einstein, Peter Fonda, Buffy Sainte-Marie, Theodore Sturgeon, Elizabeth Taylor and Milton Caniff.

Element. Pisces is the third water sign; the second was Scorpio and Cancer was the first. Pisces is distinguished from the others by its element of empathy and its retrospective vision of the world.

FOR THE CONTEMPORARY astrologer as for the contemporary Jungian psychologist, *all* of the archetypal qualities must be integrated for the individual to achieve wholeness. Each of the signs of the zodiac is Janus-faced in its bipolarity, so that the twelve signs actually consist of six archetypal figures: each sign and its polar opposite are one archetype whose countenances face in opposite directions. They may be summarized as follows:

1. Aries/Libra. Aries is the sign of self; Libra is the sign of partnership. Together these signs comprise the archetype of *Identifica-*

tion, which Aries achieves through self-assertion and Libra through relationships with others.

2. Taurus/Scorpio. Taurus is the sign of receptivity and Scorpio is the sign of passion. Together they make up the archetype of *Sense Awareness,* which Taurus expresses through its passive receptivity to the stimuli of the senses, and Scorpio through its active commitment to the object of its passion.

3. Gemini/Sagittarius. Gemini is the sign of communication, Sagittarius of idealism. Their archetype is *Ideation,* Gemini through verbal acts, Sagittarius through idealized mental structures which are the effort of the conscious will.

4. Cancer/Capricorn. Cancer is the sign of the home and early environment, Capricorn is the sign of the public or larger environment. Together they are the archetype of *Orientation,* Cancer through our first and last environment, Capricorn through the intermediate environment of society.

5. Leo/Aquarius. Leo is the sign of the king, Aquarius is the sign of the humanitarian. Their archetype is *Leadership,* Leo through a passionate desire to command, Aquarius through a dispassionate concern for humanity which requires him to take command.

6. Virgo/Pisces. Virgo is the sign of service to others, Pisces is the sign of otherworldliness. Together they are the archetype of *Selflessness,* Virgo through devoted service and Pisces through loss of self-awareness.

7   What Are the Triplicities?

"PSYCHIATRY HAS NEVER developed a satisfactory theory of personality types," Dr. White once remarked. "That's one area in which astrology has done something we haven't been able to do."

I suspect that Dr. White was thinking of the twelve zodiacal signs as personality types. It is the thesis of this book that the signs themselves represent archetypal qualities which we all have in varying degrees of emphasis; and that astrology provides personality types only when the signs are considered according to the triplicities of the four elements of alchemy: fire, earth, air and water. The grouping of signs by element results in a triangle of three signs for each of the four elements, for a total of four triangles. Each of these sets is called a trigon or, more commonly, a *triplicity*. The elements and their association to the signs of the zodiac are illustrated in figure three. Note that the sequence of elements, in the order of fire, earth, air and water, follows the sequence of the signs of the natural zodiac, commencing with Aries. Each group of signs by element constitutes one triplicity; for example, Aries, Leo and Sagittarius make up the fire triplicity.

The specific implications of the triplicities for human personality will be explored later in this chapter. For present purposes, you need only remember the basic concept that the Sun-sign emphasis by triplicity, as well as the overall planetary emphasis by triplicity, provides important clues to the native's personality.

Nonetheless, Dr. White was certainly aiming in the right direction, and his observation was thought-provoking. I remembered it when I discovered that Carl Jung had actually developed two personality typologies of his own. The first is the well-known attitude typology of introversion and extroversion, having to do with the basic direction of our psychic energy, or what Freud would call the libido.

Jung's second typology is virtually unknown and, for my purposes, far more intriguing. In it, Jung set out four types of personality

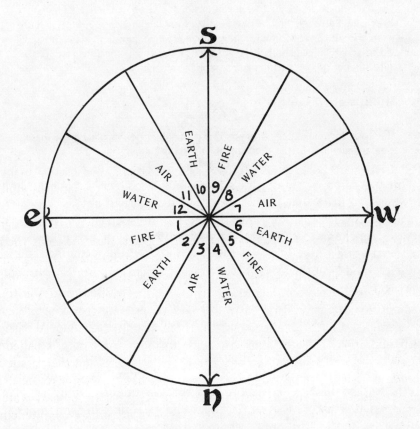

FIGURE 3. The triplicities

according to their *preferred mode of functioning*. People who function primarily by thinking are *thinking types;* people who function primarily through their present sense orientation are *sensation types*. Likewise, people who prefer to function by relying on their intuition are *intuitive types*, and people who function primarily according to their emotional evaluation of everything that happens to them are *feeling types.* [1]

The relationship of Jung's four functions of personality* to the process of individuation—a process better known today as self-actualization—has been recapitulated as follows:

---

*How Jung arrived at his functional types, and their astrological-alchemical significances, is dealt with at length in Appendix 1, "Carl Jung and the Philosopher's Stone."

If the four functions are placed equidistant from each other on the circumference of a circle, the center of the circle represents the synthesis of the four fully differentiated functions. In such a synthesis there are no superior or inferior functions and no auxiliaries. They are all of equal strength in the personality. Such a synthesis can only occur when the self has become fully actualized. Since complete actualization of the self is impossible, the synthesis of the four functions represents an ideal goal towards which the personality strives.[2]

Or, as Jung himself said:

The four functions are somewhat like the four points of the compass; they are just as arbitrary and just as indispensable.[3]

It was apparent that Jung's functional typology had impressed his colleagues so little that Dr. White either disregarded or was unaware of it. Part of the reason was Jung's interest in mysticism, which made his theories repellent to many scientists.[4] But a major reason has always been that Jung's psychological types were based upon his own clinical findings and mythical sources rather than upon experimental investigation.[5]

Until now. A recent issue of *Psychology Today* featured an article entitled "Four Types of Personality and Four Ways of Perceiving Time." The three authors, whose credentials combine expertise in psychology, sociology, neurology and psychiatry, reported their efforts to devise experiments aimed at testing Jung's typology and developing its theoretical base. On the premise that an understanding of Man's temperospatial nature is essential to an understanding of human personality—itself a thought oddly evocative of astrological principles—the three scientists approached the problem by testing for differences in the ways their experimental subjects perceived time.[6] The report of their results makes fascinating reading for anyone interested in contemporary psychology *or* astrology:

There are four realities—the thinking reality of process and ideas, the feeling reality of memories and emotions, the sensation reality of immediacy and concreteness and the intuitive reality of anticipation and visions.[7]

The tests also show the characteristic time and space orientation of each type. From the analysis of their data, the scientists concluded that Jung's functional personality types were indeed empirically valid. I agree, but for a somewhat different reason. I was summarizing this article for an attorney friend when I saw that the temperospatial orientation used in testing Jung's personality types placed his functional typology in its true context.

Jake (a pseudonym) was a classmate of mine in law school. On weekdays, he is an aggressive and extremely capable attorney. But on weekends, more often than not, he rides his prize-winning chopper with the Iron Horsemen or the Hell's Angels. There is another side to his personality which would surprise anyone who knew him only as an attorney or heavy-duty biker. That side was in evidence one Sunday when my wife and I were enjoying a leisurely brunch at his carriage house.

Jake's home had actually been a carriage house once; and the double doors of the entrance still swing wide to admit horse and carriage alike. The wood is time-darkened well beyond its original stain. From the rickety and shattered gate leading in from the street, it is an unprepossessing affair. What he has made of it, however, is something else again. Shag carpeting softens the interior in a muted terra cotta throughout, and the furnishings are an intriguing mixture of Danish contemporary and counterculture artifacts.

The muted strains of Sir Henry Purcell created an ambience of elegant contentment for our luncheon conversation. Jake's lovely blond girlfriend eyed us languidly as I expounded on the *Psychology Today* article. And Jake passed a platter of his home-made biscuits.

"They related Jung's personality types to the way people perceive time," I remember saying. "For the thinking type, time flows from the historical past in a linear way to the present. For the feeling type, on the other hand, time is circular. He evaluates events in terms of how they will appear in retrospect, more than how they affect the present. Everything that happens to him is assessed for its value as a memory, as a recollection—"

"But that's the way I am!" Jake interrupted. "Haven't I ever told you how I feel about life?" He spoke with great feeling. "I could die today, riding my bike. I realize that. So my life is always going to be the value I place on everything that has happened to me. I live in the past—and for the past."

I stared at him as he spoke. My wife, Nola, had erected Jake's chart and declared that he was first, last and always a Cancer. That had startled me at first, because of Jake's *machismo* style. But now, hearing his views on life in the warm atmosphere of his home, I could see that she was right. . . .

It was then that the light bulb went on. There it was: Jake was dramatizing the point. For me at least and now, I hope, for you, the triplicities and the Jungian personality types had merged. What had flashed upon my field of inner vision was a circle showing not Jung's four functions but the *cardinal* astrological sign associated with the *cardinal* compass direction and the appropriate element by triplicity. The result? You have it in figure three. Aries is cardinal fire, Capricorn is cardinal earth, Libra is cardinal air and Cancer is cardinal water. So Jung's types were drawn from the combined astrological and humoral concepts which produced the triplicities.

Jake is an example of what I mean. In terms of astrological types, Jake is a Cancer and thus is in the triplicity of water signs, which includes Cancer, Scorpio and Pisces. In the typology of the four humors, drawn from the four elements of alchemy, the water triplicity corresponds to the watery humor called *phlegm.* And Jake's Cancerian personality might indeed be described as phlegmatic. According to the astrological literature, individuals such as Jake, whose sign emphasis places them in the water triplicity, are characterized by an emotional, *feeling* orientation to life. That astrological datum dovetails with the results of the time-perception tests, which show that Jung's feeling type assesses everything that happens to him in terms of his emotional response, and lives in and for the past, reordering his world as a treasure chest of favored memories, as does anyone who falls within the water triplicity.

All of these associations—astrological, humoral, psychological and temperospatial—fit Jake precisely!

What then, I wondered, of Jung's other functional types? Did they correspond to specific astrological triplicities as well? Armed with the excitement of discovery and the time-perception test results, I pursued this question. Here are my conclusions:

The *thinking type* corresponds to the fire triplicity and the choleric humor with a linear orientation to time and space. A native of this type and triplicity must connect past, present and future to establish a persistent cause-and-effect relationship between time past, time present and time future.

The *sensation type* corresponds to the earth triplicity and the melancholy or bilious humor, with a time and space orientation to the present. A native of this type and triplicity lives in the eternal NOW.

The *intuitive type* corresponds to the air triplicity and the sanguinary humor, with a time and space orientation to future time. A native of this type and triplicity lives in the future.

This discovery meant a very different book from the one I had started out to write. The astrological basis of Jung's functional types, placed in the context of the applicable temperospatial orientation, provides the contemporary astrologer with new tools whose scope can at present only be guessed at. With the use of these tools, for example, the contemporary astrologer has new access to a literary tradition of enormous proportions in which the elemental characterology of the astrologer and the humoral characterology of the alchemist have been interwoven for millennia.*

NO LESS A writer than Shakespeare relied on the humors as a basis for the delineation of character, as Professor John W. Draper has demonstrated in *The Humors and Shakespeare's Characters.*

Hamlet was a *melancholy* Dane because of his preponderance of the black *bile,* the melancholy earth humor, which rooted him indecisively to the present, and which made him unable to overcome his inertia to find appropriate outlet for his rage. Depression, we are told today, is rage turned inward, against the self. Historically, such moods of depression have been described as the *black melancholia,* referencing both the humor and the color of the earth element with which it is associated.

The element *fire* translates into the humor of *choler* and Laertes, the brother of Ophelia and the slayer of Hamlet, is seen as both fiery and choleric.[8]

Some thirty-five references to the word "star" have been noted, in the context of influencing human fortune, and forty-six to "humor" in the sense of a cast of mind.[9] Shakespeare demonstrably viewed the psychology of each humor as the matter of chief importance, and knew the astrological reference as well. Thus, the "choleric man under Mars was violent" and the "phlegmatic type under Venus was luxurious . . ."[10]

Chaucer used the humors to define his characters; and that eccentric bachelor, Robert Burton, analyzed the humors in *The Anatomy of Melancholy.* Interestingly enough, Floyd Dell has observed in his introduction that

> Translated into modern terminology, Burton's title, The Anatomy of Melancholy, would read, An Analysis of Morbid Psychology. Burton was, indeed, a scholarly and humanistic precursor of Freud.[11]

---

*There is also a remarkable parallel between the triplicities, the Jungian personality types, and the four masks described in William B. Yeats' *A Vision*, which I noticed too late to include in the text. However, the reader may find Yeats' description of the masks helpful for a better understanding of the triplicities as well as Yeats' later poetry.

The very terms for the humors corresponding to the elements of astrology/alchemy have entered the language as characterological descriptions. Too much of any one humor made for dominance of that humor's characteristics, according to Galen, who developed the ancient humoral theory of medicine from Aristotle's four elements. [12] Someone was choleric if he had too much of the fiery yellow humor of choler, which produced a characteristic intellectual arrogance, and a jaundiced view of life. He was sanguine if the airy red humor of the blood predominated, and the sanguinary individual saw life through rose-colored glasses. If he was bilious or melancholy, his earthy black humor of bile was overactive, and he took a dark view of things. Phlegmatic types had too much of that watery white humor, phlegm. Such people were pale and rheumy; and rheum is synonymous with phlegm.

Now let's place these traditional concepts in their contemporary context.

Fire. For the thinking or fire type of personality, time is linear, and there must be a precise connection for any event from the detached, historical past to the present and to the future. The fiery thinking type simply cannot consider events without considering their cause. He lives according to principle. He wants to make up his mind and arrive at conclusions before he acts.

The Age of Science started with René Descartes and his conception of cause and effect related to a linear one-way time. To Descartes more than to any other individual we owe the bias of the past five centuries of Western rationalism with its mechanistic model of the universe. It is therefore exciting to the contemporary astrologer to discover that Descartes was not only an Aries by Sun sign but also that he had a stellium of three planets in that fire sign—making him a thinking time-linear type indeed.

Earth. For the sensation or earth type of personality, the time is always the present, and no effort is made to integrate past experience and present action. Reality is what is happening NOW and the sensation type has perfected his skills in perceiving that reality in depth. He acts in response to the stimuli of the present, without the forethought of the thinking type, and without the subjective evaluation of the feeling type. The earthy sensation type neither remembers nor anticipates, but senses fully the immediate present—which, after all, is always there. Falstaff was a sensation type—but then Shakespeare was himself a Taurus.

Air. For the intuitive or air type, the future is where he lives; and what will happen is more real than what is happening now. The intuitive type lives beyond the last mountain and spends his life trying to get there; but there is always another mountain. To the other personality types, the airy intuitive type appears flighty and impractical. To him, other people are frustrating, since he often finds himself waiting for events he has anticipated to catch up with them.

The airy intuitive type tends to skip rapidly from one project to another, abandoning one goal to follow the inspiration of the next, frequently letting the more Earth-bound type reap the harvest of that projective vision. Intuitive types find it hard to keep to a schedule, impossible to be punctual and frequently don't know what day it is. After all, *their* time is always tomorrow. Jules Verne, the Aquarian science-fiction writer, was an intuitive type; as is Jean-Paul Sartre, whose existentialist philosophy postulates that Man is prospective: Man can never be defined because he defines himself by the things he does and those things lie as much in the future as in the past.

Water. For the watery feeling type of personality, the experiments in time perception revealed that such persons conceive of time as circular, because their emotional past is all-important. They care little for what is unique in the present, and avoid decisions which would require a break with the past. They evaluate each event of life from the standpoint of how it will fit into their emotional past, rather than according to its present or even future effect. For this reason, feeling types assess with considerable skill the emotional tone of any event. Marcel Proust was a feeling type with a stellium of four planets in Cancer.

ASTROLOGY AND ALCHEMY have been two faces of the same coin throughout history. According to an ancient creation myth, God's right hand took a grain of dust from the whole world, a drop of water from all the waters of the universe, a little wind from all the air and a little warmth from all the fire. From these four elements God created Adam.[13] This ancient myth of Man's origins unites both alchemical and astrological conceptions; the cardinal compass points which correspond to the cardinal signs of the zodiac—Aries, Capricorn, Libra and Cancer—and the four elements of fire, earth, air and water to which these signs likewise correspond. Hermetically or mythically, the idea is the same: Man is the microcosm of the universal whole. It is an enduring concept.

The signs Aries, Leo and Sagittarius constitute the *fire triplicity*, in which intellectually compelled acts of will predominate.

The signs Taurus, Virgo and Capricorn are the *earth triplicity*, in which actions in response to present sense perceptions predominate.

The signs Gemini, Libra and Aquarius are the *air triplicity,* in which intuition and conjecture predominate.

The signs Cancer, Scorpio and Pisces are the *water triplicity,* in which feeling predominates.

The elements repeat themselves three times through the sequence of the signs, from Aries through Pisces, in the same order of fire, earth, air, water. These repetitions are required because each sign expresses its elemental characteristics differently, according to the character of the zodiacal archetype. In the fire triplicity, Aries tends to express its fiery mental energy in an egocentric, willful way; Leo in terms of showmanship or leadership and Sagittarius in terms of ideals and philosophy.

In the earth triplicity, Taurus expresses its sense-oriented qualities with more stolidity and inertia than Virgo; and Virgo shows its earth orientation by its meticulous sifting of the material present. For Capricorn, the elemental qualities are felt with both feet firmly on the ground because that is how he wants to see himself and to be seen by others.

In the air triplicity, Geminian intuition is so volatile that Gemini natives are sometimes accused of having a grasshopper mind. Libra, on the other hand, applies his intuition judiciously and equivocally, with considerable insight into interpersonal relationships. Aquarian intuition and conjecture lean toward politics, science and humanitarian goals. In the water triplicity, Cancerian feeling is directed toward nurture, Scorpio feeling to passionate commitment and Piscean feeling to his internal vision.

Planets posited in the same triplicity are often just about 120 degrees apart. This is called a trine (triangular) aspect, a geometric configuration which, when it occurs, emphasizes the elemental qualities of that triplicity.

JUNG'S FUNCTIONAL PERSONALITY types and the elemental triplicities have a common source in astrology; of that we are certain. Since all the signs are present in every horoscope, all the sign triplicities are represented. The questions are how and in what degree. We look to the positions of the planets in each chart to determine which triplicities predominate.

In the box scores at the bottom of every complete horoscope in this book, there are blanks in which the *number* of planets posited in each of the triplicities has been entered. From these data, the preferred and auxiliary modes of functioning can readily be ascertained, as well as how those elemental attitudes might be manifested through the planets. As an example, consider the following box scores:

Number	Element	Glyphs
5	Fire:	Sun, Moon, Mars, Uranus, Jupiter
4	Earth:	Mercury, Venus, Saturn, Neptune
2	Air:	Ascendant, Midheaven
1	Water:	Pluto

This breakdown shows the native as primarily a fiery thinking type, with five placements in that triplicity, including the all-important Sun and Moon. Anyone with that strong a fire emphasis will almost certainly have a passionate state of mind, subject to the vice of choler, and an overemphasis on intellectually compelled actions to the detriment of a healthy overall perspective.

With four earth placements, and a stellium of three planets in Capricorn, this native's auxiliary function is sensation, which roots him in present reality. His ambitious and critical Capricorn emphasis, coupled with a primary fire emphasis, directs his energies to career achievement, criticism of himself and therefore of others and especially intolerance of the impractical, the esoteric, the fanciful—not to mention anyone who dares to disagree with him!

There are only two placements in the air triplicity of signs, but they include the vital Ascendant and Midheaven. With Gemini on the Ascendant and Aquarius at the Midheaven of the natal chart, this native's personality and his professional attitudes are both characterized by an interest in the next, the new, the promised. The fiery will is catalyzed by the air of intuition and the native's choleric impatience with what he conceives to be the limitations of others will worsen if he is harnessed to unimaginative or repetitive tasks. He may be able to do anything once—but nothing twice.

There is but one placement in the water triplicity, and that in slow-moving Pluto, whose precise significance is still a matter of some conjecture. This singleton Pluto in Cancer reflects a definite lack of *feeling* orientation to life situations on the part of the native. While someone with a strong water emphasis will assess with exactitude the emotional, feeling value of a situation, this native is more than likely to blunder in his interpersonal relationships not only because of his lack of emphasis in the water triplicity but also because his principal fire emphasis is a stellium in the brash and outspoken sign of Sagittarius. His auxiliary earth emphasis may provide some balance, with a stellium in socially conscious Capricorn.

These box scores are taken from my chart (see fig. 13); the personality limitations are, regrettably, all too true—vindicating both the Jungian and the astrological types.

That's how it works. There are many more considerations to be dealt with before we are ready to interpret any horoscope. Still, with a proper comprehension of the triplicities, the reader has taken that important first step in considering the *total* personality of the native beyond his Sun sign alone.

8 What Are the Quadruplicities?

ALL OF US who enjoy fine wine owe a debt to dom Perignon, the spritely monk who was the cellarer during the seventeenth century of the Benedictine Abbey of Hautvillers near Epernay in France. Legend has it that it was the good dom who first took advantage of the phenomenon which is the subject of this chapter.

Many vintners had noticed the strange behavior of certain wines which turned effervescent—the French word is *petillant*—every year at the vernal equinox. One wine connoisseur of no known esoteric propensity remarked that it is almost as if these wines underwent "a primordial reawakening." It was in the seventeenth century that these *petillant* wines achieved a great vogue in England and attracted the venal interest of the French wine makers. They discovered that their wine only retained its bubbly quality if bottled during the first period of its mysterious reawakening, ideally during the first full moon of March—the period which most closely corresponded to the vernal equinox.

Obviously this phenomenon was a gift from God that Man should make good use of, and dom Perignon did just that. He experimented endlessly to discover the best varietal grapes of his district to make the best blends to produce the mysterious effervescence. Because strong bottles and stronger stoppers were needed to preserve these effects, the good dom invented the cork, the glass bottle—and of course the sparkling champagne with which the Epernay region is now identified. Thus the "primordial reawakening" which makes wine effervesce at the vernal equinox resulted in the champagne region of France, and the best champagne is still that honored ·with the name of its creator—*dom Perignon*.

Only recently has science acknowledged the existence of certain *Zeitgebers* or time-triggers which initiate certain cycles in life activity. Studies of biological rhythms show that geomagnetic forces from the

Earth, Sun and Moon act as such triggers in Man, the master biological clock.[1]

The principal *Zeitgebers,* in addition to the vernal equinox, are the summer solstice, the autumnal equinox and the winter solstice. These seasonal points of relationship between Sun and Earth correspond to zero degrees of Aries, Cancer, Libra and Capricorn. They are also our cardinal compass directions of east, north, west and south respectively. Rameses II fixed these positions as the key points of the heavens in what are now known as the *cardinal signs.*[2] "Cardinal," derived from a Latin word meaning hinge or to hinge upon, is appropriate enough for the signs which are the time-triggers or hinges of the zodiac.

As we have seen in earlier chapters, the equinoxes and the solstices were recognized for their mysterious vital force before the recorded history of Man. Indeed, the zodiac has been revised several times to keep the cardinal signs coincident with these time-triggers.

THE GROUPS OF signs now under consideration divide the zodiac into categories of *four* signs each. Because there are four signs in each set, these groups are called the *quad*ruplicities. Remember that it all adds up to twelve: three sets of *four* signs are the quadruplicities; four sets of *three* signs are the triplicities. Don't be confused by the number of sets; the number of signs in each set will help you remember whether it's a quadruplicity or a triplicity you're dealing with.

The quadruplicities divide the zodiac into cardinal, fixed and mutable signs in the sequence of the natural zodiac:

1. Aries: cardinal
2. Taurus: fixed
3. Gemini: mutable

7. Libra: cardinal
8. Scorpio: fixed
9. Sagittarius: mutable

4. Cancer: cardinal
5. Leo: fixed
6. Virgo: mutable

10. Capricorn: cardinal
11. Aquarius: fixed
12. Pisces: mutable

Note that each sign has the same quadruplicity as its polar opposite: e.g., Aries is a cardinal sign and its polar opposite, Libra, is also a cardinal sign. This was *not* true of the opposing signs in the triplicities.

The concept of the quadruplicities is simple enough. The horoscope is divided into twelve sections or houses; the points between the houses are called cusps and the first house of the horoscope commences at the point on the left-hand side of the circle marked east.

The cardinal signs are Aries, Cancer, Libra and Capricorn. These signs appear at the east, north, west and south points of the horoscope in the natural zodiac (see fig. 4). These points are also the first, fourth, seventh and tenth house cusps. In the natural zodiac, they are always Aries, Cancer, Libra and Capricorn.

The natural zodiac is based on the solar year commencing with the vernal equinox, the point on the ecliptic intersected by the celestial equator each spring. That point is always zero degrees Aries on the celestial sphere and cardinal east on the compass. Zero degrees Cancer

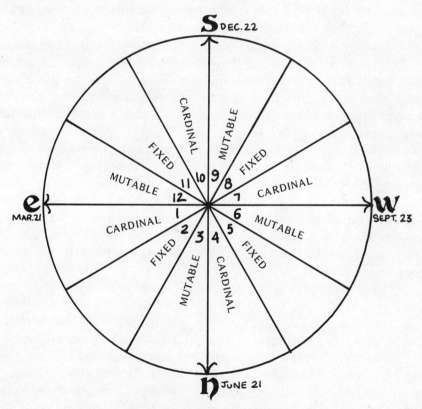

FIGURE 4. The quadruplicities

marks both the summer solstice and cardinal north. Zero degrees Libra is both cardinal west and the point of the autumnal equinox. Zero degrees Capricorn is cardinal south and the winter solstice.

The other groupings in the quadruplicities are the *fixed* and the *mutable* signs.

The quadruplicity system of sign division deals with the characteristics of the signs with regard to *action* or *change*. In the cardinal signs, action or change is initiated. In the fixed signs, change is resisted or integrated. The mutable signs are most adaptable to change.

A word of caution: some texts and even some chart forms still refer to cardinal signs as movable signs. This usage probably arose because movable means varying from year to year, as in fact the equinoxes do. However, the term is a most unfortunate synonym for the cardinal signs, since it is so easy to confuse with the term "mutable signs"—which are the antithesis of cardinal signs.

The fixed signs, Taurus, Leo, Scorpio and Aquarius, are characterized by their resistance to change—their inertia. This same fixity does have the attribute of stability, and natives with fixed sign placements predominating are the persons you look for to follow through on a project which someone else—presumably a native with cardinal sign emphasis—has already commenced.

Mutable signs are Gemini, Virgo, Sagittarius and Pisces. They are identified by their adaptability to change, as the term "mutable," meaning changeable, suggests.

"Common signs" is sometimes used for the mutable signs, in an archaic sense of the word "common," meaning obliging service. You should know the term if you run into it, but I would advise against using it because of the negative connotation which has driven it from popular usage.

The sequence of cardinal, fixed and mutable signs, each series commencing with either an equinox or a solstice, tells us that when the Sun enters a sign at a change of season, that sign will itself be characterized as an initiator of change. Thus, when the vernal equinox marks the first day of spring, the Sun enters Aries; the sign therefore signifies change. The Sun leaves Aries to enter Taurus, without a change of season or other phenomena; the changes signalled by Aries are integrated, and things stay pretty much the same. Taurus is a fixed sign.

When the Sun enters Gemini in late May, changes is in the air; there are perceptible seasonal changes, summer is not far away. Gemini is therefore a mutable sign, adaptable to the changes already on their way. The summer solstice arrives: the Sun stands still in the sky before commencing its return course in the ecliptic, and it's the first day of summer—and of Cancer. Cancer is therefore a cardinal sign, identified with change.

Just as the four elements of nature were found to have their correspondences in Man, the microcosm, so the early astrologers found correspondences between Man and the heavens through the characterization of the signs of the zodiac. Those correspondences, newly explained in terms of biorhythms and circadian cycles, remain as valid today.

How each sign manifests its particular characteristics with regard to change is best shown by example.

The Train and the Tunnel

Problem: A railroad track is being laid but a mountain is in the way. Should the track be laid around the mountain, or should a tunnel be cut straight through?

Aries: "We're putting a train straight through the mountain without delay!"

Taurus: "I wasn't hired to handle explosives, and I'm not properly equipped to do it. And I'm not getting paid enough if there's going to be danger."

Gemini: "Sounds interesting. Even if we have to fork around the mountain later because of cave-ins, I can just change the plans around."

The Paint and the Bedstead

Cancer father: "I've decided to paint Johnny's bedstead tomorrow."

Leo son: "I want it painted gold. I'll show you how!"

Virgo mother: "I don't care who does it, but do it outside and don't track paint in the house."

Each sign manifests itself in terms of the intrinsic characteristics of the sign and (1) the element of the sign, according to its triplicity; (2) the attitude toward change of the sign, according to its quadruplicity.

In the first example, Aries is cardinal fire. There are other cardinal signs and other fire signs, but there is only *one* cardinal fire and that's Aries. The Aries native would be the most likely to make the sudden, decisive judgment—and plunge straight through the mountain.

Taurus is fixed earth. He may be a slow starter, but once he starts, he's good for six months—especially if he's well paid.

Gemini is mutable air. You just don't get more volatile than that. Sure, he can rewrite the plans if a cave-in makes it necessary to do so. But watch out! He might also decide to reroute the tunnel simply to rekindle his interest in the project.

In the second illustration, Cancer is cardinal water. The Cancer father will initiate actions in areas most likely to be related to the protective, nurturing qualities of his sign.

Leo is a fixed fire sign, so the Leo son displays his majesterial qualities and his fixity by taking over the project initiated by someone else—and by demanding gold paint!

Mother is a Virgo, a mutable earth sign. So long as no mess is made (Virgo), she will go along with either of them (mutable), after sifting present realities (earth) and finding the project more or less practical.

THE TRIPLICITIES AND the quadruplicities are two systems of categorizing signs which assist the astrologer in interpretation. The triplicities provide information about how the native functions, according to Carl Jung's functional personality types. The quadruplicities provide information about the native's attitudes toward change and action. These considerations are inherent in each of the archetypes of the zodiacal signs. They may be summarized as follows:

1. Aries: cardinal fire. A cardinal sign, Aries pioneers; a fire sign, Aries functions by thinking—often impulsive and willful thinking—according to its archetype.

2. Taurus: fixed earth. A fixed sign, Taurus carries out the program already initiated and is slow to change; an earth sign, Taurus functions by reaction—particularly to his sense perceptions of the ever-present NOW.

3. Gemini: mutable air. A mutable sign, Gemini adapts readily to new programs; an air sign, Gemini is alert to the manifold possibilities in any situation.

4. Cancer: cardinal water. A cardinal sign, Cancer initiates and protects; a water sign, Cancer functions through feelings.

5. Leo: fixed fire. A fixed sign, Leo holds on course rather than take a new tack; a fire sign, he functions by conscious will.

6. Virgo: mutable earth. A mutable sign, Virgo adapts readily to change; an earth sign, he functions methodically in present reality.

7. Libra: cardinal air. A cardinal sign, Libra leads primarily through his influence on others; an air sign, he relies on intuition.

8. Scorpio: fixed water. A fixed sign, Scorpio is slow to change once his mind is made up; a water sign, he functions through his feelings about things.

9. Sagittarius: mutable fire. A mutable sign, Sagittarius readily adapts to changes; a fire sign, he functions primarily through his intellect.

10. Capricorn: cardinal earth. A cardinal sign, Capricorn is a natural leader, and likes it; an earth sign, he functions through his material senses, both feet planted firmly on the ground.

11. Aquarius: fixed air. A fixed sign, Aquarius is better in following through than in taking the lead; an air sign, he functions best at the intuitive level of conjecture.

12. Pisces: mutable water. A mutable sign, Pisces readily adapts to change. A water sign, he functions primarily through his feelings, especially feelings of compassion for others—and for himself.

9 What Is the Zodiac?

WHEN ASKED THE question, "What's your sign?" Dr. Zipporah Dobyns, a famous astrologer, pertly replies, "I have all the signs in my chart. What is it you want to know?"

Her point is well taken. For example, I do not consider myself just a Sagittarian, although that is my Sun sign; after all, I have Gemini on the Ascendant, and my wife tells me that I am hopelessly Geminian. My natal Moon position is also Sagittarian, but I have many placements in Capricorn—and Aquarius on the meridian of my birthplace, my Midheaven. However, the positions of the Sun, Moon, Ascendant and Midheaven, critically important as they are, are just the beginning.

I believe the first step to understanding the signs of the zodiac is the recognition that every human being has all twelve of these archetypal qualities functioning in some way in his natal horoscope. Some signs may be emphasized by the position of the Sun, Moon or the planets; another sign gains significance by its appearance on the natal horizon and one more sign may be speared on the cusp of the individual's natal meridian, or Midheaven.

If this is so, why do we ask each other what our "sign" is, intending only to inquire about the zodiacal position of the Sun at our birth?

The doubtful credit for this phenomenon should probably go to Paul Clancy, founder of *American Astrology* magazine. Clancy developed the device of preparing a general statement for each day of the month, keyed to the native's Sun-sign position only. This statement was based on the *transits,* or daily movements, of the Sun through the zodiac, and its possible influence on a native according to the native's own Sun-sign position. This kind of astrological analysis is indeed attenuated.

However, Sun-sign astrology has certain practical advantages. From the standpoint of the heavy competition for every inch of print space and the short attention span of the public, such vague, simplistic predictions are ideally suited to newspaper columns. Although such columns are probably harmless, they do a disservice to people who might find the subject matter interesting and worthy of study but who are turned away by vague and general analyses that could apply to anyone.

IN ORDER TO have a basic understanding of the zodiac so that you will be able to make your own interpretation of the positions of the planets and the house cusps, we should briefly consider a few celestial mechanics and terms.

The celestial sphere is a three-dimensional map of the heavens used *by astronomers* as a practical guide in locating the positions of the stars and planets. (In astrological parlance "planet" is a generic term often used to include the Sun and the Moon as well as those bodies we commonly refer to as planets.) Note that the celestial sphere pinpoints the planets' positions from the perspective of an Earth-centered universe.

To early astronomer-astrologers, the sky at night appeared to be a huge blue black dome, with one hemisphere at the rim of the visible horizon connected to the rim of another, similar hemisphere underneath the horizon. They connected these two imaginary hemispheres to create the celestial sphere, in the perspective of the heavens as a globe with the Earth at the center, and all of the stars and planets attached to the circumference.

Some time ago I purchased a celestial sphere in order to better understand some basic astrological—and astronomical—concepts. Rand-McNally makes the *Starfinder* celestial globe, which I find useful. Let us imagine that we are looking at such a celestial globe (see fig. 5). Remember that conceptually, the Earth is *on the inside*, at the center of the globe.

Notice the outside ring mounted to the stand around the center of the globe with the word "North" printed on it between the words "Taurus" and "Gemini." This is the *horizon ring*, which can be turned up or down to orient the globe in terms of your horizon. On the particular celestial globe that I am describing, the horizon ring also shows the zodiacal signs in their proper sequence of Aries through Pisces.

On the blue surface of the globe itself, as illustrated in figure five, you will see many constellations, including most or all of the ones visible to you at night. The stars in the constellations are linked by

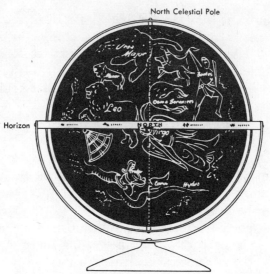

FIGURE 5. Celestial globe showing constellations
© Rand McNally & Company, R. L. 73-S-8

imaginary lines. For example, Taurus is show in the shape of a bull's head with the star Aldebaran as the bull's eye.

If you spin the globe from left to right, so that the constellation Pisces is in front of you, and then turn the globe slightly above the horizon ring, you will see that three scales printed on the globe intersect (see fig. 6).

One such scale, more or less parallel with the horizon ring, is labeled *Celestial Equator.* The celestial equator is the equator of the Earth projected outward from the Earth onto the celestial sphere. As you can see in figure six, the celestial equator measures distances eastward in hours and minutes from the point at which all three scales intersect. Thus zero on the scale of the celestial equator is both zero hours and twenty-four hours.

The *Declination Scale,* a vertical line, measures degrees north and south of the celestial equator, similar to degrees of latitude on an Earth globe.

Finally, the *Ecliptic* is a diagonal line intersecting the celestial equator and the declination scale. The scale on the ecliptic shows the position of the Sun in terms of degrees from 1 to 30 and in terms of the 12 signs of the zodiac. The ecliptic scale is a circle of 360 degrees shown in 12 units of 30 degrees each. To find the Sun's position on the ecliptic scale, we must know the sign and the degree of that sign.

Look again at the point at which all three scales intersect, shown in figure six. Notice that the scale on the celestial equator is identified

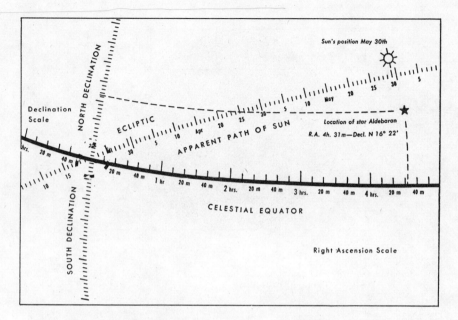

FIGURE 6. Diagram showing right ascension, declination, and ecliptic scales
© Rand McNally & Company, R. L. 73-S-8

as the *Right Ascension Scale.* The scale of the celestial equator pin-points planetary positions *to the right* of the intersecting point of the ecliptic scale: the right ascension scale shows the hours and minutes that a star or planet has apparently *ascended* above and *to the right of* the celestial equator.

EXAMINE THE DIAGRAM shown in figure six. The measurement of the right ascension scale is illustrated in terms of the location of the star Aldebaran, which, on May 30, is 4 hours and 31 minutes of right ascension, according to the scale on the celestial equator.

At this point, line up the horizon ring with the celestial equator so that the beginning of the sign Aries on the horizon ring matches the point of intersection of the ecliptic scale with the celestial equator. *It is then evident that on May 30 the Sun is in the sign Gemini according to the zodiac imprinted on the horizon ring; but the ecliptic scale clearly locates the Sun in the constellation Taurus, very close to Aldebaran, the bull's-eye star, on May 30!*

The key to the riddle may be found in the meaning of the name "Aldebaran," which is derived from two Arabic words meaning the Follower.[1] Before this most interesting star in the constellation Pleiades became generally known by its Arabic name, it was known as Aleph to

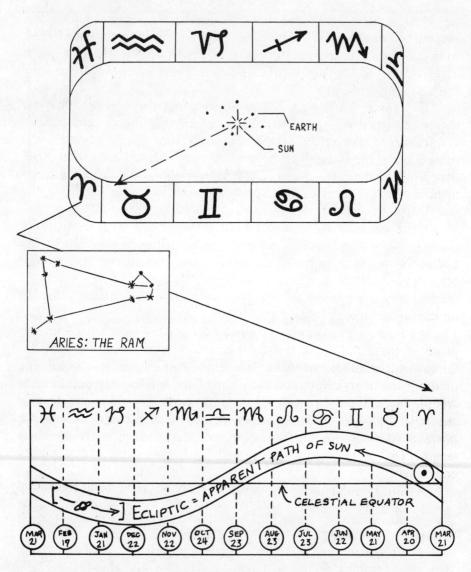

FIGURE 7. The origins of the zodiac

This figure shows how ancient astrologers saw the constellations in the apparent path of the Sun's travel throughout the year and visualized them in the configurations we recognize as the signs of the zodiac. Above is the solar system against the background of the constellations, with the sun posited in Aries from an Earth perspective. Below is the ecliptic, which rises above and falls below the celestial equator (the Earth's equator projected onto the heavens). The reason for the difference in the ecliptic and equatorial planets is shown in figure eight.

the Hebrew astrologer-prophets, and marked the vernal equinox and became synonymous with it. Since our ancestors commenced their zodiac and their year with the vernal equinox, Aleph became the first letter of one of Mankind's first alphabets, from which we derived the zodiacal sign Aries.

But about 2,300 B.C.E. it was noticed that the bull's-eye star no longer coincided with the vernal equinox, due to a phenomenon known as precession, the retreat of the equinoxes through the zodiac. As a consequence, the Hebrew astrologers adjusted the zodiac to show Aries the Ram as the constellation with which the vernal equinox commenced. Since Taurus (with its bull's eye Aleph) followed Aries, the star "Aleph" became better known as "Aldebaran," the Follower.

What causes the phenomenon of precession? Figure seven shows the ecliptic or the apparent path of the Sun through the signs of the zodiac. Notice that the ecliptic makes a wavy line through the celestial equator so that the equinoctial points of March 21 and September 23 are the only times when the ecliptic path and the celestial equator are on the same plane.

As figure eight shows, the reason for the difference between the plane of the ecliptic and the plane of the celestial equator is that the Earth is tilted about twenty-three and one-half degrees on its axis out of the plane of its orbit. This tilt is the reason why our days and nights are of unequal duration except on the vernal equinox, and on the autumnal equinox. On those dates, the plane of the ecliptic and the plane of the equator are the same, and day and night are of equal length. The term "equinox," derived from two Latin words, means equal night.

As the Earth spins on its axis, the forces of the Sun and the Moon

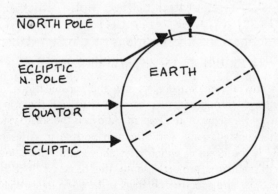

FIGURE 8. Earth's tilt on axis

cause it to move in a cone-shaped arc in space. This slow movement of the Earth in an arc along its axis of rotation is *precession*, a noun formed from the verb to precede. This precession or change of axis results in a slow change of the frame of reference of the background of stars about every twenty-one hundred years. That change is most dramatically seen in terms of the vernal equinox, which from our prehistory has always been the first day of spring and the commencement of the zodiac. That is why some five thousand years ago Aldebaran was the star in the constellation Taurus, which coincided with the vernal equinox and also why some twenty-six hundred years later the vernal equinox coincided with a point in Aries. For the same reason, the constellation Pisces is seen today against the vernal equinox. Actually, we have been moving out of the constellation Pisces for some time now, inching into the constellation Aquarius.

Remember, however, that the relationship of the plane of the celestial equator and the plane of the ecliptic always remains the same; only the background constellations are different. Indeed, the space-time continuum of the vernal equinox is regarded by astronomers as the only constant yet found in the universe. Even though the point of intersection of the vernal equinox does change at about fifty seconds on the right ascension scale a year, that change is itself a constant figure which makes the equinoxes a reliable and predictable frame of reference. For that reason astronomers adopted *sidereal time*, meaning time measured by the stars, and based it on the constancy of the vernal equinox.

The reason we talk about the Sun being in Gemini when, as we have seen, it is actually located in the constellation Taurus on, for example, May 30 of each year is that it was far easier for the ancient astronomer-astrologers to visualize three degrees of Gemini, which they could see in the night sky, than to attempt to deal with the total abstraction of sixty-three degrees of the ecliptic, which amounts to the same thing.

The ecliptic measures the positions of the Sun, Moon and planets on any given day of the year. The ecliptic does so on a scale of 360 degrees, divided into 12 units of 30 degrees each, with each unit labeled by a different zodiacal *sign*. Since the planets have varying speeds, they appear at different positions on the ecliptic with regard to the Sun, to the Earth and to each other.

Therefore, in order to erect an accurate horoscope, it is necessary to determine the exact positions for the Sun, Moon and each of the planets in the ecliptic at the precise moment of the birth of the individual whose horoscope is under consideration.

A WORD ABOUT the arguments of the sidereal astrologers, who believe that the original constellations should be the frame of reference for the zodiac, not the equinoxes and solstices.

In 1948 Irish astrologer Cyril Fagan examined the double zodiac which was originally inscribed in the Great Temple of Hathor, in Denderah, Egypt, and which was removed to the Louvre in 1821. He concluded that the constellations should be considered the basic frame of reference of the zodiac, and not the vernal equinox. So most of the principles followed by astrologers are wrong in that they are not the way the Egyptians used astrology two or three thousand years ago.

Some terms are important here, since the sidereal astrologers have their own zodiac and their own point of view. *Tropical* astrologers, the great majority, believe the equinoxes and the solstices—the *tropes* or turning points in the zodiac—are the basic frame of reference. *Sidereal* astrologers measure their zodiac by the constellations of stars, generally according to Fagan's interpretation of the zodiac-within-a-zodiac from Denderah.

The *tropical* zodiac is used in this book. The *sidereal* zodiac, reworked to match the signs with the constellations, is frequently used in *American Astrology* magazine, and can be a source of confusion if the reader doesn't know the zodiacal frame of reference.

What is the verdict on sidereal astrologers? My answer is that they have not made their case. There is no question about their integrity and their scholarship, but after having examined the evidence and having listened to the sometimes shrill arguments of Fagan, I remain unconvinced.

For one thing, the double zodiac at Denderah does not approach the evidentiary value of the adjustment of the zodiac made centuries before by the Hebrew astrologers, from whom the Egyptians learned. Indeed, the out-of-phase zodiacs of Denderah may reflect the Egyptians' recognition of the need to synchronize their zodiac to account for precession.

In any event, it is not really necessary to assume that the Egyptian or the Hebrew arrangement of the zodiac should be binding on the contemporary astrologer.

10   What Are the Planets?

ALTHOUGH THE ROMAN poet Manilius wrote about the planets and their characteristics at least a century and a half before Ptolemy wrote the first astrological treatise, *Tetrabiblos,* about 150 C.E., he "shows no great exactness in the astronomical part"[1] of his book. It remained for Claudius Ptolemy, the mathematician-astronomer who remains unique among the great synthesists of history in his willingness to credit his sources,[2] to produce the first known compendium of undisputed astrological scholarship.

With regard to the question of which planets ruled which signs, Ptolemy had an embarrassment of riches. Both the Egyptians and the Chaldeans had their own methods, and Ptolemy, conscientious scholar that he was, faulted both of them. But with the aid of "an ancient manuscript," Ptolemy devised his own system.[3]

Prior to the discovery of Uranus, Neptune and Pluto in recent times, the generally accepted attributions dating from classical antiquity were as follows:

1. Sun: Leo
2. Moon: Cancer
3. Mercury: Gemini and Virgo
4. Venus: Taurus and Libra
5. Mars: Aries and Scorpio
6. Jupiter: Sagittarius and Pisces
7. Saturn: Capricorn and Aquarius

These planetary rulerships date as far back as 2,000 B.C.E.[4] Note that with the exception of the luminaries, each planet originally ruled two signs. Now with Pluto as ruler of Scorpio, Uranus as ruler of Aquarius and Neptune as ruler of Pisces, secondary rulerships have been assigned to Mars, Saturn and Jupiter for Scorpio, Aquarius and Pisces, respectively. Only the planets Venus and Mercury continue to have unqualified rulership of two signs of the zodiac in contemporary astrology.

This historical context is important not only because the secondary rulerships are themselves a relevant factor in chart analysis but also because of the significance of the seven cycles represented by the seven traditional planets of antiquity. This significance is seen in both astrology and alchemy, and—necessarily—in the affairs of Man. Ptolemy recorded the seven ages of Man according to the sequence of the seven planetary spheres of astrological influences in *Tetrabiblos.*

The first age, Ptolemy tells us, is that of infancy, which is ruled by the Moon, and lasts four years. The second age is ruled by Mercury, to whom he allots ten years of childhood, a period in which Mercury "begins to articulate and fashion the intelligent and logical part of the soul . . ."[5]

Ptolemy's third age is eight years of youth ruled by Venus, which, Ptolemy recognizes in somewhat stilted language, "begins, as is natural, to inspire, at their maturity, an activity of the seminal passages and to implant an impulse toward the embrace of love."[6] The Sun itself rules what Ptolemy calls the middle sphere—the fourth age of early manhood—for the next nineteen years, or from age twenty-one to forty. This period is marked by "desire for substance, glory, and position, and a change . . . to seriousness, decorum, and ambition."[7]

Mars rules the fifth age of manhood, for the next fifteen years. The sixth age is ruled by Jupiter, governing the twelve elderly years. "Finally to Saturn falls as his lot old age, the latest period, which lasts for the rest of life."[8]

Although there are new planets which have justified some accommodations to the classical astrological scheme, the basic archetypal character of the planets is the same today as it was in Ptolemy's era.

THE GREEK PANTHEON was inherited by the Romans, who renamed the gods but without much independent development of their own. As received by astrology, these myths contained a heavy gloss of Orphic mysticism.

Although Orpheus is credited with the introduction of the worship of the fugitive god Dionysus in Greece, we don't know whether that legendary poet-priest ever lived. The events of his life closely parallel those of the Dionysus he worshipped; and certainly there is at least some element of poetic license in the story of his death, which relates how his severed head, tossed into the river, floated downstream, still singing. Orpheus means hidden, and I believe there is a message hidden in that myth as well.

From Orpheus we get *Orphism*, a unique brand of mysticism which combined Egyptian, Hebraic and the very earliest Christian beliefs. I anticipate that some readers may consider my mixing Old and New Testament myths with those of the Greeks, Romans and Orphics less than pious. My view is that it is just the reverse, for I believe that *all* true myths are Scripture when understood for their universal wisdom; and here, their universality is of far greater significance than their national origin.

Most myths began with the germ of an actual event; either a memorable incident of local political history, such as Theseus's acquisition of power, or a striking celestial phenomenon, such as the perturbations of the Sun which were retold as Phaethon's loss of control of the heavenly chariot. In the telling and retelling of the myths thus generated, a remarkable shaping process occurred. The historical or phenomenal event which gave rise to the myth was refined in what Joyce might call the smithy of the soul and Jung would call the collective unconscious. Jung could well have had the myth-making process in mind when he wrote that

> it is the function of consciousness not only to recognize and assimilate
> the external world through the gateway of the senses, but to translate
> into visible reality the world within us.[9]

I think that is what the making and refining of myth is all about, so that what we received in terms of our cultural inheritance was free of the incidental dross of the original event in the pure gold of true myth.

Nor is the association of Greek gods to the planets without respectable precedent. According to Rupert Gleadow, no less an authority than Plato proposed, in later life, that reverence for the pantheon of the twelve major Greek gods be replaced by the twelve signs of the zodiac.[10] With the planetary rulership of the signs, we have a proper appreciation of both.

ALL OF THE planetary glyphs have been identified for the reader in figure nine. The glyph used by astrologers to represent the Sun is called the Orphic Egg. This circle with the central dot is the basic symbol of the Orphic world-view. According to the Orphics, before the world began there was an eternal NOW of Unaging Time. Despite the diversity that was to come, it was this God-beyond-God of universal consciousness that the Orphics, Hindus and Hebrew mystics worshipped in a genuinely monotheistic sense.

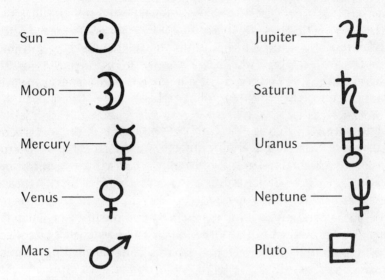

FIGURE 9. Planetary glyphs

This universal consciousness was an undifferentiated wholeness, a *One*—or, in other words, a *monad*. What followed was a *dyad:* the two polar opposites of Ether and Chaos. The whirling Ether, suggested by the Sun's courses, enclosed and gave form to Chaos, spinning off the four elements from its own essence, and shaping the cosmic egg within its coils. This world egg was personified by the feminine Moon; from the silver egg of the Moon hatched the Orphic god Phanes.* Phanes, whose name means revealer, is comparable to the Greek conception of *Logos* and the Hebrew *Memra*. All three terms connote a creative, cosmic reason, which was seen in the order of the universe and the regularity of the Sun's seasonal travels.

Notice that the feminine and maternal Moon preceded the masculine and paternal Sun. The Orphics were a matriarchal group, as were most of the earlier religions in their pristine form.

Phanes was called Phaethon, the Shining One, for the Orphics identified Phanes with the Sun itself. In contrast to the monad of preexisting universal consciousness, Phanes represented an individual-ized, albeit divine, intellect in a world of diversity: *a dyad*. Man could consciously identify with such an intellectually disposed Deity, as he

---

*As a god, the Greeks later identified him with Eros.

has done with a whole pantheon of father gods—Phanes, Zeus, Jupiter and Jehovah, among others. While that identification is an act of his rational consciousness, Man has traditionally achieved unity with the One through meditation, yoga or similar exercises or—as recent research has disclosed—by the consumption of hallucinogenic substances, especially certain mushrooms. After Aldous Huxley ingested mescaline, a derivative of the peyotyl cactus, he reported an awareness of universal consciousness which he termed Mind at Large, after the philosophy of C. D. Broad.[11]

The creation myths make more sense when we proceed on a simultaneously astronomical and mycological basis, for the mushroom was used to catalyze Man's awareness of himself as a microcosmic re-creation of the whole universe. Or, as the Hermetic astrologers expressed it: *As Above, So Below.*

In an astronomical context, the very illumination of Phanes, the Shining One, produced both Mother Night and Father Sky Uranus. The Greeks represented the upper half of this celestial division as golden, the lower half as silver, reflecting the domains of Sun and Moon respectively, with the Earth of mortal Man at the center.

In Oriental mysticism, this gold and silver dyad is known as the Yin and Yang of Tao. Yin is the yielding feminine principle ruled by the Moon; Yang is the aggressive masculine principle ruled by the Sun. Both are necessary to constitute the Tao of wholeness. Oriental mysticism and Western astrology share common premises and a common origin; the Tao is vital to our understanding the planetary rulerships of the horoscope.

Of the planets ruling the signs, only the Sun and Moon are not identified by the names of the gods of Greece and Rome, for no single-god myth could express the primary forces which these luminaries represent in astrology. Instead, the Yin and Yang of Tao provide the underlying images for the contemporary astrologer.

The role of each planet in astrology has been designated by the god of Greek and Roman myth for which it has been named. Each of these planetary gods represents one of the archetypal sources "out of which the whole social structure [of Mankind] has been developed organically"; for it has been discovered that "the mental characteristics of man are the same the world over."[12]

FROM THE UNION of Heaven and Earth came the race of Titans, the deities originally assigned to the seven known planets of the ancient world. The planetary powers were attributed as follows: Sun for illumination; Moon for enchantment; Mars for growth; Mercury for wisdom; Jupiter for law; Venus for love; Saturn for peace. From this myth we have derived the seven-day week and the basic planetary archetypes of astrology. [13]

Saturn was not always peaceful, however. The Greeks knew him as Chronos, which means time, and time is the key to the Saturn archetype. Saturn was chief among the Titans. With his sickle he first castrated and then dethroned his father, Uranus. Next Saturn consorted with his mother, inspiring Freudian theory some four thousand years later. Saturn routinely devoured all his sons until Mother Earth, representing the feminine principle, saved one son from Saturn by subterfuge. [14]

That son was Zeus, whose name means bright sky, and whom the Romans called Jupiter; he had other counterparts in the Marduk of the Babylonians and in the Enlil of the Sumerians, whom the Hebrews called El, Elohim or Jehovah.

The castration of the heavenly Uranus by time suggests the loss of the Golden Age of Man's prehistory, to which so many ancient myths, including Genesis and the *Epic of Gilgamesh,* make reference. [15] In the Genesis myth Eve is created from Adam's rib—the rib being a euphemism for the male organ. [16] With the castration of Adam, the creation of Eve and our Fall into consciousness came an awareness of time and its often cruel rulership of all life.

But with the ascendancy of Jupiter and his counterparts we had a monumental revolution in the heavens whose reverberations are still being felt by Mankind. Remember that our *first* supreme Deity was the Mother, who represented the feminine principle of Yin, which was passive, receptive and intuitive. But with Jupiter, Zeus, Marduk, El and Jehovah, we switched our allegiances, making the Yang of the male principle the primary object of our veneration. Thus Jupiter was called *Pluvius,* meaning bringer of rain, which John Allegro tells us was regarded as celestial semen. Our new supreme god was the father, the lawgiver, the inseminator and the source of all aspiration. With the rational and aggressive Yang on the ascendant, Man need no longer passively submit to the depredations of time. Thus Jupiter forced Saturn to disgorge his children with whose help Jupiter banished the Titans and dethroned his father, even as Saturn had dethroned Uranus. Jupiter then united with Mother Earth, thereby establishing his sovereignty in Heaven and on Earth. Persephone, the first-born daughter of their union, was one of the manifold appearances of the Moon, no longer the reigning monarch, but the submissive offspring of the father god.

In this episode of the creation myth we can see Man shaking off the tyranny of time by his own aspiring will, projected onto the will of the father god who made Man in his image. The same theme was explored in describing the Sagittarian archetype. And Jupiter rules Sagittarius.

AS IMPULSIVE AS the will of Man, Jupiter united with Persephone in an underground place, and his Moon-daughter gave birth to the divine child, Dionysus.

Dionysus had many honorifics. *Zagreus,* perhaps the most common, means reborn or resurrected, and is a clue to Dionysus's identification with the flycap mushrooms, which include *Amanita muscaria* and *Amanita verna.*[17] The *amanita* burst forth from the ground at night with many species at first silvery white like the Moon. *Amanita verna* is popularly known as the destroying angel. Persephone, the Moon-child and first fruit of Jupiter's underground union with Mother Earth, means bringer of destruction, which would be an apt name for the flycap mushroom as well.

AT THE INSTIGATION of Jupiter's jealous wife, Hera, the Titans destroyed Dionysus and scattered his body to the ends of the Earth. When Jupiter discovered what had happened, he salvaged his son's immortal heart (often identified with the Sun) and fed it to the goddess Semele in a glass of wine. Semele thereby became pregnant with Dionysus.

This portion of the myth contains several layers of meaning. Semele is yet another manifestation of the Moon and the myth preserves the Moon's identity as the immaculate virgin while it poetically explains the Dionysian effect of wine, which the Orphics regarded as sacred. And once again Jupiter receives primary credit as progenitor of the divine child. At the same time, the myth advises us that the body of Dionysus can be found all over the Earth; it is true that hallucinogenic mushrooms grow everywhere.

What happened next reflects the polarity which Dionysus has always generated with regard to the rule of law.

Hera means protectress,[18] but she might better have been called the Enforcer, for her role as consort to Jupiter the lawgiver was to insure that his laws were enforced impartially. The divine child— Dionysus, Christ or Buddha—has always been beyond the law, and Hera (or her many counterparts) has always implacably pursued him.

When Hera learned that Semele was carrying Dionysus, she was outraged. With malice aforethought, she convinced Semele that Jupiter should present himself to her in his true form. The duped Semele then spurned Jupiter's attentions until he agreed to show his real self; when Jupiter reluctantly appeared as thunder and lightning, Semele was consumed in his engulfing presence.

This part of the myth is a cautionary tale which warns us that we can be consumed by the immanent Godhead if we have not been properly prepared for the experience.[19] The Orphics had their own initiation rites, called the Mysteries of Eleusis (Eleusis = Dionysus), to prepare their acolytes for a safe journey into universal consciousness. In contemporary drug parlance, we might be warned of a bad trip; but eager neophytes in yogic exercises have also been cautioned about the dangerous mind-boggling consequence of their overzealousness.

Jupiter rescued the fetus of his unborn son from Semele's ashes and carried him inside his own thigh. The horns of the unborn Dionysus pricked Jupiter's thigh and caused him to limp. From his father's thigh Dionysus had his second birth.

When we are told that Jupiter permitted Dionysus to wield his royal scepter, we realize that this strange rebirth from the father presents Dionysian love as both transcendent and phallic; indeed, one particularly deadly variety of the *amanita* is called *phalloides*. The myth also reminds us that we mortals achieve rebirth through our offspring, just as mushrooms, once plucked, are magically reborn from the same ground.

This myth inspired that most Dionysian of our contemporary poets, Dylan Thomas, to write the strangely evocative poem "In the White Giant's Thigh";[20] with his Dionysian poetry, Thomas has achieved his own immorality.

The universality of the myth is its message of the relationship between the father god and his son, as a paradigm of *our* relationship to our fathers, both mortal and divine.

Jupiter in turn sired all the remaining planetary gods—Mars, Mercury and Venus—which were incorporated as such in the horoscope. Thus, in astrology, Jupiter rules Sagittarius, together with the ninth house of higher mind, which includes religion, philosophy and law.

But what of the son? Whether identified as Dionysus, Jesus or Buddha, the divine child was the incarnation of the mysteries of the intuitive and receptive Yin, which had been displaced by the ascendancy of the Yang in a reversal of the original world order. Hence the puzzlement of such rationalist philosophers as Bertrand Russell about the feminism of the Orphic worship of Dionysus; and hence the association of the divine child with the Moon and the magic mushrooms believed to be the fruit of moonlight, in contrast to every other fruit found (quite literally) *under the Sun.*

In Genesis 32, Jacob was renamed *Israel* by Jehovah after a night-long struggle with his God from which he emerged victorious but stigmatized by a lifelong limp. This limp was of course the same stigma borne by Jupiter and also by his son, Dionysus; for *Dionysus* means lame god, and *Jacob* is derived from the Hebrew word *Akeb,* meaning heel. Jacob's limp was characterized by a raised heel, a sign of divinity. The new name Jehovah bestowed on Jacob identifies him with the Jupiter-Dionysus myth even more directly, for *Israel* means God strives against *my* enemies. [21]

As the chosen son of God, Jacob is the Old Testament prototype of that sea-change in the consciousness of Western man, marking the transition from matriarchy [22] and the veneration of the feminine Yin and its acceptance of the world, to patriarchy and the veneration of the male principle of generation, the Yang of aspiration. So it was that Jacob, blessed with his new name, became the eponymous founder of the twelve tribes of Israel—corresponding, of course, to the twelve signs of the zodiac.

The triumph of Jupiter (or Zeus or Jehovah) was so complete that his son Dionysus, the god of the Yin of the feminine Mysteries, became a fugitive in Western civilization and was driven underground—from whence he has again emerged as a magic mushroom! Today once again the holistic vision of Dionysus is a force to be reckoned with. Dionysus is the patron god of contemporary astrology.

IN THIS SECTION I shall consider each planet in terms of its essential role in the horoscope and its basic astrological/alchemical correspondences to the phenomenal world.

S U N

Glyph. The Sun's glyph is a circle with a dot in the center. The dot is sometimes called the *punctum solis,* or point of the Sun. It has other meanings as well.

Metal. Gold is the metal to which the Sun corresponds in alchemy and in astrology; the glyph for gold is the same as that used for the Sun.

Function. The Sun represents the basic self in any horoscope. Jung saw the Sun's glyph as the symbol of the integration of the ego, which is a psychologist's way of saying the same thing. In the preceding section, I also identified the Sun with the Chinese Yang, or aggressive male principle.

Rulership. The Sun rules the sign of Leo in any horoscope.

Discussion. The circle with the dot in the center is the Cosmic Egg, which appears in many mythologies, including the Greek Orphic, Egyptian, Finnish, Buddhistic and Japanese.[23]

Without the central dot, the circle is the representation of the *Ain Soph* of unmanifested divine consciousness in cabalistic lore. The cabalistic Book of Formation declares that the "fiery or scintillating intelligence," which is the vital life force, comes to us in physical form as the heat and light of the Sun.[24] Put another way, the Sun represents human consciousness as a fragment of the universal consciousness which existed before Man came into being. Gold with its identical glyph symbolizes the divine spark in Man which corresponds to the Sun. [25] The color of gold is also the color of divinity, and psychologically represents the sublimation of the instincts.[26]

Oddly enough, no one seems to have commented on the fact that the central dot is quite literally a *sunspot.* The significance of that fact remains to be explored; it can only be touched upon here. The symbolism of the Sun, when traced to its earliest beginnings, adds credence to the possibility that the sunspot has played an important role in the development of human consciousness. For example, the Chinese character for the Sun includes the symbol representing a flame and that flame as a source of human thought. Likewise, the same glyph for the Sun was also the Egyptian hieroglyph for Ra, the Sun god who is equated with fire.[27]

There are other significant correlations to the Sun's glyph which illuminate its astrological function. Both Christianity and astrology are based in large part on Neoplatonism, a mixture of mysticism, asceticism and humanism traceable to the teachings of a third-century mystic named Plotinus. A reading of Plotinus's *Enneads* indicates that Christian and Hebrew mysticism have a common origin: basic to the Plotinian scheme of things is the notion of a preexisting, numberless *One,* which sounds strikingly similar to the *Ain Soph.* From the One there emanates the Intelligence, and "the Intelligence . . . is to The One . . . as a circle is to its center."[28] Intelligence is variously translated from the Greek word *Nous* as mind, intellect or intellectual principle.[29]

Following Neoplatonism came the Sun-worshipping Mithraics, who gave Christianity some serious competition in the fourth century C.E.[30] Mithraism complemented Neoplatonism and added its own contribution to astrology. According to the Mithraics, the soul yielded its essential qualities to the various planets at death, and to the Sun went the intellect.[31]

In sum, the position of the Sun in any horoscope shows how the native expresses the Yang of his own personal universe. That expression occurs principally through a fiery consciousness which distinguishes Man from all other creatures.

The Sun rulership of the sign Leo now comes clear. We have seen that Leo is the sign of the king, the paterfamilias and of Man's brain children. Just as the Sun rules the heavens, so Leo rules the Earth. Interestingly enough, astrologers find that natives with a Leo emphasis often display a strong affinity for gold.

Just as Leo is the paterfamilias, so the Sun is often said by astrologers to represent the father of the native in the horoscope. Much depends upon the context of the horoscope in this regard, for the Sun shares that role with Saturn.

MOON

Glyph. The glyph for the Moon is the familiar crescent, shown at a point between the new Moon and the first quarter.

Metal. Silver is the metal corresponding to the Moon in alchemy. As is the case with all the original planetary and alchemical correlations, the glyphs are the same.

Function. The Moon represents the native's intuitive and emotional self in any horoscope. Whereas the Sun is all conscious functions, the Moon is the native's unconscious self. As the Sun symbolizes the *Nous* or intellect, so the Moon represents the *Psyche* or Soul. In Mithraism, the Moon received the personality of the deceased just as the Sun received the intellect.

Rulership. The Moon rules Cancer in any horoscope.

Discussion. The Sun is the congealed Yang of the male principle; the Moon is the congealed Yin of the yielding, receptive feminine principle. The Moon has no light of her own but reflects the light of the Sun. Whereas the Sun's energy is necessary for growth and integration of the basic self, the Moon rules the tides of sea and spirit—in short, the emotional and intuitive side of the native.

To our ancient forefathers, the Moon was more important than the Sun: the Sun died every winter, but the Moon was eternal. The Moon's reflected light is not just a weaker form of sunlight; moonlight has its own phenomenal Yin qualities. Prague radio engineer Karel Drbal recalls a joke that soldiers played on their comrades in his service days. They would put the intended victim's straight razor on the window sill in the light of the full Moon. In the morning, the instrument was blunt although nothing but moonlight had touched the razor's edge. Why? As Drbal explains, it is because moonlight is polarized—vibrating in one direction only—and polarized moonlight is potent enough to blunt an open razor.[32]

Just as the preexisting universal consciousness of the *Ain Soph* was a single unit or monad, so the Sun and Moon are a dyad.

Prose and poetry are a good example. Poet William Empson puzzled *why* certain passages of poetry seemed beautiful. He *knew* they were beautiful, and tells us that by "teasing out" the meanings of the text, he found that he could to some extent explain his feelings about a particularly beautiful passage of verse. Yet this was not at all satisfactory, for when the individual meanings were teased out, Empson found that they "were too complicated to be remembered together as if in one glance of the eye . . ."[33] He concluded that "it is clear that this process of seeing the thing *as a whole* is particularly usual and important in language . . ."[34]

This *holistic* response to verse gives true poetry its essential ambiguity. As Robert Graves reminds us, all true poetry is a hymn to the White Goddess that is the Moon. For him there were two distinct and complementary languages, prose, which is rational, and poetry, which is intuitive and "derives its magic from the moon, not the sun."[35]

Thus the Moon and its influences are holistic, ambiguous and intuitive, just as the Sun is analytic, specific and rational. These polar forces have been termed Apollonian and Dionysian by Nietzsche.

An understanding of the dyad of Sun and Moon (expressed as Apollonian and Dionysian forces or otherwise) is fundamental to the contemporary astrologer's comprehension of the triplicities. Jung devoted an entire chapter of his *Psychological Types* to Nietzsche's concept of the Apollonian and the Dionysian. Jung's familiarity with these antipodal forces of Sun and Moon catalyzed his thinking in producing the four functional types corresponding to the triplicities.

The Apollonian archetype of the Sun is oriented to future and to linear time. The Sun as the Yang or male principle reveres the phallus of generation. The time orientation of phallic worship is to the future, for every orgasm is—as Dylan Thomas once said—an explosion of ghosts: a million new possibilities for future generations. The concept of bequeathing property bespeaks a legalistic and linear concept of time past-present-and-future. Jung's thinking and intuitive types are characteristically Apollonian.

The Dionysian archetype of the Moon, on the other hand, regards time as now-and-then. As the Yin or female principle, Moon worship reveres the feminine Mysteries which occur in the eternal NOW and which are savored as treasured memories. In his Dionysian experience of altered consciousness, Aldous Huxley found awesome the very Is-ness of things as they are NOW, just as Meister Eckhart (among other mystics) had described them some six centuries before him.[36] Feeling and sensation types are characteristically Dionysian, as are the watery and earthy triplicities to which they correspond.

MERCURY

Glyph. The glyph for the planet Mercury is the caduceus or staff carried by the god Mercury (Hermes in Greek), the winged messenger of the gods.

Metal. Mercury or quicksilver corresponds to the planet Mercury in alchemy, and has the same glyph.

Function. The function of Mercury is communication, achieved by mediating between the conscious, rational functions ruled by the Sun, and the unconscious, intuitive functions ruled by the Moon.

Rulership. Mercury rules both Gemini and Virgo in any horoscope.

Discussion. The role of Mercury in the horoscope is symbolized by the staff of the winged messenger: the caduceus consists of two snakes wound about a single staff. The snakes represent the Moon and the Sun in their courses and the integration of these Dionysian and Apollonian forces by intertwining around the staff which is Man.[37] Physiologically, the caduceus also represents the brain stem and spinal column.

Alchemists used quicksilver or cinnabar in mystic rituals revolving around the transmutation of gold and silver into the philosopher's stone of cosmic unity. Mercury was the agent used by alchemists in this work, for they regarded quicksilver as the mother of gold.[38] The union of the Apollonian and Dionysian forces represented by Sun and Moon was the goal or mysterious conjunction (*mysterium coniunctionis*), which was what the great work of the true alchemist was all about; and it was the mediation of Mercury that made such cosmic union possible.

Thus the planet Mercury rules *communication* in the broadest sense: both oral and written communication, of course; but also the inner communication of *Psyche* (Moon) with *Nous* (Sun) that makes such verbal expression possible. Simply, Mercury represents adaptation through communication—Man with his fellows and with himself.

Astronomically, Mercury is never more than twenty-seven degrees away from the Sun. As the planet which rules conscious thought processes in any horoscope, Mercury's metaphorical significance is always close as well.

The unity expressed by the intertwining serpents of the glyph is reflected in the mythical origins of the word "hermaphrodite." Biologically a hermaphrodite has the organs of both sexes. Hermaphroditus was the product of the union of Hermes and Aphrodite—the Greek counterparts of Mercury and Venus respectively. The joinder of names symbolizes the unity of mind and love in one being.

In Mithraism, the planet Mercury received the greed of the deceased—an odd notion, since we do not today think of Mercury in terms of human greed. The answer may lie in the ancient myth of the theft by Hermes (Mercury) of Apollo's cows on the very day the divine child Hermes was born. In that myth we see a metaphor by which the Greeks concluded that Man's development of manual and verbal dexterity had created a new god to whom many of the attributes formerly credited to Apollo should now be given. Thus the prowess of Mercury/Hermes includes divination, games and song. (Hermes mollified Apollo's outrage at the theft by the gift of a lyre he had devised from a tortoise shell.)

To those attributes, a sense of humor should be added. When Apollo took Hermes to answer to their father, Zeus/Jupiter, for his depredations, the father god roared with laughter at the glib tale told by his precocious son about how he stole the cattle to make appropriate obeisances to the *twelve* gods.

"Twelve!" Apollo exclaimed. "Who's the twelfth?"

"Your servant, sir." Hermes bowed modestly.[39]

So Hermes entered the pantheon of gods, after Zeus demanded that he promise not to steal or to lie. Hermes cheerfully agreed, while observing that he would not always be able to tell the *entire* truth; it was a qualification which Zeus acknowledged as reasonable.[40]

Hermes/Mercury then became the winged messenger of the gods who guided souls to the afterworld, with counterparts in Egyptian myth as Thoth and in Christian myth as the Holy Ghost.[41] Somewhat later, Hermes and Thoth were amalgamated into the patron god of alchemy, a trinity known as Hermes *trismegistos,* or literally, Hermes the *thrice-great.*[42]

Sun, Moon, Mercury; Father, mother, divine child. The concept of the trinity is pervasive in the symbolism of Man, the dream animal. It has even been found in the human brain, where the intricately convoluted cortex is divided into *two* hemispheres connected by a *single* bridge of white matter called the *corpus callosum,* which means hard body. The left hemisphere controls functions on the right side of the body, and the right hemisphere of the cerebrum controls functions on the left side of the body. The *corpus callosum* is a kind of crossover network which coordinates the two.[43] In *The Psychology of Consciousness,* Dr. Robert Ornstein has pointed out that for over a century evidence has been accumulating which shows that Man is literally of *two* minds about things: the left hemisphere of the cerebrum is rational and analytical; the right hemisphere, on the other hand, is holistic and intuitive. Or, consciousness includes the Sun and the Moon, whose astrological roles correspond to the left and right hemisphere functions. Hermetic literature supports this view: "The macrocosm has Sun and Moon; man has two eyes, the right related to the Sun, the left to the Moon."

If the *corpus callosum* is cut, the individual loses the mediatory and communicative role of Mercury and can no longer integrate his two modes of consciousness. In detailing experiments with such split-brain persons, Dr. Ornstein furnishes some striking examples of what happens when the right (hand) brain doesn't know what the left (hand) brain is doing.

Split is *skhizein* in Greek, and mind is *phren.* Together they furnish us with the roots for the term "Schizophrenia," the preeminent malady of contemporary Man.[44] The case histories discussed by Dr. Ornstein involve people who have borne such a split surgically, for compelling medical reasons. Schizophrenics, on the other hand, are split psychically between mind and heart, or rational and intuitive functions, and the results are even more severe. In either case, the *skhizein* individual lacks the mediating and communicative functions represented in Christian myth by the Holy Ghost and in classical myth and in astrology by Mercury.

JUST AS SUN, Moon and Mercury constitute a trinity, so Mars and Venus, Jupiter and Saturn each constitute a set of antipodes, or polar opposing forces.

Venus and Mars make up the antipodes of love and will. As gods they were drawn to each other, and the child of their union was Harmonia, or Harmony.[45]

♀

VENUS

Glyph. The glyph for Venus is said to be the mirror of that goddess of beauty and love; it is also a symbolic representation of the female sex organs.

Metal. Copper, the metal from which mirrors were made in earlier times, corresponds to Venus.

Function. Venus represents the affectional nature of the native, his need for harmonious relations with others and specifically his ability to give and to receive love.

Rulership. Venus rules both Taurus and Libra in any horoscope.

Discussion. Venus, Aphrodite in Greek myth, rose from the sea-foam. She was thus more a daughter of Neptune (Poseidon in Greek) than of Zeus; but Zeus adopted her as his own. Her only duty was the art of love.

In Mithraic wisdom, the planet Venus received the lust of the deceased, and the myths of Venus provide precedent for that. For example, Venus was given in marriage to the artisan god Vulcan (Hephaestus in Greek), to whom she was notoriously unfaithful. Vulcan/Hephaestus surprised his wife *in flagrante delicto* with Mars/Ares, her one true love, by capturing them in a net of his own forging.[46]

When Vulcan indignantly summoned the gods to view his wife's infidelity, their reactions were less than comforting. Apollo nudged Mercury and asked him whether he wouldn't like to be in Mars's place. Mercury loudly conceded that he would, nets and all, and both gods laughed uproariously. Venus overheard all this—she was hardly in a position to withdraw—and later had a fling with Mercury. Hermaphroditus was the child of their union.

Venus also had an affair with Dionysus, and *their* son was Priapus, a god with enormous genitals. In Priapus's generous endowment we can see the results of a union of sexual attraction (Venus) with feeling love (Dionysus).

Venus represented love both sacred and profane. In earlier Sumerian myth, Venus, like the Moon, was identified with the three aspects of the cosmic female. As the morning star, Venus was a virgin. As the evening star, she was the seducer who becomes consort of the Moon as night wears on. Finally, she was the aged crone who died with the rising Sun.[47]

Venus was Ishtar to the Egyptians, Ashtoreth to the Hebrews and Astarte to the Phoenicians and Philistines.[48] Jewish women before Nebuchadnezzar offered cakes to Astarte as the Queen of Heaven.[49] As Ishtar, Venus was revered by the Egyptians as the harbinger of bountiful harvest at the flooding of the Nile.[50]

Romans traced the sacred origins of their country to Venus in the myth of her love for the mortal King Anchises, whom she presented with that pious son, Aeneas—"Aeneas" means praiseworthy—who later brought the sacred *palladium** to Rome.[51]

We can see these many qualities of Venus in the two signs she rules. Taurus is the receptive earth sign of sense appreciation, and Venus above all is the goddess of venereal love whose beauty is irresistible. Positively manifested, Taurus is a sign of the sacred; Venus as queen mother, harbinger and kingmaker reflects these aspects of Taurus.

Libra is the cardinal air sign of beauty, harmony and balance— three words which express the same essential notion—and Venus just as clearly represents Man's striving for balance through relationship and through beauty.

MARS

Glyph. The glyph for Mars is said to represent the shield and spear of a warrior. That is a euphemism; the glyph is really an erect male organ.

Metal. Iron is the metal to which the planet Mars corresponds in alchemy and in astrology; and we still describe a strong-minded person as having an *iron* will.

Function. Mars represents what Freud would call the libido, Jung the psychic energy and Adler the *Anlage*, or aggressive instinct.

Rulership. Mars rules Aries in any horoscope. Many astrologers still consider Mars as a co-ruler or secondary ruler of Scorpio as well.

Discussion. Mars, Ares in Greek myth, was the god of war. In the Greek version, Ares was a god not even a mother could love, for Hera detested him as did all the major gods in the Greek pantheon—except, of course, Aphrodite. Ares, whose name means male warrior, was impetuous, always stirring up trouble, often drunk and enjoyed battle for its own sake.

To the Greeks, Ares personified bloodthirsty aggressive instincts and blind rage. He wasn't very bright, either, for his sister, Athena—the goddess of wisdom who sprang full-grown and in armor from Zeus's forehead—often outwitted him in war games.

Not a very attractive personality, is he? The Greeks regarded Ares as a Thracian god, an example of the technique by which one culture attributes to another country all of the qualities which it possesses but won't own up to. So the English call the condom a *French* letter,[52] and the French call the same item an *English* letter; and Daniel Webster speaks of the Devil as a *foreign* prince, until the Devil sets the record

---

*An ancient wooden statuette of Pallas Athene which was believed to have fallen from the heavens.

straight by reminding us that he arrived in this country with the first slave ships.

The Romans had no such difficulty when they assimilated Ares into Mars. In Rome, Mars ranked second only to Jupiter as the reputed father of Romulus, founder of Rome. Mars was also the patron god of agriculture and fertility and the official protector of the Roman state.[53]

In alchemy, Mars represents divine fortitude.[54] In the contemporary existential psychology of Rollo May, in a healthy person every act is a union of love and will. When we deny love in our actions, we are the belligerent, unattractive Ares; when we deny will, we are the irresponsible, promiscuous Aphrodite. When we act out of love *and* will, we unite Venus and Mars and produce the very harmony which the Greeks mythically recognized as the child of that union.

THE LAST OF the antipodes is composed of Jupiter, the planet of growth, and Saturn, the planet of limitation.

JUPITER

Glyph. The glyph for Jupiter looks something like the Arabic number four; it represents the thunderbolt which this impetuous father god was wont to throw when angry.

Metal. Tin is the metal associated with Jupiter and Zeus, his earlier Greek counterpart. *Zeus* means bright sky; and tin, a silvery white metal, was believed to be the material of which the heavens were constructed. Tin was also indispensible for producing bronze, the ideal alloy for the making of statuary at which the Greeks and Romans excelled.

Function. Jupiter represents growth and our highest goals in any horoscope.

Rulership. Jupiter rules Sagittarius. Many astrologers still assign Jupiter the co-rulership of Pisces as well.

Discussion. Jupiter is the planet of growth, development and expansion. It is a premise of Maslovian psychology that Man is a *wanting* animal; whatever he has, somehow he wants something more— or something different.

In older astrological literature the reader is likely to encounter references to Jupiter as the Greater Benefic and to Saturn as the Greater Malefic. The contemporary astrologer rejects these manipulative and judgmental terms. Instead, Jupiter is regarded today as the planet of opportunity—for increase, for expansion, for personal growth.

Another name for Jupiter is Jove, from which the English word "jovial" is derived. Joviality, or cheerful optimism, has always been a basic Jupiterian trait.

Ambition was the soul's quality which the planet Jupiter received upon death, according to Mithraic lore. Appropriately enough, for Jupiter was the father of the gods and was both omnipotent and omniscient. Each of us in his secret heart cherishes some notion of attaining such powers, and Jupiter expresses our need to grow through experience, learning and increased comprehension.

With all of his powers, Jupiter/Zeus was surprisingly human. In delineating his character in mythical exploits, the Greeks revealed great insight into the strengths and weaknesses of the highest level of Man's consciousness. Like Zeus and Jupiter, Man has the capacity to passionately embrace the world and to re-create it in his own image, and in this aspect Jupiter and Zeus reflect the highest accomplishments of Man's aspiring will. But the Greeks recognized as well the dangers of arrogance and the corruption of power in the development of such prowess. There is the potentiality for transcendence through self-knowledge in this planetary archetype, but whether or not it will be achieved is a matter of individual choice and free will.

$$\hbar$$

SATURN

Glyph. The glyph for Saturn is the scythe or sickle of Chronos, his earlier Greek counterpart who used that instrument to castrate his father, Uranus.

Metal. Lead is the metal associated with Saturn. The basest of metals, lead was commonly used for plumbing by the Romans, who called it *plumbum.*

Function. Saturn represents restriction or limitation in general and self-restraint in particular.

Rulership. Saturn rules Capricorn. Many astrologers still assign Saturn the co-rulership of Aquarius as well.

Discussion. Found in any horoscope, Saturn imposes limitations, obstacles; often the scythe of Chronos cuts down those things we think we cannot live without—and without the force of Saturn we would not discover that we *can* live without them. Saturn makes possible the kind of growth that only obstacles can bring.

Chronos' sickle later became the scythe of the figure we know today as Father Time. All myths express valuable and elemental truths and this one is no exception. *Chronos* means time and it is time which castrates us all in due course.

Once labeled the Greater Malefic, Saturn is regarded by the contemporary astrologer as the Great Teacher, who, by imposing obstacles and restrictions, gives us opportunities to grow which are needed for the fullest development of our potentialities.

Jupiter represents growth through expansion; Saturn represents growth through *limitation*. Both are necessary.

In Mithraic belief, the planet Saturn received the sloth of the deceased, a notion which fits our understanding of the nature of the planetary and mythical archetype.

URANUS, THE FIRST of the outer planets to be discovered, was sighted in the latter part of the eighteenth century when astronomer William Herschel built a seven-foot telescope to scrutinize the heavens. Traditional astrology was still reeling from the body-blows dealt by Copernicus and by Descartes when Herschel unwittingly delivered another. Since astrology is based on a seven-planet system, the scoffers asked, how can astrology have any merit if there are planets beyond Saturn?

Herschel had practiced astrology himself and had concluded from his own experience that the seven traditional planets did have an effect on human affairs; therefore it seemed reasonable to Herschel that this new planet would also. Only time, and painstaking observation, would tell.[55]

Uranus was discovered in 1781, Neptune in 1846 and Pluto not until 1930. We do not have the benefit of the accretion of myth, lore and history to delineate the archetypal nature of these planets in terms of their astrological significance; our conclusions about their correspondences to the affairs of Man must therefore be provisional.

Astrologers have reached some conclusions from the fact that the outer planets move so much more slowly than the inner planets. The orbit of Uranus around the Sun is 84 years, and that of Neptune about 165 years, whereas it takes Pluto 248.4 years to orbit the Sun.

Compare these outer-planet orbits to the slowest moving of the inner planets, Saturn, which completes its orbit around the Sun every twenty-eight to thirty years. These data have led contemporary astrologers to adjudge that the outer planets are likely to have their greatest effect on an entire generation, or era, and not just on the individual. This is particularly true in the case of Pluto, which remains from twelve to thirty-two years in each sign. However, in terms of the aspects formed between the outer planets and other planets in the horoscope, the effects of the outer planets can be seen in the individual horoscope as well.

URANUS

Glyph. The glyph for Uranus is based on the initial of its discoverer, *H*erschel, with an inverted Venus glyph stuck through the crossbar of the H.

Function. Uranus represents Man's need for change and for freedom from restraint, as well as nervous disorders.

Rulership. Uranus has been assigned the rulership of Aquarius.

Discussion. Uranus is the planet associated with astrology and with the approaching Aquarian Age. In *Virginia Woolf and the Androgynous Vision*, we learn that the British novelist sought to apply Coleridge's dictum: "The truth is, a great mind must be androgynous." Virginia Woolf believed that although every mind is potentially bisexual, most men wrote in an analytic, separative style, whereas most writers of her own sex wrote in a holistic, feminine manner. Neither literary approach was sufficient:

> In her opinion, however, to be truly creative one must use the "whole" mind. In keeping with this, the greatest writers are "androgynous": they use and harmonize the masculine and feminine approaches to truth ... in Jungian terms, they have discovered the "self," "a point midway between the conscious and the unconscious" in which there is a reconciliation of opposites.[56]

Born January 25, 1882, when the Sun and Mercury were both posited in the sign of Aquarius, Virginia Woolf was doubly ruled by Uranus; at the time of her birth, Uranus was posited in Virgo, and enjoyed a mutual reception with Mercury, her planet of communication. That is to say, each planet was posited in the sign ruled by the other, adding Uranian emphasis to her Aquarian literary method. Her androgynous vision (demonstrated, for example, by her novel *Orlando*, in which the protagonist changed sex midway through the book) is a basic characteristic of Uranus. The brotherhood of Man is not polarized into brother- and sister-hood, but is a holistic conception befitting the Uranus-ruled Age of Aquarius.

When afflicted in the natal chart, Uranus is regarded by some astrologers as an indicator of unconventional sexual attitudes. I do not view Uranus as an index of any particular sexual orientation, but rather as an indicator of Man's need for variety, of his impulse to shake off the sameness imposed by social constraints which is by no means limited to sexual expression. Uranus is the planet of inventiveness, novelty and quick changes. It is also the planet of humanitarian feeling which takes no notice of sexual distinctions.

NEPTUNE

Glyph. The glyph for Neptune is often thought to represent the trident of that Roman god of the sea whose Greek counterpart is Poseidon. Actually, the glyph may be based on the Greek letter *Psi.*

Function. Neptune represents the native's imagination, his need for fantasy and his capacity for transcendental experience.

Rulership. Neptune has been assigned the rulership of Pisces.

Discussion. In 1942, *Psi* was adopted by the Society for Psychical Research to indicate psychic function.[57] Bishop James Pike used the same symbol to represent what he described as "the transcendent aspect of the human personality."[58] For Pike, the Neptune symbol was more than a mere matter of convenience. Instead, it was a recognition that in *Psi* phenomena, there was a common theme in a score of categories, including

> telepathy, precognition, retrocognition and clairvoyance; mystical experiences, with and without psychedelic drugs; speaking with tongues; the collective or universal unconscious as well as synchronicity; telekinesis; and psychic phenomena, or apparent communication with deceased persons. To these should also be added spiritual healing, intercessory prayer, exorcism, and even ordinary dreams.[59]

Just as the gods Neptune and Poseidon rule the ever-changing seas, so the watery planet Neptune rules the mutable, watery Pisces and everything that is nebulous and ethereal in human experience.

Positively aspected, Neptune enriches our lives with imagination and fantasy. Negatively manifested, Neptune can indicate escapism and self-delusion.

PLUTO

Glyph. The glyph for Pluto is based on the initials of its discoverer, astronomer Percival Lowell.

Function. Pluto represents Man's need for regeneration.

Rulership. Pluto has been assigned the rulership of Scorpio.

Discussion. In Greek mythology, Hades was the ruler of the underworld who spirited Demeter's daughter off to his kingdom of the dead. Demeter was so upset, she refused to perform her fructifying functions, so the land grew barren and even the gods became alarmed. Jupiter/Zeus ultimately interceded: Demeter's daughter could return to the land of the living, he ruled, if she had not eaten any of the food of the dead. Unfortunately, the maiden had consumed seven pomegranate seeds; for that act, she was required to return to the land of Hades for three months every year.[60]

Demeter is the personification of the Moon in all of her manifestations; her daughter is her manifestation as the maiden of the new Moon.
The empire ruled by Hades was quite literally the underworld: that is,
everything below the visible horizon. The pomegranate was regarded as
a magical fruit because it did not rot. The seven seeds correspond to the
last seven days of a lunar month when the Moon does not appear—*i.e.,*
remains in the underworld—and these seven days were much feared by
our ancestors for that reason. [61] The three months every year in which
Demeter grieves and lets the Earth become barren are the three months
of winter, which are followed by the world's rebirth into fertility when
the virginal Moon arises anew.

The lord of the underworld is Hades, meaning sightless, but he is
better known by his honorific title, Pluto. Pluto means wealthy, and in
this title the Greeks recognized a vital truth: death meant the riches of
the harvest and the promise of rebirth in an ever-repeating cycle of
change.

The planet called Pluto has been well named, expressing as it does
that intensity of feeling related to the native's fear of death and need
for rebirth. As we saw in the discussion of Scorpio, the sign ruled by
Pluto, that intensity can be expressed in religion; in dedicated scientific
endeavor which brings some new discovery into being or in the sexual
act of procreation.

Note that Uranus represents quick and revolutionary changes,
while Pluto represents long-term, even evolutional, change. It is important to make this distinction to avoid confusion in interpreting the
influences of these two planets in any horoscope.

A PLANET IS said to be *in dignity* when it is posited in the sign which
it rules: Mars in Aries, the Sun in Leo, are in dignity in their respective
signs. When a planet is in the sign which is the polar opposite of the one
it rules, it is said to be *in detriment.* Thus, Mars is in detriment in Libra;
the Sun is in detriment in Aquarius.

There is a second relationship between sign and planet whose
origin is a matter of conjecture and whose utility is in doubt—the
so-called exaltation and fall of each planet.

A table showing the dignity, detriment, exaltation and fall of each
of the planets is found in table 1. The question of the origin of the
exaltation and fall positions of the planets is best answered in the
scholarly work of Rupert Gleadow, whose credentials as an astrologer
are supplemented by his expertise as a classicist and Orientalist.

Planet	Dignity	Detriment	Exaltation	Fall
☉	♌	♒	♈	♎
☽	♋	♑	♉	♐
☿	♊ / ♍	♐ / ♓	♒	♌
♀	♉ / ♎	♍ / ♈	♓	♍
♂	♈	♎	♑	♋
♃	♐	♊	♋	♑
♄	♑	♋	♎	♈
♅	♒	♌	♍	♉
♆	♓	♍	♋	♑
♇	♍	♉	♓	♍

TABLE 1. Planetary dignities

Gleadow points out that the word "exaltation" means hiding place; he surmises that the planetary hiding places are those parts of the zodiac in which the planets cannot be seen. That would be the sign or zodiacal position in which a planet disappears from view upon the rising of the Sun. (Such appearances and disappearances because of sunrise or sunset are called the *heliacal* risings or settings of planets or stars, as the case may be.)

For example, at the time when Gleadow estimates the system of exaltations was devised—perhaps the sixth century B.C.E., or perhaps later—Mercury was exalted in Aquarius, meaning that when Mercury was posited in that part of the zodiac, it disappeared at sunrise.[62]

In sum, the signs of detriment are opposite those of rulership or dignity; the signs of fall are opposite those of exaltation.

While I have my doubts about the usefulness of the exaltation/fall dichotomy, I have none about the dignity/detriment classifications. You should try out both systems and decide for yourself.

Remember, then, that a planet best expresses its archetypal character in the sign which it rules and in which it is *in dignity*. It also does very well in another particularly congenial sign, known as its sign of *exaltation*. The action of a planet is restricted in its sign of *detriment* and is also considered restricted in its sign of *fall*.

WHEN A PLANET is in dignity, its characteristics are apparent. However, planets may be found in any and every sign in the horoscope and their archetypal characteristics are expressed according to the house and sign positions in which the planet appears, as well as the aspects which it makes with other planets in the chart. Houses and aspects are dealt with in separate chapters of this book; however, you should now be aware of the effect of the signs on the expression of the planetary archetypes.

Take the Sun, for example. The interaction of planet and sign in this instance is one which almost everyone is familiar with, since it is the basis of the Sun-sign astrology that appears in daily newspaper columns. Thus when the Sun is posited in Leo, it evidences its essential role in the horoscope through the characteristics of that sign. When the Sun is posited in Aries (its sign of exaltation), it imparts to the basic self of the native an aggressive and self-assertive Aries character. The same synthesis takes place when the Sun is in any other sign.

In Libra, its sign of detriment, the Sun's vital energy is diffused so that the native may feel that he cannot initiate anything on his own, but must have the cooperation of others.

What about the Moon? In its own sign, Cancer, the Moon will manifest itself in terms of depth of feeling and the native's desire to nurture and to cherish those he loves. The Moon is in detriment in Capricorn, and to learn what that may mean, the astrologer must synthesize the characteristics of the sign and of the planet. In the case of a Capricorn Moon, the native may be overly concerned about his social status, or overly self-critical, depending on a number of variables yet to be considered. The Moon in Pisces, on the other hand, may suggest an individual with great sensitivity to the feelings of others and a compelling need to be needed.

Applying the same principles of synthesis to Mercury in its signs of dignity, we may infer that in Virgo the native's verbal expression would be sharply analytical, and in Gemini the native would have the ability to speak with great ease. In its signs of debility, Mercury's expression would be significantly different. In Pisces, feeling rather than thought would dominate speech; in Sagittarius, the native's mind might be dominated by mind-boggling idealism.

Since Venus rules two signs, it is in dignity both in Taurus and in Libra. In Taurus, the native's Venus finds expression in its steadfast devotion; and in Libra, in the painstaking effort to make and to maintain a harmonious relationship. Venus is also necessarily in detriment in both Scorpio and in Aries, the polar opposites of the signs of its rulership. In Scorpio, Venus is likely to be overly possessive; and in Aries, impulsive and overly aggressive in seeking the desired love object.

Mars rules Aries, and in that sign adds courage in no small measure to the native's chart. If the native's Mars is posited in Libra, its sign of detriment, the native may be overly dependent on the help of others. As the co-ruler of Scorpio, Mars adds great emotional intensity to the native's natural ardor when posited in that sign. Somewhat in detriment in Taurus, Martian energy may be diffuse, distracting the native with a desire to accumulate possessions.

Jupiter in Sagittarius is in dignity and gives the native great enthusiasm for travel and for abstract thinking. In detriment in Gemini, Jupiter's energy may become unrealistic overintellectualization unsupported by the experience which Sagittarius craves. Jupiter may also be considered a co-ruler or secondary ruler of Pisces, where its expression may find the native dedicated to spiritual goals or to charitable activities. In the antipodal sign of Virgo, Jupiter may mean a preoccupation with detail.

Saturn in Capricorn, which it rules, provides the native with an underlying stability which has great survival value, especially in stressful circumstances. In detriment in Cancer, Saturn may be reflected in the native's inability to express his true feelings even to those he loves. Saturn may be regarded as a secondary ruler of Aquarius, where its expression may find the native as a teacher with humanitarian objectives; in the antipodal sign of Leo, where Saturn may be said to be in detriment, its expression may be vainglorious and authoritarian.

Uranus is in dignity in Aquarius and natives with this sign position may be possessed of the holistic/androgynous vision which thrusts leadership upon them unbidden. In detriment in Leo, Uranus may express itself in unreasonable demands for personal freedom and preoccupation with attention-getting unconventionality.

Neptune in Pisces, which it rules, is truly inspiring: witness the great painters Georges Seurat, Vincent van Gogh and Paul Gauguin, all of whom had Neptune in Pisces. In detriment in Virgo, Neptune's expression in that sign may be a skeptical rejection of the very transcendent experiences which the native may require to achieve the healthy integration of his personality. Positively aspected, however, Neptune in Virgo may mean that the native has a very practical imagination.

Pluto rules Scorpio, a sign in which it has not been posited since its discovery. Pluto will enter Scorpio in 1984, and perhaps when Pluto's archetypal death-and-regeneration characteristics are enhanced by its entrance into its own sign, that will mark the end of the Piscean Age and the rebirth of Man's spirit in the Age of Aquarius. Or perhaps not. In detriment in Taurus, Pluto remained in that sign from 1851 to 1882. In the United States, that was a time of greedy materialism and political corruption. It was also the period of growing industrialism when the depredations of technology began the changes in our world with which we are all too familiar today.

11   What Are the Houses?

THE HOROSCOPE IS a diagram of the great circle of the ecliptic (see fig. 10) through which the planets travel in counterclockwise direction. Over that basic diagram is a series of overlays which together show the course of the year, or the Sun's position in terms of the Earth's orbital revolution.

There is the sequence of the signs themselves, commencing with Aries at the vernal equinox and moving in a counterclockwise direction. Another overlay is formed by the addition of the cardinal compass directions, in the counterclockwise sequence of east, north, west and south, to the cardinal signs and cardinal seasons. At this point, we have the following associations:

1. Aries: vernal equinox: east
2. Cancer: summer solstice: north
3. Libra: autumnal equinox: west
4. Capricorn: winter solstice: south

But the horoscope shows simultaneously the Earth's position in terms of its axial rotation. Each of the pie-shaped segments or lunes (named for the lunation cycle of approximately twenty-nine and one-half days) is a *house* which, in the Placidian house system, corresponds to two hours of time in the twenty-four-hour day. The houses deal with the affairs of life in a counterclockwise sequence which follows that of the twelve astrological months. The first house commences at the point of intersection on the east of the true horizon and the ecliptic (see fig. 10).

The horoscope also measures the Earth's daily axial rotation by the house division lines or *cusps*. The Earth is exposed to all twelve signs every twenty-four hours, and the cusps, forming a kind of sub-zodiac to record those influences, rearrange the signs to reflect the sequence of changes in the course of the day and to express transitions as they occur in nature and in Man. The house cusps go in clockwise direction, since the signs, because of the Earth's counterclockwise rotation, seem to rise on the natal horizon and culminate at the Midheaven (see fig. 10).

How can we reconcile the basic architecture of the horoscope, with its natural correlation of sign, house and season, to the house cusps, since the cusps not only confuse the starting point, but move in a different direction as well? Isn't that an awful lot to do at once? The candid answer is yes; but it is done readily by every competent astrologer who delineates a horoscope. But that facility does not come without effort. Both the solar year and the Earth's rotation must be considered and their meanings synthesized in order to interpret the significance of the house cusps for the affairs of Man.

A GREAT CIRCLE is any circle whose plane intersects the center of the Earth and can be extended to the celestial sphere.

A SMALL CIRCLE is any circle which does not intersect the center of the Earth.

The LOCAL CELESTIAL MERIDIAN is a great circle which intersects not only the center of the Earth but also the native's zenith point—*i.e.*, the point directly above the native—and his north and south horizon points.

The PRIME VERTICAL is a great circle which intersects the native's zenith point and the points of his east and west horizon.

The TRUE HORIZON is a great circle which is measured from the native's zenith point and makes a ninety-degree arc from that point at right angles to the local celestial meridian and the prime vertical.

The ECLIPTIC is a great circle twenty-three and one-half degrees from the celestial equator, which intersects the great circles of the local celestial meridian, the prime vertical and the true horizon.

The MC, MEDIUM COELI or MIDHEAVEN is the point at which the great circle of the ecliptic intersects the great circle of the local celestial meridian *above* the horizon.

The IC, IMUM COELI or UNDERHEAVEN is the point at which the ecliptic great circle intersects the local celestial meridian *below* the horizon.

The ZENITH is a *point* in the sky directly overhead. It is *not* a great circle.

The NADIR is the *point* in the celestial sphere diametrically opposite to the zenith point.

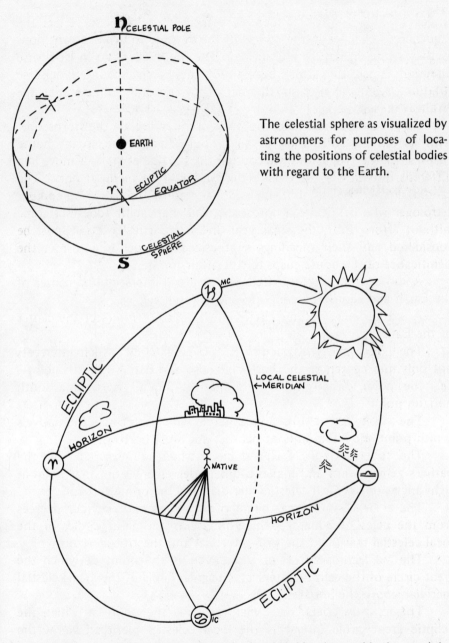

The celestial sphere as visualized by astronomers for purposes of locating the positions of celestial bodies with regard to the Earth.

The birth place and time of the native; it is pinpointed by the natal horizon and the local celestial meridian. The horizon line and the local celestial meridian are extended to the point at which they intersect the ecliptic.

FIGURE 10. The great circles

The perspective is such that the local celestial meridian appears as a vertical line, rather than as a circle; and the horizon appears as a simple horizontal line carried out to intersect the celestial ecliptic. The point at which the horizon line intersects the ecliptic on the East denotes the Ascendant (ASC). The point at which the local celestial meridian intersects the ecliptic to the South denotes the Midheaven (MC).

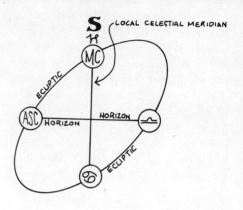

The sun [☉] has been added, and one planet, Venus, [♀] to show their positions in the celestial sphere at the natal moment.

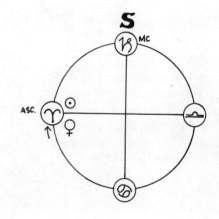

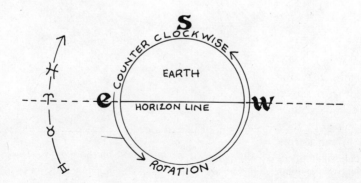

Shows why the sun and the signs appear to rise on the natal horizon due to the counterclockwise rotation of the Earth.

A clock face of a special order: in a counterclockwise direction, from the point on the East at which the horizon line of the native intersects the ecliptic, there are units numbered One to Twelve, which are termed 'Houses.' Thus the first house commences at the Easternmost point of the natal horizon, and the twelfth house ends at that same point on the ecliptic.

Contains the data set forth in the previous pictures; this time, however, the diagram is recognizable as a horoscope, with the clock face of Houses added, and certain notable omissions.

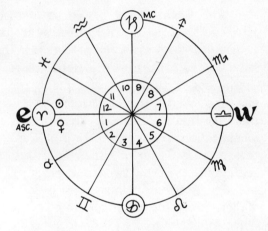

The completed horoscope. Note that the degrees of sign shown for the celestial bodies are determined by their position in the astronomers' celestial sphere and ecliptic at the moment of the native's birth.

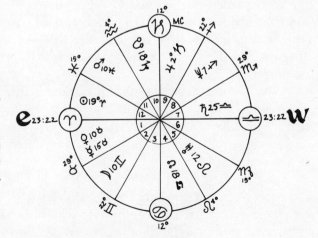

It is important that you have some notion of the different kinds of house systems as well as a grasp of the particular house system I will be using in this book. One of the greatest sources of confusion for the budding astrologer in reading astrological literature is the use of different house systems by different writers.

House systems are one of the things that astrologers like to argue about. The four basic systems of house division are as follows:

1. Equal House
2. Regiomontanus
3. Campanus
4. Placidian

The Equal House system is the oldest. It is favored by English astrologers. In the Equal House system the degree of the ecliptic at the eastern intersection of the native's true horizon is the Ascendant. That same degree constitutes the house cusps in successive signs on each of the houses in turn. For example, if the native's eastern horizon intersects the ecliptic at zero degrees Aries, zero degrees Aries is entered on the first house cusp, also known as the Ascendant. Without further computation, zero degrees Taurus is entered on the second house cusp, zero degrees Gemini on the third house cusp, and so on through zero degrees Pisces on the twelfth house cusp.

The Regiomontanus house system was the invention of Johann Müller, professor of astronomy at Vienna in the fifteenth century. When Müller moved to Italy to practice astrology, he was hailed as the King of the Mountains—*Regio Montanus*. His system of house division determines the Ascendant as the point of intersection of the ecliptic and of the true horizon—that is, ninety degrees from the zenith point— and then divides the celestial equator into six equal parts above the true horizon and six equal parts below the true horizon. Regiomontanus is little used in the United States, though it is favored by some European astrologers.

The Campanus house system is similar in concept to the Regiomontanus house system except that Johannes Campanus, a thirteenth-century mathematician, divided the houses along the prime vertical instead of along the celestial equator. The Campanus system is favored by sidereal astrologers (see fig. 11).

In the seventeenth century, Placidus de Tito, an Italian monk who was professor of mathematics at the University of Padua, developed the system in widest use today. The Placidian house system uses the same basic quadrants to determine the Ascendant, but then departs from the space concept and is based instead on time: specifically, the time it

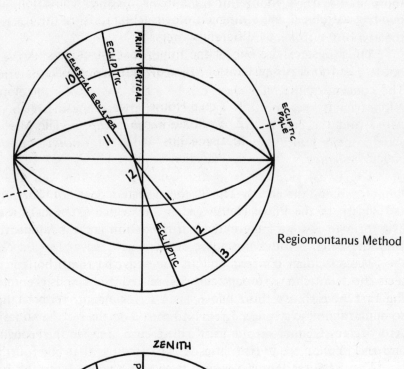

Regiomontanus Method

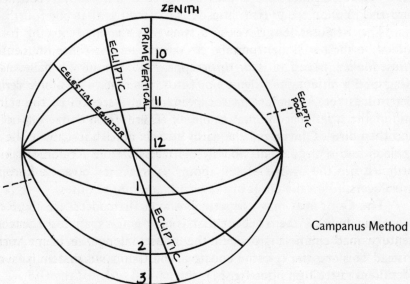

Campanus Method

FIGURE 11. Regiomontanus and Campanus house systems

takes each degree of the ecliptic to reach culmination. Placidus computed these time arcs mathematically. In the Placidian system, which is the one used throughout this book,* the Ascendant is determined in the same way as in the other systems: it is the point of intersection on the east of the true horizon and the ecliptic.

The Midheaven or MC in the Placidian system is always the tenth house cusp. Everything else is a time arc mathematically determined. The concept of the Midheaven can be a rich source of confusion. The Midheaven is the point of intersection between the meridian of the native and the ecliptic. *It is a point on the ecliptic.* The Midheaven should not be confused with the zenith, which is the *point immediately above the native.*

The Equal House system distinguishes the Midheaven, the tenth house cusp and the zenith. The Placidian system does not. The zenith is not shown in the Placidian system, a fact which often leads the new astrologer to assume incorrectly that the zenith and the Midheaven are the same thing.

The Placidian concept of Midheaven as the tenth house cusp is probably why the system is not favored by the English astrologers. Figure twelve shows these concepts in terms of a London birthplace, which is about fifty-one degrees and thirty minutes of Earth latitude. As you can see, there is a dramatic difference between the zenith point and the Midheaven at that latitude. The result is that one-fourth of a horoscope—houses ten, eleven and twelve—is crammed into this narrow arc while the remainder must be stretched over the other houses. As a consequence, two signs sometimes appear in one house, a phenomenon described as intercepted signs. For future reference you should remember that if there are two signs in a given house, there will be two signs in its opposite number. For example, if Taurus is on the cusp of the second house, Cancer on the cusp of the third house, with Gemini intercepted in the second house, Sagittarius will be intercepted in the eighth house. Also, Cancer will appear again on the cusp of the fourth and Capricorn on the cusps of the eighth and ninth houses.

Finally, it may have occurred to you that up till now you have regarded each of the twelve pie-shaped segments of the horoscopic circle as a division of signs of the zodiac in sequence from Aries to Pisces. This sequence, commencing at the point which you have now identified as the first house cusp, is the natural order of the zodiac.

---

*The Koch House System, or, more properly, the Birthplace Table of Houses, may be described as a refinement of the Placidian House System, and many contemporary astrologers such as Lillian Canaan, Zipporah Dobyns and Nola Williams used the *Hausertabellen des Geburtsortes* authored by Dr. Walter Koch and Elizabeth Schaeck. For an example of a horoscope erected with Koch house cusps, see Figure 13-A, and compare it with Figure 13.

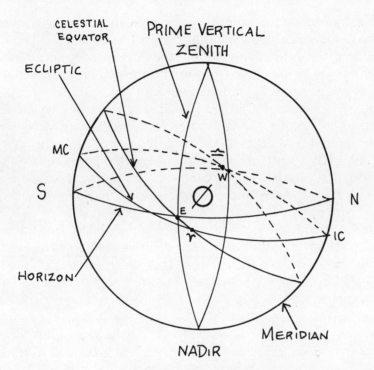

FIGURE 12. The celestial sphere
(shown at latitude for London: 51 N 32)

I hasten to add, however, that although the natural order of the zodiac represented by the Sun's yearly travel through the signs commences with Aries and concludes with Pisces, in a given horoscope the signs on the house cusps may commence anywhere in the sequence, depending on the time of the native's birth. While the signs always follow each other in the same order, the sequence may begin with any sign in the zodiac.

If the native is born at four in the afternoon eastern standard time and has his Sun in Sagittarius, he may have Gemini on the cusp of his first house, not Aries. Thus the sign sequence will start with Gemini and wind up with Taurus on the cusp of the twelfth—unless one of the signs is intercepted, in which case Aries could appear on the cusps of both the eleventh and twelfth houses, with Taurus intercepted *in* the twelfth house.

Such is the case with my own horoscope, which shows Gemini on the cusps of the first and second houses; so Sagittarius appears on the cusps of both the seventh and eighth houses, with Scorpio intercepted in the sixth house and Taurus intercepted in the twelfth house (see fig. 13).

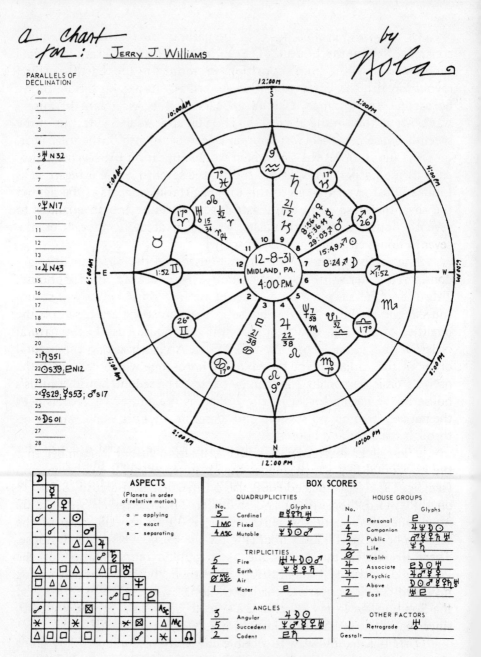

FIGURE 13. Author's horoscope

Of what importance, then, is the natural order of the zodiac in a consideration of the houses? The horoscope shows multiple concepts simultaneously: the Sun's position in terms of the Earth's orbital revolution and the Earth's position in terms of its axial rotation. In my horoscope, for instance, Gemini appears on the Ascendant because I was born at four in the afternoon. The Sun appears in Sagittarius in the seventh house because I was born on December eighth of the solar year.

Because Libra is the sign which would appear on the seventh house cusp in the natural order of the zodiac, the seventh house is regarded as Libra's house even though in this case Sagittarius appears as the sign on the seventh house cusp. Many astrologers attribute Libran qualities to seventh house planets no matter what sign actually appears on the seventh house cusp in a given horoscope.

The same is true of the other houses and the same qualities are considered in terms of the natural house sign—Aries for the first house, Taurus for the second house, Gemini for the third house and so on. Indeed, the attributes of any house in the horoscope are based on the qualities of the sign which appears on that house cusp in the natural order of the zodiac. Thus the first house, Aries's house in the natural order of the zodiac, is the house in *any* horoscope which deals with the native's basic personality as seen by others. The second house, Taurus's house in the natural order of the zodiac, is the house which deals with the native's income, possessions and senses in any horoscope. And so on through the signs and houses.

There is an easy way to visualize house division. Remember that the horizontal line which divides the circle represents the natal horizon (see fig. 13). I have placed 6:00 A.M. on the first house cusp, 8:00 A.M. on the twelfth house cusp and so on at 2-hour intervals with 12:00 noon on the cusp of the tenth house, 6:00 P.M. on the cusp of the seventh house and 12:00 midnight on the cusp of the fourth house. There you have the horoscope as a graphic representation of the 24-hour day, with 2 hours attributed to each house. I have been using my horoscope for purposes of illustration. I was born at 4:00 P.M., so the Sun appears in my chart in the seventh house as it properly should, since that is the segment of time from 4:00 P.M. to 6:00 P.M.

This is a handy way to double-check the accuracy of any given chart you have erected. If the native was born at 7:00 A.M., you know that the Sun will probably appear in the twelfth house; you certainly know that it will not appear in the fourth house. If it turns up in the fourth house, you have a good indication that something went wrong in your calculations.

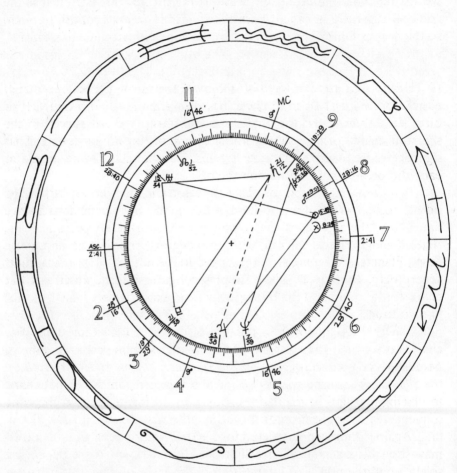

FIGURE 13A. Author's horoscope, Koch house system

In any horoscope, we know by the Sun sign approximately the time of year in which the native was born. With the help of the houses, we also know the time of day that birth occurred. However, just as the zodiacal signs tell us much more than the approximate month of birth, so the houses tell us much more than the approximate time of day.

IF THE EXACT time of birth is unknown, the astrologer may construct either a *solar chart* or a *flat chart,* based on the month, day and year of birth. In a *solar chart,* the birth time is arbitrarily set at sunrise in the sign and degree of sign shown in the ephemeris for the birth date. That sign degree is placed on the first house cusp, and the same degree of each succeeding sign is placed on the houses next in order.

A *flat chart* is erected without regard to the time of birth. The house cusps, which are the lines dividing the horoscope into twelve lunes, are labeled according to the natural sequence of zodiacal signs, Aries through Pisces, starting with zero degrees Aries on the first house cusp. Planets are entered in the appropriate houses of the flat chart accordingly. By way of illustration, see figure sixteen, which is a flat chart for a popular female singer whose exact time of birth is not known to me.

Where I do not have a reliable birth time, I have used the flat chart, rather than the solar chart, throughout this book. I have done so because of a basic astrological principle: *each house is characterized by the sign of the natural zodiac with which it is associated.* The flat chart, in placing the signs of the natural zodiac on the house cusps in the same sequence, is an application of this principle.

Again, a horoscope erected for a native whose birth time *is* known may show any degree of any sign on a given house cusp, depending solely upon the points of intersection of the natal horizon and meridian with the ecliptic at the moment of birth.

Since the entire zodiac passes over the natal horizon with every complete rotation of the Earth on its axis, and since there are 30 degrees to each of the 12 signs of the zodiac for a total of 360 degrees every 24 hours, simple arithmetic discloses that a full degree of zodiacal sign rises above the natal horizon every 4 minutes (24 hours times 60 minutes per hour = 1,440 minutes per 24-hour day; divided by 360 degrees = 4 minutes per degree). Every degree of every sign makes a difference in chart interpretation; that is why it is extremely important to have the exact time of birth.

Figure fourteen is the natal chart of a famous male singer which will serve as the illustration of *house* interpretation. I have put the word

FAMOUS MALE SINGER

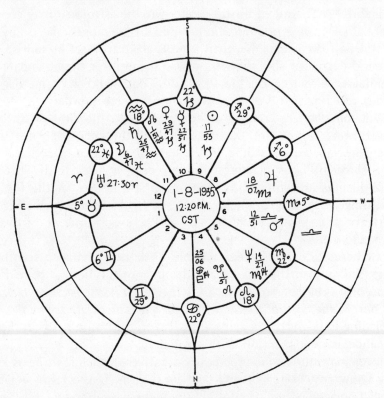

FIGURE 14. Natal chart of famous male singer

"house" in italics to emphasize that I shall resolutely ignore many other relevant considerations which are the subject of later chapters.

The sign on the first house cusp is called the Ascendant or rising sign, because it is the sign ascending or rising on the natal horizon at the moment of birth. In view of the basic astrological principle that with his first breath, every newborn child internalizes all of nature's cycles symbolized by the zodiacal sign positions, the importance of the Ascendant is apparent. Many if not most astrologers consider the Ascendant second in importance only to the Sun itself.

In the case of the famous male singer, the Ascendant is five degrees of Taurus. Notice that although the sign on the first house cusp commences with Taurus, the sequence of signs remains the same, so that Taurus is followed in counterclockwise direction by Gemini on the second house cusp, through to Aries intercepted in the twelfth house.

If I did not know the exact time of birth of the famous male singer, I would have erected a flat chart showing zero degrees Aries on the first house cusp, followed by zero degrees Taurus on the second house cusp and so on through zero degrees Pisces on the twelfth house cusp. Instead of its present position in the ninth house, the singer's Capricorn Sun would appear in the tenth house in a flat chart, since the tenth house would commence with zero degrees Capricorn instead of the twenty-two degrees of Capricorn actually shown in his natal horoscope (see fig. 14).

You can now appreciate the distinction between the flat chart and the horoscope—literally, the hour observed—erected when the exact birth time is known. Notice that the flat chart does reflect the month, day and year of the native's birth by the sign and sign degree of each planet shown in the chart.

The true horoscope incorporates the time of birth in terms of (1) sign and sign degree on each house cusp; (2) placement of planets in appropriate houses by sign and by sign degree; (3) correction of sign and sign degree of each planet for the exact moment of birth.

THE SEQUENCE OF seasons from spring to spring provides our earliest frame of reference for the affairs of the houses in the life of Man. The reader will doubtless recall that the astrological year is born at the vernal equinox, when the zodiac also begins with the sign Aries. The first house commences then as well, and it follows that the first house affairs should be expressions of the ego of the newborn.

The sign-and-season correlation to house affairs continues all the way through to Pisces, the twelfth sign and the astrological twelfth month, the month before the vernal equinox. Thus the twelfth house has traditionally been the house of destiny and hidden things, related as it was to that spooky time of year before the dead world was reborn.

With the sequence of house affairs, we can trace the development of the native from infancy to childhood, to maturity, old age, death— and, some astrologers would add, rebirth—as the postnatal ontogeny of the native recapitulates the evolution of his species from the Fall into human consciousness to his unknown destiny.

THE FIRST HOUSE OF SELF

Aries, the first sign of the zodiac, is associated with the first house of any horoscope. Aries represents Man's first existential consciousness of self as different-from-other, the native's first development of ego-awareness in infancy; hence the first house is the house of his identity. Thus, the first house is the house of self, and the affairs of life with which it deals are the way the native externalizes his ego, the expression of his personality, his appearance to others and the way in which he asserts himself.

THE SECOND HOUSE OF POSSESSIONS

Taurus, the second sign of the zodiac, is associated with the second house of any horoscope. Taurus represents the native's first awareness of his surroundings, his perception of the things he needs. It is Adam's reaching for a fig leaf; it is the infant reaching for his mother's breast. The affairs of life dealt with in the second house have to do with the native's acquisitions, his income and his possessions.

THE THIRD HOUSE OF COMMUNICATIONS AND KINSHIP

Gemini, the third sign of the zodiac, is associated with the third house of any horoscope. Gemini represents the efforts of the native to communicate, his curiosity and his versatility. It is the infant's cry for the absent breast and the short journey of the native back to the object of his immediate desire. It is everything we do to express ourselves verbally. It is also our first awareness of our brothers and sisters. The affairs of life dealt with in the third house are communications, short trips, brothers and sisters.

THE FOURTH HOUSE OF HOME

Cancer, the fourth sign of the zodiac, is associated with the fourth house of the horoscope. Cancer is our first awareness of mother as something more than her nourishing breast; our first awareness of home other than the sheltering bosom. The affairs of life dealt with in the fourth house have to do with the home and the parent who serves as mother—be that parent male or female—and with conditions at the end of life.

THE FIFTH HOUSE OF PLEASURES AND RISKS

Leo, the fifth sign of the zodiac, is associated with the fifth house of the horoscope. Leo is our first adventure into Eros; our first risk-taking ventures away from home; our first self-expression outside the protective environment. The affairs of life dealt with in the fifth house have to do with our adventures, our expression of self through children and brain children, our various gambles and pleasures. While the fifth house is traditionally known as the house of pleasure, I believe it is more accurately described as the house of risks; both terms will be used interchangeably throughout this book.

THE SIXTH HOUSE OF SERVICE AND HEALTH

Virgo, the sixth sign of the zodiac, is associated with the sixth house of the horoscope. Virgo is our recognition of the reality that to have our needs served, we must serve others; and the reality that we have a need to serve others and to be served by them as well. The proper balance of these needs means physical and emotional health. The affairs of life dealt with in the sixth house are servants, service and health.

THE SEVENTH HOUSE OF PARTNERSHIP

Libra, the seventh sign of the zodiac, is associated with the seventh house of the horoscope. Libra symbolizes our needs for partnership, for the sense of completion that can only come with a partner—which can include business as well as marriage partners. The affairs of life dealt with in the seventh house are partnership affairs; those who will not share a partnership with us are our open enemies, and the seventh house deals with them as well.

THE EIGHTH HOUSE OF SEX, LOVE AND DEATH

Scorpio, the eighth sign of the zodiac, is associated with the eighth house of the horoscope. Scorpio means death and rebirth, but such death can be the ego-loss occasioned by sex or sleep or death, or anything by which we lose, through our passionate intensity, the awareness of self. The affairs of life dealt with in the eighth house therefore include sex, love and death. The eighth house is commonly

known as the house of sex, or the house of sex, love and death, and
these terms are used in this book together with the term I think more
accurately reflects the activities of this house: *the house of ego-loss*.

THE NINTH HOUSE OF HIGHER MIND AND LONG JOURNEYS

Sagittarius, the ninth sign of the zodiac, is associated with our
need to come to terms with the trauma of sex and death. It is the sign
which represents our need to grow, to experience, beyond the limits
that our life has so far imposed, to transcend by idealism or by other
journeys away from self. The affairs of the ninth house are the higher
mind activities of religion, philosophy and law. The ninth house is also
the house of the foreign and of long journeys.

THE TENTH HOUSE OF THE PUBLIC AND CAREER

Capricorn, the tenth sign of the zodiac, represents our need for
status and achievement in a social setting. It is the resentment of Cain
for the preference shown by God the Father for Abel's gifts; it is the
martyrdom of Abel as well. It is the sign of the scapegoat, and of the
mountain goat who climbs the peaks unscathed. Affairs of the tenth
house have to do with our public role, our possible martyrdom, our
career achievement and the parent we view as our father, be he male or
female.

THE ELEVENTH HOUSE OF ASPIRATION AND FRIENDSHIP

Aquarius, the eleventh sign of the zodiac, is the sign which
represents our long view of humanity, our vision which justifies our
commanding others for their own good. Affairs of the eleventh house
have to do with our political and visionary selves, our dispassionate love
for our fellow man; it is our capacity for Agape rather than for Eros,
with which Leo, its polar opposite, is associated.

THE TWELFTH HOUSE OF DESTINATION

Pisces, the twelfth sign of the zodiac, is the sign of our otherworldliness; it is the sign of the third ear with which we listen to the
sound of Thoreau's different drummer whose faint but persistent beat
we sometimes prefer to ignore. Affairs of the twelfth house have to do
with whatever enlightenment and destiny the course of our life has
brought us. We hope our development through the stages of consciousness reflected by the twelve houses will provide us with a sense of
completion, of Oneness in the secret shared universe of Man, the dream
animal. If not, the twelfth house will indeed be the native's house of

secret sorrows, institutions and self-undoing. For those so inclined, it is the house of karmic debts. The twelfth house is variously referred to as the house of secrets; house of debts of destiny; house of the occult. I have settled upon "house of destination," which seems to include the other activities as well; however, the terms are interchangeable, and their use here depends on the context.

Taken as the development of the individual human being from infancy, the first four houses work in much the way that Dr. W. Hugh Missildine described our early psychological evolution in *Your Inner Child of the Past.* We never escape that inner child and our reactions to those early life experiences in the development of our consciousness are always very much a part of us. That level of consciousness commences with the first house of self and concludes with the fourth house of home. With the sequence of the first four houses, each of us completes one cycle of consciousness.

The second cycle commences with Leo and the fifth house of risks. At this point, the native leaves the shelter of home and seeks to assert himself as leader, paterfamilias, lover, gambler; to stand on his own two feet. The houses of service, partnership and ego-loss continue and conclude this second level of consciousness.

The third and last cycle of human consciousness commences with the ninth house of higher mind, in which astrologers have traditionally included religion, philosophy and law. The native explores his third level of consciousness through his houses of public service and his house of aspirations, and concludes with his twelfth house of destination.

The symbolism of the houses can be applied to many kinds of transition and evolution, including that of the individual, that of society or that of Mankind. The reader will find that the symbolism of the houses is a remarkably adaptive tool.

THERE ARE MANY ways in which astrologers use houses. For natal chart delineation, one useful technique has been to group planets categorically, according to activities. Consideration of planet placement by these house groups provides significant information which cannot be obtained by dealing with planetary placements in any one house alone.

1. *Personal Houses.* The twelfth through the third houses of any horoscope are the personal houses. Notice that the personal houses comprise a third of the entire chart, which for the sake of convenience I will refer to as the *first third,* even though it commences with the

twelfth house and not with the first house. (It does so because of the proximity and possible conjunction of planets posited in the twelfth house to the Ascendant, a most personal consideration.)

A native with an abundance of planets posited in personal houses does not require the companionship or participation of others in order to function well. With an overabundance of planets in personal houses, the native might comfortably be a hermit. A lack of planetary emphasis in personal houses suggests that the native may be overly dependent on the opinions and actions of others, whose presence is required for his effective functioning.

What constitutes an abundance, an overabundance or, for that matter, a lack of planetary placements in personal houses? Eventually the reader will rely on his own experience in assessing these data. As a rule of thumb, however, each of the first three house groups includes a full third of the horoscope, so that one might expect to find an average of three planets in each of these groupings. You can use the same rule (ten planets divided by number of houses in group) in assessing the average number of planets to be found in successive groupings.

I emphasize the subjective factor of the astrologer's individual experience because astrology is not all that arithmetical; it is *metempirical*. For example, recent research has shown that the peak in births occurs between the end of the night and the first hours of the day, and the trough or low point in the first hours of the afternoon.[1] That means a possibility of more planetary positions on the average in the personal houses, since the Sun at least would be posited in one of those *peak-time* houses, and probably Mercury as well, since Mercury is never more than twenty-eight degrees from the Sun. There would be correspondingly fewer planets in the trough-time houses of the early afternoon.

2. *Companionship Houses.* The second third of the horoscope, from the fourth house of home through the seventh house of partnership, constitutes the companionship houses. A native with abundant planetary placements in companionship houses needs companions and functions best in participation with others.

3. *Public Houses.* The last third of the horoscope, from the eighth house of ego-loss through the eleventh house of aspiration, constitutes the public houses. A native with abundant planetary placements in public houses needs public recognition—and will probably have it, since he will be motivated to achieve it, one way or another.

4. *Life Houses.* The first house of self, the fifth house of pleasures and risks and the ninth house of higher mind are the life houses in any horoscope. A native with an abundance of planets in life houses will

experience the *joie de vivre* more readily than the average native. A native with a lack of planets posited in life houses won't know what you are talking about when you ask him whether he enjoys life or not; he has probably never considered the question, particularly if he has an overabundance of planets in wealth houses.

5. *Wealth Houses.* The second house of possessions, the sixth house of service and the tenth house of the public and career are the wealth houses. Several planetary placements in these houses suggest that the native's opportunities and motivation for acquiring wealth will be emphasized.

6. *Houses of Association.* The third house of kinship, the seventh house of partnership and the eleventh house of friendship are the houses of association, referring to the need for *intimate* associations, in contradistinction to the need for companionship indicated by the fourth through seventh houses. Notice that the only overlap in these two groupings is in the seventh house of partnership. Heavy emphasis in houses of (intimate) association indicates the native's need for close personal friends to whom he can relate and in whom he can confide.

7. *Psychic Houses.* The fourth house of home, the eighth house of ego-loss and the twelfth house of secrets are the psychic houses. A native with emphasis in these houses often has a pronounced psychic prowess.

8. *Houses Above.* The houses above are those above the horizon; that is, the seventh house of partnership through the twelfth house of secrets. A native with a preponderance of planets posited in the houses above is likely to seek and to receive public recognition—or at least public attention. Such motivation is particularly apparent in the placements in the houses above which happen to fall in the eighth through eleventh houses, the public houses.

9. *Houses East.* The houses east are those east of the natal meridian; the tenth house of the public through the third house of communications. If the native has a preponderance of planets posited in houses east of his meridian, chances are that he is more likely to be inner-directed than other-directed. Otherwise stated, the native with emphasis in houses east will determine his own direction in life rather than let the course of his life be determined by others. It follows that a native, a preponderance of whose planets are west of his natal meridian (houses four through nine), is more likely to permit others to chart the direction of his life.

The groupings of houses by personal, companionship and public houses divide the horoscope into thirds, since they constitute groups of four houses each, commencing in order from the twelfth house. The life, wealth, association and psychic groupings of houses correspond to the triplicities. The life houses include the first house of self, the fifth house of pleasures and the ninth house of long journeys, which correspond to Aries, Leo and Sagittarius in the natural horoscope. Thus the life houses constitute the fire triplicity of signs, or in the overall gestalt of the natural horoscope association of house and sign, a grand trine in fire.

Likewise, the wealth houses include the second house of income, the sixth house of service and the tenth house of career, constituting the earth triplicity in the natural horoscope. The houses of association include the third house of kinship, the seventh house of partnership and the eleventh house of friendship, or the air triplicity. Finally, the psychic houses include the fourth house of home, the eighth house of ego-loss and the twelfth house of destiny, or the water triplicity.

All of the categories grouping signs and houses are reflected in a series of boxes on the left-hand side of the chart form. Most astrologers routinely tabulate this information as one of their first tasks in horoscope delineation (see fig. 14). The only category in the box scores with which you are not yet familiar is the classification of planets by house angle, which is the subject of the next section of this chapter.

The box scores are used by astrologers as a first step in chart interpretation. As with the consideration of all individual factors in the horoscope, the conclusions reached are provisional. All the information which the chart provides in terms of planetary positions by house, sign, aspect, house rulership, together with the house cusps and the overall gestalt, must be synthesized in the natal delineation.

Nevertheless, the box scores are an extremely handy tool. They provide immediate access to a new chart where the astrologer—especially those who are relatively inexperienced—might otherwise ponder a long time over the question of where to begin; and they stimulate the absorbing process of synthesis.

IN THE PLANISPHERE of the horoscope as it is drawn on paper the horizon appears as a horizontal line which bisects the great circle of the native's meridian, although the natal horizon is itself a great circle. Likewise, the meridian which we use to divide the ecliptic into quarters is also a great circle, even though it appears as a vertical line connecting the Midheaven and the Underheaven, known as the IC.

The horizon line creates the first and the seventh house cusps. The vertical line of the meridian creates the fourth and tenth house cusps, according to the Placidian system. The areas of life related to the houses created by this basic quadrant division of the horoscope are the most active in the chart. These areas are the first house of self, the fourth house of home, the seventh house of partnership and the tenth house of the public. Planets posited in these four houses receive their fullest expression, according to their planetary qualities and the qualities of the signs in which they appear in those angular houses.

These four houses are known as the *angular* houses, since they are the original angles created by the quadrature system of house division. All the other houses are created by trisecting each quadrant—a total of three houses for each one.

The second, the fifth, the eighth and the eleventh houses succeed the *angular* houses in the counterclockwise direction of the horoscope. For this reason, these houses are called the *succedent* houses, from the Latin verb *succedere,* which means to follow closely.

The affairs of life associated with the succedent houses also follow closely from the activities initiated in the angular houses. Thus, from the angular first house, the externalization of the self, the succedent second house deals with the native's acquisitions. Likewise, the angular fourth house, the home, leads to the succedent fifth house, dealing with the native's children, including his brain children, and his risk-taking functions. After the angular seventh house—the native's partnerships including marriage—the succedent eighth house treats activities of sex, love and death. The angular tenth house deals with the native's career and public image, and the succedent eleventh house with activities of friends, hopes and wishes.

The last set of houses created by the trisection of the quadrants is known as the *cadent* houses, from the Latin verb *cadere,* which means to fall from. The cadent houses fall from the succedent houses, with the connotation of a wider dispersion of energies. The cadent houses enlarge upon the activities initiated in the angular houses and pursued in the succedent houses. The cadent houses are the third, the sixth, the ninth and the twelfth houses.

In the cadent third house the native, by his efforts to communicate with others, more fully develops the expression of self initiated in the angular first house. In the cadent sixth house, the native, by his services, expands the home initiated in the angular fourth house and developed by children and risk-taking in the succedent fifth house. In the cadent ninth house, the native explores the mysteries of sex, love and death to which he was led in the succedent eighth house by way of initiation in the angular seventh house. In the cadent twelfth house, the native reaps the rewards of his life, from the seeds sown in the profession and in the public role he pursued in the angular tenth house, and nurtured through his friends, hopes and wishes in the succedent eleventh house.

The classification of signs by angles dovetails with the classifications by triplicity and by quadruplicity. Thus, Aries is a cardinal sign by quadruplicity, a fire sign by triplicity and the sign associated with the first house in the natural zodiac. Arien cardinal fire characteristics of pioneering spirit are paralleled by those of the angular first house as one of initiating action.

Taurus is a fixed sign by quadruplicity, an earth sign by triplicity and the sign associated with the succedent second house in the natural zodiac. Taurean fixed earth characteristics of stability, receptivity and follow-through are paralleled by those of the succedent second house angle as carrying on the activities initiated in the first house.

Gemini is a mutable sign by quadruplicity, an air sign by triplicity and the sign associated with the cadent third house in the natural zodiac. Gemini's mutable air qualities of adaptability and variety are paralleled by the characteristics of the cadent third house angle, in which the activities initiated in the first house and pursued in the second, in the native's efforts to assert and to identify himself, are widely dispersed in the third house.

And so on, through the signs and the houses of the zodiac. Once again, I urge on the reader the heuristic approach. Take one of the blank chart forms in the back of this book. Number the houses in the correct order, from one to twelve. Add the signs to the house cusps according to the natural zodiac—i.e., Aries on the first house cusp, and so on through Pisces on the twelfth house cusp.

Indicate the appropriate triplicity and quadruplicity for the sign on each house cusp in the pie-shaped segment of the house itself. This is essentially what I have done in the preceding paragraphs with the signs Aries through Gemini, the first quadruplicity, the first set of angles and three-fourths of the first triplicity. When you have added these data to the chart, you will be prepared to formulate the remainder of the parallels between house, sign, quadruplicity, triplicity and angle which I have illustrated with the first three houses.

Remember that in order to interpret the activities of each house of any horoscope you must consider the following:

1. The areas of life activity related to the house.
2. The sign associated with the house according to the natural zodiac.
3. The sign which actually appears on the cusp of the house.
4. The quadruplicity of the sign on the house cusp.

5. The triplicity of the sign on the house cusp.
6. The planet(s), if any, posited in the house, and the effect of the preceding considerations on the expression of that planet's force.
7. The sign and house position of the planet ruling the sign and house cusp, and how the preceding considerations affect the planetary ruler and hence the manifestation of the sign which it rules on the cusp of the house under consideration.

NOW, LET'S APPLY the principles outlined above to an interpretation of the houses in the natal horoscope of the famous male singer. At this point, all of the information about signs and houses contained in the box scores has been considered. Those data can now be summarized in relation to the singer.

Quadruplicities. With six placements in cardinal signs, there is a powerful emphasis in that quadruplicity, suggesting that the native is capable of initiating action, and strongly motivated to do so. His initiatory capability greatly outdistances his ability to follow the programs of others (two in fixed) or to adapt to changes of direction (two in mutable).

Triplicities. The cardinal emphasis is nicely balanced by the earth triplicity. With four planets in earth signs, plus the Ascendant and the Midheaven, the follow-through missing in the quadruplicities can here be found, together with a much-needed stability.

Angles. The four placements in angular houses, coupled with three placements each in succedent and cadent houses, indicate that the native (again) is an initiator, but here we find a balanced capacity for follow-through and for flexibility.

Personal Houses. With only the planet Uranus in personal houses, and that planet in the cadent twelfth, the native has little ability to live within himself. He would not make a good hermit.

Companionship Houses. Four placements in companions, including a debilitated Mars in Libra, suggest a felt need on the part of the native to have people around him at almost all times. This inference is emphasized by the fact that the native has but one placement in personal. It is also reinforced by the fact that Pluto, the planet of emotional intensity, is posited in the angular fourth house, in cardinal Cancer; and Jupiter, his planet of growth and beneficence, is posited in the angular seventh house in Scorpio, which Pluto rules.

Public Houses. Five placements in public houses indicate a strong drive for public recognition, particularly in view of the fact that both the Sun and Moon are not only in public houses, but the Sun is posited in Capricorn, the sign of status, together with Mercury, Venus and the Midheaven. Mercury, Venus and the north node are all in the tenth house of the public, an angular house.

Life Houses. With two placements in the three life houses, which constitute one-fourth of the horoscope, the native has an average, or less than average ability to enjoy life. Since astrology is a *holistic* expression of the personality, we cannot ignore that Sun in Capricorn, which gives him a native seriousness. I would surmise that he is at heart a serious person who, by virture of his Taurus Ascendant, externalizes—by his manner of dress, for example—much of the *joie de vivre* that he sees and perhaps envies in others.

Wealth Houses. With three placements in the three wealth houses, the native has an average or better than average interest in wealth, augmented by the Taurus Ascendant.

(Intimate) Associations. With three placements in the three houses of associations, the native feels the need for intimate relationships with others. Whether that need will be fulfilled depends on factors yet to be considered.

Psychic Houses. With two placements in the three psychic houses, the native shows some psychic or intuitive ability. For some as-yet-unexplicated reason, averages of planetary placements in psychic houses seem generally lower; therefore, I find two placements average—again, in my experience.

Houses Above. With seven placements in the six houses above the horizon, the native has a pronounced emphasis suggesting motivation to achieve public recognition. Consistent with the research on times of birth reported earlier, I have found that there are generally fewer planets in houses above the horizon than below; for this reason, seven placements in houses above qualify as an abundance. Notice also that five of those seven placements are in the public houses.

Houses East. With five placements in the six houses east of the natal meridian, this native has an almost equal planetary distribution in the hemispheres which suggest his self-direction and his direction by others.

Retrograde. With two planets retrograde at birth, the archetypal forces symbolized by those planets are more likely to be internalized, until their direct motion is achieved. The planets are Pluto and Uranus. By progression, the native's Aries Uranus achieved direct motion when the native was two, while his Virgo Neptune will remain retrograde his entire life.

The box scores show an individual, strongly motivated toward public recognition, who needs to have people around him. He doesn't like to be alone, has found his own direction in life and has an innate determination which provides him with stability.

So much for the box scores. We are now ready to consider each house in turn.

First House of Self. We look to the Ascendant for clues to the personality and the physical appearance of the native, including his interests and aptitudes and the way we might appear to others.

Five degrees of Taurus on the first house cusp suggests an individual whose personality orientation is to present sensation. Natives whose Ascendants are in early degrees of Taurus often have pleasing voices (Taurus rules the neck), an interest in music and a delight in color. Earlier, I indicated the Taurean sensuousness, but here Venus (ruler of Taurus) is posited in Capricorn in the tenth house of status, suggesting some inhibition in the native's ability to give and to receive love.

Second House of Possessions. Second house possessions include income, personal property, articles of clothing, money—just about everything but real estate. The sign on the second house cusp indicates what kind of possessions the native is likely to have, the extent of his possessory interest and his attitude toward his possessions generally.

Six degrees of Gemini on the second house cusp suggests that the native will have income from communications (hardly surprising, since he is a famous singer) and from a variety of sources. Gemini indicates also that there may be a considerable fluctuation in the state of his income, and his attitude toward his possessions is probably one of profligacy.

Gemini is the sign of communications, of versatility, of interest in many, many things and of mercurial attitudes.

Third House of Communications. This house shows how the native communicates, his attitude toward his brothers and sisters—and, for that matter, whether or not he *has* any brothers and sisters.

Since it is the sign of twins, Gemini on the third house cusp means that the native may have been one of twins. Gemini is ruling its own house, so the native probably communicates effectively. Gemini's planetary ruler, Mercury, posited in the tenth house of the public, suggests that his communications may be public or may achieve public attention. Since Mercury is in the sign of status, Capricorn, that inference is reinforced; and since Capricorn is a self-critical and idealistic sign, those characteristics may also appear in his communications—the idealism outwardly, the criticism more often than not directed within.

As you can see, all the house cusps are interrelated. The third house cusp of Gemini indicates an ability to communicate and the Gemini second house cusp suggests income from communications. The ruler of Gemini is Mercury and the ruler of Taurus is Venus. Since both planets are posited in the tenth house of the public, the native's income is related to a pleasing voice in a public role.

Fourth House of Home. Here we find the nature of the native's beginnings and home life. It is the house of the mother, or the parent who served in that role, and we look to the fourth house for the relationship between the native and that parent.

With twenty-two degrees of Cancer on the fourth house cusp, the native has Cancer ruling its own natural house. Cancer is the sign of the mother and of maternal feeling. Notice that Pluto, that planet of emotional intensity, is posited in the angular fourth house and in Cancer as well. Pluto rules Scorpio, which in this chart rules the seventh house of partnership, indicating a lifelong, deep emotional attachment between this native and his mother.

The Moon rules Cancer, and the Moon is posited in Pisces in the eleventh house of aspiration. The Moon in Pisces suggests a mother who may have been a nurse, and who is attentive to and self-sacrificing for her child. Its position in the house of aspiration means that the mother's aspirations are for her child—and vice versa. The Pisces Moon further indicates that the mother may have had musical aptitudes, somehow connected to her aspirations, perhaps given religious expression.

The south node is posited in the fourth house, in early degrees of Leo. The south node indicates areas of life in which the native requires additional effort, sometimes regarded by astrologers as lessons to be learned in life. Posited in Leo and in the house of home, the south node suggests that the native attempts to re-create the home of his childhood as a personal feifdom over which he rules; and while all of us have some impulse in that direction, for this native it represents an obstacle to be overcome. This inference is also supported by the fact that the fourth house is the house of real estate, and with acquisitive, home-loving Cancer on the fourth house cusp, the native's intense interest in his home environment is assured.

Fifth House of Pleasures and Risks. This house demonstrates how the native asserts himself and relates to his environment—perhaps another way of saying that the fifth house governs pleasures, children, brain children and gambling.

Here the native has eighteen degrees of Leo on the cusp of the fifth house, and Leo is the sign associated with the fifth house in the natural zodiac. Leo is the sign in which we identify the self by replication: the image of Narcissus looking in the pond-mirror is an accurate one. With Neptune posited in the fifth house, the native would seek recognition in an imaginative, creative way. Neptune in Virgo suggests a practical imagination and the technical musical skills often associated with Virgo. Leonard Bernstein, for example, is a Virgo.

The Sun, ruler of Leo, is posited in the ninth house of higher mind in the serious and status-oriented sign of Capricorn. From these data we can make several inferences: first, that the native's brain children will be definitely oriented to higher mind activities of religion, philosophy and law; second, that his creative efforts will have a basic core of seriousness. I note in passing Capricorn's odd quality of polarizing public opinion so that natives with this sign emphasis are frequently controversial, sometimes achieving martyrdom.

Sixth House of Service. We look to the sixth house to see how the native will serve others and also for clues to the state of his health. Virgo on the cusp of the sixth house, its natural sign association, implies good health, as well as an affirmative desire to serve others. Mercury, ruler of Virgo, is posited in the tenth house and in Capricorn, both indicating that his service will be of a public nature.

We must also take note of Libra, intercepted in the sixth house, as the co-ruler of this house. The ruler of Libra is Venus, posited in the tenth house of the public, conjunct Mercury. This configuration suggests that the native's service will be of an aesthetic nature, related to his public role; again, since we know he is a famous singer, the nature of that service seems evident. What is interesting here is that it is so clearly prefigured in the house activities of the chart, and readily ascertainable by the reader.

Mars, in detriment in Libra, is posited in the native's cadent sixth house; from these facts, we can infer that the native's service will be not only aesthetic, but energized by a sexual sublimation which could amount to debility.

Seventh House of Partnership. Here we see the kind of marriage partner the native might have, and the native's attitude toward partnerships, business, marriage or otherwise.

Five degrees of Scorpio on the seventh house cusp suggests that the native's marriage partner will have a Scorpio personality. His feelings about his relationships are intense and enduring and his loyalty steadfast. Jupiter in Scorpio is posited in the angular seventh house, implying great generosity to those with whom he feels he has a partnership. Pluto, the ruler of Scorpio, is posited in Cancer in the angular fourth house of home, suggesting that the native wishes to make all of his partnerships part of one family.

Eighth House of Sex or Ego-Loss. In this house, traditionally the house of sex, love and death, we learn how the native may seek to lose himself in the intensity of sexual passion, religious fervor or other effort at achieving Dionysian merger of the individual self with another or with the One.

Six degrees of Sagittarius on the cusp of the eighth house suggests that the native's efforts in eighth house affairs are essentially characterized by idealism. This inference is supported by the Scorpio position of Jupiter, ruler of Sagittarius, in the seventh house of partnership. Jupiter in Scorpio alone would indicate sexual relations with many partners; however, its ninth house rulership also indicates that the sexual relation would be idealized, and, since the native's seventh house activities are related to the home, sex-at-home with a marriage partner would be the ideal toward which the native would strive, successfully or otherwise.

Ninth House of Higher Mind. This house reveals the nature and expression of the native's interest in what astrology has traditionally termed the higher mind activities of religion, philosophy and law. The ninth house is also the house of the foreign and of long journeys.

Twenty-nine degrees of Sagittarius on the cusp of this house suggests that the native has a considerable interest in these activities. This inference is drawn from several factors: one, Sagittarius is the sign associated with the ninth house in the natural zodiac; two, the Sun, the native's basic self, is posited in this house. A third factor is the position of sign-ruler Jupiter in Scorpio, which can mean intense religious zeal, in the house of partnership: he would want his wife to have his religious orientation.

Tenth House of the Public. We look to the tenth house for indications of the native's public role, his public image and his attitudes toward his father.

The first consideration of the tenth house is the Midheaven, which is the tenth house cusp, and which many astrologers consider almost equal in importance to the Ascendant, the first house cusp.

Twenty-two degrees of Capricorn at the Midheaven suggests, again, that the native's public role will be controversial. There are possible overtones of martyrdom of a sort. The native is seen as essentially serious.

Both Venus and Mercury are posited in the angular tenth house and in Capricorn. These planets have been considered in relation to the signs and houses which they rule.

The north node is also posited in the tenth house in early degrees of Aquarius. The north node indicates in any chart the area of life in which things come easily for the native, and in which he is likely to find the path to achievement the smoothest. Here the north node is posited in the house of the public in the humanitarian, dispassionate sign of Aquarius. Thus the native may find it easy to love humanity as a whole, much more difficult to commit himself to a one-to-one relationship, as is further suggested by the Leo south node position.

Saturn, the ruler of Capricorn and hence the planetary ruler of the tenth house in this horoscope, is posited in Aquarius in the eleventh house of aspiration. Since Aquarius is the sign always associated with that house, and in fact rules it in this chart, we infer that public recognition is what this native hopes to achieve.

Eleventh House of Aspiration. Here are clues to the native's friends, hopes and wishes.

Eighteen degrees of Aquarius on the eleventh house cusp adds emphasis to that Aquarian influence. Important also is the influence of Uranus, ruler of Aquarius, in the aggressive, driving sign of Aries in the twelfth house.

The native's Pisces Moon and Aquarian Saturn are both posited in the eleventh house, indicating that the native regards his mother and father as his friends, somehow intimately related to his aspirations. The sign and house position of Uranus, his eleventh house ruler, indicates that these aspirations are urgent, compelling and somehow a source of secret sorrow.

Twelfth House of Destination. We look to the twelfth house for clues to the native's secret sorrows, ultimate destiny and karmic debts.

Twenty-two degrees of Pisces on the twelfth house cusp relates the sign always associated with the twelfth house to this native's twelfth house. But we must also take note of Aries as the co-ruler of the twelfth, since Aries is intercepted in that house.

Neptune, ruler of Pisces, is posited in Virgo in the fifth house of pleasures and risks. Mars, ruler of Aries, is debilitated in Libra in the sixth house of service and health. Putting these factors together, we conclude that the native has a practical, aesthetic sense which, since we know he is a famous singer, seems clearly to indicate musical aptitude; that his energies are directed more into aesthetic than into sexual channels. While he is endowed with aggressiveness and determination in the pursuit of his aspirations, his only really close friends are his mother and father, a relationship he seeks to re-create through fourth house affairs (conditions at the end of life) by the possible Leo feifdom already mentioned. Companionship and public recognition (five planets in public houses) must fill in for the truly close personal relationships which he yearns for (three in intimate associations) but which make a poor substitute for the closeness that he somehow cannot achieve. That seems to be his secret sorrow and his destiny in this lifetime.

In this analysis, I have deliberately considered only the box scores and the houses, including signs on the house cusps and their planetary rulers. Hence, the delineation of this natal chart is tentative. The aspecting of planets, for instance, is a primary consideration yet to be touched upon. It has been completely and purposely ignored here. However, even within these limitations, there is much that can be learned from the houses of any horoscope.

From the chart analysis you have just read, can you identify the singer?

THE FAMOUS MALE singer is Elvis Presley. Inferences drawn from his house cusps have been verified for the most part in biographical and critical works, especially Jerry Hopkins's biography, *Elvis*. Elvis has indeed demonstrated a drive toward and a need for public recognition. He has traditionally surrounded himself with buddies and gofers, and he is rarely alone.

His Taurus Ascendant corresponds to his popular image as well as to his biographical data—his love of colorful clothes, his precedent-shattering long sideburns and a singing voice which quite literally enraptured his audiences.

The Dionysian aspects of the Elvis Presley phenomenon are inescapable to anyone who reads Jerry Hopkins's biography, in terms of the spontaneous reactions of thousands of enraptured, screaming girls.

Elvis Presley's second house activities are well known; his love of cars, his profligacy and his mercurial attitudes.

My observation about the possibility of twins was based entirely on Gemini on the third house cusp. It troubled me, since I had never heard of a Presley twin; but, as Jerry Hopkins points out, there *was* a twin brother who died in infancy.[2]

As to the fourth house affairs, the deep emotional attachment to his mother, Gladys, who walked him to school until he was fifteen years old, is beyond question. Gladys Presley did work for a time as a nurse's aide.[3]

He learned to sing at the camp meetings, revivals and conventions of the white Pentecostal church group to which his family belonged when he was a child in Tupelo, Mississippi. And it was there, he later admitted, that he got his wiggle and the glottal click reminiscent of glossalia, or speaking in tongues, that the Pentecostal ministers displayed in their ecstatic efforts to seek direct communication with God.[4] His fifth house activities were therefore directly linked to his religious expression of creative musical talents; Elvis Presley brought Dionysian rapture to the field of popular music.

In Western civilization at least it has always been easier for men to express the Yang or verbal rational consciousness and for women to express the Yin or poetic and intuitive response. Elvis Presley was our first cultural hero to integrate both so dramatically and so completely. It was a significant step into the Aquarian Age.

Elvis Presley's sixth house activities are anticipated by his aesthetic interests related to his public role, while the particular expression of his energy, symbolized by his debilitated Mars in Libra, remains 'locked in his twelfth house of secrets.

As to his seventh house, I have been unable to find a birth date for his ex-wife Priscilla, which might have cast some light on that particular partner; but as more than one astrologer has commented, "She sure *looks* like a Scorpio!" Certainly Presley's loyalty in his partnerships is unquestioned.

Inferences about eighth and ninth house activities seem fully supported by the known facts of his highly publicized career and by what has been said thus far.

The Midheaven and tenth house deserve special comment. The polarizing, controversial and even the religious characteristics of the Capricorn archetype are evoked by Presley's Capricorn tenth house Midheaven. Presley, in whom glossalia, Pentecostal raptures, folk music and Negro spirituals combined to create a cultural hero, seemed a threat to established *mores.* Young men began to let their hair grow long to rival Elvis's scandalous sideburns, and dared to dress with the color and other affectations of adornment that have been the birthright of their sex in every species but Man.

Even while many insisted that Presley could not sing, he became the ultimate goal for creative musical genius hailing from points as far apart as Duluth, Minnesota, and Liverpool, England.

As to his eleventh house, the relationship of Presley's mother to his aspirations seems clearly established. His first record was a gift for her; his first release, "That's All Right (Mama)," remembered her. His singing was but an extension of the religious expression she had taught him from infancy. His first big home after his early success was a mansion in a wealthy section of Memphis, where Gladys Presley hung out the wash, to the outrage of her well-heeled neighbors. Their disapproval prompted a rare defiance from Presley—but this time it was his mother who was being criticized.[5]

It is noteworthy that Elvis did not marry while his mother lived; and that he and his widowed father met their future wives in Germany at about the same time.[6]

What about his twelfth house of destiny? Little can be said at this time. His marriage has ended; and today Elvis Presley seems almost an anachronism. Nevertheless, he is still the one artist, a CBS source relates, about whom stringent secrecy must be maintained whenever a new recording session is being arranged for him. Twenty years after his first success, Elvis Presley's enthusiastic fans still seek to tear him apart in classic Dionysian fashion.

12   What Are the Aspects?

"THE WONDROUS MUSIC of the spheres" was the contribution of Pythagoras, a Greek scientist who flourished in the sixth century B.C.E. He was also a philosopher and a mystic and had the unitary vision that his Orphic beliefs provided; he was the father of geometry and the religious leader of the Pythagorean Brotherhood. It is to Pythagoras that we owe the very term "cosmos." He used numbers to demonstrate the Oneness of all things, declaring that all things are numbers. The observation that "God forever geometrizes" belongs ultimately to Pythogoras. These concepts are part of the Ptolemaic synthesis found in *Tetrabiblos:*

> Of the parts of the zodiac those first are familiar one to another which are in aspect. These are the ones which are in opposition, enclosing two right angles, six signs, and 180 degrees; those which are in trine, enclosing one and one-third right angles, four signs, and 120 degrees; those which are said to be in quartile, enclosing one right angle, three signs, and 90 degrees, and finally those that occupy the sextile position, enclosing two-thirds of a right angle, two signs, and 60 degrees.[1]

Such are the aspects—a word which once had an exclusively astrological meaning—which are still used by astrologers today. The reason given by Ptolemy for using these aspects and no other is right out of Pythagorean harmonics.[2] Ptolemy does not classify the *conjunction* as an aspect, and he is technically correct, since there is no angle between planets which are conjunct; but he does use the conjunction, as do all astrologers today.[3]

In the early seventeenth century, Johannes Kepler, that perfervid astrologer/astronomer who discovered the three laws of planetary motion, invented the *minor aspects,* used by some astrologers; I use only the quincunx aspect of 150 degrees. One contemporary astrologer has surmised that Kepler would not have needed the minor aspects to account astrologically for certain phenomena, had he but known of the existence of Uranus, Neptune and Pluto.[4] Be that as it may, I adhere to the original Pythagorean conception, with the one exception noted.

An aspect, then, is the angle between planets measured in degrees of arc according to the great circle of the ecliptic. The aspects used in this chapter (and throughout this book) may be summarized as follows:

Aspect	Degree	Glyph
Conjunction	0	☌
Opposition	180	☍
Trine	120	△
Square ("quartile")	90	□
Sextile	60	✳
Quincunx	150	⊠

The trine and sextile are considered harmonious, easy or soft aspects. The square, opposition and quincunx are considered dissonant, difficult or hard aspects. The particular effect of any aspect depends on the planets involved and the signs and houses in which they are posited; so the conjunction cannot be classified as harmonious or dissonant as such.

IN DETERMINING ASPECTS, allowance is made for planets which fall short of exactitude in aspect within a given number of degrees. These allowances are called *orbs*. For example, if Mars and Venus are six degrees apart in the natal chart, a contemporary astrologer would regard them as *within orb* of a conjunction. Orbs of six degrees are allowed for the major aspects, exclusive of the Sun and the Moon, for which an orb of nine degrees is permitted. For the quincunx, an orb of three degrees is used.

In other words, if 2 planets (except the Sun and the Moon) are within 6 degrees of a conjunction, opposition, trine, square or sextile, they are within orb and those aspects are recorded on the natal chart. However, if there is a greater number of degrees of difference between these planets, they are not within orb and no aspect is formed. For example, if Mars and Venus are 129 degrees apart, they are not in trine aspect because the maximum orb is 6 degrees. Likewise, if Mars and Venus are 113 degrees apart, they are not within orb because the addition of 6 degrees—the maximum allowable orb—brings the planets only within 119 degrees of each other, and not within the required 120 degrees.

Notice that the orbs can be either added to or subtracted from the aspect within the allowable range. The same principles apply to the quincunx, with an allowable orb of 3 degrees, and to the Sun and Moon, with an allowable range of 9 degrees.

Some astrologers use wider orbs than those set out above, but the trend is toward smaller orbs. The orbs given here are those which I believe are in general use among contemporary astrologers.

I HAVE DESIGNED a new chart form for this book (see fig. 15). The major portion of the chart is taken up with three concentric circles, the innermost of which is used for the location of the planets and house cusps according to their natal positions on the great circle of the ecliptic. The chart is oriented according to cardinal compass positions, designated by *E* for east and so on; and the houses are numbered in correct sequence, one through twelve. The second circle is designed for use in entering *progressions;* and the outer circle is for the entry of *transits.*

To the left of the circles is a series of numbers, "Parallels of Declination." Parallels, as they are called, are used by some astrologers. You should know what they are so that you can try them out after you have learned the basics of chart erection and delineation. Parallels of declination are similar to latitude lines on an Earth globe, carried out to the celestial sphere. They are either north or south of the celestial equator, to which they are parallel. The allowable orb for parallels is a *maximum* of one degree. If planets are parallel and within orb, the parallel is regarded as having an effect similar to that of a conjunction *if it is in the same hemisphere,* either north or south. If the planets in parallel are in different hemispheres, the effect is comparable to that of an opposition.

My chart form is designed to simplify the notation of parallels. Each blank in the column for parallels represents a parallel of declination according to the numbered sequence, and without regard to whether the parallel is in the northern or southern hemisphere of the celestial equator. For example, if the Sun is posited at ten degrees, fifty-seven minutes south declination, the Sun's glyph would be entered at the blank numbered *ten,* followed by the letter *S* for south and by the number *fifty-seven* for the minutes. If Mars were posited at ten degrees, thirty minutes north declination, its glyph would be entered on the same line following the data for the Sun's declination, followed by the letter *N,* and by the number *thirty.* In that example, the astrologer would know immediately that the Sun and Mars were in parallel, and

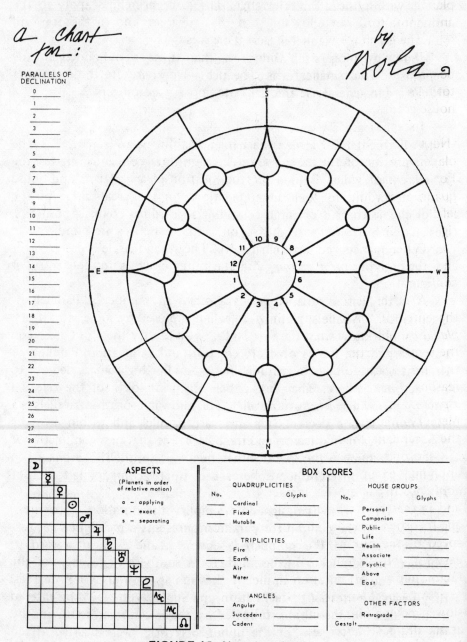

a chart for: _____ *by Nola*

FIGURE 15. New chart form

that the effect would be similar to an opposition, inasmuch as the planets were posited in different hemispheres—as indicated by the N and S notation.

The glyph for parallel is an equal sign shown vertically.

Below the wheel itself are the columns for the entry of aspects and box scores. The box scores are subdivided into two columns, one for toting up the quadruplicities, triplicities and angles, and the other for house groups.

In each case the number of planets is indicated in the Number (No.) column at the left of the particular entry, and the glyphs for the planets are entered in the column so headed to the right of the entry. For example, if Mars, Jupiter and Venus are all posited in the cardinal quadruplicity, the number three would be entered in the blank to the left of the word "Cardinal," and the glyphs for those planets to the right.

Other factors include the number of planets (if any) retrograde, and their glyphs; and the overall gestalt (if any) of the natal chart configuration.

A novel feature of this chart form is that it makes provision for the entry of the aspect glyphs for the planets *in the order of relative planetary motion.* From the Earth, the order of planetary motion is in the sequence from the Moon to Pluto, as shown in the chart. It is vital that you learn this sequence for the purpose of aspecting, for two reasons. First, the faster-moving planet is the planet which *does the aspecting* to the planets next in sequence—*e.g.,* the Moon *aspects* Mercury, Mercury *aspects* Venus and so on. All of the planets aspect the Ascendant, the Midheaven and the nodes of the Moon.

Second, there is the question whether the aspect being formed is applying, exact or separating. An aspect approaching exactitude is *applying;* it has greater impact than one which has passed that point and is therefore *separating;* and an *exact* aspect is the most potent of all. In order to make this determination, you must know the relative speed of the planets, *as seen from the Earth.* My chart form makes it easy for you. Many astrologers use the letters *a, e* and *s* to indicate this factor, adding that notation to the glyph in the appropriate box.

An aspect is applying when a faster-moving planet is approaching a slower-moving planet within orb. If the natal horoscope shows Mercury at six degrees Cancer and Jupiter at ten degrees Libra, Mercury, the faster-moving of the two planets, is in an *applying square* aspect to Jupiter. The astrologer would enter the glyph for the square aspect in the box where the vertical Mercury column intersects the horizontal Jupiter column; and he may add the letter *a* to indicate that it is an applying aspect. Notice also that Mercury is approaching an exact square to Jupiter as of the moment in time for which the horoscope is charted. When Mercury reaches ten degrees of Cancer, it will be in exact square to Jupiter and then the full impact of that square will be felt.

In addition, Mercury and Jupiter, posited in Cancer and in Libra respectively, are both in the same *quadruplicity*—specifically, the quadruplicity of cardinal signs. If you know your quadruplicities, you will find it a simple matter to spot square aspects between planets. Likewise, if you know the triplicities, you will find it easy to spot trine aspects between planets.

What if the sign positions in the above example were reversed? That would place Jupiter at six degrees Cancer and Mercury at ten degrees Libra. In such a chart configuration, Mercury, the faster-moving planet, has already passed the point of an exact square to Jupiter—which would have occurred at six degrees Libra—and is moving farther away from the slower-moving Jupiter each day. But at ten degrees Libra, Mercury is still within the six-degree orb we allow for major aspects and is therefore still in square aspect to Jupiter. However, since the point of exactitude has already occurred, the aspect is said to be *separating*, and this time we may add an *s* to the glyph for the square in the appropriate Mercury-Jupiter box on the chart form.

The distinction between applying, exact and separating aspects is of greatest significance in dealing with progressions, which chart future astrological events.

IN ASTRONOMICAL PARLANCE, a *node* is a point of intersection between the orbit of a celestial body and the great circle of the ecliptic. The Moon's orbit intersects the ecliptic at two diametrically opposite points. The north or ascending node is the point of intersection of the Moon's orbit in its travel from the southern to the northern hemisphere of the celestial sphere. The south or descending node is the point of passage from the northern to the southern hemisphere.

The north node is frequently called the dragon's head and the south node the dragon's tail, because at this point of intersection on the ecliptic, the dragon Moon swallows up the Sun whenever an eclipse occurs. Otherwise the orbit of the Moon is like the snake that swallows its own tail, a timeless symbol of world order, or cosmos.

The Moon's nodes have about three minutes' retrograde motion per day; the exact positions may be found in most ephemerides. Usually only the north node is listed, since the south node is the same degree in the polar opposite sign. So I show only the north node in my aspecting table. Notice that the glyph for the north node resembles a croquet wicket with beaded tips; the south node is the same thing upside down. There is considerable similarity between the signs for Leo and for the north node, a source of confusion for the unwary neophyte.

Traditionally, the position by sign and house in which the north node is located represents those things which come easily to the native; the position of the south node represents those affairs which require more effort on his part. Often the influence of the north node is considered analogous to that of Jupiter; the south node is analogized to Saturn.

THE EXAMPLE FOR purposes of illustrating how aspects are calculated will be Buffy Sainte-Marie, a contemporary singer of American Indian ancestry, and an adopted member of the Cree tribe, who was born February 20, 1941. Since I do not have an exact birth time for her, I have erected a flat chart (see fig. 16). The aspects have been entered in the appropriate columns; the parallels (which I won't use) have not.

In the sequence of calculating aspects, and later in delineating the chart, we start with the Sun, then the Moon and then Mercury. The remainder of the planets follow the sequence indicated on the chart for the relative speed of the planets.

Why this exception? The Sun is the most important planet in the chart, representing the basic self; the Moon is next in importance, signifying the unconscious, emotional self. Then comes Mercury, representing the mind. Sun, Moon and Mercury are the trinity in the hierarchy of planets.

Sun-Moon Aspects. Buffy's Sun is at one degree, twenty-eight minutes Pisces, which is shown the same way we show hours and minutes on the clock: 1:28. This figure is followed by the glyph for Pisces. Her Pisces Sun is within orb of a sextile to her Moon at 23:49 Sagittarius.

Notice that we have already encountered the sign change, which is sometimes a stumbling block for the beginner. Inasmuch as no aspect is formed in the given planetary positions for Sun and Moon, we must mentally add or subtract the Moon's orb of nine degrees in order to calculate whether or not the Moon forms any aspect to the Sun.

Subtracting nine degrees from the Moon's position doesn't help, since the planets will still not be within orb of any major aspect if the Moon is at 14:49 Sagittarius and the Sun at 1:28 Pisces. However, if we *add* nine degrees to the Moon's position, the Moon is then posited at

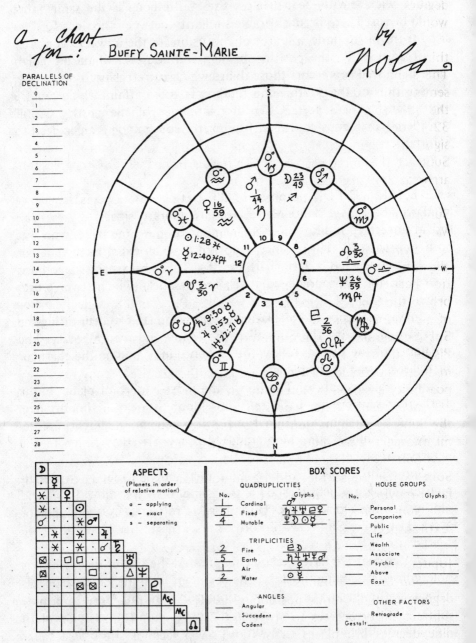

a chart for: BUFFY SAINTE-MARIE

by Nola

FIGURE 16. Flat chart for Buffy Sainte-Marie

2:49 Capricorn and the planets are in sextile aspect, since the nine degrees are clearly more than enough to give us exactitude, which would be reached at 1:29 Capricorn.

Do you see how the sign change is dealt with? Remember that thirty degrees of one sign is the same as zero degrees of the next sign. The signs themselves are just a matter of geometry, each sign representing thirty degrees of arc on the great circle of the ecliptic. Adding the allowable nine degrees orb to the 23:49 Sagittarius Moon totals 32:49 degrees of Sagittarius. Since there are only thirty degrees to a sign, this figure takes us into the next sign—that is, into Capricorn. Subtract the thirty degrees of Sagittarius from the 32:49 degrees, and arrive at 2:49 degrees Capricorn.

Accordingly, I enter the glyph for the sextile in the intersecting Sun-Moon columns, followed, optionally, by the letter *a,* since the Moon is the faster-moving luminary, and is approaching the Sun.

Sun-Mercury. With Mercury at 12:40 Pisces, it is apparent that the allowable orb of nine degrees has been exceeded insofar as a conjunction between Sun and Mercury is concerned. Adding nine degrees of orb to the Sun's position results in 10:28 Pisces, still two degrees short of a conjunction, the only possible aspect that could have been formed. Subtracting nine degrees from Mercury's position gives us 3:40 degrees Pisces—still over two degrees short of exactitude. Therefore I put a dot in the Sun-Mercury box to show that although there is no aspect, the possibility has been explored, not merely overlooked.

Sun-Venus. Venus is posited at 16:59 Aquarius, too far away from the Sun for a conjunction but not far enough away to form any other major aspect. Enter a dot in the Sun-Venus box.

Sun-Mars. At 1:44 Capricorn, Mars is within orb of a sextile to the Sun. I enter the sextile, adding the notation that, since the Sun is the faster-moving planet, the aspect is separating.

Sun-Jupiter. At 9:53 Taurus, Jupiter is within orb of an applying sextile aspect.

Sun-Saturn. At 9:30 Taurus, Saturn requires the same entry as Jupiter.

Sun-Uranus. Uranus is posited at 22:21 Taurus. Adding nine degrees to the Uranus position gives 31:21 Taurus, from which we subtract thirty degrees to arrive at 1:21 Gemini. The addition of the nine degrees orb places Uranus just seven seconds short of a square aspect; in the exercise of a wise discretion (it is applying, and it is the Sun) I allow it. I therefore conclude that there is a wide square between Sun and Uranus, applying. Some astrologers would enter the notation *a/w* beside the glyph for sextile to indicate that it is applying and that it is *wide*.

Sun-Neptune. On the chart Neptune is at 26:59 Virgo, retrograde. (The symbol druggists use to indicate prescription, ℞, is used by astronomers and by astrologers to indicate apparent retrograde motion.) Adding the allowable orb of three degrees for minor aspects places Neptune at one minute short of thirty degrees Virgo, which is the same as zero degrees Libra. That falls short of a Sun-Neptune quincunx of 150 degrees, so I place a dot in the box.

Sun-Pluto. At 2:36 Leo retrograde, Pluto is clearly within orb of a quincunx aspect and since the Sun is the faster-moving planet which will not reach 150-degree exactitude for another 1:08 degrees (the difference between the 2:36 Leo Pluto and 1:28 Pisces Sun), the aspect may be noted as applying.

The next two columns are for aspects to the Ascendant and the Midheaven. Since I am using a flat chart, these boxes are of no use. I therefore draw lines through these columns.

Sun-North Node. The last box is for the north node, which appears at 3:30 Aries—an obvious distance of thirty degrees from the Sun, well within the three-degree orb for minor aspects, in this case the semi-sextile of thirty degrees. But since we are not using this minor aspect, put a dot in this box.

I have now completed the aspecting of Sun. In like manner I have calculated the remaining aspects, all of which appear in the aspect boxes of Buffy Sainte-Marie's chart (see fig. 16). You may find it helpful to review my arithmetic before reading on.

IN THE ACTUAL delineation of a horoscope I would consider many factors which are here omitted in summarizing my interpretation of the aspects of Buffy Sainte-Marie's chart.

Moon Sextile Sun. Since the Moon is the emotional, inner self, the easy flow (sextile) between the Moon of the unconscious and the Sun of the conscious, basic self indicates that this native is in touch with her feelings and that her head knows that what her heart says is true.

Also, since the Moon is posited in Sagittarius, the sign of idealism and of the pursuit of causes, whereas the Sun is posited in Pisces, the sign of empathy and sorrow for the hurt of others, Moon sextile Sun further shows this native as someone who cares deeply about injustice to the point of a personal crusade against it. She would express her concerns according to the basic Piscean character of her Sun.

"Now That the Buffalo's Gone," a song of her own composition, is illustrative. It is a lament for her people, the American Indians, who have been the victims of countless depredations in the past, and a protest against the continued, present robbery of Indian lands as well.

"Mayoo Sto Hoon," which she sings in Hindi, mixes rain and tears in Piscean fashion and reflects her interest in Oriental philosophy; whereas "The Universal Soldier" protests against people who avert their eyes from the injustice they see to avoid the sense of personal responsibility which is properly theirs.

Pisces Sun Sextile Mars in Capricorn. Since any planet aspected by the Sun is energized, the native's aggressive energies will be more fully and harmoniously manifested by virtue of this easy aspect between Sun and Mars. Since Mars is posited in Capricorn, the native is likely to receive public attention and to perform the peculiarly Capricornian function of being an irritant in the social organism.

It is therefore no surprise to learn that, whereas her audience applaud "Now That the Buffalo's Gone," response to her second Indian protest song, "My Country 'Tis of Thy People You're Dying," is of quite a different order. Buffy remarked in a magazine interview:

> They come backstage to tell me never to sing it again. They say, "That's about my grandfather—he was a good man, a good Christian, he fought the Indians but I don't have anything to do with that." At the same time in California the big fishing interests are upset, afraid they'll lose a few extra dollars because Indians fish for salmon with their traditional nets, for food. Tell people the Bureau of Indian Affairs was set up to wipe out the Indians and they say you're mistaken. Genocide, that had to do with the Germans and the Jews, not with us. But they're wrong.[5]

That is an illustration of Sun in Pisces sextile Mars in Capricorn; it also has implications of that same Mars square both nodes.

Sun Sextile Jupiter in Taurus. With Jupiter posited in Taurus conjunct Saturn in Taurus, the energies imparted by the sextile aspect from the Sun amplify the native's opportunities for success in the areas of life suggested by the sign in which Jupiter is posited. Taurus is associated with the throat and vocal attributes. Buffy's singing voice, throaty and sensual, is prefigured by her Jupiter in a Taurus stellium, as well as by the Sun sextile Jupiter, as the key to her success.

I mention the Jupiter conjunction to Saturn out of sequence because it is impossible to ignore: the close conjunction (less than a degree) of Saturn to Jupiter may limit the opportunities otherwise indicated by Sun sextile Jupiter, but this aspect may in the long run be beneficial in that the limitations posed by Saturn, the teacher and restricter, are opportunities for growth.

Sun Sextile Saturn in Taurus. Whatever limitations are suggested by the conjunction of Saturn to Jupiter will be eased by the sextile aspect of Sun to Saturn. The Sun in a mutable water sign in harmonious aspect to Saturn in a fixed earth sign adds stability in terms of self-discipline and perseverance in accomplishing her goals.

Sun Square Uranus in Taurus. Uranus signifies quick, sometimes explosive changes in the native's life; in square aspect to the Sun and in Taurus, those changes could relate to the goals of her career or to her way of approaching those goals. There could be a sudden change, for example, from the kind of singing with which she has been identified to a style that could not properly be called protest singing at all.

Sun in Applying Quincunx to Pluto in Leo. In contrast to Uranus, which represents quick changes, Pluto signifies changes which occur over a long period of time. The quincunx aspect is often associated with illness or malaise in the area of life indicated by sign and house placement or in the part of the body identified by planet and sign placements. Here I am limited to the latter consideration. The Sun, the aspecting planet, rules the heart and the circulatory system; Pisces rules bodily fluids; Pluto, the planet receiving the aspects, rules toxic and degenerative conditions; and Leo in which it is posited, rules the cardiac system. As Buffy declared in the same interview, "I spend about a third of my time in hospitals, a problem with my blood . . ."[6]

Sun-Midheaven; Sun-Ascendant. Ordinarily, aspects of the Sun to the Midheaven and to the Ascendant would be considered at this point, but neither appears on a flat chart.

Sun-Nodes. There are no aspects from the Sun to the north or south node.

Moon-Mercury. No aspect; out of orb of a square.

Moon-Venus. With her Moon in Sagittarius in an applying sextile to Venus in Aquarius, Buffy's affectional nature (Venus) is expressed in her humanitarian feeling (Aquarius), harmonizing (sextile) her ideals (Sagittarius) and her emotions (Moon); and she is seen in that light by the public (Moon). More often than not, her affectional nature probably finds its outlet in her commitment to the Indian cause.

Moon-Mars. The Moon is in an applying conjunction to Mars. Mars is an energizing planet, and its Capricorn placement provides added forcefulness and even controversy to Buffy's public image, for the Moon not only represents the public, it is conjunct Mars in Capricorn, the sign of the public, as well.

Moon-Jupiter; Moon-Saturn. No aspect formed.

Moon-Uranus. Her Sagittarian Moon is in an applying quincunx to Uranus in Taurus, suggesting sudden changes (Uranus) in her emotions (Moon) draining (quincunx) her nervous energy (Uranus rules nervous disorders; Taurus the thyroid and metabolic system; Sagittarius the sympathetic nervous system), requiring periodic retreat from public life (Moon). Buffy confesses to being a loner; she believes that "singing exposes too much of me" and that the public will "drain your vitality from you."[7]

Moon-Neptune. This applying quincunx aspect to her Virgo Neptune suggests that her perfectionism (Virgo) and idealism (Sagittarius) could make her feel (Moon) that she always falls short of her goals, because of her unrealistic (Neptune) demands on herself.

Moon-Pluto. No aspect formed.

Mercury Sextile Jupiter. With Mercury in Pisces and Jupiter in Taurus, this applying sextile shows her considerable verbal skill in articulating her intuition, compassion and commitment. We know that she writes poetry and many of her own songs, and that she majored in English and in Oriental philosophy.[8]

Mercury Sextile Saturn. This harmonious but separating aspect to Saturn in Taurus, conjunct Jupiter which in turn sextiles Mercury, provides an additional dimension. The empathic world-view indicated by the Pisces Sun, so generously expressed in self-sacrifice shown by the sextile to Jupiter, takes a strong *teaching* direction in the Mercury sextile Saturn, positively expressed in song.

Venus Square Uranus. Here we encounter another phenomenon common to astrology: the *mutual reception*. Notice that Venus and Uranus are each posited in the sign ruled by the other: Venus, the ruler of Taurus, is posited in Aquarius; and Uranus, the ruler of Aquarius, is posited in Taurus. When the aspecting planets are each in the sign ruled by the other, astrologers say they are in *mutual reception*, which takes on the character of a conjunction, and can be either harmonious or dissonant. Since the planets are in square aspect, the interchange between the characteristics of signs and planets produces conflict rather than harmony. This applying aspect suggests that the native felt she was different from her friends and had a sense of deprivation which she sought to compensate for by identifying with others similarly deprived. Her observations about her childhood in the interview cited earlier tend to confirm this interpretation.

There are no other major aspects to Venus within the orbs I am using.

Mars Square Neptune in Virgo, Retrograde. This separating hard

aspect again reflects the problems created for the native by her energetic (Mars) overidealization of values and goals. Neptune represents
ideals and imagination; it is the planet of dreams and illusions. In hard
aspect, Neptune can mean self-delusion or, especially in Virgo, overidealization. If Buffy overidealizes her role as the rectifier of wrongs
done the Indians, *dis*illusionment (another consequence of hard aspects
to Neptune) would follow her eventual realization of the fact that what
one person can accomplish is necessarily less than everything which
someone so fiercely dedicated would desire.

Mars Quincunx Pluto in Leo, Retrograde. This applying aspect of
Buffy's Capricorn Mars to her Pluto, the planet ruling degenerative
conditions, in Leo, the sign ruler of the heart and cardiac system, adds
emphasis to the delineation of the applying quincunx of the Sun to
Leo.

Mars Square Nodes. Since the nodes are always in opposition to
the exact degree of sign, any planet which is posited at the midpoint
between them will square both nodes. Such is the case with Mars in
Buffy's chart.

Since the north node represents those things which come easily to
the native, and the south node lessons to be learned in life, any planet
squaring both nodes suggests that the lesson, which would permit the
realization of the potential of the north node, relates directly to those
things the native finds easy to do. Applying that principle to Buffy's
chart, we make the following inferences. First, those things which come
easily to her are *Libran,* since the north node is posited in Libra; and
since Venus rules Libra and is sextile the Moon, we know that these are
aesthetic accomplishments.

Second, those things which the native must work harder to
accomplish are *Arien,* since the south node is posited in Aries; and since
Mars rules Aries and has hard aspects to several planets in her chart and
is conjunct the Moon, we know that these things are her career goals.
Or, as Buffy herself put it, "My only goal is to tell the American people
how Americans are treating the Indian—whether or not they want to
hear."[9]

Mars square *both* nodes and conjunct the Moon suggests that while
her aesthetic abilities come easily, (north node in Libra), her persona
(south node in Aries) may be abrasive (south node in Aries), requiring
her to work on a public image (Moon) which will enable her to convey
her message of social injustice (Moon in Sagittarius, conjunct Mars in
Capricorn, sextile Sun in Pisces) without losing her audience.

All aspects involving Jupiter have been previously considered in
delineating aspects of the Sun and of Mercury. The conjunction of

Jupiter to Saturn was considered in the discussion of the sextile aspects of the Sun to Jupiter and Saturn.

All aspects involving Saturn have been considered in delineating aspects of other planets.

Uranus Trine Neptune. Trines are considered the most harmonious aspects because they show a relationship of two planets in the same triplicity. Here the trine is an applying aspect between Uranus in Taurus and Neptune in Virgo, both in the earth element. While too many soft aspects in a chart are considered a disadvantage by many contemporary astrologers on the theory that they can make life too easy for the native, Buffy's chart shows only one trine; and it is a chart which certainly has its share of squares, quincunxes and conjunctions.

The applying trine of Uranus in a stellium of planets in Taurus indicates the native's creative genius (Uranus in trine aspect), which is imaginatively expressed (trine to Neptune) through her singing (stellium in Taurus).

Pluto Sextile North Node. Pluto, the planet of intensity, is posited in Leo, the sign of the actress or performer, in harmonious aspect to the north node posited in Libra, the sign of aesthetics, harmony and justice. This aspect represents the native's ability to work with unswerving dedication and considerable success in combining her attributes as a performer with her aesthetic abilities and her passionate commitment to see justice done for the Indian nation.

What can now be said about Buffy Sainte-Marie on the basis of the aspects I have delineated? Since I am using a flat chart, I cannot, for example, determine the angular, succedent and cadent positions of her planets by houses, nor can I determine the Ascendant and Midheaven. I can, however, catalog the quadruplicities and triplicities, which are indicated in the box scores.

I have deliberately chosen a birth chart of someone whose birth hour was unknown to me, in order to demonstrate what aspects alone can show, even without the houses, angles and related data. Quadruplicities and triplicities, on the other hand, are closely related to aspects; indeed, they are the quickest means of determining squares and trines in the chart. I use them in summarizing my interpretations of the aspects.

With five placements in the earth triplicity and five placements in fixed signs, fixed earth characteristics predominate, with the fixity somewhat relieved by four placements in mutable signs. The dominant earth quality indicates musical ability and, in the context of the fixed sign emphasis, an unswerving dedication which is virtually indomitable. With the many sextiles of her empathic Piscean Sun to other planets, especially her idealistic Sagittarian Moon, she would project an image which combines Deidre of the Sorrows with Geronimo.

Close personal relationships may be difficult to establish and to maintain, both because her ideals are so high that few persons can meet her standards, and because of her need for personal freedom shown by the Sagittarian Moon. This inference is supported by the fact that the Moon is conjunct Mars in Capricorn, which in turn squares both nodes and Neptune—a combination which may make her appear abrasive, and which suggests that her emotional life has been sacrificed for her public life in pursuit of a cause.

So there it is—an exercise in aspecting without regard to the house positions or the additional data which an accurate birth time would provide. I selected Buffy Sainte-Marie as a public figure for whom the biographical material is not extensive. The aptitudes and problems suggested in the chart are by no means unusual, for every chart has them, in one form or another. All I have done is to indicate the particular manifestations which the aspects between the planets in this birth chart suggest.

Finally, I have tried to demonstrate the value of an orderly delineation of aspects. Once you learn the essentials of horoscope interpretation, you will find that when you look at a chart, many aspects jump out at you at first glance. Aspects which are dramatic and obvious demand immediate attention. You will do yourself a great favor, however, if you apply the positive aspects of Saturn in your own chart (however posited) to steel yourself to the self-discipline of an orderly delineation, in the proper sequence, before reaching any conclusions.

HAVING STRESSED THE orderly delineation of aspects in sequence, I now turn to what may at first appear to be a contradictory principle: the *gestalt*, or overview, of the entire horoscope.

Many contemporary astrologers believe that a preliminary consideration of any horoscope should be the overall configuration of the chart. Such an overview is called the gestalt of the chart, after the theory of contemporary gestalt psychology that each of us is a unified psychological or symbolic configuration whose properties cannot be derived simply from an analytic consideration of its parts.

As philosopher-astrologer Dane Rudhyar has observed,

> If we want to know a person as a whole, we must therefore approach
> his birth-chart in a whole act of perception. What strikes us at first is

the *gestalt* (or over-all configuration) of the chart: i.e., how it looks as a whole. [10]

There are two ways of looking at the chart as a whole, one traditional, one modern. I shall consider both of them in turn. The method Dane Rudhyar refers to is one that Marc Edmund Jones developed in his pioneering book, *Guide to Horoscope Interpretation* (1941), and expanded in a more recent work, *Essentials of Astrological Analysis*.

Jones was perhaps the first contemporary astrologer to recognize these planetary patterns, but his views quickly took hold, and have become very much a part of contemporary astrology. Although I have synthesized the ideas of many contemporary astrologers with my own in the following summary of the patterns which Jones originated, I have adhered to his terminology, since it is in widest use.

In the *Splash Pattern*, the planets are widely distributed or splashed throughout the horoscope. The overall significance of the splash pattern is that the native may have great versatility or widespread interests. However, the native must be careful to avoid spreading himself too thin.

The *Locomotive Pattern* is one in which the planets occupy two-thirds of the chart, leaving one-third or one trine of the horoscope unoccupied. (The nodes are disregarded for purposes of these configurations.) In clockwise direction, the first planet in series is the engine and the following planets the cars, so to speak.

The engine planet gives direction to the others. The locomotive pattern suggests a native who determines his own direction in life. What that direction is may be determined by the house and sign position of the engine planet and by the aspects to it.

In the *Bundle Pattern*, the planets are all posited within one-third of the horoscope, the space occupied in a trine aspect of 120 degrees. In terms of configuration, the bundle is the mirror-opposite to the locomotive pattern. In terms of interpretation, however, the bundle pattern is the opposite of the splash, for here the native is inhibited rather than versatile, and held to narrow bounds in the areas of life's opportunities. But the bundle provides a kind of tunnel-vision that may make for great concentration of activity.

In the *Bowl Pattern*, the planets are all posited in one hemisphere of the horoscope. Should that hemisphere coincide with the horizon line of the chart, the effect of the pattern is especially emphasized. The native whose chart exhibits the bowl configuration may feel excluded from the areas of life experience symbolized by the unoccupied houses of his chart, and there may be a compensatory intensity in the areas of life symbolized by the houses within the populated hemisphere.

The bowl becomes a *Bucket Pattern* when one planet is posited within the otherwise unoccupied hemisphere of the chart. This single-ton planet is the handle of the bucket, whose sign and house position may signify the direction of the native's interests. Generally, the bucket pattern suggests that the native will adopt an uncompromising and perhaps indomitable course in life. Positively manifested, his zeal can be illuminating and inspirational; negatively aspected, it can signify social and political unrest.

In the *Seesaw Pattern*, two (or more) planets are opposed to eight (or less) planets in an opposing section of the chart. Ideally, there will be two empty segments of ninety degrees each, thereby providing the symmetrical opposition of an hour-glass configuration separating two planetary clusters. Seesaw patterns with as little as a sextile of unoccu-pied arc may be allowed; however, neither planetary grouping may have more than one empty house within the cluster. Without this require-ment, the seesaw pattern could hardly be distinguished from the splash or even the locomotive pattern.

The native whose horoscope forms the seesaw pattern may have an innate sensitivity to both sides of any issue and a drive to achieve a harmonious balance between them. At its worst, however, the seesaw may signify a wasteful dissipation of life energies in the effort to reconcile such polarities.

In simplest terms, any pattern which does not meet any of the criteria already described falls into the *Splay Pattern*. That fact alone does not make a horoscope a splay pattern of any significance, how-ever. The splay pattern becomes significant when the planets fall into three stelliums, with the planets in each stellium approximating a conjunction; and ideally with some major aspect linking all three planetary groupings.

The splay pattern suggests that the native will be purposeful and individualistic, and will resist the pigeon-holing efforts of his peers. His character, like his chart, will defy convenient classification.

THE CLASSIC APPROACH to the gestalt of the horoscope is in terms of configurations based on the triplicities and the quadruplicities linked into overall patterns, called grand trines, squares, T-squares and so on. Neither approach excludes the other; most contemporary astrologers use both.

A grand trine occurs when the native has planets posited in each of the three signs of the same triplicity, within orb of a trine aspect. Since there are four triplicities, there are four kinds of grand trines: fire, earth, air and water. Each of the grand trines manifests the characteristic action of its triplicity, together with the characteristics of the trine aspect, as modified by the signs and houses in which the particular planets are posited.

A grand trine is generally regarded as a fortuitous configuration signifying an easy flow among the planets in the sign triplicity involved. However, many astrologers believe that a grand trine can be disadvantageous if the chart does not contain some balancing stress as well.

I start with the chart of Maria Magdalene, [11] born in Berlin on December 27, 1904. As prefigured by her earth emphasis, she planned a musical career, and took up the violin at an early age. However, when she was sixteen, she was ordered by her doctor to give up the violin permanently. It was then that she decided to become an actress.

On the basis of her chart and her grand trine (see fig. 17), what are her chances of success?

The grand trine has been marked with lines—a conventional astrological practice—which shows the overall configuration. Notice that Pluto is posited at 20:14 Gemini and trines Mars at 21:11 Libra, which in turn trines Venus at 17:21 Aquarius and Saturn at 18:07 Aquarius. This Aquarian conjunction of Venus and Saturn in turn trines Pluto.

There are also significant hard aspects to provide the necessary opportunities for growth. Most significant is the opposition of Jupiter to Mars, the latter being one leg of the grand trine. Since the grand trine is a self-contained unit, the Mars opposition to Jupiter provides direction to what would have been an encapsulated airiness.

The box scores also show a good balance to the air sign emphasis of the grand trine. Maria has a preponderance of cardinal signs by quadruplicity and an emphasis in earth equal to her emphasis in air, with four signs in each triplicity. These factors suggest a native of considerable initiative, with an ability to see the world in its infinite possibilities and to enjoy the present as well. There will be little looking back and little show of emotion (Neptune is her only water sign placement). With Jupiter her only fire sign placement, there will also be little in the way of a passionate idealism.

There is a nice balance between hard and soft aspects too. With Sun trine Moon in earth signs, we can infer that this lady will seek public achievement (Sun in Capricorn), but that her ambition will not separate her from an awareness of self (Moon in Virgo trine Sun).

What does the grand trine indicate in this context? Mars in Libra

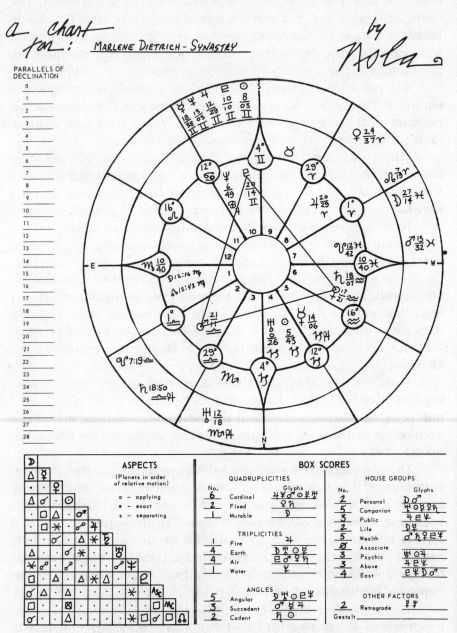

FIGURE 17. Chart for Marlene Dietrich—synastry
(Josef von Sternberg's planets in outer circle)

suggests that her aggressive energies will be softened by her aesthetic sensibilities and her innate desire for fairness. Its trine aspect to Pluto in Gemini indicates that her emotional intensity will be modified by her insatiable curiosity and wide-ranging interests. Pluto trine the Aquarian Venus means harmony in the manifestation of her intensity with her ability to give and to receive love. The conjunction of Saturn suggests that the native will always have a certain reserve in her affectional nature, but that her commitments will be deep and abiding. She will probably love her teacher—Saturn conjunct Venus, trine Mars and trine Pluto—and will be attracted to men who will somehow occupy the role of teacher in relation to her. Also, since Aquarius rules the lower legs and ankles and Saturn the skeletal system, and since Saturn conjuncts Venus and is in dignity in Aquarius, which it co-rules, she will probably have legs which are aesthetically pleasing.

If this were the only significant configuration in this native's natal chart, we might say that the native may appear detached, uncommitted and rather remote. Why? Because the grand trine is a plenum which ties up the native's aggressive energies, her emotional intensity and her affections, modulating them into an almost otherworldly detachment. With this configuration alone, the native might have no great ambition, dedication or love interest.

But notice that Jupiter is posited in Aries in opposition to that Mars in Libra. Jupiter is idealism, and is outgoing and beneficent. Aries is a fiery, impulsive and initiatory sign. Together, Jupiter in Aries suggests the person who is eager to find new fields to conquer, who is not going to watch the world go by without participating in its excitement, but who must plunge in and find expression for his (or her) ideals.

This Aries-Jupiter opposition to Mars in Libra gives the air grand trine direction and motivation. In this context, the grand trine can express itself positively, and the native will not be disadvantaged, because balance is provided by the opposing Aries Jupiter, which in turn is squared by her Virgo Moon. This last aspect suggests that the native, to achieve the successful public image (Moon in Virgo) necessary for her career, must work to overcome the obstacles imposed by her impulsive and idealistic Jupiter.

This thumbnail sketch of a native with a grand trine in air, who happens also to have her Sun and Moon in earth signs, must now be related to the events of her life.

Maria Magdalene was seen in a German musical by Josef von Sternberg, an American film director who had been born in Vienna and had traveled peripatetically from the Continent to America ever since.

Von Sternberg was one of the great directors in the 1930s and 1940s, and his films bore his visual signature more than those of any other director in that fabulous era of American cinema.

Early in 1930, Emil Jannings, the great German silent-film star, sent von Sternberg a copy of a novel about a middle-aged professor whose fatal passion for a cabaret singer destroys him. The original novel was a thinly veiled attack on the then rising Naziism. Lola Lola, the cabaret singer in the book, is the unofficial agent for a group of politicians identified in all but name with the Nazis. Because of his love for Lola Lola, the professor allows himself to be used for the political ends of her friends.

Von Sternberg liked the story, and decided to film it through a German studio which agreed to the production. However, it was now 1930, and Naziism was rampant. Whether for that reason or simply as an act of his independent artistic genius, von Sternberg decided to omit the political element of the story and make the professor's downfall the result of his sexual involvement with Lola Lola.

That meant that Lola Lola had to be something very special; someone whose fatal allure would provide believable motivation for the professor's actions. Von Sternberg refused to accept the unglamorous lady whom the studio wished cast in the part.

He launched his own search for the actress with the necessary *persona* vital to the success of his picture, and after he saw Maria Magdalene, he went backstage to her dressing room and introduced himself: his search had come to an end. A few days later Maria signed the film contract, using her stage name, and, as Marlene Dietrich, began work in *The Blue Angel.*

Compare what I have said about her chart with what you know about Marlene Dietrich, who has become a legend in her own time. I will add only a few further observations.

The elusive, mysterious sexuality she projects is, in my view, a reflection of the air grand trine, with its essential sexual ambiguity which gives it its mystery. Jean Cocteau recognized that element when he described Dietrich as "the most exciting and terrifying woman I have ever known."

Her Jupiterian idealism is revealed in her observation:

> I sometimes wonder if I just might have been the one person in the
> world who could have prevented the war and saved millions of lives. It
> troubles me a lot and I'll never stop worrying about it.

Her Sun trine Moon in earth signs and her emphasis in those signs reveal themselves in her well-known talent for making and holding on to money. Her Sun's conjunction to Uranus is manifested in terms of her famous collection of modern art, which she has herself described as her personal fortune.

Stories are told about the (assumed) contrast in her character between her fabled business acumen and her firm belief in astrology. The knack for business is seen in the Capricorn Sun and other earth placements, whereas her astrological convictions may be found in the Aquarian placements of her grand trine.

Von Sternberg was her teacher; and her Saturn conjunction to Venus was shown by their close relationship during the seven years in which he was her exclusive director; whether intimate or not, it led his wife to sue for divorce.

With Marlene Dietrich and Josef von Sternberg we have a unique opportunity to illustrate briefly one last astrological principle in aspecting: synastry (see fig. 17). Marlene Dietrich's natal chart appears in the inner circle, based on an estimated birth time, so that her Ascendant is in early degrees of Virgo and her Midheaven in early degrees of Gemini. The outer circle contains the planetary positions for May 29, 1894, the date of birth of Josef von Sternberg. Note that although the planets for von Sternberg's birth date are set out according to sign and degree of sign as they appeared on May 29, 1894, they are posited in the houses of Marlene Dietrich's chart.

Thus, in synastry, the planets of one horoscope are placed in the houses of a second horoscope; aspects between the first and second are then calculated to determine how one native may affect the life of another. In the case of Dietrich and von Sternberg, we can see that his Gemini stellium of Sun, Pluto, Jupiter, Neptune and Mercury fall in Marlene Dietrich's tenth house of profession, status and the public with at least three of them, including Pluto, conjunct her Midheaven.

From this aspect alone, we can infer that von Sternberg was destined to have a profound effect on Dietrich's public image and profession.

THE T-SQUARE IS a configuration involving three planets, two opposite each other and both squaring the third. Because the triangle thus formed contains one right angle, it is called a T-square.

See figure 18, which contains two T-squares. What I will call the first T-square involves Jupiter at 24:28 Gemini opposing Neptune at 24:30 Sagittarius. Mars, posited in the first house, squares Jupiter in the tenth house and Neptune in the fourth house. Jupiter in the tenth house of the father opposes Neptune in the fourth house of the mother, suggesting conflict between the parents which was probably internalized by the native at an early age.

Also, with Neptune, ruling the seventh house of partnership and

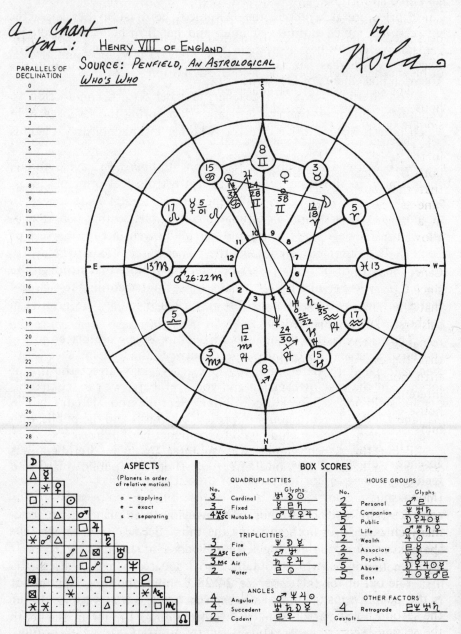

a chart for: HENRY VIII OF ENGLAND
SOURCE: PENFIELD, *An Astrological Who's Who*

by Nola

FIGURE 18. Natal chart for Henry VIII

marriage, posited in the fourth house of home in the freedom-loving sign of Sagittarius, squaring his male sexual identity in the first house of self, we could conclude that the native's marital relationship(s) might be shaky at best. This configuration indicates that once the native marries, he feels psychically castrated: his wife probably reminds him of his mother and triggers the T-square syndrome.

The outlet for this T-square would be 26:22 Pisces in the seventh house of partnership, manifested as the development of a compassionate or mystical relationship with another person.

The second T-square in the natal chart involves the Sun in Cancer in the tenth house opposing Uranus in Capricorn in the fifth house, both of which square the Moon in Aries in the eighth house. (Notice that the square aspect of the Moon to Uranus slightly exceeds the nine-degree orb permitted for the Moon. However, the Moon is posited in a cardinal sign and in applying aspect; for these reasons, I have allowed the aspect, as many, if not most, astrologers would.)

The Sun in the tenth house of the father and of the public and in Cancer may suggest a role reversal—from the viewpoint of the native— since Cancer is a maternal sign. This sign and house position also implies that the native is a facile politician, since Cancer males often excel in this area. The opposition to Uranus in the fifth house of pleasures and romance in the idealistic but conservative sign of Capricorn indicates that the parent symbolized by the tenth house restricts the native's fifth house pleasures, imposing inhibitions on his love life. This last inference is supported by the square of the Aries Moon in the eighth house of sex and death to the fifth house Uranus and the tenth house Sun.

The Moon in Aries in the eighth house indicates a mother whose absence from the home, aggressiveness or possible lack of maternal feeling for her son created stress for the native in terms of his basic self (Moon square Sun), and in terms of his ability to enjoy pleasure and romance (Moon square Uranus). The latter square in particular suggests many quick changes in the native's love life, involving new partners, and the possibility of the death of one or another of the partners (Moon in eighth house of death).

The outlet for this T-square is 12:18 Libra, the sign degree which is the polar opposite of that of the Moon, and is therefore located in the second house, which has five degrees Libra on its cusp. The ruler of the second house of possessions is Venus, which is posited in the ninth house of higher mind activity in Gemini; so the native's release, from some of the essentially sexual stresses indicated by this T-square, would possibly relate to the development of a comforting aesthetic, religious and perhaps a legal philosophy.

The native whose chart contains these two T-squares is Henry VIII, born June 28, 1491, at Greenwich, England.[12]

Various reasons have been given for the many marriages of Henry VIII. The one I find most convincing is that the King yielded to the T-squares in his natal chart, with the feelings of psychic castration they imposed. One incident seems illuminating: when the Spanish ambassador politely asked Henry, before he married Anne Boleyn, whether he really expected to produce more children, Henry's

> reaction was instantaneous, rebounding before he knew he was struck. Three times he demanded as he blazed with anger, "Am I not a man like other men? Am I not a man like other men? Am I not a man like other men?" The blood that had rushed to his face took long to pale.[13]

The outlets to the T-squares also played a significant part in Henry's life. Pisces in the seventh house: he was a skilled musician and dancer; once, when his first wife was ill, he staged a ballet for her and performed in it as well. Libra in the second house: Henry took refuge in writing both prose and poetry; and it was his treatise on Luther that first commended him to favorable papal attention.

Henry VIII was a complex monarch who lived in perilous and revolutionary times. While it would be a mistake to give too much weight to the influence of his admittedly powerful personality, I cannot help but wonder how the course of history might have been changed had the man who was King of England early in the sixteenth century had a little more insight into the compulsions which he permitted to drive him.

THE GRAND CROSS or grand square consists of two sets of opposing planets whose squares to each other link them in a cross or square configuration. As the grand trine can occur in any triplicity, so the grand cross can occur in any quadruplicity. Thus astrologers speak of a *cardinal, fixed* or *mutable* grand cross. The nature of the obstacles reflected by the overall configuration is characterized by the quadruplicity involved.

The grand cross is relatively rare, and the one good illustration which I was able to retrieve from our files is the chart of a Cancer male (see fig. 19). The lines connecting the Moon in Libra in the second house; Saturn in Capricorn in the fifth house; Uranus in Aries in the eighth house; Jupiter in Cancer in the eleventh house form the overall square configuration of a cardinal grand cross.

Because the native whose chart contains this cardinal grand cross is

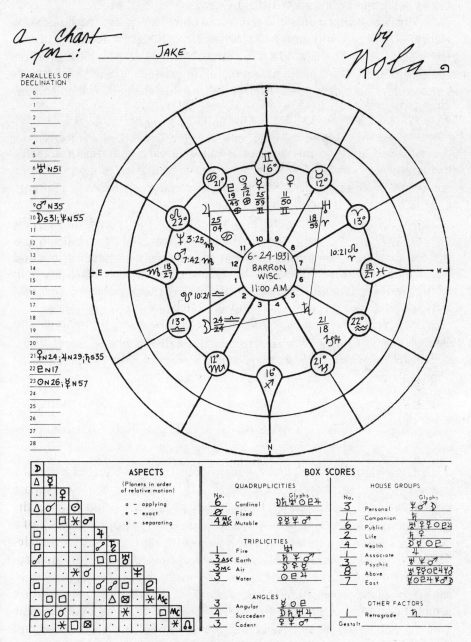

FIGURE 19. Natal chart for Jake

so well known to me, I prevailed upon Lillian for her opinion. The following observations are essentially hers.

The Moon represents the mother, women generally, the home, the emotions and, in this case, the native's friends (the Moon rules the eleventh house) and his partners (the Moon is in Libra). The Moon is also posited in the second house, and therefore operates principally in the area of possessions and income, as well as how the native spends his income. (Good enough: the native is a lawyer.)

Jupiter represents expansiveness, generosity, joy and, in this case, one of the parents, since Jupiter rules the fourth house and is posited in the sign of Cancer. Jupiter in the eleventh house operates principally in the area of friends. The square to the Moon indicates a parent who could not become a friend or a friend who could not become a parent. (The native verified that both statements are true.)

Saturn represents the forbidden; it is the inhibitor, the disciplinarian, the voice of authority, maturity and fear. It is in dignity in the sign of Capricorn, augmenting its impact, and it is posited in the fifth house of pleasures in opposition to Jupiter. This aspect means that joy of Jupiter begets guilt and gloom of Saturn: the native feels that joy must be paid for by regret, guilt and loss. ("Hmm," said the native.)

Uranus is the maverick and the native's desire to be free. In the sign of Aries, Uranus acts to demand the native's independence from responsibility. In the eighth house, that demand for freedom especially applies in the area of sex. ("That's fair enough," the native commented obliquely.)

The square of Uranus to Saturn indicates that the native may have experienced periods of repression—almost to the point of emotional and physical (sexual) starvation—and then suddenly the extreme opposite. Quite literally, feast or famine. He may have gone without food as a youngster. ("Quite literally," confirmed the native.)

The opposition of Saturn to Jupiter also suggests that his greatest fear is of being alone, bringing with it the strongest kind of frustration and (Uranus square Jupiter) an urgent need to get away from the place of isolation. (He said he would have to think about that.)

The opposition of Uranus to the Moon suggests many love affairs, and many changes of mood or feeling born of a desire for freedom. Yet the square and opposition aspects to Jupiter bring the reaction of isolation in turn and the need to find friends and new partners.

Uranus in Aries in the eighth house, ruling the sixth house of illness and health, is particularly powerful. Thus aspected and posited, Uranus places the native in physical danger because of an urgent need for freedom after long periods of Saturnian repression—even if it brings death, the final freedom. When Uranus is in charge, anything goes.

Later, when Saturn takes control, the native's very acts terrify him. (No comment from the native.)

The native is Jake, the attorney whom I introduced in the discussion of triplicities. It was Jake who said, "I could die today, riding my bike. I realize that. So my life is always going to be the value I place on everything that has happened to me." With two serious motorcycle accidents to date, one which caused a near-fatal head injury and the second, a long period of hospitalization, it is notable that while his stable of motorcycles and nubile female companions grows ever larger, Jake continues to ride without a helmet.

In delineating the grand cross, Lillian placed one or another planet in a predominant role at different times in the native's life. This concept applies to all planetary configurations and involves the triggering effect on a given planet or planetary configuration of *progressions* and of *transits*.

THERE ARE A number of ways of progressing the natal chart in order to forecast future events in the native's life. Some of them involve relatively complicated mathematics; I will avoid them here. Two of the best happen also to be the easiest: *secondary progressions and one-degree directions*.

There is a great deal of confusion in terms particularly because the word "progressions" is used as a collective term. Here I shall use the term "secondary progressions" to refer to a method of forecasting in which the astrologer counts one day for each year of life with reference to an ephemeris which shows the actual planetary position for that advanced day in the natal year. I shall use the term "one-degree directions" to refer to a method of forecasting in which one degree of celestial longitude is added to the natal position of a planet for each year of the native's life *without reference to the actual ephemeral position of the planet*.

For example, if the native was born on May 6, 1856, his natal Mars would be posited at 3:31 Libra, retrograde. In order to progress his natal Mars to his eighth year of life by secondary progression, we would add eight days to his birth date, and then consult the ephemeris for the position of Mars on May 14, 1856. In doing so, we would find the entry "3D4," which means that on May 14, Mars was posited at 3:04 Libra, with the "D" advising that Mars went direct on that date.

In using the same birth date to progress natal Mars by one-degree directions, we would simply add eight degrees to the natal position of 3:31 degrees Libra. By this method of forecasting, the native's directed Mars would be posited at 11:31 Libra in his eighth year of life.

In either case, the result is theoretical, since the advanced position does not record the actual position of the planet for the future year; and even though secondary progressions require reference to the ephemeris, the ephemeral position arrived at is not the actual position of the planet for the future year.

Notice also that both secondaries and one degrees are based on one day or one degree for one year of life. Some astrologers claim scriptural justification for these formulas, pointing to passages in Ezekiel and in Numbers in which the equation of "a day for a year" is used; but astrologers who prefer transits to progressions for forecasting insist that these passages have no astrological content. In my view, both transits and progressions work (for whatever reason), and that is sufficient justification for using them.

Whether you are dealing with one-degree directions or secondary progressions, remember that the aspect formed by the progressed planet to the natal planet is significant. For example, if in the natal chart Jupiter is posited at five degrees Sagittarius in the second house of income, with the Sun posited at twenty-five degrees Sagittarius in the third house of communications, the one-degree method tells the astrologer at a glance that at the age of twenty the native's directed Jupiter will conjunct his natal Sun. However, its full effect is not felt or experienced until the directed, one-degree planet has separated a degree from the natal planet, or, in this example, when Jupiter reaches twenty-six degrees of Sagittarius, representing his twenty-first year of life. Depending on other aspects, such a forecast may presage good fortune for the native in areas relating to communications, to short journeys or to both.

Secondary progressions often confirm what is indicated by one-degree directions; sometimes they tell us more. Take Mars, in the earlier example, which achieves direct motion for the first time in the native's eighth year. That is a highly significant event in the native's life; for the first time there may be some outward manifestation of his aggressive sexual energies.

The orb allowed for progressions and directions is generally one degree or less. Many contemporary astrologers believe that the maximum effect of secondary progressions occurs just before exactitude. Keep in mind, however, that by the one-degree method the full effect is felt as the directed planet separates by one degree from the aspect to the natal planet.

THE TERM "TRANSIT" is used by astronomers to indicate the passage of a celestial body across a particular point, such as a meridian. It is used the same way by astrologers. Thus, in the example for progressions, if on a given date the ephemeris shows that Jupiter will be posited at twenty-five degrees Sagittarius, and that the position of the Sun in the natal chart is also twenty-five degrees Sagittarius, an astrologer would say that transiting Jupiter is conjuncting the natal Sun.

The degree positions of transiting planets refer to the actual positions of those planets according to their passage through the skies at a particular time. Progressions are theoretical and arithmetically computed; transits are not. Astrologers use both.

A colleague had his Moon transiting through his fifth house of pleasures and risks at the same time conjuncting his south node of lessons to be learned in life. Also on that day transiting Jupiter quincunxed natal Jupiter; transiting Mars conjuncted his natal Sun; transiting Saturn was but one degree from an exact opposition to his natal Sun. Astrology buffs carefully consider such transiting aspects as warnings to use extra caution in the areas of life affected by such transits.

ONLY RECENTLY WE have discovered that Archaic Man had a vast and sophisticated knowledge of astronomy. The distinguished astrophysicist Sir Fred Hoyle has concluded that Stonehenge was even more than the neolithic computer designed to predict eclipses that Gerald Hawkins, himself a professor of astronomy, had postulated in *Stonehenge Decoded.*

Hoyle says that Stonehenge is itself a model of the great circle of the ecliptic, whose very monolithic existence compels the conclusion that thousands of years ago, Mankind knew many things about the geometry of our celestial sphere that we have only recently rediscovered, and perhaps some things we have not.[14] Professor Hawkins has found evidence of a universal knowledge of celestial geometry throughout the world which antedates our written history.

No better evidence of such ancient lore can be found than in the Great Pyramid of Cheops. As a theodolite, or surveying device to measure vertical and horizontal angles, it is so precise that surveyors check their own instruments against it. The sides of the pyramid run precisely east-west, pointing to the sunrise at the vernal equinox.[15] And it is at least four thousand years old.[16]

Less than a mile away, the Sphinx stares squarely toward the horizon. Squarely, indeed: at a ninety-degree angle east of north. But on the first day of spring, when the Sun rises at a declination of zero degrees, there is an exact sextile of sixty degrees at midday along the axis of the Sphinx.[17] An astronomer has concluded that its half-lion, half-virgin construction symbolizes the junction of the constellations of Leo and Virgo which occurred at the summer solstice—in the fourth millennium B.C.E.[18]

We find it difficult to believe that such a body of knowledge could have existed in our so distant past. But the Great Pyramid—and other artifacts discovered all over our Earth—are solid evidence that such was the case. It is just as clear that the use to which this knowledge and those structures were put was astrology. Only now are we beginning to relearn the importance of the celestial geometry, the ceaselessly changing aspects of astrology, to our daily lives.

There are many possible points of departure in tracing the rediscovery of the principles of the Pythagoreans, embodied in Ptolemy's *Tetrabiblos*, but the publication in 1887 of *The Rhythm of Life: Foundations of an Exact Biology* is perhaps as good as any.[19] Its author, Dr. Wilhelm Fliess, was a nose and throat specialist, later president of the German Academy of Sciences, but with a wide range of interests, as his written works demonstrate. One reviewer was astounded at his "knowledge of medicine, mathematics, genealogy, botany, zoology, astrology and psychology."[20]

The omission of numerology is surprising, for Fliess was a modern Pythagorean who believed that all things were number; and it was his numerological expertise which he combined with astrology and his medical skills in postulating his theory of *periodicity*. Fliess's text was premised on the theory that human beings are essentially bisexual and that there are two basic organic rhythms reflecting this fact. One rhythm is feminine, relating to our emotional responses, with a twenty-eight-day period; the second is masculine, relating to our physical energies, with a period of twenty-three days. His work was extensively documented with observations of the periodicity of illness, recovery and relapse of patients under his supervision.

The Rhythm of Life was a pioneering work in a field which is now known as the study of biorhythms. Today it is fashionable to diminish Fliess's contribution; Gay Gaer Luce, for example, refers to Fliess's formulation as childish,[21] but does concede evidence of a 28-day biorhythm cycle which "suggests lunar influence."[22]

However, the Fliess thesis encouraged others—including at least one contemporary, Dr. Hermann Swoboda, who confirmed Fliess's periods—and in the 1920s was supplemented by the discovery of yet a third period.[23] Independent research on both sides of the Atlantic led to the conclusion that a thirty-three-day rhythm of mental alertness also existed, together with the physical and emotional rhythms documented by Fliess and Swoboda.

The study of biorhythms has led to an extensive literature of its own, with the finding of a wide variety of rhythms in addition to the three principle ones of physical, emotional and mental activity. The twenty-eight-day emotional cycle is indeed keyed to the Moon; somehow the twenty-three-day cycle of physical energy is related to the Sun; the thirty-three-day mental cycle is related to Mercury, the third luminary in our celestial trinity.

That dedicated astrologer Sir Isaac Newton pointed out the Moon's effect on the tides; it is a simple step from there to the lunar effect on the menstrual cycle. The relationship between the Sun and physical health and energy, or between Mercury and mental alertness, is, however, best explained in terms of what we have learned in recent years about the powerful relationship between biology and numbers.

John H. Nelson is an electrical engineer who was hired by RCA in 1942 to do something about unpredictable magnetic disturbances which were interfering with radio reception. Nelson was not then, and is not now, an astrologer, but he succeeded where others had failed, by consulting that basic tool of astrologers, the ephemeris.[24]

An ephemeris is a table which shows the positions of the planets on any given day of a given year according to the degree and sign of the zodiac. While it was known that most magnetic storms occurred as the result of sunspot activity, no one knew why the sunspots occurred or when to anticipate them. Nelson discovered that the hard aspects of the square and the opposition triggered such sunspot activity, but that the soft aspects of trines and sextiles did not.

Nelson eventually succeeded in making magnetic disturbances which caused radio interference predictable within 93 percent accuracy by determining the positions of the planets as astrologers have done for millennia.[25] (It should be noted, however, that Nelson used heliocentric aspects for his charts.)

Just as significant to our understanding of aspects was his development of a system of prediction which he calls "simultaneous multiple harmonics." Nelson found that in addition to hard and soft aspects, the harmonics of the basic angles were needed to perfect his system and to give his forecasting its high degree of reliability.[26] Twenty-five hundred years after Pythagoras, John Nelson may have at last found the true meaning of the harmony of the spheres.

There remains the question of how such harmonious and dissonant planetary relationships affect human behavior.

Space is filled with a variety of force fields, not the least of which is the electromagnetic energy of the Sun itself, or what astronomers call the *solar wind*: a constant stream of charged particles, whose velocity reaches several hundred miles per second and increases during solar activity. The solar wind directly affects the Earth's own magnetic field.[27]

But the Sun is not alone in doing so. Frank A. Brown, Morrison Professor of Biology at Northwestern University, has been working for twenty-five years on testing the ways in which life may be influenced by remote environmental factors. He has succeeded in demonstrating that all life is sensitive to extremely subtle stimuli, for organisms isolated under constant and unvarying conditions in test chambers continually produced rhythms that proved their sensitivity to environmental phenomena.[28]

The conclusion is inescapable: *all* of the planets (Sun and Moon included) produce disturbances which reverberate on Earth;[29] possibly by creating disturbances in our electromagnetic field[30] which may influence bodily function as well.[31]

One scientific explanation for the correlation between the activities of the human nervous system and the solar system echoes the basic tenet of Hermeticism: the human body and the Earth have a comparable composition of 80 percent water and 20 percent mineral.[32]

Forty years of research by Dr. Harold Saxton Burr at the Yale University School of Medicine have established that all organisms have electrodynamic fields surrounding them. Called L-fields for short, these phenomena have been studied by Dr. Burr in both animal and vegetable organisms. Years of research into the L-fields of trees have established that their development varies with the cycles of day and night, the cycles of the Moon, sunspots and magnetic storms as well.[33]

What, then, about human organisms? Dr. Burr observes:

> As extraterrestrial forces, such as solar flares and sun-spot activity, influence the L-fields of trees it seems most unlikely that human L-fields are unaffected by such forces.[34]

The results of Dr. Burr's research on some 500 human beings indicate that the electromagnetic fields of healthy people vary in cyclical rhythms over periods of weeks; and from some 50,000 measurements, it became evident that the regularity of these rhythms made prediction of future health and emotional states of the experimental population a reality.[35]

THE FIELDS OF life may answer one of the most ancient questions posed by philosophers, and provide valuable insights into the workings of astrology as well. Why, asked Aristotle, do acorns always produce oak trees? Why not fig trees or perhaps even horses? What is there in the seed that determines the ultimate form of the organism?

Aristotle postulated an entelechy, a vital force which urged the organism to growth according to nature's intended purpose. Aristotle also believed that the inborn entelechy was set in motion by the *pneuma*—usually translated as soul—at the moment of birth.

The philosophy of vitalism became a source of debate among philosophers for centuries, but without significant attempts at empirical proofs until the sixteenth century. It was then that an alchemist whose Latin name was Paracelsus became the first modern medical scientist. [36] Paracelsus's conviction that the macrocosm of nature was repeated in the microcosm of his patient's body led him to seek natural, rather than supernatural, explanations for medical phenomena. Because of his empirical methodology and his insistence on naturalism, Paracelsus is credited with creating a revolution in medicine which turned magic into science.

But not without loss. Paracelsus was also skilled in astrology, and a kind of astrological vitalism was basic to his method. At the moment of birth, he explained, the external heaven engraved on the individual a heaven within—the *astrum*, or astral body—which constituted his basic character. The astrum could not be perceived by our senses, and our higher instincts belonged to it.[37]

Thus the entelechy of Aristotle became the *astrum* of Paracelsus, and in turn was lost as alchemy became science with a narrowing of its vision to a mechanistic empiricism. The astral body became the *aura* of the occultists—a derisive term applied to any scientist who dared explore its validity.

One such scientist was a respected chemist and physicist, Baron Karl von Reichenbach, whose *Physico-Physiological Researches on the Dynamics of Magnetism, etc., in Relation to the Vital Force* caused a sensation in 1845. Using scientific methods, von Reichenbach discovered a magnetic force which he called od, and which both streamed about the human organism and permeated the universe.[38] But odic forces or auras were contrary to the prevailing scientific mood, and von Reichenbach's findings were dismissed as an exercise in occultism—despite the fact that they were never disproved and were in fact duplicated by other scientists.

Dr. John Kilner, an electrotherapist who joined a London hospital in 1869, had read the work of von Reichenbach. Kilner discovered a way of making the human aura visible to the naked eye by means of tinted glass in order to diagnose and treat a variety of complaints. When he published his findings in 1911, Kilner received much the same treatment as his mentor. "Dr. Kilner has failed to convince us that his aura is more real than Macbeth's visionary dagger," the *British Medical Journal* commented.[39]

In philosophy, vitalism has had a similarly uneven career. It was revived in this century by Henri Bergson, whose most popular work, *Creative Evolution,* was published in 1907. Bergson's philosophy would supplement the thesis of Darwinism with a creative vital force which could be far better understood by intuition (Bergson was a Libran), he believed, than by scientific proofs.

Hans Driesch, a scientist and a contemporary of Bergson's, commenced orthodox scientific investigations to show that evidence for the entelechy of Aristotle (somewhat reformulated by Driesch) did in fact exist.

Although Driesch's work became steadily more metaphysical as it progressed, Dr. Burr's research into the fields of life is respectably scientific. Dr. Burr concludes that L-fields are a "guiding factor which not only makes the acorn grow into the oak tree but also induces a characteristic pattern of organization, of which the physiological functional activities are known as behaviour."[40] This description dovetails not only with vitalist philosophy, but also supports the evidence of auras or odic forces, not to mention the orgone energy of Wilhelm Reich, yet another martyr to scientism.

Recently, Russian experiments in what has been termed Kirlian photography have shown von Reichenbach's odic force just as he described it—a kind of light streaming from the finger tips—and even more recently such experiments have been duplicated in the United States.[41]

As the acorn is to the oak, so the birth chart is to the fully-realized native whose entelechy, animated by his first breath—the literal translation of the Greek *pneuma*—it describes. Or as Lillian and other contemporary astrologers often remark, the birth chart shows the natal promise which the individual has always been given the opportunity to fulfill or to deny, notwithstanding the influence of his immediate or celestial environment.

13   What Is Delineation?

THE DELINEATION OF the horoscope is a process of interpretation by which the seventeen hundred or so factors in every natal chart are synthesized. In the following example, the aspects used will be the major aspects and the quincunx. The orbs allowed are nine degrees for the Sun and the Moon and six degrees for the planets in all major aspects. The orb allowed for the quincunx is three degrees.

In the process of synthesis, an analysis of the overview of the chart is related to considerations of the chart in terms of sign, house, planet and aspects. These factors can be integrated in many ways. After such a basic analysis, reality considerations intrude. In an actual delineation, we would ask the native about certain basic facts of his (her) life in order to determine his direction and to pin down other aspects of the delineation. In this chapter, those data will be supplied.

The first consideration is a holistic overview of the chart (see fig. 20). Here we see the *bucket pattern*, with a retrograde Mars in Libra, its sign of detriment. Note that Mars is the handle of the bucket: thus the debilitated and retrograde Mars is the most powerful influence in the chart, and will have a great deal to do with the action expressed in this native's horoscope. Remember that the handle of the bucket indicates the direction of the native's interest.

In the box scores we see that, in the quadruplicities, the native has a strong emphasis in fixed signs with four planetary placements, plus both the Midheaven and the Ascendant. This fixity is somewhat relieved by four placements in mutable signs, providing needed flexibility.

By triplicity, the native's strongest emphasis is in earth signs, suggesting stolidity, which corresponds to the fixed emphasis in the breakdown by quadruplicity. Three placements in air ease that stolidity somewhat, providing an outlet through the native's intuition.

In the house positions, there is equal distribution between angular and succedent houses—four and four—with two cadent house place-

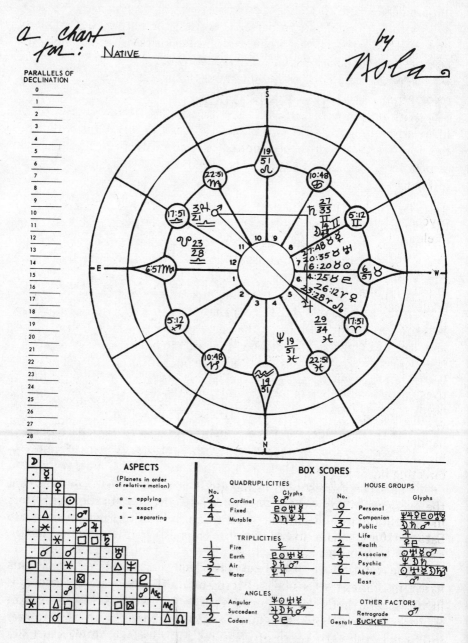

FIGURE 20. "Native's" chart

ments. This breakdown indicates that the native has the power to initiate change and to pursue it as well.

With no placements in personal houses, the native does not function well alone; with seven companionship positions, the complementary need for associations with others is shown.

Three placements in public houses suggest a need for public recognition.

With only one placement in life houses, the native's joy of living is likely to be limited. With two planets in wealth houses, his opportunities for wealth are probably limited as well. With four placements in associations, the native probably needs close personal ties with intimates.

Three psychic house placements suggest that the native has some psychic ability; and six placements above the horizon indicate the likelihood of the desired public recognition.

With only one planet in the eastern hemisphere of the chart, this native will probably rely on his companions and intimates a great deal in determining the direction of his life. Finally, with one planet retrograde (Mars) we are reminded to check the ephemeris to see at what age that planet may have gone direct.

What can be said about this native on the basis of the box scores and the overall bucket pattern of his chart? We may observe that the native has a great deal of dogged determination in pursuing his objectives, with some relieving adaptability and intuition. We can also say he needs the participation of others to provide direction for his life goals. We can surmise that he has a desire for public recognition and, with a handle on his bucket pattern being a retrograde Mars in detriment, that his sexual feelings will play a great part in coloring his life and in directing his objectives.

The aspects are shown in the boxes at the bottom of the chart. In the overview of the aspects, we find a T-square configuration with Mars in opposition to Jupiter and square Saturn; Jupiter in turn is square Saturn. The T-square adds additional emphasis to the profound significance of Mars in this native's chart.

The open end of the T-square, which may be the outlet for this native insofar as the tensions reflected by the T-square are concerned, is in the second house of possessions at about twenty-seven degrees of Sagittarius. Note that this T-square involves an opposition from Jupiter in Pisces in the fifth house of pleasures and romance, to Mars in Libra in the eleventh house of friends, hopes and wishes; and that Saturn in Gemini in the eighth house of sex, love and death completes the T-square by squaring both Mars and Jupiter.

Thus, the T-square involves friends, hopes, wishes and (especially) sexuality as symbolized by Mars in the eleventh; romance and pleasure as symbolized by Jupiter in the fifth; the brooding omnipresence of a Saturn parental figure restricting his sexual outlets as symbolized by Saturn in the eighth. We may immediately conclude that the native will have some difficulty in the area of sexual expression.

We may also infer that the tensions related to sex, love and romance come to some sort of culmination at the age of twelve or thirteen when, by one-degree directions, Saturn exactly conjuncts the natal Moon. This inference is reinforced by the fact that thirteen is probably the age the native reached puberty. The age of thirteen therefore brought the native the realization that he had to live with certain feelings of limitation in the area of sex. How he resolved that conflict will be determined by other aspects, sign and house placements.

The native's Sun is in Taurus, a fixed earth sign. The box scores show that the primary sign emphasis in the chart is in terms of earth (four placements) and even more so of fixity (four placements plus the Midheaven and Ascendant). From these factors we conclude that the native, in terms of his basic self, is oriented to an acute perception of present reality and is slow to change a perspective once it has been established. His sense perceptions are excellent in terms of aesthetic response and in terms of any sense orientation. Natives with a Taurus sign emphasis are ordinarily thought to be sensuous and this native is no exception. However, we have already seen that the T-square imposes limitations on any *expression* of such sensuousness.

The Sun is posited in the seventh house of marriage and other partnerships and Taurus is on the cusp of that house. Since the Sun is the basic self, its position in the seventh house suggests an element of narcissism in the native's search for a love partner. This influence is supported by the fact that the natal Uranus, that planet of desire for the unusual, and Mercury, the planet representing the native's mind and communication (both within oneself and with others), are also posited in the seventh house with Sun conjunct Uranus and Uranus conjunct Mercury.

The conjunction of the Sun to Uranus, with Uranus in turn conjunct Mercury, suggests that the native will have a taste for the offbeat and even the bizarre, which will involve the senses (all placements are in Taurus), and about which he will attempt to communicate with partners, particularly in close relationships.

The Sun is sextile Neptune, which is posited in the fourth house of home and conditions at the end of life; Neptune is also in the sign of Pisces, which it rules—a most comfortable placement for Neptune. As with the conjunction to Uranus, this Sun-sextile-Neptune aspect is applying rather than separating, so the native probably has an intuitive and compassionate regard for the problems of humanity which may find mystical expression as an outlet for the pressures elsewhere reflected in the chart. The fourth house placement of Neptune implies that this mystical and compassionate orientation was very much a part of the native's early home environment.

The Sun is square Midheaven, an applying aspect in Leo, a fixed fire position, which suggests that the native will have conflict relating to public recognition. Inasmuch as Leo is a front-and-center sign of leadership, it further indicates that the native will achieve a position of leadership in his field of interest, but not without considerable conflict.

The Sun is also in opposition to the natal Ascendant, a separating aspect. While the Sun is in Taurus, a fixed earth sign, the two other sign positions dealing with the native's personality and public image— Midheaven and Ascendant respectively—are in fixed signs as well. This opposition to the Ascendant in the fixed water sign of Scorpio represents conflict between the native's basic self, as shown by his Sun position, and the externalization of the personality, as shown by the Scorpio Ascendant. In this particular instance, the Ascendant indicates intensity, secretiveness and depth of feeling and purpose. A Scorpio Ascendant is often associated with the scientist and with the religious zealot—two fields not so far apart as is commonly supposed. The conflict shown in the opposition is perhaps related to the intensity of the endeavor toward which the Ascendant may orient the native.

There is an applying opposition between the Ascendant and the ruler of the Ascendant, Pluto. Pluto is posited in the sixth house of service and health in Taurus. Pluto expresses intensity and long-term changes culminating in rebirth. This aspect underscores the ambivalence reflected in the Sun-Ascendant opposition: somehow the native's basic self, oriented toward a superb appreciation of present reality which the native does not wish to disturb, is necessarily jolted by the probing and impassioned role that the Ascendant plays in this chart.

The Moon, posited in the eighth house of sex, in the inquisitive and versatile sign of Gemini, suggests that the native has an inquiring mind and that, unconsciously, his attitude toward women is more curious than emotional. Also, his mother may have been Geminian in her attitude toward the native. The Moon's position underscores the inference that the native's sexual responses to women may have had a frequency which reflects more curiosity than involvement. In addition, the Moon, posited in the eighth house, rules the ninth house of higher mind, with motherly Cancer on the ninth house cusp.

The Moon has an applying square aspect to Neptune, posited in the fourth house. This aspect indicates that the native's mother may have been an early obstacle to the fullest expression of his sexual feelings involving women. Since Neptune is an idealistic sign, imaginative when positively aspected and self-deluding when negatively aspected, this square also suggests that the native may have been deluded by an overidealization of his mother and her role in his early life.

The applying sextile aspect of Moon to Midheaven indicates that the native's curiosity about women, including his mother, may somehow have supported his public role and his leadership in that public role (Leo Midheaven).

Mercury is posited in Taurus in the seventh house. There is an applying trine aspect to Mars in the eleventh house of friends. Although the expression of Mars energy is in detriment in Libra, the trine brings an easy flow of Martial energy to the native's mind and ability to communicate. The applying sextile from Mars to Jupiter in the fifth house of pleasures adds further facility to that ability, indicating a mystical higher consciousness, which may provide some outlet through communication for his besieged Jupiter.

The conjunction of Mercury to Uranus adds brilliance to the native's mind.

Venus is posited in Aries—its sign of debility—in the sixth house of service and health. Venus is the native's ability to give and to receive love and here finds its expression in service to others, with limitations on the native's ability to give and receive love. There is an applying sextile from Venus in the sixth house of health to Saturn in the eighth house of death. This positive aspect also suggests that the native's affectional nature may have been directed toward a father figure or, since Saturn is in Gemini, toward a variety of father figures.

Venus has a separating trine to the Midheaven, softening somewhat the obstacles reflected by Sun square Midheaven by permitting the native's more attractive, affectionate side to appear to the public to some extent as well.

Venus conjunct the north node provides some easing of the Aries sign position of Venus and, inasmuch as the north node reflects an area of life in which the native's opportunities for achievement may fall, this conjunction may indicate that his service to others may be his greatest opportunity for success, especially since the north node conjunct Venus is in the sixth house as well.

Mars is posited in Libra in the eleventh house of friends, hopes and wishes. Mars is the native's sexuality and his masculine aggressive energy. It is a singleton planet, the only one in the eastern hemisphere of the horoscope, and it is separated from the other planets by the ninth and tenth houses on the one hand and by the twelfth through the third houses on the other.

Mars is the most significant planet in the native's chart. It is retrograde at birth and in its sign of detriment, Libra. It is one leg of the T-square, squaring Saturn and opposing Jupiter. Mars in Libra, since it is the sign of detriment, reflects in the male some difficulty in expressing his sexual feelings and because of that strain, and the strain reflected by the debilitated Venus, the native may find homosexual expression an easier outlet in some circumstances. This possibility is indicated by the square to Saturn in the eighth house of sex and the opposition to Jupiter in the fifth house of pleasures and romance. However, I must hasten to add that such a potentiality should not be confused with the popular notions of homosexual-versus-heterosexual as a mutually exclusive dichotomy. There is a quincunx from Mars to Pluto, that planet of intensity, with Pluto posited in the sensuous sign of Taurus; and Pluto rules the Scorpio Ascendant and is the natural ruler of the eighth house of sex. A quincunx also reflects a strain, thus adding credence to the possibility of a homosexual outlet for this native's sexuality.

Jupiter is posited in Pisces in the fifth house of pleasures, romance and children—including brain children. In any event, Pisces is a most comfortable position for Jupiter, the planet of good fortune, growth and general beneficence. Ordinarily the sign and house position of Jupiter in this chart would suggest that the native would give free expression to love and to his sexual feelings. However, the hard aspects to Jupiter in this chart profoundly affect its expression: Jupiter forms the other leg of the T-square with a separating opposition to Mars and a separating square to Saturn. As I have noted, this T-square restricts the free expression of the native's sexuality, and the applying sextile to Mercury provides some outlet for this restriction. In this chart, Jupiter is the ruler of the second house, the outlet for the T-square. Since Jupiter is in the sign of Pisces, bespeaking an expression of mysticism or higher consciousness, and since the fifth house is the house of brain children, the native's outlets may well be brain children or creative productions of higher consciousness, the true possessions indicated by the native's second house, which has Sagittarius, the sign of higher mind activities, on its cusp.

Saturn is posited in the eighth house of sex, love and death in the inquisitive sign of Gemini and rules the native's third house of communications. Saturn is the third leg of the natal T-square, squaring Mars and Jupiter. There are no aspects to Saturn other than those already delineated. Saturn is regarded as the father in the natal horoscope (unless there is a role reversal of the parents) especially in early life. For many astrologers Saturn is still a co-ruler or secondary ruler of Aquarius—and Aquarius is the sign on the cusp of this native's fourth house.

Although the Moon and Saturn are too wide for a conjunction, both planets are posited in Gemini in the eighth house of sex, love and death.

Uranus is posited in Taurus in the seventh house of partnership, conjunct the Sun and conjunct Mercury as well. Uranus has a trine aspect to Neptune, separating, which implies an inventive imagination, particularly with regard to the native's Piscean concern about the problems of humanity and the conditions of his early life. The applying square aspect to the native's Midheaven suggests that the native's inventiveness as a characteristic of his basic self and his communication of his mental efforts (Uranus is conjunct the Sun and conjunct Mercury) will create conflicts in his quest for public recognition.

Neptune is posited in Pisces, which it rules, in the fourth house of home. In this native's chart, Neptune rules the fifth house of pleasures, romance, children and brain children. Neptune represents the native's idealism and his imagination. The only aspect to Neptune not previously considered is the quincunx aspect to the native's Midheaven. A quincunx can indicate illness or a general feeling of malaise which may be entirely unconscious, in the areas of life indicated by the house and sign placements. Here the quincunx from Neptune is to the Leo Midheaven, which is the tenth house parent, ordinarily the father. Leo on the cusp of the tenth house suggests a powerful father figure, at least insofar as the native is concerned, from the perspective of his afflicted Neptune. The native may overidealize the power of the father figure, sustaining a delusion from which he could not be shaken, similar to the native's illusions about his mother by virtue of the applying square of the Moon to Neptune. These hard aspects to Neptune by parental figures underscore the native's difficulties in experiencing the *joie de vivre* which his fifth house Jupiter should otherwise express.

Pluto is posited in Taurus in the sixth house of service and health and rules the native's Scorpio Ascendant, to which it has an applying opposition. Thus the native's intensity and depth of feeling, which would otherwise be oriented to an appreciation of present sense reality (Pluto in Taurus), show ambivalence. As mentioned earlier, the outlet for the tension thus created may be in service to others in the area of scientific research, religion or mysticism.

The Midheaven or the tenth house cusp is in the sign of Leo, ruled by the Sun in Taurus to which it has an applying square. There are no aspects to the Midheaven not previously considered. It should be noted, however, that whereas Saturn already represents the native's father in early life, that representation ordinarily is transferred to the Sun as the native approaches and achieves adulthood. Here the natal Sun opposes the natal Midheaven, which it rules, inviting the inference that the native's father continued to pose a problem for the native, in the native's perspective. His view of his father may have been exaggerated: there is a quincunx of Neptune to the Midheaven, which I have already considered.

The native's north node is posited in the sixth house at 23:28 Aries. This sign and house position indicates that those areas of life in which the native is most readily able to excel are in the area of service to others, perhaps also relating to health. The conjunction of the north node to the natal Venus suggests that the native's affectional nature is related closely to the area of service in which he is likely to excel. The trine from the natal Venus to the Midheaven and from the north node to the Midheaven as well implies that the native's public image will be favored by the close relationship of his service to others and his ability to give and to receive love.

The south node is somewhat analogous to Saturn in the natal chart, just as the north node is in some respects comparable to natal Jupiter. Here the south node is posited in the sign of Libra in the twelfth house of secret sorrows, karmic debts and institutions. The south node represents the areas of life in which the native must work for achievement.

Here the native's secret sorrows relate to other people and partnerships (Libra), to institutions and to love and marriage. The south node has a sextile aspect to the Midheaven, since there is a trine from the north node to the Midheaven. This aspect indicates that the native's efforts in dealing with his secret regrets somehow enhance his public role.

What can we say about the inferences drawn from the delineation of the natal chart? Obviously some basic information about the native is needed to flesh out the tentative observations.

The native lived in an Eastern European community most of his life and, being Jewish, was exposed to anti-Semitism. He regarded his father as "the most powerful, wisest and wealthiest man" in the world, at least up to the age of twelve. He recalls that at the age of seven or eight he defied his father by urinating in his parents' bedroom and in their presence.

His angry father exclaimed, "That boy will never amount to anything!" The natal Mars went direct at the age of eight, an event which would prompt the very kind of male assertiveness this defiant act represents.

The native's exaggerated view of his father is borne out by the squares of Saturn to Mars and Jupiter in the natal T-square and the quincunx of Neptune to the Leo Midheaven as well as the square of the natal Sun to the Leo Midheaven, which it rules.

The native recalls that the father's retort was a terrible affront to his ambition, so that justifying himself in his father's eyes became one of the most compelling motivations in his life—and the basic incentive to his intensive study, resulting in significant scientific discoveries. The native also recalls considerable hatred of his father, related directly to his overwhelming love of his mother. As the native once remarked, "A man who has been the indisputable favorite of his mother keeps for life the feeling of a conqueror." He confesses that his awareness of his mother's undivided love was the foundation of his emotional life— which also meant tremendous jealousy of his father and a lifelong desire to triumph over him.

There is another reality factor which must be built into the synthesis of this native's chart: the native's family, being of Eastern European Jewish origin, reflected the characteristics of that culture. As Martha Wolfenstein has observed, maternal attitudes in this cultural background tend to establish a fixation of the mother-child relationship at the earliest stages of infancy.[1]

Wolfenstein points out that the Jewish religion has as a major motive the consolidation of the father-son relationship by establishing at an early age that there is one God, the father, whose authority is pervasive. For that reason it was customary to separate sons from their mothers at an early age in order to induce submission to the parental father, the representative of the parental Deity. Rebellious impulses in the son appeared as doubts about religious rules.

Also, traditional Jewish life involved strong defenses against sexual impulses with minimal eroticism, particularly for the wife, so that the great sexual experience for the mother was childbirth, thus emphasizing the strong attachment of mother to son in infancy.

The role of Saturn as the "brooding omnipresence of the father" by virtue of the T-square has been noted. Saturn in Gemini indicates that the native, if he had brothers and sisters, would find trauma there as well—as indeed he did. As the native himself observes, his self-confidence was undermined when he was almost a year old by the appearance of his baby brother, a resentment which became self-reproach when his brother died within the year.

In the native's chart Saturn, posited in the eighth house of death, rules the third house of brothers and sisters. His feelings about his younger brother lingered in his unconscious to the extent that *at the age of fifty-six* he had sudden fainting spells which he traced to his remorse over his infantile hatred of his little brother.

Synthesizing the native's cultural background with his own observations about his attitudes toward his mother and father and with the delineation of his chart, we may conclude that the native did indeed overidealize the role of his mother and greatly exaggerated the seeming omnipotence of his father. It seems clear also that these attitudes, which persisted at least to some extent throughout his life, were a substantial limitation on his ability to enjoy a sexual relationship or simply to enjoy life, as prefigured by the T-square.

The native married a woman whom he fell in love with at the age of twenty-six, and his wish to marry her led him to take up the general practice of medicine. He had to give up research in physiology, a less lucrative field, which was his first interest—and which is certainly indicated by his Scorpio Ascendant and the Pluto aspects.

Whatever the success of that marital relationship, we do know that the native yearned for "a master key to open all female hearts" and that he felt that he "stood helpless at the strange design of the lock" and was forced to "torment" himself "to discover a suitable key to it."

When the native was twelve or thirteen, Saturn exactly conjuncted his natal Moon by one-degree progression. He seems to have recognized then that he was to feel the denial of sex with love (Jupiter in Pisces in the fifth house of pleasures, square Saturn and the Moon in the eighth house of sex; opposition Mars in the eleventh house of wishes): that he therefore had to know intellectually why such restrictions must be. This desire to know is indicated by the curiosity of Gemini on the eighth house cusp and by the fact that Jupiter in Pisces in the fifth house rules Sagittarius on the cusp of the second house of possessions. The Sun in Taurus is a sensuous position indeed; the native must have felt a deep sense of chagrin in recognizing that he must learn how to do without: (1) sex with love (Mars opposition Jupiter in the fifth); (2) the fuller sexual expression of his manhood (Mars in detriment in Libra); (3) sex for the joy of sex (Saturn square Mars square Jupiter in the eighth).

The resolution of this natal deprivation is strongly oriented to the zero in personal house placements. He had no personal hermitage where he could escape the externally imposed sexual inhibitions of his parents; and he also had the ability to view objectively why that was so. He was in a very real sense his first patient.

At the age of twelve or thirteen, when the native entered puberty and by progression the Moon conjuncted Saturn, the natal T-square was activated, causing him to discover great pleasures in either writing or talking about his total frustration in these areas, coupled with a desire *to lead the field,* exemplified in his Leo Midheaven (Saturn rules the third house of expression). Since the Moon symbolizes mother, all the native's personal agony could have been avoided if the mother had not imposed upon the native her own standards of sexual behavior. She succeeded in castrating the native emotionally; because the father could have sex with the mother but the native could not, the father was a better man than he was.

Because of the absence of personal house placements, the native's thoughts in these areas of sex, imposed on him when he was young, later became self-denial. He accepted these thoughts also because of the emphasis in his chart on *fixity* and because of his inability to find a self-image otherwise. Rather than change—which the native could not do readily with six placements in fixed signs, including both the Sun and the Ascendant—he could analyze and understand. In this regard, note that the ruler of the Ascendant is Pluto—and that Pluto, by one-degree progressions, conjuncted the Sun at the same time that the Moon, by one-degree directions, conjuncted Saturn.

The native was *twelve years old* when his father told him about an episode in which an anti-Semite knocked his hat off and directed him off the sidewalk and into the street. When the native asked what his father had done, his father calmly replied that he had retrieved his hat and walked on. The native admits feelings of contempt for his father's response, and remembers that ever since that episode, he fantasized about Hannibal, whose father made his son swear vengeance against the Romans. From that event we can trace the native's desire for intellectual leadership in his field.

We also know that as an adult the native suffered acute depressions and that he sought to analyze himself as a cure for his depression and, hopefully, to develop a therapeutic method that would help others. He was candid enough to admit that his new approach at least held out the promise of permitting him to make a living—an economic difficulty was one realistic source of his depression—if it were successful. Both economic benefit and self-understanding are seen in the Pisces Jupiter rulership of Sagittarius on the cusp of the second house of possessions and income. His desire for leadership in a field of his own creation can be seen in the Leo Midheaven.

By scrupulous self-analysis, the native ultimately recognized that his love for his mother and his envy and hatred of his father (all of which are shown in the natal chart) characterized not only his sexual orientation but his very identity as well. He was indeed able to apply this self-knowledge to second house affairs of possessions and income.

In still another way the native worked out his feelings of deprivation of sexual love. He candidly relates that in treating a female patient one day for her neurotic symptoms, she suddenly flung her arms around his neck. From this event, the native determined that there was indeed an *erotic* basis to his therapeutic method which was the key to its effectiveness.

The native had discovered something which, as one biographer observed, was far more than a simple intellectual exercise. It was in fact "a master key to open all female hearts." Once again the native's determination to achieve self-discovery related to his second house affairs. In this case, however, it was related to his Venus sextile Saturn in the sixth house of service as well.

In the delineation I spoke of a possible homosexual outlet for the stresses indicated by the T-square, especially as seen in the afflicted natal Mars. The native did have strong emotional attachments to other men, although there is no evidence of any overt sexual activity as such. One remarkable relationship deserves comment. For fifteen years the native shared a high degree of mutual admiration with another doctor, a contemporary whose unorthodox ideas subjected him to ridicule from the medical profession, but whom the native staunchly supported.

Ultimately the native understood his feelings for his friend, following the breakup of the relationship (which had aspects of a lovers' quarrel) when he remarked to another male companion, "A part of the homosexual cathexis has been withdrawn and made use of to enlarge my own ego."

The native's emotional attachments to other men can also be seen as an effort to overcome the omnipotent father, as seen in the T-square of the natal chart. Thus, the series of emotional attachments became father substitutes, just as the rigorous self-analysis was a way of intellectualizing away the effect of the Saturnian father.

A third way is suggested by the Leo Midheaven: in a very real sense the native *became his own father*, excelling by his achievements anything his father had ever done, spurred by his father's spontaneous exclamation that he would never amount to anything.

There is still another way in which the native handled the Saturn squares to Mars and Jupiter in his chart. He had a lifelong obsession about Moses the lawgiver, certainly a father figure in Jewish religion. In early life he dealt at length with the Moses of Michelangelo, journeying to Rome to gaze at the statue. His musings appeared in a journal he edited but were carefully disguised to ensure the native's anonymity—one instance of the secrecy characteristic of his Scorpio Ascendant. In that essay he concluded that the figure of Moses sculpted by Michelangelo was the Moses who had overcome his wrath against his people for violating the law and was in repose.

At the end of his life the native concluded that Moses was an Egyptian, thereby ultimately resolving his obsession by making Moses a Gentile, so that he was not the native's religious father at all.

Finally the native *created* his own father along more satisfactory lines, thereby totally displacing the original model. He groomed one of his colleagues as his successor in his particular brand of therapy. The anointed successor was both a Gentile, oriented to Christian mysticism, and an individual whose Sun and Uranus were in the sign of Leo—the sign placement on the native's Midheaven, and the house of the father.

The native's emotional involvement in this effort is demonstrated by the fact that, when the intended successor showed signs of defection (which ultimately occurred), the native argued him back into the fold on two occasions—and fainted after each such event!

At this point I have covered most of the indications in the natal delineations except perhaps for the native's secrecy, shown by the Scorpio Ascendant and his orientation toward mysticism, shown by his Neptune and Jupiter in Pisces. The native was deeply rooted in the Jewish mystical tradition, and his work reflects the lore of the Kaballah. Because of the anti-Semitism prevalent at the time the native developed his ideas, Jewish mysticism, the basic source of his therapeutic methods, was deliberately concealed.

THE NATIVE WHOSE chart I have delineated is Sigmund Freud, who was born at 6:30.P.M. on May 6, 1856, in Freibert, Moravia, now a part of Czechoslovakia; and whose family moved in 1860 to Vienna, where Freud grew up and lived most of his life. Indeed, Freud's Taurian fixity is nowhere better demonstrated than by his unwillingness to leave Vienna even when the sickness of anti-Semitism became the plague of Naziism in the 1930s. It took enormous efforts at persuasion by his closest friends to induce him to leave the country in 1938, following the Nazi invasion.

The therapeutic principles developed by Freud are the principles of psychoanalysis, which Professor David Bakan has shown are essentially derived from the Jewish mystical tradition.

I have noted specifically the theory of *transference,* in which Freud recognized the erotic basis of the therapeutic relationship; and the greatest product of his genius, the discovery of Man's unconscious, so brilliantly delineated in *The Interpretation of Dreams.*

His dream analysis also led to his formulation of the theory of the Oedipus complex, which he discovered in himself first and which involved the development of earlier notions about the essential bisexuality of Man which he derived from the theory of biorhythms developed by his friend, Dr. Wilhelm Fliess, the gentleman he referred to in his remark about his "homosexual cathexis."[2]

Freud's conclusions about Moses are set out in his final work, *Moses and Monotheism,* published when he was eighty-three. His intended successor was, of course, Carl Jung, born July 26, 1875, Sun in Leo, (see fig. 21) who broke with Freud to follow his Leonine inclinations by founding his own school of psychoanalysis. Although Jung has

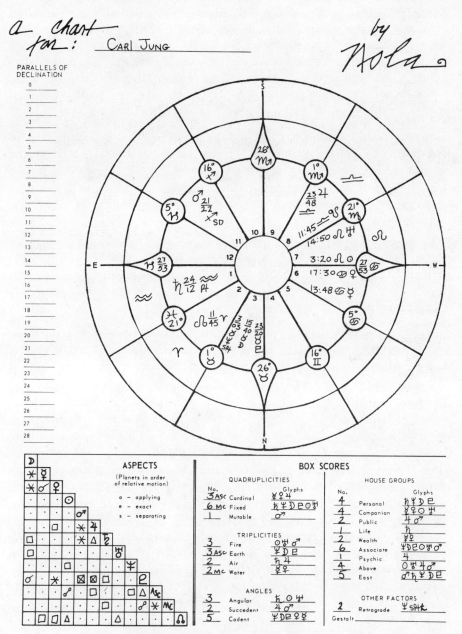

FIGURE 21. Natal chart for Carl Jung

recounted the story of their breakup in terms of Freud's supposed antipathy to the occult or to any expression of mysticism, Freud wrote to his principal biographer and lifelong friend, Ernest Jones, in 1929 that he was so impressed in reading about Gilbert Murray's telepathy experiments that "I am ready to give up my opposition to the existence of thought transference . . . I should even be prepared to lend the support of psychoanalysis to the matter of telepathy."[3]

According to Erich Fromm, Freud's aim was the liberation of Man from the thralldom of our rationalist Judeo-Christian religious heritage by creating a new religion of his own devising. Fromm believes that Freud succeeded in striking a deathblow to Western rationalism with the discovery of the timeless unconscious, showing that our conscious thoughts control our actions only to a small degree and that our unconscious motives are beyond our powers of inspection.

BECAUSE OF THE loss of the mythical frame of reference which gave meaning to our world before the Age of Rationalism, the reader may have had no experience to which to relate the task of synthesizing and interpreting the seventeen hundred factors which he must consider in the delineation of a horoscope. *Finnegans Wake*, with its universal symbols, encoded messages of multiple significance and portmanteau words, synthesizes virtually all of the premises of astrology. As such it is a paradigm of chart formulation and delineation.

Finnegans Wake begins in mid-sentence:

> riverrun, past Eve and Adam's, from swerve of shore to bend of bay, brings us by a commodius vicus of recirculation back to Howth Castle and Environs.

The last sentence reads, in its entirety, "A way a lone a last a loved a long," completing the physical book, and at the same time starting it anew. What Joyce demonstrates by the circle of his prose, the astrologer shows by the circle of his horoscope.

How often the neophyte astrologer may stare at a horoscope with unseeing eyes (we have all done it), before the chart begins to yield its many clues. Yet they are all there, just as they are in *Finnegans Wake*. "A commodius vicus of recirculation" is our first clue to the master plan of the work. "Vicus" refers to Giambattista Vico, an eighteenth-century scientist-historian on whose metaphysics of the recirculation of world history Joyce's book is structured.

As Vico saw it, the world began with a thunderclap which brought us out of chaos by setting free religion in its earliest form. A four-part cycle then commenced, as religion produced a progression from anarchy to despotism, feudalism, democracy and back to anarchy with the attendant chaos which starts the whole thing over again. Hence Joyce's reference to a "commodius vicus"; Commodus was the emperor of Rome at the time of its first unmistakable signs of decay.[4]

Finnegan, in one of his many incarnations, can be identified with Gwion, since *Gw* is the Celtic equivalent of *F*; and Gwion is in turn identifiable with the miraculous Taliesin of the early Irish *Romance of Taliesin*.[5] Taliesin was a miraculous child who possessed a secret doctrine that nobody could guess; but the reader can, for he is another incarnation of the fugitive god, Dionysus.[6] At an early period of Christian influence, the wine sacrament was substituted for those seemingly ubiquitous magic mushrooms of Dionysian initiation in order to reconcile the tales of Taliesin/Gwion/Finn with Christian orthodoxy. It is an interesting example of the layers of myth working like the astrological palimpsest: rebirth from magic mushrooms becomes rebirth from the wine sacrament of communion, and ultimately a raucous tale about a wake at which the deceased is reborn not from wine but from whiskey, the real sacrament of every true Irishman.

Finnegan is also closely related to Humpty Dumpty, whom Lewis Carroll characterizes as the embodiment of the maxim, Pride Goeth Before a Fall. This absurd nursery-rhyme figure is an appropriate enough image for Joyce, however, since Humpty Dumpty's fall is but another retelling of the Fall of Man (this time through the pride of Lucifer), with connotations of the crack in the Cosmic Egg as well.

All of these concepts are embodied in the horoscope, which commences with the Fall into human consciousness at the first house cusp, and the corresponding natural zodiac commencing with zero degrees Aries; and concludes with the twelfth house cusp corresponding to thirty degrees Pisces, which is the same as zero degrees Aries and the beginning of a new cycle. Or, as Samuel Beckett said in appreciation of Joyce's application of Vico:

> The consciousness that there is a great deal of the unborn infant in the lifeless octogenarian, and a great deal of both in the man at the apogee of his life's curve removes all the stiff inter-exclusiveness that is often the danger in neat construction.[7]

The image of the horoscope is implicit in Beckett's metaphor: the apogee is the point of a planet's orbit most distant from the Earth—or, in Beckett's literary sense, the highest point reached by Man at the tenth house position of his life cycle. The lifeless octogenarian/unborn infant would both be located at the point on the chart which is at once Ascendant and the twelfth house cusp. Unwittingly, perhaps, Beckett has shown *Finnegans Wake* for what it is: the horoscope as literature.

Vico's contribution goes farther. Holding that all things are ultimately identified with God, Vico saw the universe as a monad in an
essentially Orphic conception of creation, which is directly symbolized
by the planisphere of the horoscope and the four parts of *Finnegans
Wake.* Consistent with his universal monad, Vico also saw the world in
terms of its polarities, which the horoscope expresses in archetypes of
bipolar opposing signs and which *Finnegans Wake* expresses in its
archetypal characters. Again, Beckett sums it up well:

> Thus we have the spectacle of a human progression that depends for its
> movement on individuals, and which at the same time is independent of
> individuals in virtue of what appears to be a preordained cyclicism.[8]

What individuals? The protagonist of *Finnegans Wake* is Humphrey
Chimpden Earwicker, often simply called HCE, whose sleeping consciousness flows with the riverrun and whose dreams, together with
those of his wife and children, form the substance of *Finnegans Wake.*

As in the horoscope of any male, Earwicker the individual is also
identified with Everyman and with the male principle; he has many
other correlations as well. The first such correspondence is in the
reference to *H*owth *C*astle and *E*nvirons, in which HCE appears in the
initials of the Dublin landmark where stood the sentinels of the legendary Irish hero Finn MacCool, the model for Finnegan and Earwicker
as well.

Earwicker's wife is Anna Livia Plurabelle, called ALP, who is
identified with the feminine principle, the psyche and the Eternal
Mother—again, just as any individual female whose horoscope is charted
embodies all of these conceptions.

In the horoscope we find the male and female principles of Yang
and Yin in the Sun and the Moon and in the horizon diameters of the
chart; and the horoscope reflects all of the associations by which Joyce
characterizes HCE and ALP.

Anna Livia Plurabelle's first appearance in *Finnegans Wake* can be
found in the first word, *riverrun*, for just as the Moon controls the
tides, so ALP is the flow of water, especially the River Liffey. We first
see her as she seductively swerves by the shore and the headland bay,
where the male fixity of the castle's structure counterpoints her
fluidity.

Anna Livia Plurabelle embodies all three of the manifestations of
the Moon as virgin, temptress and crone which have been drawn from
myth and embodied in the Moon's role in astrology. The first chapter
devoted to ALP commences with a prayer to Anna Livia Plurabelle as
the Mother of the World, and is modeled after the more familiar prayer
known in our Judeo-Christian heritage as Our Father.

ALP's manifold appearances in the book include an incarnation as Earwicker's daughter and her twenty-eight little companions; in this image we see the Moon and the twenty-eight days of the original lunar month. As the Moon, ALP keeps the flux of life in eternal motion.

ALP and HCE: These two acronyms appear again and again throughout *Finnegans Wake* as a kind of code by which all manner of things are related to the Mother and the Father, the chief archetypes of the novel. Merged into one, HCE and ALP constitute the anagrammatic CHAPEL, a nondenominational church. Fittingly enough, for *Finnegans Wake* is affirmatively nondenominational, combining as it does all the religions of the world in its litany to ALP.

But for Joyce one meaning is never enough; and I note that the cognate or root-meaning of chapel is HEAD. Thus HCE and ALP, the archetypal parents, together make up the Godhead, with correlations to the *mysterium coniunctionis* of alchemy, the right and left brain hemispheres, the conscious and unconscious roles of Sun and Moon, the two hemispheres of the horoscope united by the diameter of the horizon into a circular whole.

As Godhead, ALP and HCE produce two sons, Shem and Shaun, introvert and extrovert, penman and postman. More specifically, they are two brothers named Jerry and Kevin. As Shem and Shaun, the brothers are polar opposites engaged in Cain and Abel's eternal battle. As in the horoscope of any individual, the specific context of the situation presented determines the symbolic identification of the characters. Just as Kevin is sometimes Shaun and Jerry, Shem, so HCE is presented variously as Adam, Lucifer, Finn MacCool and many other mythical figures. Likewise, ALP shares archetypal roles as Eve, Isis, Iseult and many others.

To understand Joyce's delineation of character, we must read *Finnegans Wake* in the same manner as a horoscope, for Joyce's work seeks to explore our collective unconscious and embodies the concepts of the eternal return, the complementary nature of polar opposites, the microcosm of Man reflecting the macrocosm of Vico's monad.

Just as the horoscope uses a special symbolic language to express this theme, so Joyce found it necessary to develop a language of his own, "like a portmanteau—there are two meanings packed up into one word."[9]

One illustration must suffice. Immediately following the introduction of HCE and ALP in the opening paragraph, Joyce announces that Sir Tristram has arrived to fight "his penisolate war." Tristram is the hero of that great medieval cycle of tales which incorporates a host of legends; Joyce draws upon them to relate HCE to Tristram's—and Mankind's—plight of guilty love; and especially to the cosmic theme of love and war, "the constant life expressions of that polarized energy which propels the universe round."[10]

Penisolate can be a *late war of the penis*, precipitated by Tristram's elopement with Iseult, the wife of the king; it can also mean *pen-isolated*, referring to the literary struggles of Tristram as an introverted poet. Finally, it may also incorporate a passing reference to the *Peninsular* War waged by that great Dubliner, the Duke of Wellington, against Napoleon.[11]

Even the book's title suggests such correlations of meaning; Finn is reborn as *Finn Again*, or Finnegan, and *wakes* at his own Wake. For that matter, all of Mankind is in the flowing wake of the endlessly resuscitated Finn and Finn again.

By means of such portmanteau words, Joyce avoids the linear trap of language itself; instead, *Finnegans Wake* is a giant *holon:* each thing-in-itself is also a recapitulation of the whole of which it is a part. Such is the ultimate message of the horoscope. And, as critic Edmund Wilson observed in describing Joyce's technique:

> The style he has invented for his purposes works *on the principle of a palimpsest:* one meaning, one set of images, is written over another.[12]

That is the master analogue for astrology. Clearly the integration of even a portion of such a palimpsest of symbols and meanings does not come without effort, as a glance at Rex Bills's *Rulership Book*—with its listings of astrological correspondences by planet, house and sign, as well as parts of the body—will show. But the learning experience is rewarding for its own sake, for like *Finnegans Wake*, it permits the individual greater insight into himself and into the world of which, he again discovers, he is very much a part.

THE HOROSCOPE HAS been considered objectively, in terms of its diagrammatic structure, and subjectively, in terms of the interpretation of the symbolism which that structure reflects. Now, the horoscope will be viewed psychologically, as the architectonic of human personality. Psychologist Raymond Cattell will serve as our point of departure.

Using factor analysis, Cattell has isolated sixteen factors as the basic components of human personality, each of which he identifies by letters of the alphabet in sets of opposites, *e.g.:* relaxed-tense, conservative-experimenting, practical-imaginative and so on. The idea is, the less one extreme is found, the more there is of the other.[13]

Cattell reports that the personality profiles thus obtained have proved useful in determining the compatibility of marriage partners. I do not find that surprising, since the underlying concept of Dr. Cattell's sixteen personality factors is identical to that of bipolar opposites found in the twelve zodiacal signs.

Psychologist Gardner Murphy speaks of a continuum of individual personality as a kind of gyroscopic development on a time-growth axis, based on universal laws by which the human personality develops everywhere, at all times. [14]

Cattell's sixteen factors are bipolar opposites, which can be viewed as spokes of a wheel rotating on a common axis. These factors are a palimpsest on Murphy's microcosm of time and human growth, which is in turn governed by the universal laws outlined by Dr. William H. Sheldon's continuum of human consciousness. [15]

The result is the reassembling from various psychological theories of personality the architecture of the horoscope. Cattell's factors are bipolar opposites in the same sense as the signs of the zodiac (although there are more of them); the field continuum is a microcosm with the basic cyclical structure expressed in the microcosm of the horoscope; Sheldon's five panels of consciousness correspond (sometimes with amazing accuracy) to the sequence of signs and houses.

In conventional psychology, we must pick and choose from various disparate sources to erect a structure. Astrology alone furnishes an *archetectonic* of human personality in terms of the horoscope, which integrates the development of human personality in a time-growth continuum governed by universal laws, and expressed in individual terms of bipolar opposing factors—not to mention the circadian rhythms which set it all in motion.

And what does the horoscope give us? In Cattell's words, "The personality of an individual is that which enables us to predict what he will do in a given situation." [16].

If astrology, properly practiced, is in any sense a predictive discipline, the key to such prediction lies in the understanding of the character of the individual personality, whether set out in sixteen personality factors symbolized by letters of the alphabet, or by the original astrological symbols from which the alphabet is itself derived.

FIGURE 21-B, FREUD'S natal chart in the inner circle and Jung's planets in the outer circle, shows how Jung appeared to Freud. Figure 21-A shows how Freud appeared to Jung. Lillian comments below.

Jung's natal chart (fig. 21) shows he wanted help in his work (Moon, conjunct Pluto, rules both his seventh house of partners and his sixth house of service, Pluto rules his tenth house of profession) and financial security (Neptune in Taurus in the second) obtainable with the help of a collaborator (Sun in the seventh). Jung would get help but many obstacles between his collaborator and himself would have to be

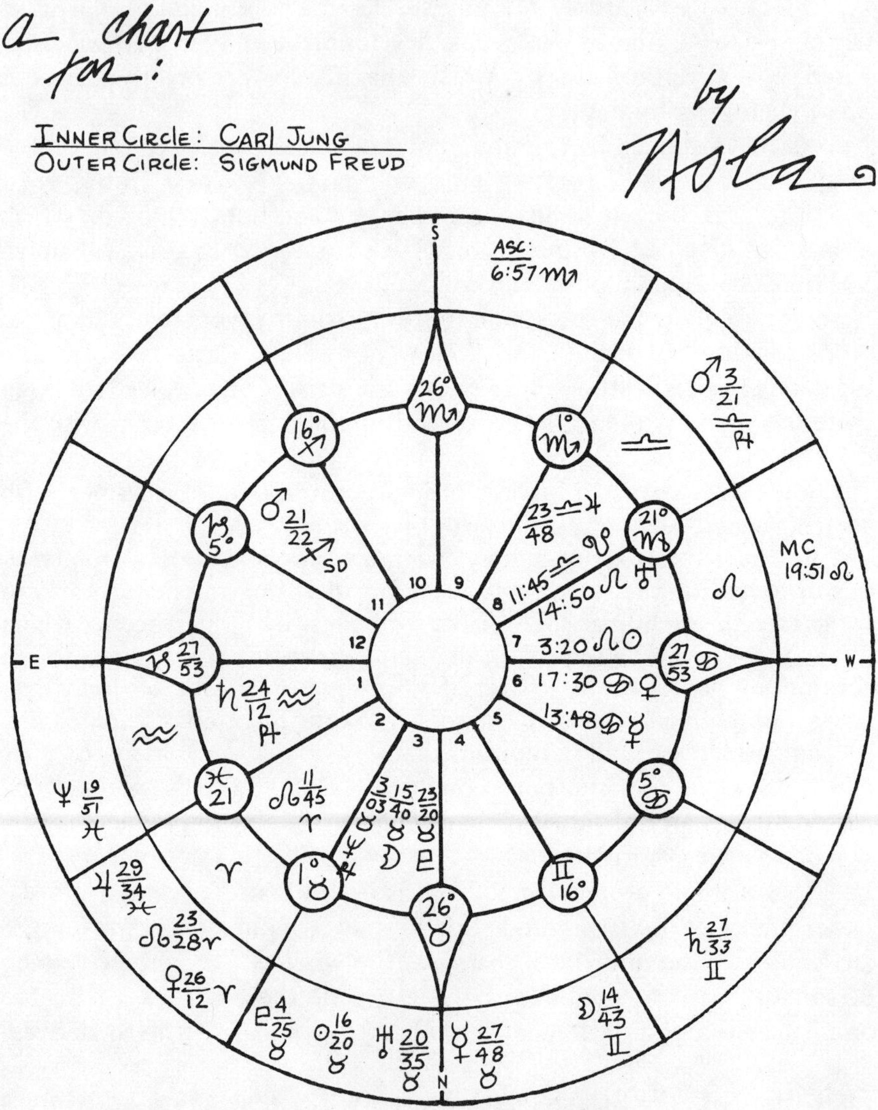

FIGURE 21A. Jung/Freud synastry

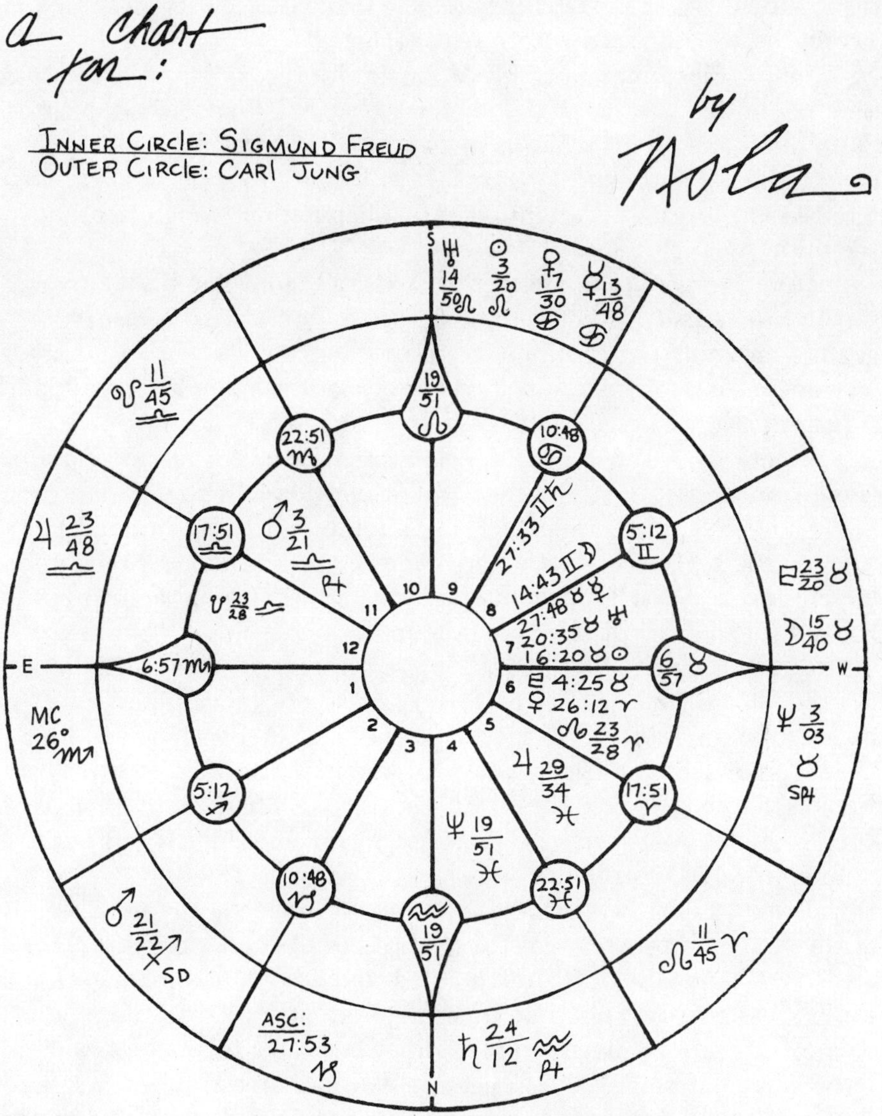
a chart for:
INNER CIRCLE: SIGMUND FREUD
OUTER CIRCLE: CARL JUNG
by Nola
S
N
E
W
MC 26°
ASC: 27:53
SD

FIGURE 21B. Freud/Jung synastry

overcome (exact square of Sun to Neptune). It had to be Freud's way (Uranus in the seventh co-rules the first, Aquarius intercepted in the first) and it was, because Jung *needed* financial security (Neptune in Taurus in the second; Capricorn Ascendant).

Jung's Pluto, conjunct his Moon in Taurus, rules the ninth and signifies both intensity and long-term changes. Freud's Ascendant is Pluto-ruled and Freud's Sun is in Taurus. Freud was his teacher; Jung *had* to meet Freud—and later break with him. Jung deliberately flattered Freud to gain his attention and collaboration (Jung's Neptune in the third, square his Sun).

Jupiter rules Jung's eleventh, exactly quincunx his Pluto and square his Ascendant. If friendship posed any threat to his professional goals, Jung could not continue the relationship. Jung's work was always foremost (Capricorn Ascendant, ruled by Saturn in the first, posited in Aquarius). He felt responsible for people.

Figure 21-A shows that Jung selected Freud for his collaborator (Freud's MC in Jung's seventh) and knew intuitively how to approach him (Jung's Neptune conjunct Freud's Pluto in Jung's third and Pluto rules Freud's Scorpio Ascendant). And Jung understood Freud completely: he saw that Freud's interest was not in making money, but in living through other people (Jung's Moon conjunct Freud's Sun).

But Freud (fig. 21-B) saw Jung as a threat to his personal image (Jung's MC in Freud's first) of which he was possessive (Pluto, his first house ruler, in Taurus). Although the sextile of Freud's Moon to Jung's Uranus shows Freud's great curiosity about Jung's work in astrology, Freud's Scorpio secretiveness and fixity, plus the square aspects of Jung's Uranus to Freud's Scorpio Ascendant and Taurus Sun, would not permit Freud to admit it.

I think Lillian was right. Jung's near-sycophancy toward Freud is demonstrated in the early epistolary stages of their relationship.[17]

As Charles Rycroft has pointed out, Freud's "lifelong Grand Design was to construct a science of mind analogous to the physical sciences . . . strictly determinist . . . in which all explanations were in terms of causation."[18] But Jung, a mystic and an astrologer, wrote to Freud, "I make horoscopic calculations in order to find a clue to the core of psychological truth. Some remarkable things have turned up which will certainly appear incredible to you."[19] They certainly did. As biographer Ernest Jones pointed out, "It was an area in which Freud was a complete unbeliever."[20]

Or was he?

PART TWO

How to Do It

Then the Lord answered Job out of the tempest:
"Can you bring out the signs of zodiac in their
season or guide Aldebaran and its train?"

Job 38:32

14 How Do I Figure the Houses?

MANY BOOKS HAVE tables in them to show the *approximate* positions of the planets, Ascendant and Midheaven. This is not such a book. It is my goal to show you how to erect and interpret your own horoscope precisely the way a professional astrologer would. Hence you will need the basic tools of a professional astrologer, an ephemeris and a table of houses. Although not essential, you will eventually find helpful a book showing time changes in the United States, and one showing longitude and latitude variations from standard time. However, for purposes of erecting your own chart and learning the correct procedure, you will need only the ephemeris for the year of your birth, and the table of houses.

An ephemeris is a table which shows the positions of the planets for each month and day of a given year. Ephemerides have been used by astrologers since astrology began. The most prestigious ephemerides have been published continuously since 1820 by Raphael in England. However, Raphael's ephemerides are relatively expensive in the United States and are not always readily available.

Recently, computerized ephemerides have been introduced, which calculate planetary positions (including, of course, the Sun and the Moon) all the way back to 601 B.C.E.![1]

However, the ephemerides I will use here are published by the Rosicrucian Fellowship, Oceanside, California 92054; they are inexpensive and available at most large bookstores. In any event, don't worry about getting your ephemeris right now. For purposes of these instructions, two pages from the ephemerides are reproduced here (see fig. 22).

Finally, note that the ephemerides used are for the *tropical* system of astrology. That means you must check before purchasing any ephemeris to make sure that the tropical zodiac is being used; and also that the *Placidian house system* is being used in the table of houses. The

Rosicrucian publications are based on the tropical and Placidian systems.

To erect your own chart, along with the appropriate ephemeris for the year of birth, you must have a table of houses to show you the Ascendant, Midheaven and other house cusps for the latitude and sidereal time of your birth. The Rosicrucian Fellowship supplies this volume as well. However, as with the ephemerides, tables of houses are now generally available at most bookstores.

The next reference works are optional, but their use will be explained in case of your future need. Doris Chase Doane has performed a memorable service to astrologers with the preparation of her *Time Changes in the U.S.A.*, published by Professional Astrologers Inc., P. O. Box 2616, Hollywood, California 90028; and also sold by the Church of Light, Box 1525 Main Office, Los Angeles, California 90053. While *Time Changes* is not absolutely essential, it certainly helps solve one of the astrologer's greatest headaches: determining what time changes, if any, were in effect at the native's time of birth.

Over the years we have had standard time, daylight-saving time, war time and other variations established by state law or by local ordinance. Certainly, local inquiry can determine whether or not any time changes were in effect on a given birth date, but if you pursue your interest in astrology, you will eventually want to purchase this book and probably her companion volumes, *Time Changes in Canada and Mexico* and *Time Changes Throughout the World*.

The American Federation of Astrologers, 6 Library Court, S.E., Washington, D.C. 20003, has performed a great service with the publication of *Longitudes and Latitudes in the United States*, by Eugene Dernay. The book is available from the American Federation of Astrologers and at most large bookstores. Again, *Longitudes and Latitudes* is not absolutely essential, since there is a formula for providing the information which Dernay has codified, and I will give you that formula. Nevertheless, all practicing astrologers with whom I am acquainted use *Longitudes and Latitudes* for quickly determining accurate variations from standard time and Greenwich mean time for any city of significant size in the United States.

YOUR FIRST OBJECTIVE in erecting any horoscope is to find the true local time of birth for the native whose chart you plan to erect. Unless your native was born right at the degree of Earth longitude which is used to set the time for the entire time zone, the birth time reflected by the standard time of the time zone is only an approximation.

The time of day is based on the time at which the Sun appears directly overhead from one day to the next. In astronomical terms, that means two successive transits of the local celestial meridian. When the Sun appears to cross or transit your local meridian or overhead point, it is high noon where you live. Two of these transits, from noon one day to noon of the next, equal twenty-four hours. Note that this system means that *every community has its own local time,* since, in the course of a twenty-four hour circuit, high noon changes continuously as the Sun passes overhead from east to west.

Time begins at Greenwich, England, at zero degrees of Earth longitude, and moves west at the rate of one hour of clock time for each 15 degrees of longitude. (In the discussion of the celestial sphere, the right ascension hour circles which correspond to Earth longitude follow the same formula.) In the United States, each of the four time zones is pegged to a specific degree of longitude. Thus the eastern standard time zone is based on 75 degrees west longitude; the central standard time zone, 90 degrees west longitude; the mountain standard time zone, 105 degrees west longitude; the Pacific standard time zone, 120 degrees west longitude. As you can see, each of the time zones reflects 15-degree increments of longitude.

Clearly, there are variations of time within a time zone, according to the number of degrees away from the longitude degree of the time zone that any given community is located. That variation must be considered in order to establish the true local time of birth for chart erection.

In sum, we are (thus far) dealing with four different kinds of time. *Apparent time* is time measured by the real Sun, according to its appearance overhead at high noon. Since the Sun's movement is not uniform from day to day, apparent time is not satisfactory for accurate measurement.

Mean time is the apparent Sun time averaged out to take account of the day-to-day variations of apparent time.

Standard time is the mean time of a specific location which is used as the standard clock time over a geographical area of fifteen degrees of longitude.

Local mean time is the mean time of any particular place within the time zone.

Since one hour of clock time equals fifteen degrees of Earth longitude, it follows that local mean time varies four minutes per degree of longitude in either direction from the longitude to which the time zone is pegged. Astrologers have used this formula to make the necessary corrections from standard time of birth to get the local mean time of birth, and you may do so also.

Los Angeles, for example, is located at 118 degrees and 15 minutes of west longitude. This figure is written "118 W 15." You know that the Pacific standard time zone is based on 120 degrees of west longitude. Therefore, high noon in Los Angeles occurs a little earlier than the standard time for the Pacific time zone. The difference between 120 W 00 and 118 W 15 degrees longitude is a simple matter of subtraction (but don't forget to change 120:00 to 119:60, so you can subtract 118:15 from it). Subtraction yields 1:45 degrees of difference. Since one degree of longitude equals four minutes of clock time, and since 45/60 of a degree reduces to 3/4 of a degree, 4 times 1-3/4 equals seven minutes. Seven minutes is therefore the local mean time variation from Pacific standard time in Los Angeles. Since the Sun is overhead at noon in Los Angeles *before* it is overhead at 120 degrees of longitude, seven minutes must be *added* to any time of birth given for Los Angeles in Pacific standard time. Why? Because Pacific standard time is seven minutes *later* than true local time in Los Angeles.

THE NATIVE WHOSE chart we shall erect was born November 12, 1934, in Cincinnati, Ohio. His given time of birth is 4:40 P.M. Our first step is to determine whether the given time of birth is standard time for that time zone or whether daylight-saving time or some other departure from standard time was in effect in Cincinnati on that day.

Reference to *Time Changes* shows that daylight-saving or war time was observed from 1920 to 1941 in some areas of Ohio, but not in others. So we must turn to local ordinance listings for all the cities in Ohio.

The local ordinance listing for Cincinnati indicates that daylight-saving time or war time was observed from 1922 through 1926. There are no other entries for Cincinnati, so we conclude that 4:40 P.M. is the standard time of this native's birth.

At the end of this chapter you will see a form summary for natal chart erection. Put the birth date and the place of birth in the appropriate blanks. In the blank for given time of birth put 4:40 P.M. Copy this figure in the blank for standard time of birth, and delete the "A.M."

The next entry on the form calls for longitude and latitude of birthplace.

Pages three through thirty-seven of the Rosicrucian table of houses set out the latitudes and longitudes of all principal cities in the United States. This information can also be obtained from an atlas or gazetteer, and is available in *Longitudes and Latitudes*, which I will assume you are using.

At page seventy-nine of *Longitudes and Latitudes,* we find that Cincinnati is located in Hamilton County at eighty-four degrees and thirty-one minutes west longitude and at thirty-nine degrees and six minutes north latitude. Copy this information into the blanks for longitude and latitude. If you are using the Rosicrucian table of houses to obtain this information, you will find it on page twenty-six, where it is shown as thirty-nine north latitude. Note that the table of houses rounds off the minutes to the nearest degree.

The next entry on the chart erection form is for the local mean time variation from the standard time of birth.

Cincinnati is located in the eastern standard time zone, as you can confirm by any map or atlas. The longitude for that time zone, as set out in these instructions, is seventy-five degrees west. The difference in longitude is nine degrees and thirty-one minutes of Earth longitude, expressed as 9:31 degrees.

Our formula tells us that each degree of longitude equals four minutes of clock time. Applying the formula to nine degrees, we get thirty-six minutes of time; and rounding off thirty-one minutes of longitude to one-half degree gives us two more minutes of clock time, or a total of thirty-eight minutes of local mean time variation for the city of Cincinnati, Ohio.

We should be able to confirm that figure by reference to *Longitudes and Latitudes.* The entry for Cincinnati next to its longitude and latitude is headed "LMT Variation From Standard Time," followed by a subheading "m" for minutes; the other "s" for seconds. Together, the entries in the "LMT Variation" column show the minutes and seconds by which the listed cities vary from standard time within the time zone. Notice too that there is a plus or a minus signature before each entry which tells us whether the minutes and seconds of LMT variation must be added to or subtracted from the standard time of the time zone.

Since we have seen that Cincinnati is west of, or later than, the time zone center of seventy-five degrees west longitude by 9:31 degrees, the LMT variation for Cincinnati must be subtracted from the standard time of birth.

In *Longitudes and Latitudes,* the entry for Cincinnati shows an LMT variation of a *minus* thirty-eight minutes and four seconds. (That extra minute of longitude, discarded in rounding off nine degrees and thirty-one minutes of longitude to nine and one-half degrees, shows up here as four seconds of clock time.)

Copy the LMT variation onto your chart erection form as "0:38:04," to show that you have taken hours, minutes and seconds into account. (If you make your computations without *Longitudes and*

Latitudes, you won't have the seconds; don't worry about it.) Be sure to line out the "plus" in the blank, leaving the "minus" to remind you to subtract the LMT variation from the standard time of birth.

You now have all the information you need to calculate the actual local mean time of birth for this native within his time zone. Take a sheet of scratch paper and write down 4:40:00 P.M., the standard time of birth. Under that write 0:38:04, preceded by a minus sign. Make the necessary subtraction. Enter the result in the space provided on the form and delete the "A.M. " reference following that blank.

You have now completed the important first step, establishing the local mean time of birth, A.M. or P.M., of the native whose chart you are erecting.

YOU NOW KNOW that the native's local mean time of birth is 4:01:56 P.M. Your next step is to figure out the difference in time between Greenwich, England, and Cincinnati, Ohio, in terms of the hours and minutes of the Sun's travel. You need this information, since all of the planets' positions in the ephemerides are shown as of noon at Greenwich. Corrections must be made to show the actual planetary positions when the native was born at Cincinnati.

Also, we use the ephemeris to find the sidereal time for the date of birth, and we determine the house cusps from the table of houses on the basis of that sidereal time and the latitude of birth. Again, the sidereal time shown in the ephemeris is as of noon at Greenwich, and must be adjusted to reflect the difference between Greenwich mean time at noon, and the time at the native's birthplace.

The Greenwich mean time variation is the difference in hours, minutes and seconds of clock time between Greenwich and the birthplace of the native. Added to the local mean time of birth, it produces the equivalent time, in hours, minutes and seconds, that it was in Greenwich when the native was born in Cincinnati. That figure is sometimes referred to as the "equivalent Greenwich mean time," or "EGMT."

Remember that eastern standard time is pegged to 75:00 west longitude—or 75 degrees of longitude *west of Greenwich, England.* Since we know the Sun travels at the rate of 4 minutes of clock time for each degree of longitude, and since 4 minutes times 75 degrees equals 300 minutes, or 5 hours, we know that eastern standard time is 5 hours earlier than Greenwich mean time.

You already know that Cincinnati is 9:31 degrees of longitude west of the time zone center of seventy-five degrees. That means the

Sun still has farther to go to get to Cincinnati after it has passed the longitude of the time zone center. Therefore, to calculate the Greenwich mean time variation, take the hour equivalent of the time zone from Greenwich, and add or subtract the local mean time variation, depending on whether the place of birth is east or west of the time zone center. As a practical matter, this means reversing the signature on the LMT variation.

You are now concerned about the *total amount of time* it takes the Sun to travel from Greenwich, England, our ground zero, to Cincinnati, Ohio. To determine the time it takes the Sun to travel that distance, we must add up all of the time west of Greenwich—from time zone to time zone, plus any additional time west of that to the birthplace. In the case of our native, whose 9:31 degrees of longitude west of the time zone center we have already converted to thirty-eight minutes and four seconds of clock time to find the LMT variation, that means that the total number of hours, minutes and seconds that it takes the Sun to travel from zero degrees longitude at Greenwich, England, to Cincinnati, Ohio, is the five hours from Greenwich to the time zone center of seventy-five degrees, *plus* the additional thirty-eight minutes and four seconds for the Sun to travel the 9:31 degrees farther to Cincinnati. Total time of the Sun's travel is therefore 5:38:04 hours, the Greenwich mean time variation.

Let's confirm this calculation with *Longitudes and Latitudes.* Turn to Cincinnati again; look at the right-hand column, headed with the legend, "To obtain GMT, add to LMT." The subheading calls for hours, minutes and seconds of time. For Cincinnati, the entry is a *plus* 5:38:04, which means a GMT variation of five hours, thirty-eight minutes and four seconds. Note that in the United States, all GMT variations will be *plus* figures, inasmuch as the United States is in its entirety west of Greenwich.

Copy 5:38:04 into the blank on the chart erection form next to the entry "GMT variation in U.S." You have now completed the second step in erecting a natal chart.

Thus far, we have confirmed that the native's given time of birth is also his standard time of birth. We have established the longitude and latitude of birth by checking a map or the Rosicrucian table of houses. We have double-checked these coordinates with Dernay's *Longitudes and Latitudes.*

Using only the longitude of birth obtained from a map or from the table of houses, we have calculated the local mean time variation and the local mean time of birth of the native in his birthplace. Using the local mean time variation, we have calculated the Greenwich mean time variation as well. We confirmed all our calculations by using *Longitudes and Latitudes,* and established that either the formula method or the reference-book method could be used to make these essentially simple calculations, depending on individual preferences.

Having performed these tasks, and having entered the results in the form for chart erection, you are now prepared to find the GMT interval.

THE EQUIVALENT GREENWICH mean time at birth, or EGMT, is the sum of the local mean time of birth and the Greenwich mean time variation. In the sample chart, that means adding the GMT variation of 5:38:04 hours to 4:01:56 P.M., the LMT of birth. The sum of these figures is the EGMT, which in this case is 9:40:00 hours. Enter this figure on the form in the space for EGMT; be sure to include the double zero for seconds, so that you will not later become confused as to whether 9:40 means hours and minutes or minutes and seconds.

Remember that EGMT represents the time in Greenwich, England, when the native was born in Cincinnati, Ohio. The EGMT is expressed in hours, minutes and seconds of time which, unlike our conventional clock system, may amount to more than 12:00:00 hours.

THE GREENWICH MEAN time interval is the difference between noon at Greenwich and the equivalent mean time of birth. Therefore, for births which occur *before* noon according to the local mean time of birth, noon (expressed as 12:00:00, 11:60 or 11:59:60) must be subtracted. Note that if noon is a larger figure than the EGMT, the result of the subtraction will be a *minus* Greenwich mean time interval; and if noon is a smaller figure, the result of the subtraction will be a *plus* GMT interval.

In the case of a birth time in which the LMT of birth is *later* than noon at the birthplace, we do not subtract noon, because that factor has already been taken into account. Note that in the case of an LMT of birth after noon, the EGMT and the GMT interval are the same figure—which is always a plus figure.

If you will remember that the Greenwich mean time *interval* calls for the interval of time before or after noon at Greenwich, England, you should have no difficulty in erecting charts for A.M. or P.M. births. That is why it is so important to remember to carry down the A.M. or P.M. signature from the given time of birth, through the standard time of birth, all the way to the local mean time of birth: it is the A.M. or P.M. signature on the local mean time of birth which is controlling. If the signature on the LMT is an A.M. signature, noon must be subtracted from the EGMT to get the GMT interval; and if noon is the larger figure, for purposes of subtraction, the result will be a minus figure in terms of the GMT interval.

Enter the GMT interval of 9:40:00 in the space provided in the chart erection form. Be sure to line out the minus sign, so that you will remember that this native was born nine hours and forty minutes *after* noon, Greenwich mean time.

You now have the Greenwich mean time interval for the native, and you are ready to determine his correct sidereal time of birth.

SIDEREAL TIME IS time measured by the stars. A sidereal day is based on one complete rotation of the Earth in relation to any star. Astronomers measure the sidereal day by the time it takes for two successive meridian transits of the vernal equinox, which means two midday crossings from one day to the next. You and I think of that time as 24 hours. Astronomers know better: it is 23 hours, 56 minutes and 4:09 seconds. The difference occurs because at the same time the Earth is rotating on its axis, it is revolving around the Sun. Our clock time is based on the time it takes for the Sun to appear overhead from noon to noon, one day to the next. However, that period includes both the time for the Earth's rotation and for the Earth's revolution around the Sun.

Because of the Earth's revolution around the Sun, we don't stay in the same place from one day to the next—we have moved in space so that it takes an extra three minutes and fifty-six seconds every day for the Sun to appear overhead at high noon.[2] The sidereal day is based on the Earth's rotation on its axis alone; it is therefore three minutes, fifty-six seconds shorter than the solar day. Up to now, all of the time we have considered, be it Greenwich, local, standard or apparent, has been *solar* time.

We are now using sidereal time in order to use the table of houses which shows the house cusps according to sidereal time.

The ephemeris shows us the sidereal time for each day of the month in the year of the native's birth. The sidereal time shown is—once again—the equivalent of mean noon at Greenwich, England. Obviously we have some work to do to correct the sidereal time shown for November 12, 1934, to account for the fact that the native was not born at noon GMT.

Notice too that sidereal time is not divided into "A.M." and "P.M." time figures; it runs continuously from zero hours to twenty-four, just as it does in the military.

There are two corrections to be made to the sidereal time figure shown in the ephemeris. The first is to account for the difference between the sidereal time equivalence to Greenwich time at noon, and the actual time of birth of the native. We make this first correction by determining the local mean time interval, which is the difference in time, before or after noon, between the LMT of birth and noon in the native's own time zone.

By way of example: if we were dealing with a birth time which occurred in the A.M., we would subtract that birth time from noon (expressed as 12:00:00, 11:60 or 11:59:60 as needed), in order to get the interval between the local mean time of birth and noon. Thus, if the native were born at 4:01:56 *a.m.*, the local mean time interval would be 7:58:04, a *minus* figure, which would mean that the difference between the LMT and noon was a minus 7:58:04 hours.

However, the actual LMT of the native's birth was 4:01:56 P.M., meaning that he was born 4:01:56 hours *after* noon. As you can see, for afternoon LMT's the LMT interval is the same as the LMT of birth and for the same reason: our conventional time system which calls for twelve hours in the A.M. and twelve hours in the P.M. automatically tells us the hours and minutes *after* noon in the case of a P.M. birth time.

On the chart erection form, simply enter in the space for "LMT after noon" the same plus figure you entered for the P.M. LMT at birth.

You are now ready to use the ephemeris. The pages for November 1934 of the Rosicrucian ephemeris are set out in figure twenty-two.

We are interested in sidereal time for November 12, 1934, and we find this information on the second page in the farthest column on the left headed "D" for "day." Reading down the column to the twelfth day, we look at the entry next to twelve in the column headed "S.T." (sidereal time): fifteen hours and twenty-four minutes. The remainder of the columns deal with declinations of the planets; we have no present need for this information, so simply copy the sidereal time for November 12, 1934, onto your form as 15:24:00.

You are now prepared to make the first correction to the given sidereal time figure. The purpose of this first correction is to adjust the given sidereal time for noon in Greenwich to take account of the actual time of this native's birth. Simply add the LMT interval, which you found in the last step, to the given sidereal time and enter the result in the appropriate space on the form, "S.T. with first correction."

For future reference you should be aware of the fact that in the event of a minus LMT interval, the LMT interval would be *subtracted* from the figure showing sidereal time in the ephemeris, just as the minus signature directs.

SIMPLIFIED SCIENTIFIC

EPHEMERIS OF THE PLANETS' PLACES

Calculated for Mean Noon at Greenwich

November, 1934

New Moon November 7, 4:44 A. M., in ♏ 14° 06'

Longitude of the Planets

Day	☉ ♏		♀ ♏		☿ ♏		☽ ♍		♄ ♒		♃ ♏		♂ ♍		♅ ♈		♆ ♍		☊ ♒	
	°	'	°	'	°	'	°	'	°	'	°	'	°	'	°	'	°	'	°	'
Th 1	8	23	4	00	12ʀ14		1	41	21	32	4	38	8	22	29ʀ05		14	00	5	27
F 2	9	23	5	16	10	59	13	44	21	32	4	51	8	56	29	03	14	02	5	24
S 3	10	23	6	31	9	41	26	01	21	33	5	05	9	31	29	00	14	03	5	21
Su 4	11	23	7	46	8	25	8 ≏ 35		21	34	5	18	10	05	28	58	14	04	5	17
M 5	12	23	9	01	7	13	21	28	21	35	5	31	10	39	28	56	14	06	5	14
Tu 6	13	23	10	17	6	08	4 ♏ 42		21	36	5	44	11	13	28	53	14	07	5	11
W 7	14	24	11	32	5	10	18	13	21	37	5	57	11	47	28	51	14	08	5	08
Th 8	15	24	12	47	4	22	2 ♐ 00		21	38	6	10	12	21	28	48	14	10	5	05
F 9	16	24	14	03	3	44	15	57	21	40	6	23	12	55	28	46	14	11	5	02
S 10	17	25	15	18	3	19	0 ♑ 02		21	41	6	36	13	29	28	44	14	12	4	58
Su 11	18	25	16	34	3	04	14	10	21	43	6	49	14	03	28	42	14	13	4	55
M 12	19	25	17	49	3	01	28	19	21	44	7	02	14	36	28	39	14	15	4	52
Tu 13	20	26	19	04	3 D 10		12 ♒ 26		21	46	7	15	15	10	28	37	14	16	4	49
W 14	21	26	20	20	3	28	26	31	21	48	7	28	15	43	28	35	14	17	4	46
Th 15	22	27	21	35	3	55	10 ♓ 33		21	50	7	41	16	17	28	33	14	18	4	42
F 16	23	27	22	50	4	32	24	32	21	52	7	54	16	50	28	31	14	19	4	39
S 17	24	28	24	06	5	16	8 ♈ 25		21	54	8	06	17	23	28	28	14	20	4	36
Su 18	25	28	25	21	6	07	22	10	21	57	8	19	17	56	28	26	14	21	4	33
M 19	26	29	26	37	7	04	5 ♉ 46		21	59	8	32	18	29	28	24	14	22	4	30
Tu 20	27	29	27	51	8	07	19	09	22	02	8	45	19	02	28	22	14	23	4	27
W 21	28	30	29	07	9	14	2 ♊ 17		22	04	8	58	19	34	28	20	14	24	4	23
Th 22	29	30	0 ♐ 23		10	25	15	09	22	07	9	10	20	07	28	18	14	25	4	20
F 23	0 ♐ 31		1	38	11	39	27	43	22	10	9	23	20	40	28	16	14	25	4	17
S 24	1	31	2	54	12	56	10 ♋ 01		22	12	9	36	21	12	28	14	14	26	4	14
Su 25	2	32	4	09	14	17	22	06	22	15	9	48	21	44	28	12	14	27	4	11
M 26	3	33	5	24	15	38	4 ♌ 00		22	18	10	01	22	16	28	10	14	28	4	08
Tu 27	4	34	6	40	17	05	15	49	22	22	10	13	22	48	28	09	14	28	4	04
W 28	5	35	7	55	18	27	27	36	22	25	10	26	23	20	28	07	14	29	4	01
Th 29	6	35	9	11	19	54	9 ♍ 28		22	28	10	38	23	51	28	05	14	30	3	58
F 30	7	36	10	26	21	21	21	30	22	31	10	51	24	24	28	03	14	30	3	55

Pluto, Longitude, November 1, ♋ 26° 02'

FIGURE 22. Rosicrucian ephemeris
Reprinted by permission of the Rosicrucian Fellowship

SIMPLIFIED SCIENTIFIC

EPHEMERIS OF THE PLANETS' PLACES

Calculated for Mean Noon at Greenwich

November, 1934

Full Moon November 21, 4:26 A. M., in ♉ 28° 11′

Declination of the Planets

D	S.T. H.M.	Dec. ☽ ° N ′	D	⊙ ° S ′	♀ ° S ′	☿ ° S ′	♄ ° S ′	♃ ° S ′	♂ ° N ′	♅ ° N ′	♆ ° N ′
1	14 40	8 48	1	14 18	11 51	16 29	15 42	12 07	9 54	10 38	7 08
2	14 44	3 31	3	14 56	12 44	15 02	15 41	12 16	9 29	10 36	7 07
3	14 48	1 s 59	5	15 34	13 36	13 35	15 40	12 25	9 04	10 34	7 06
4	14 52	7 31	7	16 10	14 27	12 19	15 39	12 33	8 39	10 33	7 05
5	14 56	12 53	9	16 45	15 16	11 21	15 38	12 42	8 14	10 31	7 04
6	15 00	17 48	11	17 19	16 03	10 45	15 37	12 50	7 49	10 29	7 03
			13	17 52	16 49	10 31	15 36	12 59	7 24	10 28	7 03
7	15 04	21 56	15	18 23	17 34	10 37	15 35	13 07	6 59	10 26	7 02
8	15 08	24 56	17	18 54	18 16	11 01	15 33	13 06	6 35	10 25	7 01
9	15 12	26 27	19	19 22	18 56	11 38	15 31	13 24	6 10	10 23	7 00
10	15 16	26 17	21	19 50	19 35	12 24	15 30	13 32	5 45	10 22	7 00
11	15 20	24 25	23	20 16	20 11	13 17	15 28	13 40	5 21	10 20	6 59
12	15 24	21 01	25	20 41	20 44	14 14	15 26	13 48	4 57	10 19	6 59
13	15 28	16 22	27	21 04	21 16	15 12	15 23	13 56	4 32	10 18	6 58
			29	21 25	21 45	16 12	15 21	14 04	4 08	10 17	6 58
14	15 32	10 52									
15	15 36	4 49									

Latitude of the Planets

16	15 39	1 N 24	D	☽ ° S ′	♀ ° N ′	☿ ° S ′	♄ ° S ′	♃ ° N ′	♂ ° N ′	♅ ° S ′	♆ ° N ′
17	15 43	7 31	1	2 13	1 04	1 00	1 26	1 01	1 34	0 34	0 55
18	15 47	13 13	3	3 53	1 01	0 19	1 26	1 01	1 35	0 34	0 55
19	15 51	18 12	5	4 52	0 57	0 N 21	1 26	1 00	1 36	0 34	0 55
20	15 55	22 11	7	4 52	0 54	0 58	1 26	1 00	1 38	0 34	0 55
			9	3 46	0 50	1 29	1 25	1 00	1 39	0 34	0 55
21	15 59	24 57	11	1 44	0 46	1 53	1 25	1 00	1 40	0 34	0 55
22	16 03	26 21	13	0 N 44	0 42	2 10	1 25	1 00	1 41	0 34	0 55
23	16 07	26 22	15	3 01	0 37	2 20	1 25	1 00	1 42	0 34	0 55
24	16 11	25 03	17	4 33	0 38	2 23	1 25	1 00	1 44	0 34	0 55
25	16 15	22 34	19	5 02	0 29	2 22	1 25	1 00	1 45	0 34	0 55
26	16 19	19 09	21	4 25	0 24	2 17	1 25	1 00	1 46	0 34	0 55
27	16 23	15 00	23	2 56	0 19	2 09	1 24	1 01	1 47	0 34	0 55
			25	0 57	0 15	1 59	1 24	1 01	1 49	0 34	0 55
28	16 27	10 17	27	1 s 09	0 10	1 47	1 24	1 01	1 50	0 33	0 55
29	16 31	5 11	29	3 04	0 05	1 34	1 24	1 01	1 51	0 33	0 56
30	16 35	0 s 10									

Pluto Declination. November 1, N. 22° 33′

The second correction to sidereal time is known as *acceleration on interval.* Since the sidereal day is four minutes less than the solar day, the sidereal hour is ten seconds less than the hour we use in our twenty-four-hour clock system. To figure acceleration on interval, first round off the GMT interval to the nearest hour. If the minutes of the GMT interval are more than thirty, add another hour; if less, disregard them. Either way, you now have a specific number of hours. Multiply that number of hours times ten seconds. The result gives you the seconds of time which you must add to sidereal time to correct for the number of hours later than Greenwich mean time at noon that this native's birth actually occurred.

Again, note for future reference that, if we were dealing with a *minus* GMT interval that minus number of hours times ten seconds would result in a *minus* number of seconds to be subtracted from sidereal time.

You now have the correct sidereal time of birth, which you should enter in the appropriate blank on the chart erection form.

LOGARITHMS ARE AN easy and useful tool to simplify the process of chart erection. For our purposes, the logarithm of any number is a whole number plus a decimal. Since we are using a base of ten, the logarithm of a given number is the exponent to which ten must be raised to obtain that number. The table of logarithms does all the work for us.

In the back of each of the Rosicrucian ephemerides you will find a table of proportional logarithms and that heading the words "Hours or Degrees." That means that any of the figures given can be read either way. For our purposes, consider them degrees. (For your convenience, a table of proportional logarithms is included as figure twenty-three.)

The GMT interval should be +9:40. Look at the logarithm table. The degrees column is read horizontally from zero through twenty-three. The "9" column is the one we want. Holding your place in the "9" column, look at the minute column, which runs vertically from the top of the page at zero to the bottom of the page at fifty-nine. Since we are dealing with forty minutes, find the corresponding entry to "40" in the minute column, to "9" in the degrees column: it is 3949. If you will look at the second degrees column you will see that at two degrees and twenty-four minutes—reading down from the "2" degrees column and across from the "24" minute column—the entry 1.0000 appears. Everything after two degrees and twenty-four minutes is a log figure of *less than one.* That means we must always supply a decimal for all entries in the log table corresponding to anything larger than two

TABLE OF PROPORTIONAL LOGARITHMS

Min.	0	1	2	3	4	5	6	7	8	9	10	11	Min.
0	3.1584	1.3802	1.0792	.9031	.7781	.6812	.6021	.5351	.4771	.4260	.3802	.3388	0
1	3.1584	1.3730	1.0756	.9007	.7763	.6798	.6009	.5341	.4762	.4252	.3795	.3382	1
2	2.8573	1.3660	1.0720	.8983	.7745	.6784	.5997	.5330	.4753	.4244	.3788	.3375	2
3	2.6812	1.3590	1.0685	.8959	.7728	.6769	.5985	.5320	.4744	.4236	.3780	.3368	3
4	2.5563	1.3522	1.0649	.8935	.7710	.6755	.5973	.5310	.4735	.4228	.3773	.3362	4
5	2.4594	1.3454	1.0614	.8912	.7692	.6741	.5961	.5300	.4726	.4220	.3766	.3355	5
6	2.3802	1.3388	1.0580	.8888	.7674	.6726	.5949	.5289	.4717	.4212	.3759	.3349	6
7	2.3133	1.3323	1.0546	.8865	.7657	.6712	.5937	.5279	.4708	.4204	.3752	.3342	7
8	2.2553	1.3258	1.0511	.8842	.7639	.6698	.5925	.5269	.4699	.4196	.3745	.3336	8
9	2.2041	1.3195	1.0478	.8819	.7622	.6684	.5913	.5259	.4690	.4188	.3738	.3329	9
10	2.1584	1.3133	1.0444	.8796	.7604	.6670	.5902	.5249	.4682	.4180	.3730	.3323	10
11	2.1170	1.3071	1.0411	.8773	.7587	.6656	.5890	.5239	.4673	.4172	.3723	.3316	11
12	2.0792	1.3010	1.0378	.8751	.7570	.6642	.5878	.5229	.4664	.4164	.3716	.3310	12
13	2.0444	1.2950	1.0345	.8728	.7552	.6628	.5866	.5219	.4655	.4156	.3709	.3303	13
14	2.0122	1.2891	1.0313	.8706	.7535	.6614	.5855	.5209	.4646	.4149	.3702	.3297	14
15	1.9823	1.2833	1.0280	.8683	.7518	.6600	.5843	.5199	.4638	.4141	.3695	.3291	15
16	1.9542	1.2775	1.0248	.8661	.7501	.6587	.5832	.5189	.4629	.4133	.3688	.3284	16
17	1.9279	1.2719	1.0216	.8639	.7484	.6573	.5820	.5179	.4620	.4125	.3681	.3278	17
18	1.9031	1.2663	1.0185	.8617	.7467	.6559	.5809	.5169	.4611	.4117	.3674	.3271	18
19	1.8796	1.2607	1.0153	.8595	.7451	.6546	.5797	.5159	.4603	.4109	.3667	.3265	19
20	1.8573	1.2553	1.0122	.8573	.7434	.6532	.5786	.5149	.4594	.4102	.3660	.3258	20
21	1.8361	1.2499	1.0091	.8552	.7417	.6519	.5774	.5139	.4585	.4094	.3653	.3252	21
22	1.8159	1.2445	1.0061	.8530	.7401	.6505	.5763	.5129	.4577	.4086	.3646	.3246	22
23	1.7966	1.2393	1.0030	.8509	.7384	.6492	.5752	.5120	.4568	.4079	.3639	.3239	23
24	1.7781	1.2341	1.0000	.8487	.7368	.6478	.5740	.5110	.4559	.4071	.3632	.3233	24
25	1.7604	1.2289	0.9970	.8466	.7351	.6465	.5729	.5100	.4551	.4063	.3625	.3227	25
26	1.7434	1.2239	0.9940	.8445	.7335	.6451	.5718	.5090	.4542	.4055	.3618	.3220	26
27	1.7270	1.2188	9.9910	.8424	.7318	.6438	.5706	.5081	.4534	.4048	.3611	.3214	27
28	1.7112	1.2139	0.9881	.8403	.7302	.6425	.5692	.5071	.4525	.4040	.3604	.3208	28
29	1.6969	1.2090	0.9852	.8382	.7286	.6412	.5684	.5061	.4516	.4032	.3597	.3201	29

FIGURE 23. Table of proportional logarithms

	0	1	2	3	4	5	6	7	8	9	10	11	
30	1.6812	1.2041	0.9823	8361	7270	6398	5673	5051	4508	4025	3590	3195	30
31	1.6670	1.1993	0.9794	8341	7254	6385	5662	5042	4499	4017	3583	3189	31
32	1.6532	1.1946	0.9765	8321	7238	6372	5651	5032	4491	4010	3577	3183	32
33	1.6398	1.1899	0.9737	8300	7222	6359	5640	5023	4482	4002	3570	3176	33
34	1.6269	1.1852	0.9708	8279	7206	6346	5629	5013	4474	3995	3563	3170	34
35	1.6143	1.1806	0.9680	8259	7190	6333	5618	5003	4466	3987	3556	3164	35
36	1.6021	1.1761	0.9652	8239	7174	6320	5607	4994	4457	3979	3549	3157	36
37	1.5902	1.1716	0.9625	8219	7159	6307	5596	4984	4449	3972	3542	3151	37
38	1.5786	1.1671	0.9597	8199	7143	6294	5585	4975	4440	3964	3535	3145	38
39	1.5673	1.1627	0.9570	8179	7128	6282	5574	4965	4432	3957	3529	3139	39
40	1.5563	1.1584	0.9542	8159	7112	6269	5563	4956	4421	3949	3522	3133	40
41	1.5456	1.1540	0.9515	8140	7097	6256	5552	4947	4415	3942	3515	3126	41
42	1.5351	1.1498	0.9488	8120	7081	6243	5541	4937	4407	3934	3508	3120	42
43	1.5249	1.1455	0.9462	8101	7066	6231	5531	4928	4399	3927	3501	3114	43
44	1.5149	1.1413	0.9435	8081	7050	6218	5520	4918	4390	3919	3495	3108	44
45	1.5051	1.1372	0.9409	8062	7035	6205	5509	4909	4382	3912	3488	3102	45
46	1.4956	1.1331	0.9383	8043	7020	6193	5498	4900	4374	3905	3481	3096	46
47	1.4863	1.1290	0.9356	8023	7005	6180	5488	4890	4365	3897	3475	3089	47
48	1.4771	1.1249	0.9330	8004	6990	6168	5477	4881	4357	3890	3468	3083	48
49	1.4682	1.1209	0.9305	7985	6975	6155	5466	4872	4349	3882	3461	3077	49
50	1.4594	1.1170	0.9279	7966	6960	6143	5456	4863	4341	3875	3455	3071	50
51	1.4508	1.1130	0.9254	7947	6945	6131	5445	4853	4333	3868	3448	3065	51
52	1.4424	1.1091	0.9228	7929	6930	6118	5435	4844	4324	3860	3441	3059	52
53	1.4341	1.1053	0.9203	7910	6915	6106	5424	4835	4316	3853	3435	3053	53
54	1.4260	1.1015	0.9178	7891	6900	6094	5414	4826	4308	3846	3428	3047	54
55	1.4180	1.0977	0.9153	7873	6885	6081	5403	4817	4300	3838	3421	3041	55
56	1.4102	1.0939	0.9128	7854	6871	6069	5393	4808	4292	3831	3415	3035	56
57	1.4025	1.0902	0.9104	7836	6856	6057	5382	4799	4284	3824	3408	3028	57
58	1.3949	1.0865	0.9079	7818	6841	6045	5372	4789	4276	3817	3401	3022	58
59	1.3875	1.0828	0.9055	7800	6827	6033	5361	4780	4268	3809	3395	3016	59

TABLE OF PROPORTIONAL LOGARITHMS

Min.	Hours or Degrees												Min.
	12	13	14	15	16	17	18	19	20	21	22	23	
0	3010	2663	2341	2041	1761	1498	1249	1015	0792	0580	0378	0185	0
1	3004	2657	2336	2036	1756	1493	1245	1011	0788	0577	0375	0182	1
2	2998	2652	2330	2032	1752	1489	1241	1007	0785	0573	0337	0179	2
3	2992	2646	2325	2027	1747	1485	1237	1003	0781	0570	0363	0175	3
4	2986	2641	2320	2022	1743	1481	1234	0999	0777	0566	0364	0172	4
5	2980	2635	2315	2017	1738	1476	1229	0996	0774	0563	0361	0169	5
6	2974	2629	2310	2012	1734	1472	1225	0992	0770	0559	0358	0166	6
7	2968	2624	2305	2008	1729	1468	1221	0988	0766	0556	0355	0163	7
8	2962	2618	2300	2003	1725	1461	1217	0984	0763	0552	0352	0160	8
9	2956	2613	2295	1998	1720	1460	1213	0980	0759	0549	0348	0157	9
10	2950	2607	2289	1993	1716	1455	1209	0977	0756	0546	0345	0153	10
11	2945	2602	2284	1989	1711	1451	1205	0973	0752	0542	0342	0150	11
12	2938	2596	2279	1984	1707	1447	1201	0969	0749	0539	0339	0147	12
13	2933	2591	2274	1979	1702	1443	1197	0965	0745	0535	0335	0144	13
14	2927	2585	2269	1974	1698	1438	1193	0962	0742	0532	0332	0141	14
15	2921	2580	2264	1969	1694	1434	1189	0958	0738	0529	0329	0138	15
16	2915	2575	2259	1965	1689	1430	1185	0954	0734	0525	0326	0135	16
17	2909	2569	2254	1960	1685	1426	1182	0950	0731	0522	0322	0132	17
18	2903	2564	2249	1955	1680	1422	1178	0947	0727	0518	0319	0129	18
19	2897	2558	2244	1950	1676	1417	1174	0943	0724	0515	0316	0125	19
20	2891	2553	2239	1946	1671	1413	1170	0939	0720	0511	0313	0122	20
21	2885	2547	2234	1941	1667	1409	1166	0935	0717	0508	0309	0119	21
22	2890	2512	2229	1936	1663	1405	1162	0932	0713	0505	0306	0116	22
23	2874	2536	2223	1932	1658	1401	1158	0928	0709	0501	0303	0113	23
24	2868	2531	2218	1927	1654	1397	1154	0924	0706	0498	0300	0110	24
25	2862	2526	2213	1922	1649	1393	1150	0920	0702	0495	0296	0107	25
26	2856	2520	2208	1917	1645	1388	1146	0917	0699	0191	0292	0104	26
27	2850	2515	2203	1913	1640	1384	1142	0913	0695	0488	0290	0101	27
28	2845	2509	2198	1908	1636	1380	1138	0909	0692	0485	0287	0098	28
29	2839	2504	2193	1903	1632	1376	1134	0905	0688	0481	0283	0094	29

	12	13	14	15	16	17	18	19	20	21	22	23
30	2833	2499	2188	1899	1627	1372	1130	0902	0685	0478	0280	0091
31	2827	2493	2183	1894	1623	1368	1126	0898	0681	0474	0277	0088
32	2821	2488	2178	1890	1619	1363	1123	0894	0678	0471	0274	0085
33	2816	2483	2173	1885	1614	1359	1118	0891	0674	0468	0271	0082
34	2810	2477	2168	1880	1610	1355	1115	0887	0670	0464	0267	0079
35	2804	2472	2161	1875	1605	1351	1111	0883	0667	0461	0264	0076
36	2798	2467	2159	1871	1601	1347	1107	0880	0664	0458	0261	0073
37	2793	2461	2151	1866	1597	1343	1103	0876	0660	0451	0258	0070
38	2787	2456	2149	1862	1592	1339	1099	0872	0656	0451	0255	0067
39	2781	2451	2144	1857	1588	1335	1095	0868	0653	0448	0251	0064
40	2775	2445	2139	1852	1584	1331	1092	0865	0619	0444	0248	0061
41	2770	2440	2131	1848	1579	1327	1088	0861	0616	0441	0245	0058
42	2764	2435	2129	1843	1575	1322	1084	0857	0642	0437	0242	0055
43	2758	2430	2124	1838	1571	1318	1080	0854	0639	0434	0239	0052
44	2753	2424	2119	1834	1566	1314	1076	0850	0635	0431	0235	0048
45	2747	2419	2114	1829	1562	1310	1072	0846	0632	0428	0232	0045
46	2741	2414	2109	1825	1558	1306	1068	0843	0629	0424	0229	0042
47	2736	2409	2104	1820	1553	1302	1064	0839	0625	0421	0226	0039
48	2730	2403	2099	1816	1549	1298	1061	0835	0621	0418	0223	0036
49	2724	2398	2095	1811	1545	1294	1057	0832	0618	0414	0220	0033
50	2719	2393	2090	1806	1540	1290	1053	0828	0614	0411	0216	0030
51	2713	2388	2085	1802	1536	1286	1049	0824	0611	0408	0213	0027
52	2707	2382	2080	1797	1532	1282	1045	0821	0608	0404	0210	0024
53	2702	2377	2075	1793	1528	1278	1041	0817	0604	0401	0207	0021
54	2696	2372	2070	1788	1523	1274	1037	0814	0601	0398	0204	0018
55	2691	2367	2065	1784	1519	1270	1034	0810	0597	0394	0201	0015
56	2685	2362	2061	1779	1515	1266	1030	0806	0594	0391	0197	0012
57	2679	2356	2056	1774	1510	1261	1026	0803	0590	0388	0194	0009
58	2674	2351	2051	1770	1506	1257	1022	0799	0587	0384	0191	0006
59	2668	2346	2046	1765	1502	1253	1018	0795	0583	0381	0188	0003

degrees and twenty-four minutes. In this case, since we are dealing with nine degrees, our log figure is actually 0.3949. Note also that for ease of reading, in degrees and minutes smaller than 2:24, the initial digit before the decimal point is repeated only at intervals; we must remember to supply it as and when appropriate.

The logarithm for the GMT interval is known as the *constant log number;* in this case, it is 0.3949. Enter the constant log number in the space provided on the chart erection form. You will use the constant log to make corrections for planets' positions in entering their positions on the chart. You might note for future reference that the number of degrees and minutes which corresponds to the log number is called the *antilogarithm.*

You have now completed the form for natal chart erection and you know the correct sidereal time for this native's birth. You are ready to enter the house cusps on the horoscope.

TO DETERMINE THE house cusps, including the vital Ascendant, which is the first house cusp, we need only the latitude of the birthplace and the corrected sidereal time of birth. We now have both of these pieces of information. Look at your table of houses for thirty-nine degrees north latitude (the pages you will need are reproduced in figure twenty-four).

Your fully corrected sidereal time of birth should be 19:27:36. The closest figure shown for the corrected sidereal time at thirty-nine degrees north latitude is 19:26:34. Reading across from the left-hand column headed "Sider'l Time" at 19:26:34, the right-hand column headed "Latitude 39° N" provides the house cusps for the tenth through the third houses. Enter the house cusps as shown on the horoscope blank. Note that although zodiacal signs are set out under the numbers 10, 11, 12, Asc., 2, 3, in several instances there are *sign changes* within the columns which must be noted.

For example, the column headed "Asc." shows Aries immediately underneath it, but three entries above the one we're looking for, there is a sign change to Taurus so that the native whose chart we are erecting has Taurus, and not Aries, as his first house cusp. Remember, always look for sign changes within the columns for the house cusps!

The house cusps for the native are as follows:

Ascendant: 4:49 degrees Taurus
Second house: 6 degrees Gemini
Third house: 29 degrees Gemini

SIMPLIFIED SCIENTIFIC TABLES OF HOUSES

Sider'l Time H M S	Latitude 37° N. 10 ♑	11 ♑	12 ≈	Asc ♈ ° ′	2 ♉	3 ♊	Latitude 38° N. 10 ♑	11 ♑	12 ≈	Asc ♈ ° ′	2 ♉	3 ♊	Latitude 39° N. 10 ♑	11 ♑	12 ≈	Asc ♈ ° ′	2 ♉	3 ♊
18 0 0	0	22	20	0 0	10	8	0	22	19	0 0	10	8	0	22	19	0 0	11	8
18 4 22	1	23	21	0 46	11	9	1	23	20	0 48	11	9	1	23	20	0 50	12	9
18 8 43	2	24	23	1 32	12	10	2	24	21	0 36	12	10	2	24	21	0 40	13	10
18 13 5	3	26	24	5 17	14	11	3	25	23	23	14	11	3	25	23	29	14	11
18 17 26	4	27	25	5 3	15	12	4	27	25	11	15	12	4	27	25	19	16	12
18 21 48	5	28	26	5 48	17	13	5	28	26	58	17	13	5	28	26	8	18	13
18 26 9	6	29	29	33	18	14	6	29	28	44	18	14	6	29	28	56	19	14
18 30 30	7	♒	2	17	20	15	7	♒	29	30	19	15	7	♒	29	44	21	15
18 34 51	8	1	4	0	21	16	8	1	♓	16	21	16	8	♓	♓	32	22	16
18 39 11	9	2	15	44	22	17	9	2	3	0	22	16	9	1	1	18	23	17
18 43 31	10	3	4	17	23	18	10	3	3	45	23	17	10	3	3	4	24	19
18 47 51	11	4	5	8	24	19	11	4	4	28	24	19	11	4	4	49	25	20
18 52 11	12	5	6	20 49	26	20	12	5	5	21 10	26	20	12	5	6	21 33	26	21
18 56 31	13	7	8	22 29	27	21	13	6	7	22 52	27	21	13	6	8	23 16	28	22
19 0 50	14	8	9	24 24	28	22	14	7	9	24 33	28	22	14	7	9	24 59	29	23
19 5 8	15	9	11	25 46	29	23	15	9	11	26 12	29	23	15	9	11	26 40	♊	24
19 9 26	16	10	12	27 23	♊	24	16	10	12	27 51	♊	24	16	10	12	28 20	1	25
19 13 44	17	11	14	0	1	25	17	11	14	29 28	1	25	17	11	14	29 59	3	26
19 18 1	18	12	16	35 0 ♉	3	26	18	13	16	18	3	26	18	14	16	18	4	27
19 22 18	19	14	17	2	4	27	19	14	17	2	4	27	19	15	17	3 13	5	28
19 26 34	20	15	18	43 3	5	28	20	15	18	4	5	28	20	18	18	4 49	6	29
19 30 50	21	16	19	15 5	6	29	21	16	20	48 5	6	29	21	16	20	23 6	7	♋
19 35 5	22	17	21	45 7	8	♋	22	17	21	20 7	8	♋	22	17	21	56 8	8	1
19 39 20	23	18	23	15 8	9	1	23	18	23	50 8	9	1	23	18	23	27 9	9	2
19 43 34	24	20	24	44 9	10	3	24	20	25	10 9	10	3	24	19	25	58 10	10	3
19 47 47	25	21	26	11 10	11	4	25	21	26	48 11	11	4	25	20	26	27 11	11	4
19 52 0	26	22	28	38 11	13	5	26	22	28	15 13	13	5	26	21	28	55 13	13	5
19 56 12	27	23	29 ♈	13 12	14	6	27	23	♈	41 14	14	6	27	22	♈	21 14	14	6
20 0 24	28	24	27	15 14	15	7	28	24	2	5 15	16	7	28	24	1	46 15	16	7
20 4 35	29	26	1	16 49	15	8	29	26	2	17	17	8	29	25	2	18 10	17	8

Houses	4	5	6	7	8	9	4	5	6	7	8	9	4	5	6	7	8	9
	Latitude 37° S.						Latitude 38° S.						Latitude 39° S.					

FIGURE 24. Table of houses

Tenth house: 20 degrees Capricorn
Eleventh house: 15 degrees Aquarius
Twelfth house: 18 degrees Pisces

The table of houses has provided the house cusps for the tenth through the third houses. We determine the others ourselves by noting the polar opposites for the given house cusps:

Seventh house: 4:49 degrees Scorpio
Eighth house: 6 degrees Sagittarius
Ninth house: 29 degrees Sagittarius
Sixth house: 18 degrees Virgo
Fifth house: 15 degrees Leo
Fourth house: 20 degrees Cancer

As you can see, the determination of the other six house cusps is a matter of recalling the polar opposite signs in the exact degrees of the given sign. Record the cusps in the spaces provided for them on one of the blank chart forms at the end of the book.

Now take a look at what you have done. Notice anything odd? You should: there are two signs missing! Here is an example of *intercepted signs.* All thirty degrees of Libra are intercepted in the sixth house and it necessarily follows that all thirty degrees of Aries are intercepted in the twelfth house. Write in the glyph for Libra outside the circumference of the outer circle and midway between the sixth and seventh house cusps; do the same with Aries midway between the twelfth and first house cusps.

You now have the beginnings of a horoscope with all house cusps entered on the horoscope blank. If you feel your pulse quicken with anticipatory excitement at this point, you have the makings of a true astrologer!

FINDING LOCAL MEAN TIME (LMT) OF BIRTH:

Native: _____

Birth date: Month_____Day_____Year_____

Place of birth: City_____ State_____

Given time of birth: _____ A.M./P.M.

Standard time of birth:_____ A.M./P.M.

Latitude:_____ N_____   Longitude:_____ W_____

LMT Variation from standard time: +/-_____

Local mean time of birth: _____ A.M./P.M.

FINDING GREENWICH MEAN TIME INTERVAL:

Local mean time of birth _____ A.M./P.M.

GMT variation in U.S.:   +_____ hrs.

EGMT at birth _____

1.   If LMT of birth is A.M., subtract EGMT from noon.

   a)   If EGMT is *less* than 12:00:00 noon, the resulting
          figure is a *minus* GMT interval: -_____

   b)   If the EGMT is *more* than 12:00:00 noon, the resulting
          figure is a *plus* GMT interval: +_____

2.   If LMT is P.M., the EGMT and the GMT interval are the same
       figure and carry a *plus* signature:

              EGMT = GMT interval: +_____

FINDING SIDEREAL TIME OF BIRTH:

Local mean time interval:

    1.   If LMT is before noon, subtract LMT from noon
        to get minus LMT interval: -_____

    2.   If LMT is after noon, LMT = plus LMT interval: +_____

Sidereal time from ephemeris for birth date: _____S.T.

First correction: S.T. plus or minus LMT interval:

_____S.T. with first correction.

Second correction: S.T. as corrected, plus or minus acceleration
on interval.

    1.   Acceleration on interval: GMT interval times 10 seconds:

      +/- $\dfrac{\rule{4cm}{0.4pt}}{\text{acceleration on interval}}$

    2.   S.T. with first correction plus or minus acceleration
        on interval:

      _____
      S.T. with second correction

Sidereal time as corrected:_____

Constant logarithm: Log corresponding to GMT interval in table
of proportional logarithms: _____
                              constant log

15 How Do I Figure the Planets?

NOW THAT YOU have determined the positions of the natal horizon relative to the ecliptic, which is what the house cusps basically show, you are ready to add the planets in their proper houses.

To do so, we must take into account the fact that the planetary positions set out in the ephemeris are shown for noon, Greenwich mean time. Since the native was born some hours later than noon, Greenwich mean time, the planets will have moved from their noonday positions as of the actual time of the native's birth.

To simplify the arithmetic involved in calculating the position for each of the planets according to the actual time of birth, we will use the table of proportional logarithms (see fig. 23). The log table will be used for the following steps in correcting each of the planetary positions. 1. *Daily motion log.* The difference in planetary position, by degree and minute of ecliptic longitude, on the birth date and the day after or on the birth date and the day before is the planet's daily motion. The logarithm which corresponds to those degrees and minutes of difference is called the daily motion log. 2. *Birth time log.* To determine the location of the planets at the moment of birth, we add the daily motion log to the constant log and find the log in the table which comes closest to this combined log number. We call this new number the birth time log. 3. *Antilogarithm.* We now find the figure on the log table which corresponds to the birth time log. This figure is the antilogarithm—*i.e.*, "opposite the log," which it literally is—which tells us in degrees and minutes the planetary motion which has occurred from the GMT noon position of the planets in the ephemeris.

These are the three steps used to correct each of the planets' positions as shown in the ephemeris to account for the difference in the ephemeral positions as of noon, GMT, and the actual positions of the planets at the moment of the native's birth.

Turn to the Rosicrucian ephemeris for November 12, 1934 (fig. 21). This time we shall use the page which shows the ecliptic longitude of the planets for each day of the month. Remember that the ecliptic longitude is expressed in twelve thirty-degree units in the sequence of the signs of the zodiac. Thus each sign of the zodiac equals thirty degrees of ecliptic longitude (see table 2).

Still looking at the same page in the ephemeris, note that the left-hand column headed "Day" shows the days of the month, numbered one through thirty in a vertical tabulation. Run your finger down the column to twelve, and place a bookmark at this point so that you can keep your place for ready reference.

The Sun's positions for November 1934 are tabulated in the next column. As you can see, the Sun is shown at 19:25 degrees Scorpio for November 12.

Use a separate sheet of paper to jot down this information. That is the position of the Sun as of GMT at noon. Since the native was born at a later hour, we must correct the 19:25 degrees Scorpio Sun position at noon to find the actual position of the Sun at nine hours and forty minutes GMT *after noon*—which is the GMT interval.

Since we are dealing with a P.M. birth in terms of equivalent Greenwich mean time, our first step is to find the total motion of the Sun for one full day, from the twelfth to the thirteenth as shown in the ephemeris: 20:26 degrees Scorpio. From this figure subtract 19:25 degrees Scorpio, the position on the twelfth. The result is 1:01 degrees, the full amount of the Sun's daily motion from the twelfth to the thirteenth of November.

Now we are ready to determine what part of that motion occurred as of the GMT interval, and the log table assists us (see fig. 23). Look for the figure "1:01" in the degrees column on the log table. Remember that "Hours or Degrees" runs across the top of the page from zero to twenty-three, and that for our purposes it reads "Degrees" only. The "1" column is the column we need. In the column which shows minutes, meaning for our purposes "minutes of degrees," locate the second entry, which is, again, "1." Using a piece of paper as a guide, find the point at which the "1" in the hours column intersects the "1" in the minutes column. Note the number: that is the logarithm corresponding to 1:01 degrees. It's log 1.3730, the daily motion log for the Sun.

Our next step will be to find out what part of that daily motion had occurred nine hours and forty minutes after noon GMT when the native was born in Cincinnati according to the GMT interval. The log table again comes to our rescue. The constant log is the logarithm for

Note that 30 degrees of any sign equal zero degrees of the next sign. Example: 30 degrees Aries equals zero degrees Taurus.

TOTAL DEGREES	DEGREES OF ♈	°	♉	°	♊	°	♋	°	♌	°	♍	°	♎	°	♏	°	♐	°	♑	°	♒	°	♓
0	0	30	0	60	0	90	0	120	0	150	0	180	0	210	0	240	0	270	0	300	0	330	0
1	1	31	1	61	1	91	1	121	1	151	1	181	1	211	1	241	1	271	1	301	1	331	1
2	2	32	2	62	2	92	2	122	2	152	2	182	2	212	2	242	2	272	2	302	2	332	2
3	3	33	3	63	3	93	3	123	3	153	3	183	3	213	3	243	3	273	3	303	3	333	3
4	4	34	4	64	4	94	4	124	4	154	4	184	4	214	4	244	4	274	4	304	4	334	4
5	5	35	5	65	5	95	5	125	5	155	5	185	5	215	5	245	5	275	5	305	5	335	5
6	6	36	6	66	6	96	6	126	6	156	6	186	6	216	6	246	6	276	6	306	6	336	6
7	7	37	7	67	7	97	7	127	7	157	7	187	7	217	7	247	7	277	7	307	7	337	7
8	8	38	8	68	8	98	8	128	8	158	8	188	8	218	8	248	8	278	8	308	8	338	8
9	9	39	9	69	9	99	9	129	9	159	9	189	9	219	9	249	9	279	9	309	9	339	9
10	10	40	10	70	10	100	10	130	10	160	10	190	10	220	10	250	10	280	10	310	10	340	10
11	11	41	11	71	11	101	11	131	11	161	11	191	11	221	11	251	11	281	11	311	11	341	11
12	12	42	12	72	12	102	12	132	12	162	12	192	12	222	12	252	12	282	12	312	12	342	12
13	13	43	13	73	13	103	13	133	13	163	13	193	13	223	13	253	13	283	13	313	13	343	13
14	14	44	14	74	14	104	14	134	14	164	14	194	14	224	14	254	14	284	14	314	14	344	14
15	15	45	15	75	15	105	15	135	15	165	15	195	15	225	15	255	15	285	15	315	15	345	15
16	16	46	16	76	16	106	16	136	16	166	16	196	16	226	16	256	16	286	16	316	16	346	16
17	17	47	17	77	17	107	17	137	17	167	17	197	17	227	17	257	17	287	17	317	17	347	17
18	18	48	18	78	18	108	18	138	18	168	18	198	18	228	18	258	18	288	18	318	18	348	18
19	19	49	19	79	19	109	19	139	19	169	19	199	19	229	19	259	19	289	19	319	19	349	19
20	20	50	20	80	20	110	20	140	20	170	20	200	20	230	20	260	20	290	20	320	20	350	20
21	21	51	21	81	21	111	21	141	21	171	21	201	21	231	21	261	21	291	21	321	21	351	21
22	22	52	22	82	22	112	22	142	22	172	22	202	22	232	22	262	22	292	22	322	22	352	22
23	23	53	23	83	23	113	23	143	23	173	23	203	23	233	23	263	23	293	23	323	23	353	23
24	24	54	24	84	24	114	24	144	24	174	24	204	24	234	24	264	24	294	24	324	24	354	24
25	25	55	25	85	25	115	25	145	25	175	25	205	25	235	25	265	25	295	25	325	25	355	25
26	26	56	26	86	26	116	26	146	26	176	26	206	26	236	26	266	26	296	26	326	26	356	26
27	27	57	27	87	27	117	27	147	27	177	27	207	27	237	27	267	27	297	27	327	27	357	27
28	28	58	28	88	28	118	28	148	28	178	28	208	28	238	28	268	28	298	28	328	28	358	28
29	29	59	29	89	29	119	29	149	29	179	29	209	29	239	29	269	29	299	29	329	29	359	29

TABLE 2. Table of correspondences: degrees of the ecliptic to degrees of sign

the GMT interval, log 0.3949. Add the constant log to the daily motion log for the Sun: the sum is log 1.7679, the birth time log.

Refer again to the log table. This time we look for a log number, not a degree number. Specifically, we are looking for the log number in the table which comes closest to our birth time log or log 1.7679. In the first ("0 degrees") column we find log 1.7604 and log 1.7781. Which of these is closer to log 1.7679? Often we can tell simply by looking at the numbers. In case of doubt, we must find the difference between the birth time log and the two numbers which appear closest. Here, the difference between log 1.7679 and log 1.7604 is 0.0075; and between log 1.7781 and log 1.7679 is 0.0102, a larger number. Therefore, log 1.7604 is closest to our birth time log; hence the one we will use.

In the log table, the antilogarithm for log 1.7604 is 25 minutes, the Sun's corrected motion. Since we are dealing with a plus GMT interval, 25 minutes must be added to the Sun's position of 19:25 degrees Scorpio. Make that addition now: the result, 19:50 degrees Scorpio, was the actual position of the Sun at the time of the native's birth. Underscore, circle or otherwise annotate this figure so that you will be able to find it readily when you are ready to enter the Sun on the horoscope blank.

We make no entries on the actual chart until all of the planetary positions have been calculated in order to make sure that we have enough room on the chart form in the appropriate houses in which the planets must be placed.

If the native's equivalent Greenwich mean time at birth had been less than 12:00:00 hours, his GMT interval would have been a *minus* figure. In that event the actual position of the Sun at the native's time of birth would be *earlier than* GMT at noon and the following steps would account for the true Sun's position:

1. We would look for the Sun's position on the date before the birth date in the ephemeris and record that position on scratch paper; then subtract the Sun position of the day before from the Sun position on the birth date.

2. We would find the log number for the difference thus obtained and add it to the constant log, producing the birth time log.

3. We would find the log number closest to the birth time log.

4. We would then find the *antilog* corresponding to the new log number in the log table. The antilog constitutes the degrees and minutes of daily motion applicable to the GMT interval.

5. We would *subtract* the degrees and minutes of the daily motion of the antilog from the degrees and minutes of the Sun's position as shown for the birth date.

If the GMT interval is a plus figure, we correct the planets' places by *adding* the proportionally correct amount of degrees of arc for the position as shown on the birth date in the ephemeris. But if the native's equivalent Greenwich mean time interval is a minus figure, the GMT interval will be a minus number of hours and minutes, which requires us to *subtract* the proportionate number of degrees and minutes of daily motion found by using the log table.

THE NEXT PLANET shown in the ephemeris is Venus, which presents no special problems. Repeat the steps you learned to correct the Sun's position and enter the result on scratch paper.

Mercury, which follows Venus in the ephemeris tabulation, introduces new considerations. Note the R at the top of the column. That means that Mercury was retrograde for all dates following the R up to the date at which a D appears. In this case, the D appears at the entry for November 13.

When a planet is in retrograde motion is it (apparently) moving backward relative to the Earth's velocity in its orbit around the Sun. This occurs because the Earth and all the other planets move at varying speeds depending on their positions in their orbits. When a planet orbits closest to the Sun it moves the fastest; when a planet is farthest from the Sun in its orbit, it moves the slowest.

The phenomenon of retrograde motion can be illustrated: if you were on a fast-moving train passing a slower-moving train on the next track going in the same direction, the slower-moving train would appear to be moving backward. For the same reason Mercury appears to be in retrograde motion.

The rules for correcting planetary positions for retrograde planets are the same as those for correcting positions for planets in direct motion, with one exception: where you would ordinarily *add* the proportionate amount of daily motion in the case of a *plus* GMT interval, you would subtract it in the case of a retrograde planet; where you would ordinarily *subtract* the proportionate amount of daily motion in the case of a *minus* GMT interval, in the case of a retrograde planet you would add it.

Mercury has been in retrograde motion since October 23, 1934, as shown on the previous page of the ephemeris. Mercury continues its retrograde motion, according to the ephemeris, through November 12. *However, on November 13, Mercury goes direct!*

When, between the twelfth and thirteenth, did retrograde motion become direct motion? We can see from looking at the ephemeris positions that Mercury's retrograde motion was slowing down; indeed, between November eleventh and twelfth, the entire daily motion amounted only to three minutes of retrograde motion. On the other hand, the ephemeris shows that between November twelfth and thirteenth, there were nine minutes of *direct* motion. It therefore appears that while Mercury was not in direct motion as of GMT at noon on November twelfth, Mercury commenced its direct motion not long after noon on that date, since: (1) Mercury's retrograde motion had slowed from twenty-five minutes on November tenth to fifteen minutes on November eleventh, to three minutes on November twelfth, a decreasing interval which suggests little, if any, retrograde motion beyond the known position for November twelfth; and (2) Mercury's position on November thirteenth was 3:10 degrees of *direct* motion, nine minutes more than its position on the twelfth and three times the amount of retrograde motion between November eleventh and twelfth.

For these reasons, we elect to treat Mercury as having achieved direct motion on the twelfth of November, a decision supported as a practical matter by the fact that the native was born nine hours and forty minutes later than the noon position shown in the ephemeris when Mercury was still retrograde. Now we can make the simple calculations that we would for any other planet. Note the result on a separate sheet of paper, and circle it for future reference.

THE BIRTH DATE November 12, 1934, presents just about all of the novelties you are likely to encounter in chart erection. Note that the Moon, the fastest-moving planet, changes signs between November twelfth and thirteenth. On the twelfth the Moon is posited at 28:19 degrees Capricorn; on the thirteenth, however, the Moon has moved to 12:26 degrees *Aquarius*. How do we account for this sign change in our calculations?

Since each sign of the zodiac represents thirty degrees of arc, 12:26 degrees Aquarius is mathematically equivalent to 42:26 degrees Capricorn—the sign we want to use for subtracting the degree of sign on November twelfth from the degree of sign on November thirteenth. Therefore subtract 28:19 degrees from 42:26 degrees; the result is 14:07 degrees daily motion. Correct the 14:07 degrees of the Moon's daily motion just as you would any other daily motion figure.

Subtraction shows that there are only two minutes of daily motion for Saturn between November 12 and 13. This amount of motion will not make a difference, a fact which you can confirm by use of the log table. The logarithm which is the sum of the constant log and the daily motion log cannot be found there.

For Jupiter, the daily motion figure, although less than a degree, will make a difference because of the length of the GMT interval. The daily motion for Jupiter is thirteen minutes and the corresponding log number is 2.0444. Adding that to the constant log of .3949 produces the birth time logarithm 2.4393.

The closest log to the birth time log is log 2.4594, whose anti-logarithm is five minutes. Therefore five minutes is the motion for Jupiter which must be added to the 7:02 degrees Scorpio shown for November 12.

Follow the same steps in correcting the ecliptic longitude position for Mars which I have described for the preceding planets. There are no unusual features which will cause you any problems.

There are only two minutes of daily motion for Uranus, not enough to make a difference. You should also note that Uranus is in retrograde motion and the retrograde symbol should be used when you enter Uranus on the horoscope.

There is but one minute of daily motion for Neptune; again, not enough to make a difference and no correction is required.

The north node is shown at 4:52 degrees Aquarius. Note that the nodes are always in retrograde motion. Here the difference between November 12 and 13 is only 3 minutes, not enough to require correction. Don't forget to jot down the south node position, which is not shown in the ephemeris because it is always exactly opposite the north node position—here, 4:52 degrees Leo.

Pluto moves so slowly that its position is not usually shown in the daily tabulation. It is either set out in the opening pages of the ephemeris for that year or at the bottom of the page of the ephemeris for the date in question. For November 1934, the ephemeris shows Pluto's longitude on November 1 at 26:02 degrees Cancer. How much motion is there from November 1 to November 12? On the next page of the ephemeris (not shown here), Pluto's longitude on December 1 was 25:54 degrees Cancer. Thus the total motion for Pluto between November and December is 8 minutes. Notice that this is retrograde motion, although the ephemeris does not bother to show it as such.

This figure does not really require use of the log table. Since for the entire month of November there were only 8 minutes of motion for Pluto and since the native was born on the twelfth, we need only find 12/30 or 2/5 of 8 minutes of motion. Two-fifths of 8 minutes is slightly more than 3 minutes, which we *subtract* from the motion shown for November 1, inasmuch as Pluto is in retrograde motion. This subtraction places Pluto at 25:59 degrees Cancer retrograde, on November 12.

You have now corrected all of the planets and are prepared to enter them in the appropriate house positions. Note all of the planets you will be placing in Scorpio: Sun, Venus, Mercury and Jupiter. When entering these four planets on the chart, keep in mind the fact that you must allow room for all of them in the seventh house except Mercury, which falls in the sixth house. Remember the correct sequence of the signs and you will have no difficulty in placing the planets in the proper houses. Mercury is a good example: since Mercury is at 3:05 degrees Scorpio, whereas the seventh house cusp is 4:49 degrees Scorpio, Mercury falls in the sixth house, because the first 4:49 degrees of Scorpio are in that house and the remainder are in the seventh house. The other Scorpio planets are all located in the remaining 25:11 degrees of Scorpio, which are in the seventh house.

Enter all planets and the nodes in the correct houses, together with degree and minute of sign and retrograde motion glyph, where applicable. When you are done, compare your chart with figure twenty-five, the actual chart of the native.

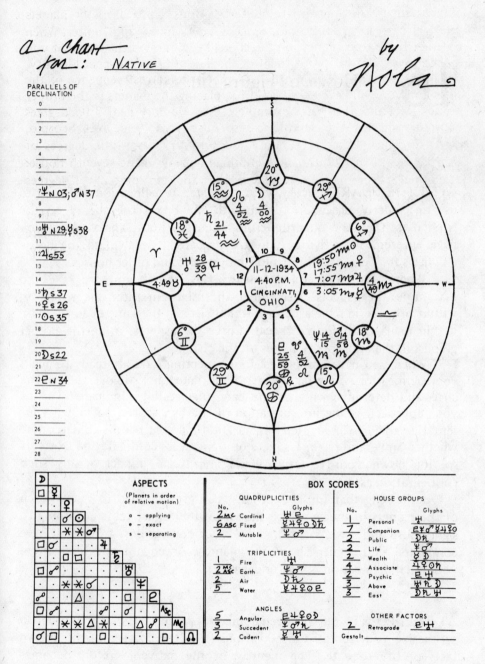

FIGURE 25. "Native's" chart

16 How Do I Figure the Native?

WITH THE CHART erected, your next step is delineation. It is best to use an orderly procedure. Start with the box scores based on the triplicities, then the quadruplicities, then the house angles. After you have entered these figures you are prepared to calculate the house emphasis for personal, companionship, public and other houses.

When you have completed the box scores you are ready to determine the aspects. Remember that signs in the same triplicity, within orb, are in *trine* aspect; and that signs in the same quadruplicity, within orb, are in *square* aspect. Enter the aspects, using the proper glyphs, in the appropriate boxes on the chart.

When you have completed your aspecting, you are ready to begin your delineation of the natal chart. First, take a holistic overview of the chart and determine whether any particular gestalt is indicated. Part of your approach is the interpretation of the box scores. Jot down your tentative analysis on scratch paper. The final step here is to determine whether any grand trine, T-square or grand cross configuration exists. If so, jot down your tentative views about the impact of any such configuration as well.

Following that initial synthesis, you are prepared to discuss each of the planets in the sequence shown on the aspect table according to sign, house and aspects. Again, note your conclusions. When you have completed your synthesis of the planets, Ascendant and Midheaven, your natal delineation is well under way.

AT THIS POINT you will need some facts about the native in order to synthesize your tentative observations from the chart with the known facts of life to date. The identity of the native therefore becomes relevant.

The chart is that of Charles Manson, whose face you probably saw on the cover of the Dec. 19, 1969 *Life* Magazine or in one of the many reprints of that startling photograph of a bearded longhair whose fixed stare made him look both ferocious and deranged. When you saw that photograph you may have shuddered (as I did, when attempting to help Dr. White), and concluded that the man who led the Family charged with the responsibility for the gruesome deaths of so many people must indeed be a monster.

What do you think now? Perhaps you think that I have played a trick on you by choosing a sensational and distasteful example for your first chart erection.

I hope not. As I stated at the outset, my view is that contemporary astrology is a *humanism;* as such, the astrologer does not concern himself with abstract judgments of good and evil, but seeks instead to discover in each chart the potentialities and problems of the native.

To dismiss any human being (Manson included) as a monster is to devalue humanity itself. *Nothing human is foreign to me,* Terence said, and this might well be the operating principle of the contemporary humanistic astrologer.

In that perspective, the maniacal stare of Manson from the cover of *Life* is reduced to its human terms: a stereotype deliberately contrived by Manson to bait the press and to compromise public opinion, another vindication of his contempt for the society he believed had mistreated and rejected him.

As I see it, the task of the contemporary astrologer is to view the horoscope as the life of a human being who warrants our consideration for that fact alone. As astrologer Rod Chase observed, "Astrology is a way to understand people and see the heaven that is in them."[1] Or as Omar Khayyám put it, "I myself am Heaven and Hell."

With the chart of Charles Manson, human being, born illegitimate on November 12, 1934, who spent most of his life in institutions of one kind or another, and who at this writing resides in the last institution he is likely to visit in this lifetime, you have your first challenge as a contemporary humanistic astrologer.

APPENDIX ONE
Carl Jung and the Philosopher's Stone

UNTIL OUR SCIENTISTS undertake to review the fabulous unread library of books and manuscripts on alchemy, the knowledge contained in them is lost to us. So says Louis Pauwels, who with Jacques Bergier authored *The Morning of the Magicians*, a reexamination of the alchemical tradition. Is it possible, Pauwels asks rhetorically, that so many scholars of such unquestioned dedication would have labored in a tradition more than a thousand years old, if they had been engaged in promoting mere fraud and delusion?

Pauwels doesn't think so and neither do I. But if alchemy was all that worthwhile, what happened to alchemy and all the alchemists?

The short answer is that today they are doctors, psychologists, astrologers, astronomers, physicists, metallurgists, chemists and the like; probably in about the same proportion of conscientious and sincere men to thieves, frauds and scoundrels as existed in the alchemical tradition.

Each branch of modern science can be charted back to its source in alchemy; and in each case the principal distinguishing features between the scientist and the alchemist are the same. Viewing Man as a part of a universal whole, the alchemist maintained a pious reverence for life and for matter alike.

The Rosicrucians began with the Brotherhood of the Rosy Cross, a society of alchemists and Christian mystics, early in the seventeenth century.[1] With the publication of their astronomical calculations in ephemerides and in house tables, the Rosicrucian Society practices its own brand of Hermetic astrology in the alchemist tradition of piety and of scholarship.

Alchemy reached its fullest flowering in the seventeenth century, as Jung tells us; but that is when it also began its headlong decline, because of the Age of Science, otherwise identified as the Copernican Revolution. The rationalist orientation, coupled with the guild system of protecting the territorial imperatives common to the halls of academe and scientism, insured a tunnel-vision view of the universe.

While this perspective has permitted many achievements in technology, it lost us the alchemist's holistic perspective with its attendant mysticism. In Jung's apt phrase, the dominance of the thinking type of function has resulted in a godless *hubris* which is still the predominant attitude in scholarship and in science.

In an age of specialists, only the archaeologist reads the alchemical literature; and he has stared at it with unseeing eyes these past three centuries. What we need, Pauwels and Bergier rightly insist, are experts from other disciplines with a different perspective to undertake the Herculean task of reviewing the scholarship of alchemy.

Carl Jung remains the only scientist in this century who has had both the moral courage and the holistic vision to attempt this task.

JUNG REGARDED *MYSTERIUM CONIUNCTIONIS* as the culmination of his efforts[2] and it was a book over which he labored for ten years. Dr. Mircea Eliade, internationally recognized scholar of religious history, has declared that *Mysterium* "is a rich and valuable book" whose cultural impact "may prove to be independent of Jung's psychological theory."[3]

The opacity of the prose notwithstanding, *Mysterium* is indeed the culmination of Jung's work in the arcane disciplines of alchemy, astrology and psychology. In the face of his colleagues' scorn, Jung resolutely set about to provide a thoughtful and detailed examination of the alchemist tradition.

Alchemists deliberately wrote in dense, symbolic language, it now seems clear, because of their fears about what would happen if their knowledge fell into the hands of the impious. In our own time, all of those fears appear to have been amply justified.

Jung's analysis of the literature of alchemy involves both psychology and astrology, although it is problematical whether or not he was fully aware of that fact. Thus he remarks that he finally hit upon his criteria for his four functional personality types this way:

> I simply framed my concepts of the psychic functions from the notions expressed in current speech, and used them as my criteria . . .[4]

This is not a credible statement of the origin of his functional typology, when placed in the context of the events leading up to the development of the theory.

His personality types were developed during a period of time in which he was preoccupied with alchemy and astrology; when his recurrent dreams took him into the fabulous library of alchemical incunabula in an unknown wing of his house; when he admittedly envied the simplicity of the "astrological criteria" of personality as well as the closely related humoral criteria of Galen.

Jung's 1928 lecture at the Congress of Swiss Psychiatrists in Zurich became a chapter of *Psychological Types* and, in slightly different form, a chapter in *Modern Man in Search of a Soul* in 1933. It was also in 1933 that Jung published a lecture entitled "A Study in the Process of Individuation," which appears in revised form as a chapter in *The Archetypes and the Collective Unconscious.* In the latter work he deals at length with mandala symbolism, where he observes "a transformation process divided into four stages of three parts each, analogous to the twelve transformations of the zodiac and its division into four."[5]

Then there is the famous episode in which Jung compared the horoscopes of marriage partners in order to determine their compatibility. Using the conjunctions and oppositions of Sun, Moon, Mars, Venus, Ascendant and Descendant, Jung found such a meaningful coincidence of Moon conjunctions in the compared horoscopes as to amount to "a minor miracle."[6]

If we had any lingering doubts about Jung's true sources for his functional personality types, they were fully dissipated by the observations made in *Mysterium,* which he commenced in 1941. Consider this passage:

> Alchemy is inconceivable without the influence of her elder sister astrology and the statements of these three disciplines must be taken into account in any psychological evaluation of the luminaries.[7]

Luminaries is the astrological term for the Sun and Moon; and the *three* disciplines referred to must be astrology, alchemy and psychology.

In *Mysterium,* Jung also takes note of the seven colors associated with the planets, for their astrological and their corresponding psychological significance; he concludes that "the planets correspond to individual character components."[8] Gold symbolizes intellect, the principal formative agent in the alchemical process, just as choler corresponds to yellow, which is called *citrinatas* in alchemical parlance.

Jung decides that the other three principal colors also denote *psychological functions*—and that is the term he uses. The elements of fire, earth, air and water were colored yellow, black, red and white respectively. Jung correlates them in identical fashion, commencing with the yellow for choler—and for intellect.[9] Likewise, Jung deduces that the seven colors denote the seven astrological components of human character:

> Consequently, the synthesis of the four or seven colors would mean nothing less than the integration of the personality, *the union of the*

four basic functions, which are customarily represented by the color quaternio blue-red-yellow-green.[10]

As Jung himself explains in the opening chapter of *Mysterium,* the *quaternio* or quaternity division of the circle into four quarters refers to the union of opposites reflected in the four elements, the four seasons and the four cardinal compass directions. Each of these correspondences is astrological in origin and in application.[11] Later in the same treatise, Jung observes that "the alchemical symbols are saturated with astrology."[12]

When I finally conquered the prose style, it seemed self-evident that Jung's theory of personality (including his four personality types based on four basic functions and his notion of the need for integrating these four functions by what he termed the process of individuation*) culminated in *Mysterium Coniunctionis;* and that that work showed conclusively that his personality theory originated in alchemy and astrology.

I also concluded that *Mysterium,* as the fullest expression of his astrological theory of personality, was likely to have all of the impact foreseen by Eliade, and perhaps even more.

IT IS GENERALLY assumed that the alchemists were engaged in a spurious kind of metallurgy in which they purported to change base metals into gold; and that the particular brand of snake oil they used to gull the unwary public was something they called the philosopher's stone.

Jung's conclusions are vastly different from these popular assumptions; he pursued his research with the same conviction of Silberer before him, that the sincere alchemist wasn't interested in *aurum vulgaris*—vulgar gold—but only in the gold of transcendence. After all, alchemist authors *do* repeatedly remind their readers that "our gold is not your (vulgar) gold."

In the Jungian conception, the philosopher's stone was that mysterious something, variously described by the alchemists, by which Man could transcend his base and corporeal form to achieve the true gold of Oneness, self-integration and insight into the unity of all things.

Whether or not any alchemists ever found the philosopher's stone is a matter of some debate. The question seems moot to me; for, with the body of his writings in alchemy and astrology and his resultant

---

*Now more commonly referred to as self-actualization.

theories of human personality, Jung has himself produced the philosopher's stone, in a form comparable to the Rosetta Stone.

As Rosetta Stone or philosopher's stone, Jung's achievements permit us to translate the language of alchemy into any number of disciplines, be they mystical or rationalist-empirical, to permit the practitioner to achieve whatever form of transcendence the outside limitations of his discipline may permit.

Jung's philosopher's stone may ultimately give us the insight to see all areas of Man's inquiry as essentially a unified whole, for *The Secret of the Golden Flower,* dealing with Oriental alchemy, reflects the same secret preserved by Western alchemists and astrologers, who, with their Eastern counterparts, strove for the holistic vision. Jung himself expressed the hope that his commentary to that work would "build a bridge of psychological understanding between East and West."[13]

Just as the unbroken Oriental mystical tradition proved invaluable to Hugh Moran in tracing the alphabet to its astrological origins, so the similarly unbroken tradition of Chinese medicine enables us to trace the origins of Oriental alchemy. The authors of the university text, *Chinese Medicine,* assure us,

> In medicine it will appear neither astounding nor impossible to compare the ancient *Nei-ching* (The Classic of Internal Medicine) with a recent work compiled in accordance with the standards of contemporary scientific medicine; it would even be possible for the latter to be regarded as inspired by the *Nei-ching.*[14]

This is a startling statement when we consider that the earliest fragments of the *Nei-ching* date from the fifth to the third century B.C.E.[15]

Until the recent popular interest in acupuncture, the *hubris* of Western science has been such that we gave little attention to what had been accomplished by doctors of Chinese medicine, much less to the principles of astrology and alchemy upon which so much of it is based.

Since Western medicine has no adequate explanation for the workings of acupuncture, Western doctors would prefer to ignore it. Its continued (and increasing) popularity is at least annoying, if not just a little threatening. Inevitably, traditional tactics have been tried to dispatch this latest threat to medical orthodoxy and the territorial imperatives upon which it is based.

Jung's philosopher's stone would suggest a different approach, more constructive and ultimately more rewarding. A gloss of *Acupuncture,* a widely reprinted report by Dr. Felix Mann, English physician and acupuncturist, considered together with *The Yellow Emperor's Classic of Internal Medicine,* the ancient text which inspired contemporary Chinese medicine, makes clear that the underlying concepts of astrology, alchemy and acupuncture are the same in the Oriental tradition.

In Oriental alchemy the human body is viewed as having four elements. A fifth element, the Earth itself, lies outside the body. This element may have been added principally to satisfy the Oriental fascination with the number five; but it also has its counterpart in Western alchemy.[16]

As in Western astrology, the four elements of Oriental alchemy are correlated to the four cardinal compass directions in the microcosmic orbit that is Man; *and the body also has twelve meridians* through which the life energy (*qi* or *chi*) flows in that microcosmic orbit. As Dr. Felix Mann points out, the Chinese view the course of this *chi* energy as being regulated in two ways; first, according to the cycles of the seasons; and second, according to the cycle of the twenty-four-hour day.[17]

Although drawn from Oriental alchemy, this view of Man is virtually identical to the basic concept of Western astrology, in which the twelve segments of the horoscope represent the cycles of the seasons and the cycle of the twenty-four-hour day as well.

It is a basic premise of acupuncture that each of the twelve meridians commences its activity according to a specified order of bodily organs and at a specified time period triggered by the flow of *chi* energy.

Hopefully, one day we in the West will know more about the relationship of the meridians of acupuncture to the houses of astrology, and the relationship of both to what Teilhard de Chardin has aptly described as the phenomenon of Man.

WHY DIDN'T JUNG admit his sources?

Arthur Koestler has pointed out that Jung was not always generous about acknowledging his intellectual debts. Jung's famous essay, "Synchronicity: An A-Causal Connecting Principle," owes much to Paul Kammerer, whose Law of Seriality Jung adopts and mislabels synchronicity.[18] It was Kammerer who first postulated acausality, a principle important both to astrology and to astrophysics. Jung's essay quotes Kammerer at length, and only then "pays somewhat grudging tribute to him," according to Koestler.[19]

Likewise, Herbert Silberer, a colleague of Jung's, pioneered in developing the psychoanalytic aspects of alchemy in *Problems of Mysticism and Its Symbolism.* Jung acknowledges rather obliquely that he had read the book: "Oddly enough, I had entirely forgotten what

Herbert Silberer had written about alchemy." Again, after a somewhat grudging tribute, Jung adds this less than charitable thought: "As his tragic death shows, Silberer's discovery of the problem was not followed by insight into it."[20] The reference is to Silberer's suicide, which Jung mentions in footnote to this statement. Kammerer was also a suicide and I wonder in what order that coincidence should be catalogued!

But Jung did acknowledge his debts to Kammerer and to Silberer, however reluctantly, and that is something that other scientists have not always done for greater intellectual obligations than his. Since Jung's Sun and Uranus were both posited in Leo, perhaps he deserves some credit for his willingness to share the limelight at all; at least, that would be the astrological way of looking at it. Besides, it wasn't an intellectual debt to a colleague that was involved in this instance. For these reasons, I believe that Jung's unwillingness to confess his astrological sources for *Psychological Types* lies elsewhere.

Jung had looked back longingly at the astrological criteria in pondering where he would find his own criteria for personality types, and he sternly reminded himself that "our scientific conscience does not permit us to revert to these old, intuitive ways of thinking."[21] Yet he worked for years to develop just such intuition, but he often failed. Jung struggled for years to understand the *Tibetan Book of the Dead*, gradually moving in the direction of a commitment to the "wisdom and superior reality of internal perceptions" but doing so "cautiously and with the ambivalent reservations of the psychiatrist *cum* mystic."[22]

Ralph Metzner, a co-author of *The Psychedelic Experience*, whose own *Maps of Consciousness* is a significant contribution to contemporary astrology, would probably agree. Acknowledging Jung's pioneering advances in recognizing the importance of the alchemical tradition, Metzner declares that "Jung fell victim to the inherent trap of the intellectual approach: that of assuming that mental knowledge is true understanding."[23]

But I think that in *Psychological Types* Jung overcame "the ambivalent reservations of the psychiatrist *cum* mystic" and avoided the "inherent trap of the intellectual approach" of what he himself called our "scientific conscience," by using his intuition to synthesize traditional astrological principles with his own contributions of analytical psychology, in order to produce the first genuinely useful theory of personality types since Galen.

APPENDIX TWO

How to Construct
a Three-Dimensional Model of a Horoscope

FIGURE TWENTY-SIX SETS out the templates and diagrams for this model, but I suggest you follow along step by step, according to the following directions.

1. Use three index cards. Trace a circle on each card with a jar lid just small enough to fit whatever size card you are using.

2. Label one circle *Meridian*. Label another circle *True Horizon*. Label the third circle *Prime Vertical*.

3. With a pencil, trace a diameter on each of the circles.

4. Draw a second diameter perpendicular to the first on the meridian circle. Write *Z.* for Zenith at the top of the vertical diameter, and *Na.* for Nadir at the bottom. (Refer to figure 26 for an illustration.) On the right-hand edge of the horizontal diameter, write *N* for North; and on the left-hand edge, write *S* for South.

5. Write *horizon* on the horizontal diameter line of the meridian circle. At the center of the horizon line, draw a small circle; half of the circle should be above the horizon line, and half below the line. Shade in the circle with pen or pencil. That's the Earth at the center of the meridian, which the plane of the meridian intersects at the Earth's center. Finally, about halfway between the S and the zenith, write *MC* at the edge of the circle. (You may find another glance at the illustration helpful at this point.)

6. Take a pair of scissors. Starting at the north point on the meridian paper circle, cut *only* halfway into the horizon line—up to the point of intersection with the vertical diameter.

7. Now take the true horizon great circle. Draw a second diameter, perpendicular to the first. Label the edges of the diameter *N,S,E,W* in sequence for compass directions.

8. Take your scissors. Cut *only* halfway into the north-south diameter line of the true horizon great circle, starting at the south edge of the diameter, and cutting only to the intersection of the vertical diameter.

9. Insert the true horizon circle into the meridian circle, slipping one paper cut into the other; position the card circles at right angles to each other.

10. Look at your handiwork. You now have a model of the true horizon and the meridian as they appear in two-dimensional diagrammatic form on any Placidian horoscope.

11. Cut the prime vertical circle in half; lay the unlabeled half aside. With scissors, cut into the middle of the prime vertical semicircle starting from the diameter; cut *only* halfway into the circle.

12. Take the meridian circle. Cut halfway down into the meridian circle from the Z of the zenith point. Insert the prime vertical cut into the meridian cut at right angles.

13. Look at what you have done. You now have a model of the celestial sphere which shows how the prime vertical intersects the center of the Earth at right angles to the great circles of the meridian and the true horizon. Note that the prime vertical is also a great circle and actually goes all the way through the meridian. Solely for convenience, I am using only the upper half of the prime vertical in this model.

14. Now take the other half of the paper circle you used to construct the prime vertical and label it *Ecliptic*. Cut with scissors halfway into the ecliptic semicircle, starting at the middle of its diameter.

15. Cut a similar line halfway into the meridian at the point you have labeled MC, in between the horizon and the prime vertical. This cut should be at about a thirty-degree angle from the horizon line on the meridian circle.

16. Insert the ecliptic semicircle into the meridian semicircle at the cuts. This places the ecliptic at about a thirty-degree angle to the horizon.

17. Your model now shows the relationship of the ecliptic to the native's meridian, the true horizon and the prime vertical. For convenience, I have used only that half of the ecliptic great circle which appears above the horizon, just as I did with the prime vertical. However, the ecliptic is a great circle which intersects the center of the Earth and appears below the horizon as well as above it, as does the prime vertical.

You may wish to use a bit of cellophane tape to fix the great circles at the proper angles to each other.

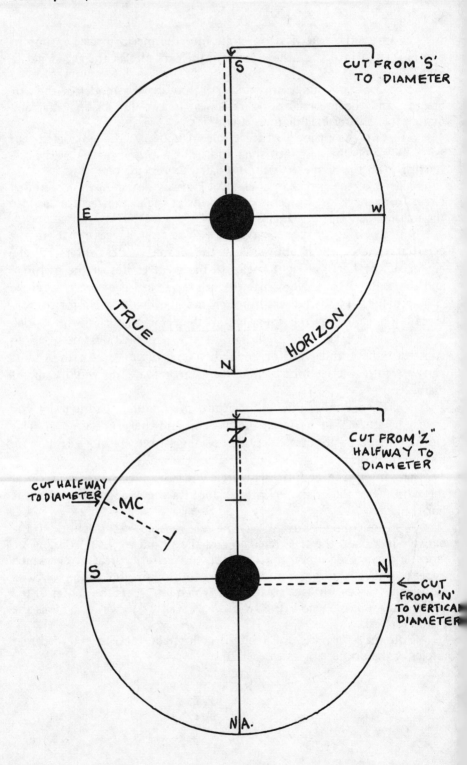

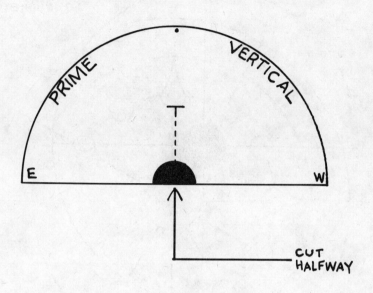

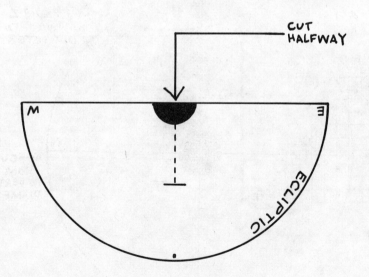

a chart for: _____

by Nola

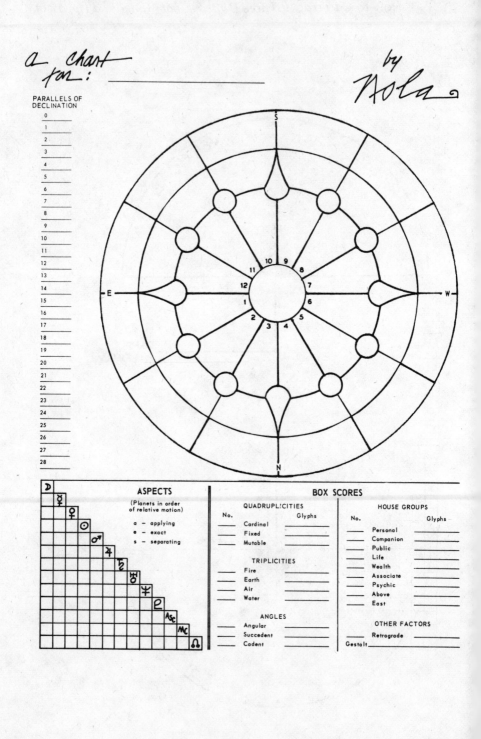

PARALLELS OF DECLINATION

0
1
2
3
4
5
6
7
8
9
10
11
12
13
14
15
16
17
18
19
20
21
22
23
24
25
26
27
28

ASPECTS

(Planets in order of relative motion)

a — applying
e — exact
s — separating

BOX SCORES

QUADRUPLICITIES

No.		Glyphs
___	Cardinal	_____
___	Fixed	_____
___	Mutable	_____

TRIPLICITIES

___	Fire	_____
___	Earth	_____
___	Air	_____
___	Water	_____

ANGLES

___	Angular	_____
___	Succedent	_____
___	Cadent	_____

HOUSE GROUPS

No.		Glyphs
___	Personal	_____
___	Companion	_____
___	Public	_____
___	Life	_____
___	Wealth	_____
___	Associate	_____
___	Psychic	_____
___	Above	_____
___	East	_____

OTHER FACTORS

___	Retrograde	_____
Gestalt		_____

a chart for: _____

by *Nola*

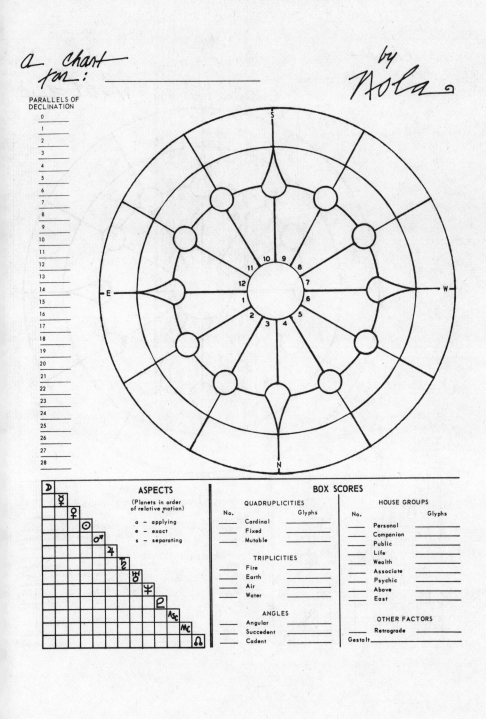

PARALLELS OF DECLINATION

0
1
2
3
4
5
6
7
8
9
10
11
12
13
14
15
16
17
18
19
20
21
22
23
24
25
26
27
28

S

E   W

N

10 9 8
11   7
12   6
1   5
2 3 4

ASPECTS

(Planets in order of relative motion)

a — applying
e — exact
s — separating

BOX SCORES

QUADRUPLICITIES

No.		Glyphs
___	Cardinal	_____
___	Fixed	_____
___	Mutable	_____

TRIPLICITIES

Fire	_____
Earth	_____
Air	_____
Water	_____

ANGLES

Angular	_____
Succedent	_____
Cadent	_____

HOUSE GROUPS

No.		Glyphs
___	Personal	_____
___	Companion	_____
___	Public	_____
___	Life	_____
___	Wealth	_____
___	Associate	_____
___	Psychic	_____
___	Above	_____
___	East	_____

OTHER FACTORS

Retrograde	_____
Gestalt	

a chart
for: _____

by
Nola

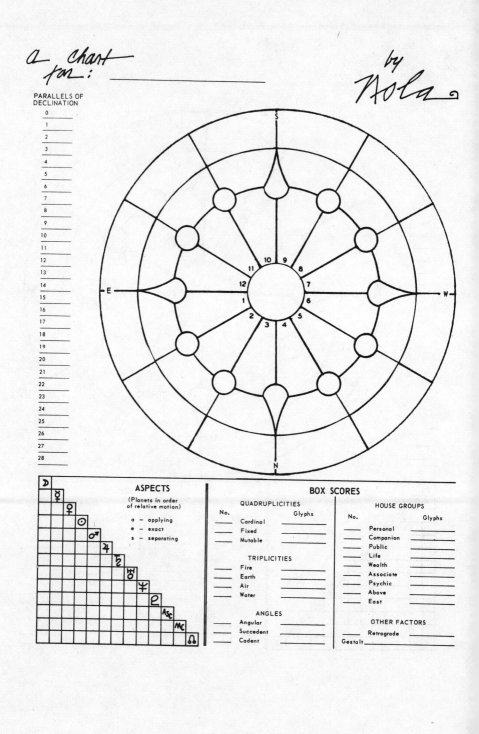

PARALLELS OF
DECLINATION

0
1
2
3
4
5
6
7
8
9
10
11
12
13
14
15
16
17
18
19
20
21
22
23
24
25
26
27
28

S

E

W

N

10 9
11   8
12   7
1   6
2   3   4   5

ASPECTS

(Planets in order
of relative motion)

a – applying
e – exact
s – separating

BOX SCORES

QUADRUPLICITIES

No.		Glyphs
___	Cardinal	___
___	Fixed	___
___	Mutable	___

TRIPLICITIES

___	Fire	___
___	Earth	___
___	Air	___
___	Water	___

ANGLES

___	Angular	___
___	Succedent	___
___	Cadent	___

HOUSE GROUPS

No.		Glyphs
___	Personal	___
___	Companion	___
___	Public	___
___	Life	___
___	Wealth	___
___	Associate	___
___	Psychic	___
___	Above	___
___	East	___

OTHER FACTORS

___	Retrograde	___
Gestalt		

a chart for: _____

by Nola

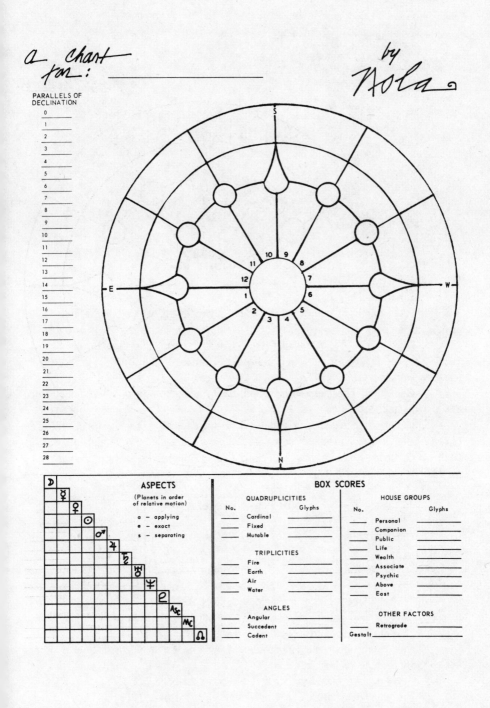

PARALLELS OF DECLINATION

0
1
2
3
4
5
6
7
8
9
10
11
12
13
14
15
16
17
18
19
20
21
22
23
24
25
26
27
28

ASPECTS

(Planets in order of relative motion)

a — applying
e — exact
s — separating

BOX SCORES

QUADRUPLICITIES

No.		Glyphs
___	Cardinal	___
___	Fixed	___
___	Mutable	___

TRIPLICITIES

___	Fire	___
___	Earth	___
___	Air	___
___	Water	___

ANGLES

___	Angular	___
___	Succedent	___
___	Cadent	___

HOUSE GROUPS

No.		Glyphs
___	Personal	___
___	Companion	___
___	Public	___
___	Life	___
___	Wealth	___
___	Associate	___
___	Psychic	___
___	Above	___
___	East	___

OTHER FACTORS

___	Retrograde	___
Gestalt	___	

Chapter Notes

Notes to Chapter 1

1. Leviticus 16.

2. "Air, Earth, Fire and Water," *Sybil Leek's Astrology Journal*, March 1972, at pages 8-9.

3. Novak, *The Experience of Nothingness*, Harper Colophon Books edition, 1970, at page 83, quoting May, "The Significance of Symbols," *Symbolism in Religion and Literature.*

4. Campbell, *The Hero With a Thousand Faces*, Bollingen Paperback edition, 1972, at page 256.

5. Benét, *The Reader's Encyclopedia*, third edition, s.v. "humanism." *See also* Colin Wilson, *Introduction to the New Existentialism*, Houghton Mifflin Company, 1967; Julian Huxley, especially "Evolutionary Humanism," *New Bottles for New Wine*, Harper & Brothers, 1957, at pages 279-312.

Notes to Chapter 3

1. Dane Rudhyar, *The Astrology of Personality*, Doubleday Paperback edition, 1970, at page 32.

2. A. T. W. Simeons, M.D., *Man's Presumptuous Brain*, Dutton Paperback edition, 1962, especially at pages 35-6. *See also* N. J. Berrill, *Man's Emerging Mind*, Fawcett Premier Books edition, 1965, at pages 228-30; Loren Eiseley, *The Immense Journey*, Random House Vintage Books edition, 1959, at page 109.

3. Eiseley, *The Immense Journey*, at page 26.

4. Edna Sarah Beardsley, *The Word: A Philosophy of Words*, Filmer Brothers Press, 1958, at page 262.

5. Berrill, *Man's Emerging Mind*, cited *supra*, at page 221.

6. Eiseley, *The Immense Journey*, cited *supra*, at page 120.

7. Gustav Davidson, *A Dictionary of Angels*, The Free Press, 1967, at pages 20-1, hereinafter cited as *Angels. See also* John McKenzie, S.J., *A Dictionary of the Bible*, Macmillan Company, 1965, at pages 30-2.

8. Davidson, *Angels*, at page 298.

9. *Ibid.*, quoting G. D. Smith, *The Teaching of the Catholic Church.*

10. Kramer, *History Begins at Sumer*, Doubleday Anchor Books edition, 1959, at page xix.

11. *Id.* at pages 76-7.

12. John Allegro, *The Sacred Mushroom and the Cross*, Doubleday and Company, 1970, at pages 20-1, hereinafter cited as *Sacred Mushroom*.

13. Gaston Bachelard, *The Psychoanalysis of Fire*, Beacon Press paperback edition, 1968, at pages 22-4.

14. Allegro, *Sacred Mushroom*, at page 20.

15. *Essays on a Science of Mythology*, Bollingen Paperback edition, 1971, at pages 10-2.

16. *The Alphabet and the Ancient Calendar Signs: Astrological Elements in the Origin of the Alphabet*, Pacific Books, 1952, at page 17, hereinafter cited as *The Alphabet*.

17. A. Alvarez, *The Savage God*, Random House, 1972, at page 244.

18. Durkheim, *Suicide: A Study in Sociology*, John A. Spaulding and George Simpson, trans., The Free Press of Glencoe, 1951, at page 15.

19. Julius Gould and William L. Kolb, eds., *A Dictionary of the Social Sciences*, The Free Press of Glencoe, 1964, at page 29.

20. Eliade, *The Myth of the Eternal Return*, Bollingen Paperback edition, 1971, at page 103.

21. *Ibid.*

22. *Id.* at page 104.

23. Moran, *The Alphabet*, cited *supra*, at pages 18-20, 32.

Other works consulted in the preparation of this chapter include: John Allegro, *The Dead Sea Scrolls*, Pelican edition, 1964; *Archaeological Discoveries in the Holy Land*, compiled by Archaeological Institute of America, Bonanza Books edition, 1967; David Bakan, *Sigmund Freud and the Jewish Mystical Tradition*, Schocken Books paperback edition, 1969; Albert Camus, *The Myth of Sisyphus and Other Essays*, Random House Vintage Books edition, 1955; C. W. Ceram, *Gods, Graves, and Scholars*, Bantam Books edition, 1972; W. E. LeGros Clark, *History of the Primates*, fifth edition, University of Chicago Press, 1971; Hippolyto Joseph da Costa, *Sketch for the History of the Dionysian Artificers*, introductory essay by Manly P. Hall, Macoy Publishing and Masonic Supply Company, 1936; Loren Eiseley, *The Invisible Pyramid*, Charles Scribner's Sons, 1970; Mircea Eliade, *The Sacred and the Profane*, Harvest Books edition, 1959, and *The Two and the One*, Harper Torchbooks edition, 1971; Henri F. Ellenberger, *The Discovery of the Unconscious*, Basic Books edition, 1970; Erich Fromm, *You Shall Be As Gods*, Fawcett Premier Books edition, 1969; Robert Graves, *The Greek Myths*, 2 vols., Pelican edition, 1960, and *The White Goddess*, Noonday Press edition, 1972; Gerald S. Hawkins, with John B. White, *Stonehenge Decoded*, Delta Books edition, 1965; Alexander Heidel, *The Gilgamesh Epic and Old Testament Parallels*, University of Chicago Press, Phoenix Books edition, 1971; Joseph L. Henderson and Maud Oakes, *The Wisdom of the Serpent: The Myths of Death, Rebirth and Resurrection*, Collier Books edition, 1971; S. H. Hooke, *Middle Eastern Mythology*, Pelican edition, 1971; C. G. Jung, *Aion*, Bollingen edition, 1959, and *The Archetypes and the Collective Unconscious*, Bollingen edition, 1959, and *Psychology and Alchemy*,

Bollingen edition, 1953; Colin McEvedy, *The Penguin Atlas of Ancient History*, 1967; Christopher McIntosh, *The Astrologers and Their Creed: An Historical Outline*, Frederick A. Praeger, 1969; Desmond Morris, *The Naked Ape*, McGraw-Hill, 1967; Sabatino Moscati, *The Face of the Ancient Orient*, Doubleday Anchor Books edition, 1962; *Plutarch's Lives*, Modern Library, undated edition; J. B. Priestly, *Man and Time*, Dell Laurel edition, 1968; Hans Reichenbach, *From Copernicus to Einstein*, Philosophical Library, 1947; M. C. Richard, *Centering: In Pottery, Poetry, and the Person*, Wesleyan University Press, 1972; Bertrand Russell, *A History of Western Philosophy*, Simon & Schuster, 1945; Hugh J. Schonfield, *The Bible Was Right*, Signet Books edition, 1959; Herbert Silberer, *Hidden Symbolism of Alchemy and the Occult Arts* (former title: *Problems of Mysticism and Its Symbolism*), Dover Publications, 1971; Lionel Tiger, *Men in Groups*, Random House, 1969; Norman Winski, *Understanding Jung*, Sherbourne Press, 1971; Yaker, Osmond and Cheek, eds., "Time in the Biblical and Greek Worlds," *The Future of Time: Man's Temporal Environment*, Doubleday and Company, 1971, at pages 15-33; Louise B. Young, ed., *The Mystery of Matter*, Oxford University Press, 1965; Swami Sri Yukteswar, *The Holy Science*, seventh edition, Self-Realization Fellowship, 1972.

24. Eliade, *The Eternal Return*, cited *supra*, at pages 112-37.

Notes to Chapter 4

1. Bertrand Russell, *A History of Western Philosophy*, Simon & Schuster, 1945, at pages 14-21, hereinafter cited as *Western Philosophy*.

2. *Id.* at pages 21, 22.

3. Robert Graves, *The Greek Myths*, vol. 1, Pelican edition, 1969, at page 57, hereinafter cited as *Myths I* (or *Myths II*).

4. Graves, *Myths I*, at page 56.

5. René Dubos, *So Human an Animal*, Charles Scribner's Sons, Lyceum edition, 1968, at pages 103-4, quoting Nietzsche, *The Birth of Tragedy;* C. G. Jung, *Psychological Types*, Bollingen edition, 1971, at page 140.

6. Graves, *Myths I*, at page 349.

7. *Id.* at pages 110, 119.

8. Graves, *The White Goddess*, Noonday Press edition, 1972, at page 45.

9. Allegro, *Sacred Mushroom*, cited *supra*, at page 86.

10. McKenzie, *A Dictionary of the Bible*, cited *supra*, at pages 432-6.

11. Allegro, *Sacred Mushroom*, at pages 34-5.

12. Ernest Wood, *Vedanta Dictionary*, Philosophical Library, 1964, at pages 16, 31-4. *See generally* Clive Johnson, ed., *Vedanta: An Anthology of Hindu Scripture, Commentary and Poetry*, Harper & Row, 1971.

13. Lu K'uan Yü (Charles Luk), *Taoist Yoga: Alchemy and Immortality*, Samuel Weiser, 1972, at page 67.

14. William James, *The Varieties of Religious Experience*, Modern Library, 1929, at pages 370-2.

15. Aldous Huxley, *The Doors of Perception*, Harper & Brothers, 1954, at pages 78-9.

16. Russell, *Western Philosophy*, at page 525.

17. *Id.* at pages 525-40, 557-68.

18. Gilbert Ryle, *The Concept of Mind*, Barnes & Noble Everyday Handbooks, 1971, at pages 15-8.

19. David Bakan, *Sigmund Freud and the Jewish Mystical Tradition*, Schocken Books paperback edition, 1969, at page 3.

20. *Time*, April 28, 1973, at page 83.

21. *Ibid.*

22. Willis Harman, "The New Copernican Revolution," *Stanford Today*, Winter 1969, at page 7.

23. E. A. Burtt, *The Metaphysical Foundations of Modern Science*, Doubleday Anchor Books edition, 1954, at pages 27, 305.

24. Schrödinger, *What Is Life?*, Cambridge University Press, 1967, at page 93.

25. *Time*, cited *supra*, at page 86.

26. Harman, "The New Copernican Revolution," cited *supra*, at page 8.

27. Fromm, *You Shall Be As Gods*, Fawcett Premier Books edition, 1969, at page 50.

28. Aldous Huxley, *The Doors of Perception*, cited *supra*, at page 9.

29. Leary, Metzner and Alpert, *The Psychedelic Experience: A Manual Based on the Tibetan Book of the Dead*, University Books, 1969, at page 12. *See also* Bernard Aaronson and Humphry Osmond, *Psychedelics*, Doubleday Anchor Books edition, 1970; William Braden, *The Private Sea: LSD and the Search for God*, Bantam Books edition, 1968.

30. Alan Watts, *The Joyous Cosmology*, Random House Vintage Books edition, 1970, at page 3.

31. Weil, *The Natural Mind*, Houghton Mifflin Company, paperbound edition, 1973, at page 19.

32. *Id.* at page 184.

33. *Today's Health*, December 1972, at page 8.

34. Edward R. Dewey, with Og Mandino, *Cycles: The Mysterious Forces that Trigger Events*, Manor Books edition, 1973, at page 159.

Notes to Aries

1. Fromm, *You Shall Be As Gods*, cited *supra*, at page 125.

2. Homer W. Smith, *Man and His Gods*, Grosset's Universal Library edition, 1956, at pages 245, 251.

3. Carlo Fiore, *Bud: The Brando I Knew*, Delacorte Press, 1974.

4. Parmenia Migel, *Titania*, Random House, 1967.

Notes to Taurus

1. A. Huxley, *The Doors of Perception*, cited *supra*, at page 17.

2. Higham, *The Films of Orson Welles*, University of California Press, 1970, at page 4.

3. *Id.* at page 1.

4. Koch, "The Night the World Came to an End—Almost," album notes to *War of the Worlds*, Evolution Records.

5. Andrew Sarris, ed., *Interviews with Film Directors*, Avon Discus Books, 1967, at page 547.

Notes to Gemini

1. Gaddis and Gaddis, *The Curious World of Twins*, Hawthorn Books, 1972, at page 156.

2. Richard Hinckley Allen, *Star Names: Their Lore and Meaning*, Dover Publications, 1963, at page 224, hereinafter cited as *Star Names*.

3. *Ibid.*

4. Graves, *Myths I*, cited *supra*, at page 248.

5. *Id.* at page 65.

6. Sartre, *The Words*, Fawcett Premier Books edition, 1968, at page 34.

7. *Id.* at pages 145-6.

Notes to Cancer

1. Moran, *The Alphabet*, cited *supra*, at page 43.

2. *See* Georges Cattaui, *Marcel Proust*, Minerva Press, 1967.

3. Hemingway, *A Moveable Feast*, Charles Scribner's Sons, 1964, at pages 18-21.

4. Carlos Baker, *Hemingway: A Life Story*, Charles Scribner's Sons, 1969, at page 184.

Notes to Leo

1. Moran, *The Alphabet*, cited *supra*, at pages 59, 60.

2. Norman O. Brown, *Love's Body*, Random House Vintage Books edition, 1966, at page 136.

3. *Id.* at page 135.

4. D. H. Lawrence, *Apocalypse*, Viking Press, 1960, at page 169.

5. R. G. H. Siu, *The Portable Dragon*, MIT Press, 1968, at page 11. *See also* Henderson and Oakes, *The Wisdom of the Serpent*, Collier Books edition, 1963; Neumann, *The Origins and History of Consciousness*, Bollingen Paperback edition, 1971, at pages 5-38.

6. Lawrence, *Apocalypse*, cited *supra*, at pages 177, 178.

7. Nancy Milford, *Zelda: A Biography*, Harper & Row, 1970, at page 25.

8. *Id.* at page 39.

9. *Id.* at page 313.

10. Zelda Fitzgerald, *Save Me the Waltz*, Southern Illinois University Press, Arcturus Books edition, 1967, at page 38.

11. *Id.* at page 227.

12. Milford, *Zelda*, at pages 153, 211.

13. Henri F. Ellenberger, *The Discovery of the Unconscious*, Basic Books edition, 1970, at pages 447-8. *See also* Ellenberger, "Freud in Perspective," *Psychology Today*, March 1973, at page 58.

14. Clive Johnson, ed., *Vedanta: An Anthology of Hindu Scripture, Commentary and Poetry*, cited *supra*, at page 1.

15. Grover Smith, ed., *Letters of Aldous Huxley*, Harper & Row, 1969, at pages 862-5.

Notes to Virgo

1. Moran, *The Alphabet*, cited *supra*, at page 61.

2. Allen, *Star Names*, cited *supra*, at page 454.

3. Jess Stearn, *The Search for a Soul: Taylor Caldwell's Psychic Lives*, Doubleday and Company, 1973, at page 20, hereinafter cited as *Psychic Lives*.

4. Taylor Caldwell, *On Growing Up Tough*, Fawcett Crest Books edition, 1971, at page 118.

5. Stearn, *Psychic Lives*, at page 311.

6. *Id.* at page 1.

7. *Id.* at pages 5-6.

8. *Id.* at page 314.

9. *Id.* at page 310.

10. *Id.* at page 70.

11. *Id.* at page 315.

12. *Id.* at page 311.

13. *See generally*, *On Growing Up Tough*, cited *supra*.

14. Stearn, *Psychic Lives*, at page 311.

15. Taylor Caldwell, introduction to *Dear and Glorious Physician*, Bantam Books edition, 1962, at page 1.

16. Stearn, *Psychic Lives*, at pages 313-15.

17. Works consulted for the biographical sketch of D. H. Lawrence include: Ford Madox Ford, "D. H. Lawrence," *Portraits from Life*, Henry Regnery Company, Gateway edition, 1937, at pages 93-120; George H. Ford, *Double Measure: A Study of the Novels and Stories of D. H. Lawrence*, The Norton Library, 1969; Horace Gregory, *D. H. Lawrence, Pilgrim of the Apocalypse*, Grove Press, 1957.

18. Harry T. Moore and Warren Roberts, *D. H. Lawrence and His World*, Viking Press, 1966, at page 111.

19. Mark Schorer, *D. H. Lawrence*, Dell Publishing Company, 1968, at page 67.

20. Aldous Huxley, ed., *The Letters of D. H. Lawrence*, Viking Press, 1932, at page xv.

21. Plato, *Symposium*, *The Philosophy of Plato*, Erwin Edman, ed., Modern Library, 1958, at pages 368-9.

22. Rollo May, "The Daemonic: Love and Death," *Psychology Today*, February 1968, at pages 16-7.

23. *Ibid.*
24. Schorer, *Lawrence,* cited *supra,* at page 89, italics mine.
25. *Ibid.*
26. May, "The Daemonic: Love and Death," cited *supra,* at page 20.
27. *Id.* at page 23.
28. Aldington, *D. H. Lawrence,* Collier Books edition, 1967, at page 53.

Notes to Libra

1. Moran, *The Alphabet,* cited *supra,* at page 65.
2. Edward Albertson, *Understanding the Kabbalah,* Sherbourne Press, 1973, at page 19.
3. Homer W. Smith, *From Fish to Philosopher,* Natural History Library edition, 1961, at pages 38, 141.
4. David Bakan, *Sigmund Freud and the Jewish Mystical Tradition,* cited *supra,* at pages 282-5. *See also* Penelope Balogh, *Freud: A Biographical Introduction,* Charles Scribner's Sons, 1971, at pages 42-53; Freud, *The Interpretation of Dreams,* Modern Library, 1950, at page 268; Ernest Jones, *The Life and Work of Sigmund Freud,* Doubleday Anchor Books edition, 1963, at page 258; C. G. Jung, "Approaching the Unconscious," *Man and His Symbols,* Dell Laurel edition, 1972, at pages 3-95, and *Psychology and Alchemy,* Bollingen edition, 1953, at pages 109, 233, and "The Structure of the Psyche," *The Portable Jung,* Joseph Campbell, ed., Viking Press, 1972, at pages 23-46.
5. Omar V. Garrison, *Medical Astrology,* University Books, 1971, at page 171. For another view, *see* Gavin Arthur, *The Circle of Sex,* University Books, 1966.
6. Works consulted for the biographical sketch of F. Scott Fitzgerald include Morley Callaghan, *That Summer in Paris,* Coward-McCann, 1963; Malcolm Cowley, ed., *The Stories of F. Scott Fitzgerald,* Charles Scribner's Sons, 1953; F. Scott Fitzgerald, *The Crack Up,* New Directions paperback edition, 1956; Sheilah Graham and Gerold Frank, *Beloved Infidel,* Bantam Books edition, 1959; Aaron Latham, *Crazy Sundays: F. Scott Fitzgerald in Hollywood,* Pocket Books edition, 1972.
7. Arthur Mizener, *The Far Side of Paradise,* Houghton Mifflin Company, 1951, at pages 117-8.
8. *Id.* at page 185.
9. Milford, *Zelda,* cited *supra,* at pages 114-5.
10. *Id.* at page 55.
11. Calvin Tomkins, *Living Well Is the Best Revenge,* Signet Books edition, 1972, at page 115.
12. *Id.* at page 12.
13. *Id.* at page 13.
14. Andrew Turnbull, *Scott Fitzgerald,* Charles Scribner's Sons, 1962, at pages 268-9, 312-3.

15. Turnbull, ed., *The Letters of F. Scott Fitzgerald*, Bodley Head, 1964, at pages 308-11.

Notes to Scorpio

1. Moran, *The Alphabet*, cited *supra*, at pages 63-5.
2. Leonard, *Education and Ecstasy*, Dell Publishing Co., Delta Books edition, 1968, at page 4.
3. Hans Heibert, *Ibsen: A Portrait of the Artist*, University of Miami Press, 1967, at page 129.
4. Rossell Hope Robbins, *The Encyclopedia of Witchcraft and Demonology*, s.v. "Vampire."
5. Bram Stoker, *Personal Reminiscences of Henry Irving*, vol. 1, William Heinemann, 1906, at page 30.
6. *Id.* vol. 1 at page 31.
7. *Ibid.*
8. *Id.* vol. 1 at page 56.
9. *Id.* vol. 1 at page 123.
10. *Ibid.*
11. *Id.* vol. 2 at pages 122-4.
12. *Id.* vol. 2 at page 130.
13. *Id.* vol. 1 at page 370.
14. Raymond T. McNally and Radu Florescu, *In Search of Dracula*, New York Graphic Society, 1972, at page 178.
15. *Id.* at page 177.
16. *Id.* at page 11.
17. Stoker, *Dracula*, Doubleday and Company, 1973, at page 58.
18. Stoker, *Personal Reminiscences of Henry Irving*, vol. 2, at page 130.
19. Leonard Wolf, *A Dream of Dracula*, Little, Brown & Co., 1972, at page 206.
20. *Id.* at page 254.
21. *Id.* at page 248.
22. R. D. Laing, *The Divided Self*, Penguin Books edition, 1965, at page 38.
23. A. R. Jones, "On 'Daddy,' " *The Art of Sylvia Plath*, Indiana University Press, Midland Books edition, 1971, at page 234.
24. A. Alvarez, *The Savage God*, cited *supra*, at page 26. The author credits Michael Bakunin with the quoted statement.
25. May, "The Daemonic: Love and Death," cited *supra*, at page 17.
26. May, *Love and Will*, W. W. Norton and Company, 1969, at page 319.
27. Also consulted for the biographical note on St. Augustine: John Fines, *Who's Who in the Middle Ages*, Anthony Blond Ltd., 1970, at pages 25-9.
28. Stephen Erlewine, *The Circle Book of Charts*, Circle Books, 1972, at page 3.

29. St. Augustine, *Confessions*, F. J. Sheed, trans., Sheed and Ward, 1950, at page 41.

30. *Id.* at page 170.

31. Russell, *Western Philosophy*, cited *supra*, at pages 351-2.

Notes to Sagittarius

1. Moran, *The Alphabet*, cited *supra*, at pages 29, 35-6, 69-70.

2. *The Tragedy of Doctor Faustus*, Folger Library Pocket Books edition, 1971, at page 71.

3. Goethe, *Faust: A Tragedy*, Miss Swanwick, trans., Thomas Y. Crowell and Company, 1882, at page 436.

4. Gunther S. Stent, *The Coming of the Golden Age*, Natural History Press, 1969, at pages 82-6, hereinafter cited as *Golden Age. See also* Joseph Campbell, *Myths to Live By*, Viking Press, 1972, at pages 82-3; Oswald Spengler, *The Decline of the West*, Arthur Helps, ed., Alfred A. Knopf, 1962, at page 165.

5. *See* Barbara Watters, *Horary Astrology and the Judgment of Events*, Valhalla Publishing Company, 1973, at page 208; and *Sex and the Outer Planets*, Valhalla paperback edition, 1971, at page 83, hereinafter cited as *Outer Planets. See also* Doris Chase Doane, *Horoscopes of the U.S. Presidents*, second edition, Professional Astrologers, 1971, at page 13.

6. Watters, *Outer Planets*, at page 84.

7. Sybil Leek, *Astrological Guide to the Presidential Candidates*, Ace Books, 1972, at page 16.

8. Leon Wolff, *Lockout*, Harper & Row, 1965.

9. Leo Rosten, *People I Have Loved, Known or Admired*, Pocket Books edition, 1973, at pages 63-4.

10. Muggeridge, "The Totemization of Sir Winston Churchill," *Esquire*, October 1973, at page 482.

11. Dorothy M. Johnson, *Western Badmen*, Ballantine Books edition, 1973, at pages 94-113.

12. Dee Brown, *Showdown at Little Big Horn*, Berkeley Medallion Books edition, 1972, at page 190.

13. Works consulted for the biographical sketch of Samuel Clemens include: *The Autobiography of Mark Twain*, Charles Neider, ed., Harper & Brothers, 1959; Van Wyck Brooks, *The Ordeal of Mark Twain*, revised edition, Dutton Paperback, 1970; Bernard DeVoto, *Mark Twain's America* and *Mark Twain at Work*, Sentry editions, 1967; Margaret Duckett, *Mark Twain and Bret Harte*, University of Oklahoma Press, 1964; Paul Fatout, *Mark Twain on the Lecture Circuit*, Indiana University Press, 1960; Hamlin Hill, *Mark Twain: God's Fool*, Harper & Row, 1973; Mark Twain, *Letters from the Earth*, Bernard DeVoto, ed., Fawcett Crest edition, 1963.

14. Fiedler, *Love and Death in the American Novel*, revised edition, Stein & Day, 1966, especially at pages 47-55, hereinafter cited as *Love and Death.*

15. Graves, *The White Goddess*, cited *supra*, at page 24.

16. Fiedler, *Love and Death*, at pages 142, 270-89.

17. Justin Kaplan, *Mr. Clemens and Mark Twain*, Simon & Schuster, 1966, at page 364, hereinafter cited as *Mr. Clemens*.

18. Fiedler, *Love and Death*, at page 115.

19. Frederick Anderson, ed., *A Pen Warmed-up in Hell: Mark Twain in Protest*, Harper & Row, 1972, at page x, hereinafter cited as *Protest*.

20. *Id.* at page xvi.

21. Kaplan, *Mr. Clemens*, at pages 258, 261-2.

22. Anderson, ed., *Protest*, at page 4.

23. Janet Smith, ed., *Mark Twain on Man and Beast*, Lawrence Hill & Co., paperbound edition, 1972, at page 213.

24. Mark Twain, *The Mysterious Stranger*, William M. Gibson, ed., University of California Press, paperbound edition, 1970, at page 11, hereinafter cited as *Mysterious Stranger*.

25. *The Family Mark Twain*, biographical summary by Albert Bigelow Paine, Harper & Brothers, undated edition, at page 1181. *Cf. Mysterious Stranger*.

26. *Mysterious Stranger*, at pages 1-3.

27. Kaplan, *Mr. Clemens*, at page 326.

28. *Id.* at pages 352-3.

29. Milton Meltzer, *Mark Twain Himself*, Bonanza Books edition, 1960, at page 288.

30. Helen Kazantzakis, *Nikos Kazantzakis: A Biography Based on His Letters*, Amy Mims, trans., Clarion Books edition, 1970, at page 81.

31. *Id.* at page 83.

32. Colin Wilson, *Introduction to the New Existentialism*, Houghton Mifflin Company, 1967, at page 43.

33. Colin Wilson, *New Pathways in Psychology: Maslow and the Post-Freudian Revolution*, Taplinger Publishing Company, 1972, at page 41, hereinafter cited as *New Pathways*.

34. *Id.* at pages 26, 34.

35. Maslow, *Religions, Values and Peak Experiences*, Viking Compass Books edition, 1970, at pages vii-xii, hereinafter cited as *Peak Experiences*. *See generally* Maslow, *Toward a Psychology of Being*, second edition, Van Nostrand Reinhold Company, 1968; *New Knowledge of Human Values*, Maslow, ed., Henry Regnery Company, Gateway edition, 1970.

36. Maslow, *Peak Experiences*, at pages 59-68.

37. Wilson, *New Pathways*, at page 15.

38. *Id.* at page 41.

39. Maslow, "Self-Actualizing People," *The World of Psychology*, vol. 2, G. B. Levitas, ed., George Braziller, 1963, at page 528.

40. Anderson, ed., *Protest*, cited *supra*, at page 183.

41. Meltzer, *Mark Twain Himself*, cited *supra*, at page 288.

42. Stent, *Golden Age*, cited *supra*, at pages 87-8.

43. *Id.* at page 89.

44. *Id.* at page 95.

45. *Id.* at page 123.

46. *Id.* at pages 137-8.

47. Jonas, *Visceral Learning,* Viking Press, 1973, at page 131.

Notes to Capricorn

1. Moran, *The Alphabet,* cited *supra,* at pages 73-4.

2. T. H. White, *The Bestiary,* Capricorn Books edition, 1960, at pages 40-2.

3. José Torres, *Sting Like a Bee,* Curtis Books edition, 1971, at page 91; *Current Biography,* 1963, at pages 72-5.

4. Torres, *Sting Like a Bee,* at page 148.

5. *The Compleat Astrologer,* McGraw-Hill Book Company, 1971, at page 124.

6. Robert Graves and Raphael Patai, *Hebrew Myths: The Book of Genesis,* McGraw-Hill Paperback edition, 1966, at page 116, hereinafter cited as *Hebrew Myths. See also* Jung, *Symbols of Transformation,* Bollingen edition, 1956, at page 198.

7. S. H. Hooke, *Middle Eastern Mythology,* Pelican edition, 1971, at pages 40-58; Graves and Patai, *Hebrew Myths,* at page 29.

8. Hooke, *Middle Eastern Mythology,* at pages 26-7.

9. *Id.* at page 29; Graves and Patai, *Hebrew Myths,* at page 23.

10. Hooke, *Middle Eastern Mythology,* at pages 44-5; Graves and Patai, *Hebrew Myths,* at page 23.

11. Graves and Patai, *Hebrew Myths,* at pages 23, 24. *See also* Heinrich Zimmer, *Myths and Symbols in Indian Art and Civilization,* Joseph Campbell, ed., Princeton University Press, paperback edition, 1972, at pages 3, 52, 123-4.

12. Paramahansa Yogananda, *Autobiography of a Yogi,* tenth edition, Self-Realization Fellowship, 1969, at page 4, hereinafter cited as *Autobiography.*

Other works consulted for the biographical note on Paramahansa Yogananda include the following, published by the Self-Realization Fellowship: *The Life Story of Dr. M. W. Lewis,* 1960; Paramahansa Yogananda, *Metaphysical Meditations,* 1967, and *Science of Religion,* 1953; Swami Sri Yukteswar, *The Holy Science,* seventh edition, 1972. Other references include: W. Y. Evans-Wentz, *Tibetan Yoga and Secret Doctrines,* Oxford University Press, 1971; Charles Johnston, *The Yoga Sutras of Patanjali,* Stuart & Watkins, 1968; *The Song Celestial or Bhagavad-Gita,* Sir Edwin Arnold, trans., Routledge & Kegan Paul Ltd., 1972; an interview with Sister Karan Lanza of the Self-Realization Fellowship at the Mt. Washington headquarters.

13. Yogananda, *Autobiography,* at pages 18-9.

14. *Self-Realization Fellowship: Golden Anniversary,* Self-Realization Fellowship, 1970, at page 20. This work is relied upon for all dates of events in the life of Yogananda.

15. Yogananda, *Autobiography,* at page 230.

16. *Id.* at page 363.

17. *Id.* at page 445.

18. *Id.* at page 400.

19. *Paramahansa Yogananda: In Memoriam,* Self-Realization Fellowship, 1958, at page 16, hereinafter cited as *In Memoriam.*

20. *Id.* at page 24.

21. *Id.* at pages 43-4.

22. *Id.* at page 44.

23. *Time,* August 4, 1952, at page 57.

24. Yogananda, *Autobiography,* at pages 209-10; *In Memoriam,* at pages 93-6.

25. *See, e.g., Self-Realization* Magazine, Fall 1973, at pages 21-5, 28-33.

26. *Christian Century,* April 9, 1947, at page 464.

27. *Time,* March 17, 1947, at pages 108-9.

28. Yogananda, *Autobiography,* at page 339.

29. *The Teachings of Don Juan: A Yaqui Way of Knowledge,* Ballantine Books edition, 1971, at page 1, hereinafter cited as *Teachings.*

30. *Time,* March 5, 1973, at page 38.

31. *Id.* at page 43.

32. *Ibid.*; Sam Keen, "Sorcerer's Apprentice," *Psychology Today,* December 1972, at pages 90-102.

33. *Journey to Ixtlan,* Simon and Schuster, 1972, at page 220.

34. *Ibid.*

35. Works consulted for this section on our Capricorn presidents include: Samuel Hopkins Adams, *The Godlike Daniel,* Sears Publishing Company, 1930; Thomas A. Bailey, *Presidential Greatness,* Appleton-Century, 1966; Wilfred E. Binkley, *The Man in the White House,* Johns Hopkins Press, 1958; Marcus Cunliffe, *The American Heritage History of the Presidency,* 1968, and *American Presidents and the Presidency,* American Heritage Press, 1972; Doris Chase Doane, *Horoscopes of the U.S. Presidents,* second edition, Professional Astrologers, 1971; Samuel Eliot Morison, *The Oxford History of the American People,* 1965; Allan Nevins, *Ordeal of the Union, Fruits of Manifest Destiny, 1847-1852,* vol. 1, Charles Scribner's Sons, 1947; Frank H. Severance, ed., *Millard Fillmore Papers,* 2 vols., Kraus Reprint Company, 1970; Tim Taylor, *The Book of Presidents,* Arno Press, 1972; David C. Whitney, *The American Presidents,* Doubleday and Company, 1967.

36. Mazlish, *In Search of Nixon,* Penguin Books edition, 1973, at page 146.

37. *Id.* at pages 146-7.

38. *See* William L. Shirer, "The Hubris of a President," *The Nation,* January 22, 1972, at pages 105-8.

Notes to Aquarius

1. Vera W. Reid, *Towards Aquarius,* Arc Books edition, 1971, at page 13. *Cf.* Swami Sri Yukteswar, *The Holy Science,* Self-Realization Fellowship, 1972, at pages x-xvi.

2. J. Robert Evans, "Plug-In Happiness," *San Diego* Magazine, December 1972, at page 73.

3. Constance A. Newland, *Myself and I*, Signet Books edition, 1962.

4. Marcia Moore and Mark Douglas, *Astrology: The Divine Science*, Arcane Publications, 1971, at page 4.

Notes to Pisces

1. Yogananda, *Autobiography*, cited *supra*, at page 177.

2. Robert Graves, *King Jesus*, Farrar, Straus & Cudahy, 1946, at page 3.

3. Darrach, "The Day Bobby Blew It," *Playboy*, July 1973, at page 150.

4. *Ibid.*

5. *Ibid. See also* Thomas Powers, "Showdown in Reykjavik: Bobby Fischer Prepares for His Most Important Match," *The Rolling Stone Reader*, Warner Paperback Library edition, 1974, at pages 283-301.

6. Romola Nijinsky, *Nijinsky*, Pocket Books edition, 1972, at page 15.

Other works consulted for the biographical sketch of Nijinsky include: Richard Buckle, *Nijinsky*, Simon & Schuster, 1971; Romola Nijinsky, *The Last Years of Nijinsky*, Victor Gollancz Ltd., 1952; Romola Nijinsky, ed., *The Diary of Vaslav Nijinsky*, University of California Press, 1971; John Percival, *The World of Diaghilev*, Studio Vista/Dutton Pictureback, 1971.

7. Romola Nijinsky, *Nijinsky*, at page 293.

8. *Id.* at page 347.

9. Jung, "Sign of the Fishes," *Aion*, Bollingen edition, 1959, at pages 80-1.

10. *Id.* at page 87.

11. Bucke, *Cosmic Consciousness*, Dutton Paperback edition, 1969, at page 9.

12. *Id.* at unpaginated introduction.

13. *Id.* at page 17.

14. Introduction to *Cosmic Consciousness*, quoting *Proceedings and Transactions of the Royal Society of Canada*, 1872, at pages 159-96.

15. Bucke, *Cosmic Consciousness*, at page 9.

16. *Id.* at unpaginated introduction.

17. *Ibid.*

18. Wallace, ed., *Macmillan Dictionary of Canadian Biography*, third edition, 1963, at page 91.

19. Pike, *The Other Side*, Doubleday and Company, 1968, at page 211.

20. *Id.* at page 212.

21. Dean Jennings, *We Only Kill Each Other*, Fawcett World Library edition, 1967, at pages 20, 209.

22. *Id.* at page 29.

23. *Id.* at page 39.

Notes to Chapter 7

1. Calvin S. Hall and Gardner Lindzey, *Theories of Personality*, John Wiley and Sons, 1970, at pages 88-9.

2. *Id.* at page 90.

3. C. G. Jung, *Modern Man in Search of a Soul,* Harvest Books edition, 1933, at page 93.

4. Hall and Lindzey, *Theories of Personality,* at page 111.

5. *Ibid.*

6. Harriet Mann, Miriam Siegler, Humphry Osmond, "Four Types of Personality and Four Ways of Perceiving Time," *Psychology Today,* December 1972, at page 76.

7. *Id.* at page 84.

8. Draper, *The Humors and Shakespeare's Characters,* Duke University Press, 1945, at page v.

9. *Id.* at page 10.

10. *Id.* at page 14.

11. Robert Burton, *The Anatomy of Melancholy,* Floyd Dell and Paul Jordan-Smith, ed., Tudor Publishing Company, 1927, at page xiii.

12. *See Galen on the Natural Faculties,* Arthur John Brock, trans., Loeb Classical Library, 1963.

13. Graves and Patai, *Hebrew Myths,* cited *supra,* at page 64.

Notes to Chapter 8

1. Still, *Of Time, Tides and Inner Clocks,* Stackpole Books, 1972, at pages 59-60.

2. P. I. H. Naylor, *Astrology: An Historical Examination,* Robert Maxwell, 1967, at page 24.

Notes to Chapter 9

1. Allen, *Star Names,* cited *supra,* at page 383.

Notes to Chapter 10

1. *The Five Books of M. Manilius,* National Astrological Library, 1953, at page 155.

2. Lancelot Hogben, *Mathematics in the Making,* Macdonald and Company Ltd., 1960, at page 140.

3. Ptolemy, *Tetrabiblos,* W. G. Waddell and F. E. Robbins, trans., Loeb Classical Library, 1971, at pages 103-7.

4. Titus Burkhardt, *Alchemy,* Penguin Books edition, 1971, at page 88.

5. Ptolemy, *Tetrabiblos,* at page 443.

6. *Id.* at pages 443-5.

7. *Id.* at page 445.

8. *Id.* at page 447.

9. C. G. Jung, *Psychological Reflections,* Bollingen Edition, 1970, at page 39.

10. Rupert Gleadow, *The Origin of the Zodiac,* Castle Books, 1968, at pages 84-5. *Cf. Epinomis* in *Collected Dialogues of Plato,* Bollingen edition, 1971, at pages 1517-1533.

11. Aldous Huxley, *The Doors of Perception*, cited *supra*, at pages 22-4.

12. Joseph Campbell, *The Hero With a Thousand Faces*, Bollingen Paperback edition, 1972, at page 18, n.18, hereinafter cited as *Thousand Faces*.

13. Graves, *Myths I*, cited *supra*, at page 29.

14. *Id.* at page 39.

15. *Id.* at pages 35-7.

16. Allegro, *Sacred Mushroom*, cited *supra*, at page 104.

17. Graves, *Myths I*, at pages 9-10.

18. *Id.* at page 51.

19. Manly P. Hall, "The Myth of Dionysus," introduction to Hippolyto Joseph da Costa, *Sketch for the History of the Dionysian Artificers*, Macoy Publishing and Masonic Supply Company, 1936, at pages xlii-xliii.

20. *Collected Poems of Dylan Thomas*, New Directions Books, 1953, at page 197.

21. Graves and Patai, *Hebrew Myths*, cited *supra*, at page 229.

22. Graves, *The White Goddess*, cited *supra*, at page 161, n.1; McKenzie, *A Dictionary of the Bible*, cited *supra*, at page 718.

23. Campbell, *Thousand Faces*, at pages 276-7.

Other works consulted in the preparation of this and the following sections of this chapter include: J. E. Cirlot, *A Dictionary of Symbols*, Philosophical Library, 1962; Bergen Evans, *Dictionary of Mythology*, Dell Laurel edition, 1970; *Larousse Encyclopedia of Mythology*, Prometheus Press, 1960; J. E. Zimmerman, *Dictionary of Classical Mythology*, Bantam Matrix edition, 1971.

24. *See* Paul Foster Case, *The Tarot*, Macoy Publishing Company, 1947, at pages 29-30.

25. Burkhardt, *Alchemy*, cited *supra*, at page 91.

26. Norman O. Brown, *Life Against Death*, Wesleyan University Press, 1970, at page 281.

27. Wallace Budge, *The Gods of the Egyptians*, vol. 2, Dover Publications, 1969, at page 97, and vol. 1 at page 78.

28. Elmer O'Brien, S.J., *The Essential Plotinus*, Mentor Books edition, 1964, at page 217. *See also* Grace Turnbull, *The Essence of Plotinus*, Oxford University Press, 1934, at pages 14-5.

29. Turnbull, *The Essence of Plotinus*, at page 14.

30. P. I. H. Naylor, *Astrology: An Historical Examination*, cited *supra*, at page 37.

31. *Ibid.*

32. Ostrander and Schroeder, *Psychic Discoveries Behind the Iron Curtain*, Prentice-Hall, 1970, at page 341.

33. *Seven Types of Ambiguity*, Meridian Books edition, 1960, at page xi.

34. *Id.* at pages xi-xiii, emphasis added.

35. Robert Graves, *The White Goddess*, cited *supra*, at pages 448, 480.

36. Aldous Huxley, *The Doors of Perception*, cited *supra*, at page 17. *See, e.g., Meister Eckhart*, James M. Clark and John V. Skinner, trans., Fontana Library edition, 1963, at pages 64-7.

37. Burkhardt, *Alchemy*, cited *supra*, at pages 44-8, 64-5, 130-8.

38. *Id.* at page 89.

39. Graves, *Myths I*, cited *supra*, at page 64.

40. *Ibid. See also* Norman O. Brown, *Hermes the Thief: The Evolution of a Myth*, Random House Vintage Books edition, 1969.

41. Campbell, *Thousand Faces*, cited *supra*, at pages 72-3.

42. *Id.* at page 73, n.31.

43. Isaac Asimov, *The New Intelligent Man's Guide to Science*, Basic Books edition, 1965, at pages 757-9. *See also* Asimov, "Our Cerebrum," *The Human Brain*, Signet Books edition, 1965, at pages 161-94.

44. *See* Aldous Huxley, *Heaven and Hell*, Harper Colophon Books edition, 1963.

45. Graves, *Myths I*, at pages 67, 73.

46. *Id.* at page 68.

47. Campbell, *Thousand Faces*, at pages 302-3.

48. *Id.* at pages 213-4; Graves and Patai, *Hebrew Myths*, cited *supra*, at pages 26-7; Allen, *Star Names*, cited *supra*, at page 339; Joseph Kaster, *Putnam's Concise Mythological Dictionary*, fourth edition, s.v. "Ashtart."

49. Graves and Patai, *Hebrew Myths*, at page 27.

50. Campbell, *Thousand Faces*, at page 214.

51. Graves, *Myths I*, at page 71.

52. Wayland Young, *Eros Denied: Sex in Western Society*, Grove Press, 1964, at page 32.

53. *Bray's Universal Dictionary of Mythology*, Apollo edition, s.v. "Mars"; Kaster, *Putnam's Concise Mythological Dictionary*, s.v. "Ares."

54. *Brewer's Dictionary of Phrase and Fable*, s.v. "Mars."

55. Watters, *Outer Planets*, cited *supra*, at pages 80-1.

56. Nancy Topping Bazin, *Virginia Woolf and the Androgynous Vision*, Rutgers University Press, 1973, at page 3.

57. Margaret Hone, *The Modern Text-Book of Astrology*, L. N. Fowler and Company, 1971, at page 35.

58. Pike, *The Other Side*, cited *supra*, at page 209.

59. *Ibid.*

60. Graves, *Myths I*, at pages 89-92.

61. Moran, *The Alphabet*, cited *supra*, at page 26.

62. Rupert Gleadow, *The Origin of the Zodiac*, Castle Books edition, 1968, at page 211.

Notes to Chapter 11

1. Michel Gauquelin, *The Cosmic Clocks*, Henry Regnery Company, 1967, at pages 181-2.

2. Hopkins, *Elvis: A Biography*, Warner Paperback Library, 1972, at page 23, hereinafter cited as *Elvis. See also* Eisen, ed., *The Age of Rock*, 2 vols., 1969-1970; esp. Booth, "A Hound Dog to the Manor Born," vol. I, at pages 16-27.

3. *Elvis,* at page 45.
4. *Id.* at pages 26-7.
5. *Id.* at pages 123-4.
6. *Id.* at page 249.

Notes to Chapter 12

1. Ptolemy, *Tetrabiblos,* cited *supra,* at page 73.
2. *Id.* at pages 73-5.
3. *Id.* at page 72, n.2.
4. Charles E. Luntz, *Vocational Guidance by Astrology,* Llewellyn Publications, 1971, at pages 24-5.
5. Edwin Miller, "They Talk About Freedom," *Seventeen Interviews: Film Stars and Superstars,* Macmillan Company, 1970, at pages 278-9.
6. *Id.* at page 282.
7. *Ibid.*
8. *Id.* at pages 281-2.
9. *Id.* at page 280.
10. Rudhyar, *First Steps in the Study of Birth Charts,* Humanistic Astrology Series, no. 4, 1970, at page 8.
11. References consulted for the biographical note on Marlene Dietrich include: John Baxter, *Hollywood in the Thirties,* Paperback Library edition, 1970; Leslie Frewin, *Dietrich,* Avon Publishing Company, 1972; Sarris, ed., *Interviews with Film Directors,* cited *supra,* at pages 479-500; Herman G. Weinberg, *Josef von Sternberg,* Dutton Paperback edition, 1967.
12. Marc Penfield, *An Astrological Who's Who,* Arcane Publications, 1972, at page 221.
References consulted for the note on Henry VIII include: Bowle, *Henry VIII,* Little, Brown and Company, 1964; Marie Louise Bruce, *Anne Boleyn,* Warner Paperback Library, 1972; *Columbia Encyclopedia,* third edition, s.v. "Henry VIII."
13. N. Brysson Morrison, *The Private Life of Henry VIII,* Paperback Library edition, 1972, at page 143.
14. Fred Hoyle, *From Stonehenge to Modern Cosmology,* W. H. Freeman and Company, 1972, at page 51.
15. Hawkins, *Beyond Stonehenge,* Harper & Row, 1973, at page 216.
16. *See* Peter Tompkins, *Secrets of the Great Pyramid,* Harper & Row, 1971, at page xiii.
17. Hawkins, *Beyond Stonehenge,* at page 216.
18. Tompkins, *Secrets of the Great Pyramid,* at page 33.
19. Works consulted for this note on periodicity and biorhythms include: Michel Gauquelin, *Cosmic Influences on Human Behavior,* Stein & Day, 1973; Marvin Karlins and Lewis M. Andrews, *Biofeedback,* Warner Paperback Library, 1973; Huburtus Strughold, M.D., *Your Body Clock,* Charles Scribner's Sons, 1971; Ritchie R. Ward, *The Living Clocks,* Alfred A. Knopf, 1971.
20. George Thommen, *Is This Your Day?,* Crown Publishers, 1964, at page 19.

21. Gay Gaer Luce, *Body Time: Physiological Rhythms and Social Stress,* Pantheon Books edition, 1971, at page 25.

22. *Id.* at page 55.

23. Thommen, *Is This Your Day?,* at pages 25-6.

24. John Anthony West and Jan Gerhard Toonder, *The Case for Astrology,* Coward-McCann, 1970, at pages 178-80; Gauquelin, *The Cosmic Clocks,* cited *supra,* at pages 111-2.

25. West and Toonder, *The Case for Astrology,* at page 181.

26. J. H. Nelson, "Short Wave Radio and Planetary Arrangements," *American Federation of Astrologers Bulletin,* vol. 35, no. 5, May 1973, at pages 43-5.

27. Ake Wallenquist, *Dictionary of Astronomical Terms,* Sune Engelbrektson, ed. and trans., Natural History Press edition, s.v. "solar wind."

28. Lyall Watson, *Supernature,* Anchor Press, 1973, at pages 28-9. *See also* Gauquelin, *The Cosmic Clocks,* at page 113.

29. Gauquelin, *The Cosmic Clocks,* at page 313.

30. Watson, *Supernature,* at pages 29-30, 38.

31. *Id.* at page 53.

32. Marilyn Ferguson, *The Brain Revolution: The Frontiers of Mind Research,* Taplinger Publishing Company, 1973, at page 27.

33. Dr. Harold Saxton Burr, *The Fields of Life,* Ballantine Books edition, 1972, at page 6.

34. *Id.* at page 130.

35. *Id.* at pages 11-2.

36. Pachter, *Magic Into Science,* Henry Schuman, 1951; *Paracelsus: Selected Writings,* second revised edition, Guterman, trans., 1969, at page xlvii.

37. *Paracelsus,* at pages 18, 248-9.

38. Karl von Reichenbach, *The Odic Force,* O'Byrne, trans., University Books, 1968, at pages 91-3. *See also* Colin Wilson, *The Occult,* Random House, 1971, at pages 537-9.

39. John Kilner, *The Aura,* Samuel Weiser, 1973, at pages ii-iii.

40. Burr, *The Fields of Life,* at page 116.

41. *See* Krippner and Rubin, eds., *Galaxies of Life,* Gordon and Breach, Interface Books edition, 1973. *See also* Ostrander and Schroeder, "Kirlian Photography—Pictures of the Aura?," *Psychic Discoveries Behind the Iron Curtain,* Prentice-Hall, 1970, at pages 186-198.

Notes to Chapter 13

1. Wolfenstein, "Two Types of Jewish Mothers," *The World of Psychology,* vol. 2, cited *supra,* at page 209.

2. Penelope Balogh, *Freud: A Biographical Introduction,* Charles Scribner's Sons, 1971, at pages 43, 47.

3. *Id.* at page 99. Additional works consulted for biographical information about Sigmund Freud include Ellenberger, *The Discovery of the Unconscious,* Basic Books edition, 1970; Freud, *The Origins of Psycho-Analysis: Letters to Wilhelm*

Fliess, Basic Books edition, 1954; *C. G. Jung Letters,* Gerhard Adler, ed., with Aniela Jaffé, vol. 1, Princeton University Press, 1973; *The Freud/Jung Letters,* William McGuire, ed., Princeton University Press, 1974.

4. Joseph Campbell and Henry Morton Robinson, *A Skeleton Key to Finnegans Wake,* Viking Compass Books edition, 1963, at pages 25-6, hereinafter cited as *Skeleton Key.*

5. Graves, *The White Goddess,* cited *supra,* at pages 74-5, 123.

6. *Id.* at page 141.

7. Beckett, "Dante ... Bruno. Vico. . Joyce," *James Joyce/Finnegans Wake: A Symposium,* New Directions Paperback, 1972, at page 8.

8. *Id.* at page 6.

9. Martin Gardner, *The Annotated Alice,* Bramhall House, 1960, at page 271.

10. Campbell and Robinson, *Skeleton Key,* at page 27.

11. *Ibid.*

12. Wilson, *Axel's Castle,* Charles Scribner's Sons, 1948, at pages 234-5, italics mine.

13. Peter Koenig, "Man and the Universal Equation, A Sketch of Raymond B. Cattell," *Psychology Today,* July 1973, at page 43.

14. Gardner Murphy, *Personality: A Bisocial Approach to Origins of Structure,* Harper & Brothers, 1947, at pages 899-902.

15. William H. Sheldon, *Psychology and the Promethean Will,* Harper & Brothers, 1936.

16. Koenig, "Man and the Universal Equation," cited *supra,* at page 43. *See generally,* Cattell, *The Scientific Analysis of Personality,* Aldine Publishing Company, 1965.

17. *See The Freud/Jung Letters,* William McGuire, ed., Princeton University Press, 1974; *C. G. Jung Letters,* Gerhard Adler, ed., with Aniela Jaffé, vol. I, Princeton University Press, 1973.

18. Charles Rycroft, "Is Freudian Symbolism a Myth?," *The New York Review of Books,* January 24, 1974, vol. XX, nos. 21 & 22, at page 13.

19. *C. G. Jung Letters,* at page 24.

20. *The Life and Work of Sigmund Freud,* vol. 3, Basic Books edition, 1957, at page 388.

Notes to Chapter 14

1. Tuckerman, *Planetary, Lunar and Solar Positions: 601 B.C. to A.D. 1,* The American Philosophical Society, 1962.

2. *See* Rudaux and de Vaucouleurs, *Larousse Encyclopedia of Astronomy,* second edition, s.v. "combined effects of rotation and revolution," "the sun's rotation."

Notes to Chapter 16

1. Chase, "Aquarian Wave of Love," *The Journal of Astrological Studies,* Fall 1970, at page 242.

Notes to Appendix 1

1. H. Stanley Redgrove, *Alchemy: Ancient and Modern*, University Books, 1959, at pages 61-5. For a sympathetic view of Rosicrucianism, *see* A. E. Waite, *The Brotherhood of the Rosy Cross*, University Books, undated edition; in contrast, *see* Mervyn Jones, "The Rosicrucians," *Secret Societies*, Norman MacKenzie, ed., Collier Books edition, 1971, at pages 109-27.

2. Aniela Jaffé, *From the Life and Work of C. G. Jung*, R. F. C. Hull, trans., Harper Colophon Books edition, 1971, at page 70.

3. Eliade, *The Forge and the Crucible*, Harper Torchbooks edition, 1971, at page 196.

4. Jung, *Modern Man in Search of a Soul*, Harvest Books edition, 1933, at page 89.

5. Jung, *The Archetypes and the Collective Unconscious*, cited *supra*, at page 310.

6. Jung, "On Synchronicity," *The Portable Jung*, Joseph Campbell, ed., Viking Press, 1972, at page 517.

7. Jung, *Mysterium Coniunctionis*, Bollingen edition, 1970, at page 179.

8. *Id.* at page 287.

9. *Id.* at page 287, n.113.

10. *Ibid.*, italics mine.

11. *Id.* at page 3.

12. *Id.* at page 350, n.353.

13. Jaffé, *From the Life and Work of C. G. Jung*, at pages 51-2.

14. Pierre Huard and Ming Wong, *Chinese Medicine*, McGraw-Hill World University Library edition, 1972, at pages 9-10.

15. *Id.* at page 38.

16. Lu K'uan Yü (Charles Luk), *Taoist Yoga*, cited *supra*, at pages 30-1, nn.2,3.

17. Mann, *Acupuncture*, Random House Vintage Books edition, 1972, at page 28.

18. Koestler, *The Case of the Midwife Toad*, Random House Vintage Books edition, 1973, at page 142.

19. *Ibid.*

20. Jung, *Memories, Dreams, Reflections*, Aniela Jaffé, ed., Richard and Clara Winston, trans., Random House Vintage Books edition, 1963, at page 204.

21. Jung, *Psychological Types*, cited *supra*, at page 532.

22. Leary, Metzner and Alpert, *The Psychedelic Experience*, cited *supra*, at page 23.

23. Metzner, *Maps of Consciousness*, Collier Books edition, 1971, at page 85.

Index